Eckhart, Heidegger,
and the Imperative
of Releasement

SUNY series in Contemporary Continental Philosophy

Dennis J. Schmidt, editor

Eckhart, Heidegger, and the Imperative of Releasement

Ian Alexander Moore

Published by State University of New York Press, Albany

© 2019 State University of New York

All rights reserved

Printed in the United States of America

No part of this book may be used or reproduced in any manner whatsoever without written permission. No part of this book may be stored in a retrieval system or transmitted in any form or by any means including electronic, electrostatic, magnetic tape, mechanical, photocopying, recording, or otherwise without the prior permission in writing of the publisher.

For information, contact State University of New York Press, Albany, NY
www.sunypress.edu

Library of Congress Cataloging-in-Publication Data

Names: Moore, Ian Alexander, author.
Title: Eckhart, Heidegger, and the imperative of releasement / Ian Alexander Moore.
Description: Albany : State University of New York Press, [2019] | Series: SUNY series in contemporary continental philosophy | Includes bibliographical references and index.
Identifiers: LCCN 2018054672 | ISBN 9781438476513 (hardcover : alk. paper) | ISBN 9781438476520 (pbk. : alk. paper) | ISBN 9781438476537 (ebook)
Subjects: LCSH: Heidegger, Martin, 1889–1976. | Eckhart, Meister, –1327— Influence. | Ontology. | Metaphysics.
Classification: LCC B3279.H49 M586 2019 | DDC 193—dc23
LC record available at https://lccn.loc.gov/2018054672

10 9 8 7 6 5 4 3 2 1

Meinen Meistern gewidmet.

Contents

ACKNOWLEDGMENTS   xi

GENERAL INTRODUCTION   xiii

Part One

CHAPTER 1
The Thinker and the Master: Heidegger on Eckhart   3

Part Two

INTRODUCTION   35

CHAPTER 2
Thinking, Being, and the Problem of Ontotheology in Eckhart's Latin Writings   39

CHAPTER 3
Become Who You Are: The Oneness of Thinking and Being as Releasement in Eckhart's German Writings   61

CHAPTER 4
Eckhart's Strategies for Cultivating Releasement   81

Part Three

Introduction — 91

Chapter 5
The Middle Voice of Releasement in Heidegger's Lecture Courses, 1928–30 — 97

Chapter 6
Violent Thinking and Being in Heidegger's *Introduction to Metaphysics*, 1935 — 111

Chapter 7
Releasement as the Essence of Thinking and Being in Heidegger's First "Country Path Conversation," 1945 — 123

Conclusion — 139

Appendix One
Materials on Heidegger's Relation to Eckhart — 145
  §1. Editions of Eckhart Consulted, Owned, or Referenced by Heidegger — 145
  §2. Locations of Heidegger's References to Eckhart and Pseudo-Eckhart — 146
  §3. Heidegger's Citations of Eckhart and Pseudo-Eckhart — 148
  §4. Heidegger's Marginalia und Underlining in His Personal Copies of Eckhart — 167
  §5. Summary of Eckhart's/Pseudo-Eckhart's Texts Read or Cited by Heidegger — 179
  §6. Reports on Heidegger's Relation to Eckhart — 180
  §7. Heidegger's Evaluation of Käte Oltmanns's Dissertation on Eckhart — 187
  §8. Heidegger's Notes on Käte Oltmanns's Oral Examination — 190

Appendix Two
"Essentiality, Existence, and Ground in Meister Eckhart," by Käte Oltmanns — 191

Appendix Three
"Nietzsche's Zarathustra and Meister Eckhart," by Nishitani Keiji — 195

NOTES	219
BIBLIOGRAPHY	283
PUBLISHED PRIMARY SOURCES	283
UNPUBLISHED SOURCES	296
SECONDARY SOURCES	297
INDEX	317

Acknowledgments

Many institutions and individuals have provided vital support for this project. I thank the Fulbright Commission for awarding me a 2015–16 German Research Fellowship. I am grateful to the American Friends of Marbach for a 2016 Max Kade Summer Research Grant to conduct archival research at the Deutsches Literaturarchiv Marbach. Among the many archivists who helped me locate and decipher Heidegger's manuscripts, I am especially indebted to Gudrun Bernhardt, Heidrun Fink, and Ulrich von Bülow. Ted Kisiel and Peter Trawny also provided helpful guidance. I thank Alfred Denker and Holger Zaborowski for the Martin-Heidegger-Fellowship, which allowed me to live in the Meßkirch castle while conducting research at the Martin-Heidegger-Archiv der Stadt Meßkirch. The Josephine de Karman Fellowship Trust and DePaul University also provided crucial financial support.

I would like to thank especially Heidegger's grandson and literary executor, Arnulf Heidegger, for permitting me to consult unpublished manuscripts and correspondence of his grandfather, and for allowing me to publish transcriptions and translations of his grandfather's reports and notes on Käte Oltmanns's dissertation and oral examination. I am also deeply grateful to Friedrich-Wilhelm von Herrmann, who generously allowed me to examine Heidegger's personal copies of Eckhart and to incorporate Heidegger's underlining and marginalia into the book.

This book would not have been possible without the conversation and critique that are essential to all philosophy. Although there are too many to name here, I would nevertheless like to single out, in addition to those mentioned above, Peg Birmingham, Tobias Keiling, Sean Kirkland, Rick Lee, Josh McBee, Will McNeill, Lisa Moore, Mary Moore, and Denny Schmidt.

Chapter 2 first appeared under the title "The Problem of Ontotheology in Eckhart's Latin Writings," in *Epoché: A Journal for the History of Philosophy* 22, no. 2 (Spring 2018): 317–44. Portions of chapters 5 and 7 were published in "*Gelassenheit*, the Middle Voice, and the Unity of Heidegger's Thought," in *Perspektiven mit Heidegger: Zugänge—Pfade—Anknüpfungen*, ed. Gerhard Thonhauser (Freiburg: Karl Alber, 2017), 25–39. A shorter version of Appendix One appeared as ". . . 'Seit 1910 begleitet mich der Lese- und Lebemeister Eckehardt': Materials on Heidegger's Relation to Meister Eckhart," in *Bulletin heideggérien* 6 (2016): 186–218. I thank the publishers of these texts for permission to reprint this material.

I am also grateful for the permission to publish, in Appendix Two, my translation of Käte Oltmanns, "Wesenheit, Dasein und Grund bei Meister Eckehart," in *Heideggers Schelling-Seminar (1927/28). Die Protokolle von Martin Heideggers Seminar zu Schellings 'Freiheitsschrift' (1927/28) und die Akten des Internationalen Schelling-Tags 2006. Lektüren F. W. J. Schellings I*, ed. Lore Hühn and Jörg Jantzen in cooperation with Philipp Schwab and Sebastian Schwenzfeuer, *Schellingiana* 22 (Stuttgart-Bad Cannstatt: frommann-holzboog, 2010), 356–62, 437–38. I thank S. P. K. Cerda and Hiroshi Abé for their translation of Nishitani's text, and Nishitani's daughter Toshiko Yada and Masaaki Kuboi of Sōbunsha publishing house for the permission to publish it in Appendix Three. Finally, I would like to express my gratitude to Karl von der Luft for preparing the index.

General Introduction

We begin with a precondition, perhaps the greatest precondition ever set on seekers of wisdom. You wish to know the truth? Then you must do but one thing: you must be the truth you wish to know.

Thus runs the general imperative of Meister Eckhart's teaching and preaching. As he puts it in a German homily: "[I]f you are unlike this truth of which we want to speak, you cannot understand me" (DW 2: 487,6–7/ ES 199 Pr. 52 ["Beati pauperes spiritu"]). The primary task of this book is twofold: to explore how this imperative functions in Eckhart's philosophy, and to show how Martin Heidegger creatively appropriated it at several stages of his career.

Eckhart specifies his imperative with the language of releasement or letting-be (*gelâzenheit* in Middle High German). If what being truly *is* is releasement, then to know this most fundamental of truths, it is imperative that I release myself. "No one," preaches Eckhart, "can hear my word or my teaching unless he has released himself" (DW 1: 170,1–2/TP 264 Pr. 10 ["In diebus suis"]; trans. mod.). But this is not all. I must also come to see that, fundamentally, releasement comprises my essence too. In this respect Eckhart is a successor of Parmenides. Thinking and being, or, for Eckhart, the essence of the soul and the Godhead, are the same.

Yet how can Eckhart even speak of such matters? If I cannot understand him unless I release myself, of what avail is his language? It will be necessary to show that Eckhart does not just describe releasement. Nor does he simply argue for it. Through various deconstructive and extradiscursive linguistic strategies, Eckhart also puts his language in service of releasement. He tries to provoke letting-be.

In these respects, Heidegger is indebted to Eckhart above all else. For Heidegger, as for the "master of letters and life" (as Heidegger would occasionally refer to him), ontology is dependent on what I would like to call, following Reiner Schürmann, a "practical apriori." By this, I mean that, in order properly to understand being, one must first engage in the proper *activity* of thinking. This activity will, in turn, reveal being to be the same as that very activity. We will see that Heidegger follows Eckhart here not only in terms of form, but also, at times, in terms of content. Especially (though not exclusively) in Heidegger's later thought, it is only in letting be that I may come to understand that being, too, prevails as letting be. And, as with Eckhart, many of Heidegger's notoriously peculiar linguistic devices will become more comprehensible when we view them as facilitating releasement.

It may seem strange to characterize Heidegger's later thought in terms of a search for essences, whether of being or of the human being. However, our inquiry into Heidegger's relation to Eckhart will reveal that, even when Heidegger turns to the "history of being," he never entirely abandons his early project of a "hermeneutics of facticity." That is, he never entirely gives up on the attempt to explicate an infra-historical sense of being that is always already at work, albeit implicitly, in our everyday life. If, as Heidegger writes in *Being and Time*, phenomenological hermeneutics involves "the discovery of the meaning of being and the basic structures of Dasein" (SZ, 37/35), then on a certain level Heidegger always remained a hermeneut. He also remained true to two masters he once identified as constant companions on his path of thought: Parmenides and Eckhart (MH/KJ, 181–82/172). For Heidegger, as for his Greek and German predecessors, the essence of being and the essence of the thinking human being are in some sense the same.

Heidegger's relation to Eckhart is not just confined to these issues, however. Rather there is ample historical evidence, much of it unpublished or only recently available in German, to suggest that Heidegger consulted Eckhart again and again throughout his career to develop or support his own thought. The secondary task of the book before you is to reconstruct this relation. Part One, chapter 1 does so by examining the important references to Eckhart in Heidegger's corpus, as well as numerous authors who were influenced by Eckhart and who either mediated this influence to Heidegger or tell us something significant about Heidegger's relation to Eckhart. By situating these references and relationships within their intellectual and sociopolitical milieu, we will see that Heidegger's debt to Eckhart runs deeper than anyone has yet to establish in the secondary literature. The Appendices corroborate the results of chapter 1. Appendix One documents when and where Heidegger cites or references Eckhart, which editions he used, what his underlining and marginalia in his personal copies of Eckhart look like, secondary reports on his relation to Eckhart, and his evaluation of his student Käte Oltmanns's dissertation and oral examination on Eckhart from 1934. I have also, in Appendix Two, translated the basis for Oltmanns's dissertation, namely, a presentation Heidegger assigned her to write on Eckhart for his 1927–28 seminar on Schelling. Appendix Three comprises the first English translation of Nishitani Keiji's seminal essay on Eckhart and Nietzsche's Zarathustra, which was first given as a presentation in one of Heidegger's classes in 1938.

In Parts Two and Three of the book, I focus on a specific aspect of Eckhart's wide-ranging influence on Heidegger: the unique way in which being and thinking are connected in Eckhart's thought. Part Two examines this connection in the Meister's Latin and German writings. Chapter 2 looks at two ostensibly opposed positions in Eckhart's Latin texts. On the one hand, Eckhart presents an intellectualist approach to the question of God, arguing in favor of God as understanding as opposed to God as being. On the other hand, he contends that being is God. I argue that these claims are not as incompatible as they initially appear, and that, in certain respects, both resist Heidegger's sweeping charges of ontotheology. Nevertheless, although Eckhart does deploy several strategies to strip off a few layers of Scholastic oversimplification, neither of his approaches in the Latin writings suffices to unfold the deepest implications of his thought. For that we must turn to his German texts.

Chapter 3 draws on Eckhart's German tractates and sermons to show that the relationship between the spark of the soul and the Godhead or between thinking and being is best understood in terms of *gelâzenheit,* which not only names their implicit oneness, but also is the way in which we can explicitly appropriate or own up to such oneness.

However, as mentioned above, it is important to note that Eckhart does not simply describe being as *gelâzenheit.* He also endeavors to prepare his listeners and readers to experience it. In chapter 4, I accordingly supplement my analysis of Eckhart's deconstructive strategies in his Latin writings by examining a few ways in which Eckhart cultivates his readers for *gelâzenheit,* namely, his dialectical logic with respect to the terms *nothing* and *something,* his paradoxical prayer that God make him void of God, and his peculiar mistranslation of Luke 9:23.

Part Three then shows how the connection between thinking and being in Eckhart is formally operative throughout Heidegger's career, even if the content of that connection differs from one stage of Heidegger's thought to the next. I focus on three stages between the years 1928 and 1945. Chapter 5 analyzes two lecture courses Heidegger delivered in Freiburg after taking over Edmund Husserl's chair: the 1928–29 course *Einleitung in die Philosophie* and the 1929–30 course *The Fundamental Concepts of Metaphysics*. I argue that the being of Dasein's transcendence involves several layers of operative letting-be that can be made thematic only if Dasein lets be. None of these senses should be understood in terms of the active or the passive voices, however. Rather, both the primordial happening of Dasein's transcendence *as letting-be*, and the *Gelassenheit* that makes this manifest, are middle voiced. The chapter then looks at how the tension between activity and middle-voiced letting-be plays out in the 1929–30 course with respect to philosophy, and argues that letting-be must take precedence. In particular, it shows how this tension is itself part and parcel of the methodological strategy of the course to unsettle the principle of noncontradiction.

If, at the end of the 1920s, an ambiguity between letting-be and activity pervades Heidegger's discourse, in the first half of the 1930s (during which time Heidegger joins the Nazi Party, assumes rectorship over the University of Freiburg, is compelled to resign, and is placed under surveillance), Heidegger opts resolutely for activity, indeed to such an extent that he is taken in by the language of violence and voluntarism. Chapter 6 addresses this change by examining Heidegger's 1935 course *Introduction to Metaphysics*. Although Heidegger's willful, violent language couldn't be farther from Eckhart's language of *gelâzenheit*, I argue that Heidegger nevertheless deploys the same method as he had in the late 1920s. To understand that being prevails as overwhelming violence, human beings must use violence against it. Only in doing so will they come to understand that they too are essentially violent. As in his courses of the late 1920s, Heidegger also deploys a number of strategies here to awaken us to the connection between being and the human being.

In chapter 7, I undertake a close reading of Heidegger's first "Country Path Conversation" (1945), which is most representative of his later understanding of letting-be. After examining the problem of the will and thus the problem of Heidegger's own position in the first half of the 1930s, I show how the essence of the human being is best understood as *Gelassenheit*. However, unlike in chapter 5, which starts from the perspective of Dasein's transcendence, here it is only on the basis of a conception of being itself as a form of *Gelassenheit* that the essence of the human being can be characterized as *Gelassenheit*. Yet this may become manifest only insofar as the human being lets being prevail *as* letting-be. Through various strategies such

as dialogical and poetic writing, circular reasonin[g]
and oxymoron, Heidegger endeavors to disrupt o[ur thinking]
(including that of his own earlier thought) and [open it]
to the event of being as letting-be. At no poi[nt is he]
influenced by Eckhart.

Before moving on, I should say a few wo[rds about referring to]
Eckhart's work above as philosophy. While th[is may seem strange,]
Eckhart himself believed that it was philosophy that could best [unlock the]
seals of the Bible. He even went so far as to claim that, in terms of content, the teachings of both Testaments differed not a whit from the teaching of Aristotle (LW 3: 155, no. 185, In Ioh.). The borders between philosophy and theology were of as little interest to Eckhart as were the borders between immanence and transcendence, reason and revelation, faith and knowledge.

And yet, Eckhart's philosophy, for all that, is no conventional philosophy. For it relies on what I would like to call a "mystical foundation." I use this phrase with caution, as mysticism is surely one of the most vexed terms in vocabulary of Western thought and spirituality. Indeed, its meaning seems to remain as hidden as the hidenness to which the term is supposed to point: *mysticism*, from the Greek *muein,* to initiate into a mystery before which you must close your eyes and shut your mouth. If you wish to speak of it, merely murmur and mumble. Direct discourse will only lead you astray.

Nevertheless, I do think the term befits the practical condition that philosophy must meet if it is to fulfill its task. To think truly, you must truly *be*. To know, you must first *do*. There is something hidden within each of us that may be revealed only if we obey these practical imperatives. Yet what is revealed by such being and doing is nothing extraordinary. It is rather the most ordinary thing in our lives. We just fail, for the most part, to heed it. Few philosophies are essentially founded on a practical apriori. Eckhart's and Heidegger's are. It is in this sense, and only in this sense, that I will call them mystical.

PART ONE

1

The Thinker and the Master

Heidegger on Eckhart

It has long been known that Heidegger was, and indeed saw himself as, a successor to Meister Eckhart. Hannah Arendt, for example, believed Heidegger's later thought to be "entirely influenced by him," whereas Hans-Georg Gadamer took Eckhart to be a crucial source for the early development of Heidegger's questions about being. Otto Pöggeler, in contrast, has contended that it was in between these two periods, when Heidegger was trying to liberate himself from the hegemony of Western metaphysics, that he depended on Eckhart. Judging from a remark Heidegger made at age fifty-nine, however, all three commentators seem to be right. For, as he said then, "Since 1910, the master of letters and life, Eckehardt, has accompanied me" (MH/KJ, 181–82/172; trans. mod.). Thus, we would not be overstating matters if we were to claim, with Jacques Derrida and Werner Beierwaltes, that Heidegger is hardly legible without an appreciation of his Eckhartian heritage.[1]

Not surprisingly, therefore, many parallels have been drawn between Eckhart's thought and Heidegger's: from the sameness of their vocabulary (*abgrunt/Abgrund, gelâzenheit/Gelassenheit, abegescheidenheit/Abgeschiedenheit, wesüng/Wesung*), to the similarity of their core relata (the spark of the soul and *Dasein*, the Godhead and *Sein*); from their linguistic creativity to their philosophical concerns (the verbal character of being, life without why, truth as deeper than correspondence); from their critiques to their contributions. While some of these connections surely have merit, and indeed will receive corroboration over the course of this study, in this chapter I am less interested in speculating about possible lines of influence than in examining when and where Heidegger himself cites or refers to Eckhart. This preliminary philological work on the Heidegger/Eckhart connection is especially necessary today, since only recently have many of Heidegger's references to Eckhart become available to researchers. There is also crucial archival material that must be discussed if we are to have a more complete

3

picture of Heidegger's relation to Eckhart. Given the fact that Heidegger cites or makes reference to Eckhart nearly one hundred times throughout his career, however, I cannot hope to discuss all of the relevant passages here. Instead, this chapter will examine the most significant places in which Heidegger mentions Eckhart, as well as material that has only recently come to light. Proceeding more or less chronologically, I will also mention various figures in Heidegger's life whose own knowledge of Eckhart will help us to better understand Heidegger's. This should help us to appreciate how Heidegger could see in Eckhart not just a great theologian, philosopher, and mystic, but a great thinker as well. This will, in turn, provide a degree of orientation for the chapters to follow, when I focus on the distinctive way in which being and thinking are connected in the work of both men.

1. Heidegger's Early Eckhartianism

The earliest indication available for Heidegger's engagement with Eckhart comes from a lecture course Heidegger took with the archaeologist, theologian, and art and church historian Joseph Sauer at the University of Freiburg in Winter Semester 1910–11. The course was called "Geschichte der mittelalterlichen Mystik" (History of Medieval Mysticism) and took place two hours per week (HAD, 14). Although it is possible that Eckhart was neither read nor discussed during Sauer's course, it is extremely unlikely that the towering figure of medieval German mysticism would have been omitted, especially in light of Sauer's 1911 bibliography of the history of mysticism in the Middle Ages, which contains many entries on Eckhart.[2] What is more, in a letter to Karl Jaspers from 1949 that was cited above, Heidegger writes that it was since 1910, the very year Heidegger began Sauer's course on medieval mysticism, that Eckhart had accompanied him. Sauer's course might well have influenced Heidegger's eventual critique of Scholasticism as well as his efforts toward a phenomenology of religious life. For, as will be the case for Heidegger several years later, Sauer saw in mysticism "a certain compensation for the loss of religious immediacy that resulted from the historical relativization of the beginnings of Christianity."[3]

Heidegger and Sauer would remain in contact over the years, although a serious intellectual exchange between the two men after Heidegger's student days seems doubtful. Nevertheless, it is worth nothing that, around the time when Heidegger was compiling notes for a work on the phenomenology of religious life and planning a lecture course on the foundations of medieval mysticism (1916–19), Sauer, along with his colleague (and Heidegger's close friend) Engelbert Krebs, was also working on mysticism. In Winter Semester 1917–18, for example, Krebs delivered a popular lecture course on mysticism, and in Summer Semester 1919, Sauer offered a course on mysticism and art.[4]

Although Heidegger most likely began reading Eckhart in Sauer's course, there are no references to Eckhart in Heidegger's corpus until 1915. Nonetheless, we know that Heidegger continued to work on Eckhart in the interim, as he later recollects: "My previous study of Aristotle over the years facilitated my first attempt in 1913–15 at thinking alongside Meister Eckhart, who belongs in the slim kinship [*geringe Verwandtschaft*] of the first thinkers" (GA 97: 436). Indeed, as he later clarifies, it was particularly with the help of Franz Brentano's *On the Several Senses of Being in Aristotle* and Hermann Lotze's *Metaphysik* that "I learned for myself to read Eckhart" (GA 97: 470).[5] These recollections—which, mind you, were not, like many of his other references to Eckhart, intended for immediate publication or reception, and would thus attenuate any attempt to see Heidegger's later tributes to Eckhart as a mere self-rebranding—reveal Heidegger as a careful reader of Eckhart, indeed at a time when many philosophers hardly took Eckhart seriously.[6] They also indicate that, in Heidegger's own view, Eckhart was one of the few great thinkers of the premodern Occident. Later he will even call Eckhart a "master of thinking" (GA 79: 15/14–15).

As mentioned, it was in 1915 that Heidegger began to refer to Eckhart explicitly in his writings. In a local newspaper article, he notes the appearance of new editions of Eckhart and of the latter's disciples John Tauler and Henry Suso (KT, 22/51).[7] In the main portion of his *Habilitationsschrift*, Heidegger mentions the epigraph that his director Heinrich Rickert took from Eckhart for his essay "Das Eine, die Einheit und die Eins" (One, Oneness, and the Number One).[8] For his qualifying lecture "The Concept of Time in the Science of History," which was required in order to be able to teach as a *Privatdozent* (unsalaried lecturer) at the university, Heidegger himself selected an Eckhart-quote for the epigraph (GA 1: 415/49). And in a footnote to the 1916 conclusion of his *Habilitationsschrift*, Heidegger projects future work on his German predecessor: "I hope to be able to show on another occasion how *Eckhartian mysticism* is given its proper philosophical interpretation and assessment only from this point of view and in connection with the metaphysics of the problem of truth" (GA 1: 402, n. 2/187, n. 4).[9] Thus, already at the very beginning of his professional career, Heidegger is thinking about Eckhart with regard to topics as wide ranging as number theory, time, and truth.

He is also thinking about the central role of detachment (*abegescheidenheit*) in Eckhart's corpus. This may be seen indirectly in a note that has survived from Heidegger's Winter Semester 1915–16 lecture course "Grundlinien der antiken und scholastischen Philosophie" (Basic Trends of Ancient and Scholastic Philosophy), and directly in his 1916–19 notes for a work on the phenomenology of religious life. Although there is no explicit mention of Eckhart in the extant portions of the 1915–1916 course, there is one passage in which Heidegger no doubt had Eckhart in mind.[10] The note deals with one of the fundamental themes of Eckhart's preaching: detachment (DW 2: 528,5–6/ES 203 Pr. 53 ["Misit dominus mahum suam"]). Heidegger speaks of the detached man's ignorance of (or perhaps indifference to) his city and its customs. He speaks, with Nicholas of Cusa, of opposites coinciding.[11] And he speaks of detachment from both self and world. He then alludes to Matthew 18:3 and Genesis 1:2. When detachment has been realized, and philosophy has reached its summit, we return back to our origins: we "become like little children," and "the spirit of God" again comes to "hover over the waters."

Without more context, it is difficult to determine how exactly detachment should be understood here. Heidegger seems to intend not only a prerequisite detachment from the world and from our selves—insofar as they are plagued by the distinction of *hoc et hoc,* this and that—but also how our relationship to the world will change as a result of this. In true detachment, we are able to see and be in the world as but an unfolding of the contraries that are one in God. Things no longer appear as distinct and opposed, but as unified, indeed *as* God. "All things," preaches Eckhart in a sermon that Heidegger will later cite, "become pure God to you" (DW 4: 488,136/Davies 228 Pr. 103 ["Cum factus esset Iesus annorum duodecim"]).[12]

For our part, teleology is suspended, our knowing transforms into an unknowing, and, like children, our relation to God becomes a relation of *play.* As Heidegger writes in a note for a phenomenology of religious life from 1916, quoting (Pseudo-)Eckhart: " 'The Father thus conveys His word to the soul and the soul, again in the word, conveys itself to the Father. Let us nurture this eternal play in God, so help us God' (Pfeiffer 1857, 479, 25f.)."[13] The note is titled "Original Sense of Spirituality in its Central Vitality," and contains several other quotations from Pfeiffer's edition of Eckhart that are now thought to be spurious. One of Heidegger's main concerns in this note, as well as in others that would come to be published in GA 60, is to find out where and how the divine reveals itself. With respect to the "where," Eckhart entertains several options in another passage cited by Heidegger, including (1) reason, (2) the will, (3) the spark of the soul,[14]

(4) the concealment of the heart (*verborgenheit des gemüetes*), and (5) "the most intimate essence of the soul—where all the powers of the soul are first born *in a divine taste*, [which manifests] each power in its essence." Eckhart opts for the fifth, but brings it together with the fourth when he writes of the *"concealment of the heart* as a concentration of all divine gifts in the innermost essence of the soul, like a bottomless spring of all divine goods."[15] It is here that the Son is born in the soul and we are one with God, where there is no ultimate reason but only that childlike, "eternal play."

How this transpires is addressed in other notes from Heidegger's work on a phenomenology of religious life, where the term *detachment* again takes center stage, this time with direct reference to Eckhart. Generally speaking, what we need is a detachment that is not just "negative," but has a "positive" side, one that is at work even as we direct ourselves to the world. This positive unification through detachment would primarily not be of a theoretical nature, but rather of a lived, "emotional," "religious" experience. There is thus something "irrational" about this "[c]entral concept: 'detachment'" (GA 60: 308/234, 314/239; trans. mod.). Heidegger develops what this means for Eckhart in a three-and-one-half-page note from 1917 titled "Irrationality in Meister Eckhart."

Though interpreted in the potentially misleading language of subjectivity and objectivity, Heidegger rightly notes that detachment for Eckhart involves a suspension of "multiplicity," "opposition," and "difference," including "space and time" as "forms of the multiple and oppositional," as well as a suspension of "the understanding, as judging, pulling apart into the duality of subject and predicate." Doing so enables access to the "eternal 'now [*Nu*]'" (GA 60: 318/241; trans. mod.),[16] and lets the subject behold the pure "objectness" of the object, that is, "the primordial object *kat'exochēn*, the absolute." It also lets the subject overcome its own imbrication in opposition. "Only in this way," Heidegger writes, "does the mystical-theoretical meaning of the central concept of *detachment* first become clear" (GA 60: 317–18/241; trans. mod.).

The term *mystical-theoretical* should not be misunderstood here. Although Eckhart does employ speculative terminology borrowed from the Schools, there is still something "irrational" about Eckhart's mysticism (GA 60: 315/239). Yet the term *irrational,* for its part, does not mean what lies prior to all determination, awaiting rationalization (GA 60: 311/236), nor what is beyond all apprehension and analysis, at least insofar as these fall under what Heidegger calls "phenomenological understanding" in contrast to "scientific study."[17] Nor, however, can the term *irrational* be conflated with the holy, as in Rudolf Otto's *das ganz Andere* (the wholly Other).[18] Rather, the irrational is "that which is essentially without determination in general," "the ever-expanding exclusion of particularizations from the form, out of the magnified emptiness of the same." It is, in other words, the absolute attained through detachment. And since the ground of the soul and the ground of God are one for Eckhart, there is an "[a]bsoluteness of object and subject in the sense of radical unity and as such unity of *both: I am it, and it is I*. From this the namelessness of God and ground of the soul" (GA 60: 316/240).

Such namelessness is, importantly, not to be reached through the faculties. "In this sphere," Heidegger writes, there is "no opposition—and therefore the problem of the precedence of *intellectus* or *voluntas* no longer belongs to this sphere." Hearkening back to his note from 1916 on the proper place of the soul for the manifestation of the divine, Heidegger writes that "Eckhart is not in favor of theoretical reason as juxtaposed to the will, but rather of the primacy of the soul's ground, which is, mystical-theoretically, ranked above both" (GA 60: 316/240, 318/241; trans. mod.). When we take Eckhart's whole corpus into consideration, we cannot readily place it on one side of the medieval debate about the primacy of will or intellect (even if in texts such as the early Parisian Questions Eckhart will argue along with the Dominicans in favor of the intellect against the Franciscan emphasis on the will). Such a line should certainly lead one to question just how serious Heidegger is when he later has an interlocutor in the first "Country Path Conversation" relegate Eckhart's thought to the domain of the will. I will return to this issue later. In any event, Heidegger does notice an ambiguity in Eckhart, for, despite his move beyond the faculties, Eckhart nevertheless "sees precisely in free will, by virtue of its freedom and devotion to value [*Werthingegebenheit*], the axiologically superior 'faculty' [*das wertüberlegene 'Vermögen'*]" (GA 60: 316, 318/240–41; trans. mod.).[19] Heidegger is thus clearly aware of the difficulties surrounding Eckhart's doctrine of the soul, where, at the most fundamental level, even the term *faculty* is out of place.

Heidegger also takes note of what might be called the epistemological dimensions of such a doctrine. If it is true that like is known only by like, then, taken radically, I can only know God if in some sense I am God. Knowledge, at the level of the ground of the soul and of God, is such that subject and object, knower and known, must be the same. Here it is not a question of the relative feebleness of the human intellect in comparison to God, nor thus of the intellect's dependency on phantasms or its discursiveness. Knowledge, here, is not a result, but a primordial state, prior to the more familiar subject/object distinction:

> An opinion that grasps the subject-correlate of the absolute as summation, as the totality of specific achievements and faculties,

and correspondingly views the value of the holy as some kind of result of the true, good, and beautiful, is entirely misguided. . . .

Eckhart's "fundamental conception"—"you can only know what you are"—becomes conceivable only from out of the specific concept of cognition. Here cognition determines subject and object. (GA 60: 316–17/240)[20]

Although Eckhart's "progression to the subject" or, better, to the originary ground of the soul, is not a theoretical enterprise, and although Heidegger suggests that it advances beyond the medieval problem of universals, Heidegger nevertheless seems to complain that "Eckhart seeks to grasp it rationally and thus places it into theoretical contexts" (GA 60: 317/240). One might argue that Eckhart accordingly falls prey to the Scholastic tendencies of his epoch,[21] and that it was Heidegger's reservations about the theoretical superstructure in Eckhart's work that led him to abandon further work on Eckhartian mysticism around this period. Rather than deconstructing the Eckhartian edifice, Heidegger would have simply moved on to other, less fortified structures.

The problem with such a reading, however, is that Heidegger speaks, not of a mystical superstructure that is also theoretical (as if the latter were facultative), but of a mystical-theoretical superstructure that "*stems from* living religiosity."[22] Heidegger's wording here suggests that this superstructure is not an external imposition, but rather an outgrowth of primordial religious life. Thus, a few years later Heidegger is still able to exempt Eckhart and Tauler from the Scholastic obfuscation of primal Christianity, suggesting that they remain viable candidates for work on the phenomenology of religious life (GA 58: 61–62/47–48; GA 61, 7/7).

2. God and Godhead in the 1920s and Beyond

And yet, after 1920 there will not be a single reference to Eckhart in Heidegger's corpus until the *Basic Problems of Phenomenology* (Summer Semester 1927). Although this may be due to a certain incompatibility between Eckhart's speculative-mystical thought and Heidegger's attempt to give phenomenology a scientific footing, a report by Gadamer assures us that Heidegger never stopped reading the Dominican master:

> Meister Eckhart played a particularly great role for Heidegger. At that time (1924), the *Opus tripartitum,* Meister Eckhart's Latin

magnum opus, had just been reedited. Heidegger was completely fascinated by it, evidently because the dissolution of the concept of substance in regards to God pointed in the direction of a temporal and verbal sense of being, when it was said that: "Esse est Deus." At that time, Heidegger may have suspected an ally in the Christian mystic.[23]

Only later will Heidegger explicitly acknowledge his debt to Eckhart's understanding of being.[24] His interpretation of Eckhart in the *Basic Problems of Phenomenology*, which draws closely (and tacitly) on Adolf Lasson's 1868 book on Eckhart,[25] nonetheless confirms Gadamer's report about his interest in this topic. After claiming that "[t]he mystical theology of the Middle Ages, for example, that of Meister Eckhart, is not even remotely accessible without comprehension of the doctrine of essentia and existentia," Heidegger notes a distinctive feature of medieval mysticism, namely, "that it tries to lay hold of the being [*Seiende*] that is rated ontologically as the properly essential being [*das eigentliche Wesen*], God, in its very essentiality [*Wesenheit*]." What is strange about this, Heidegger explains, is that it treats essence, which is *of* a being, as though it were *itself* a being, and considers a being's possibility, not its actuality, to be what really *is*. (Here too, we might add, does possibility stand higher than actuality.) This "ontologization" of essentiality and possibility is necessary for what Heidegger refers to as "mystical speculation." Yet it is not, for all that, ontotheological. Strictly speaking, it is neither theological nor ontological, as Heidegger goes on to show with reference to Eckhart:

> Meister Eckhart speaks mostly of the "superessential essence [*überwesentlichen Wesen*]"; that is to say, what interests him is not, strictly speaking, God—God is still a provisional object for him—but Godhead. When Meister Eckhart says "God" he means Godhead, not *deus* but *deitas*, not *ens* but *essentia*, not nature but what is above nature, the essence—the essence to which, as it were, every existential determination must still be refused, from which every *additio existentiae* must be kept at a distance. Hence he also says: "Spräche man von Gott er ist, das wäre hinzugelegt." "If it were said of God that he is, that would be added on." Meister Eckhart's expression "das wäre hinzugelegt" is the German translation, using Thomas' phrase, of: it would be an *additio entis*. "So ist Gott im selben Sinne nicht und ist

nicht dem Begriffe aller Kreaturen." Thus God is for himself his "not"; that is to say, he is the most universal being, the purest indeterminate possibility of everything possible, the pure nothing [*das reine Nichts*]. He is the nothing over against the concept of every creature, over against every determinate possible and actualized being.

Heidegger then notes the similarity between Eckhart and Hegel on the identification of being with the nothing, before concluding this remarkable passage with the comment that medieval mysticism ought not to be understood in terms of the way in which mysticism is typically understood, but rather "in a preeminent sense" (GA 24: 127–28/90–91; trans. mod.).

This passage shows Heidegger's awareness of the crucial distinction between the Godhead (*gotheit, deitas*) and God (*got, deus*) in Eckhart's thought.[26] Eckhart is so committed to God's unique, radical otherness that he is willing to distinguish the Godhead as a single oneness (*ein einic ein*) from God the Father, from God the Creator, and from God as Person of the Trinity. Indeed he is so committed to such otherness that, at times, even the term *being* falls short. For the danger looms that God's essence would still be understood in terms of creation. Instead, sheer nothingness would be a better description, as would terms such as *abyss* and *desert*.

Heidegger's passage on Eckhart, and especially the distinction between Godhead and God, can also help us to make better sense of later references to Eckhart in Heidegger's corpus. Allow me to mention three. First, in a letter to the historian Rudolf Stadelmann from November 1945, Heidegger comments that certain theological circles in Freiburg are beginning to recognize that what seems to be nihilistic about Heidegger's thought is actually something more akin to the nothingness of Eckhart's Godhead (GA 16: 406).[27]

Second, in his 1949 text "The Pathway," Heidegger writes of his beloved trail in Meßkirch:

> The expanse of all growing things, which while along the pathway, bestows world. In the unspoken of their language is—as Eckehardt, the old master of letters and life, says—God first God.
>
> Die Weite aller gewachsenen Dinge, die um den Feldweg verweilen, spendet Welt. Im Ungesprochenen ihrer Sprache ist, wie der alte Lese- und Lebemeister Eckehardt sagt, Gott erst Gott. (GA 13: 89/35; trans. mod.)[28]

Here Heidegger seems to have in mind Eckhart's 109th German sermon ("Nolite timere eos").²⁹ In this sermon Eckhart explains that "when all creatures speak God forth: there 'God' is born [*Dô alle crêatûren gotes sprechent, dô wird got*]" (DW 4: 771,56/Davies 234). Although not contained in the manuscripts, the inverted commas supplied by the translator here point to the difference between God and the Godhead, which "are as far apart from each other as heaven and earth" (DW 4: 767,34–768,35/Davies 233). God is representable, relatable to creatures, whereas the Godhead is beyond all representation and relation.³⁰ The Godhead only becomes "God" in creation: "When I was still in the ground, in the depths, in the river and source of the Godhead, no one asked me where I wished to go or what I was doing. But as I flowed forth, all creatures uttered: 'God' [*Dô ich ûzvlôz, dô sprâchen alle crêatûren got*]" (DW 4: 771,56–772,59/Davies 234; trans. mod.).³¹ Of God creatures may speak, yet the Godhead remains unspoken.

This process may be reversed, however, when "God 'unbecomes' [*entwirt got*]" (DW 4: 773,68/Davies 234). For it is not just to God that we may return from his bubbling-out (*ebullitio*) into creation. In what Eckhart calls the "breakthrough [*durchbrechen*]" (DW 4: 773,64/Davies 234), we may return to the Godhead from the latter's inner-bubbling (*bullitio*) into God. If we listen closely, if we release ourselves to the Godhead and "follow God" not in richness, but "in poverty and in exile," then truly may we let God be God (DW 4: 774,74/Davies 235). Then is God first truly God, the Godhead.

Lastly, the passage from the *Basic Problems of Phenomenology* bears on the final session of Heidegger's 1968 seminar in Le Thor, where Heidegger shows how this emergence of God from out of the Godhead can be understood in terms of being (which is used transitively). Heidegger is reported to have concluded his reflections with a discussion of God in Eckhart and Hegel as a way to elucidate the nature of a speculative statement. He begins his elucidation with Aquinas's proposition, *Deus est ipsum esse*, God is being itself. This, Heidegger contends, is merely a metaphysical statement. It only becomes speculative when the terms are switched, as one finds in Eckhart's *Opus tripartitum*: *esse est deus*, being is God. What emerges from this inversion is not simply a reversal, however. It does not simply mean that everything that *is* is now also God. Rather, this reversal is more of a "*counter-blow*" in which the function of the copula is also transformed. "Now," Heidegger continues,

> what does "is" mean when overturned in this manner? Meister Eckhart said: *Istic-heit*. Being is God, now understood specula-

tively, means: Being "*istet*" God, that is, Being lets God be God. "Is" speaks here in the transitive and the active. The unfolded Being itself [*Das entfaltete Sein selbst*] (as it is unfolded in Hegel's *Logic*) first makes possible (in a speculative recoil) being-God [*Gott-sein*]. (GA 15: 325/34)[32]

While *wesen* (Middle High German for "being") does appear in Eckhart's corpus in the transitive passive voice,[33] it seems less obvious that *isticheit* ("isness" or, more properly, the "thatness" of self-identity) has a transitive sense.[34] One passage Heidegger might have had in mind, however, is from Eckhart's 12th German sermon ("Qui audit me"), where the language of letting is quite prominent. Eckhart speaks of St. Paul letting go of God for God's own sake, such that God was able to remain for him "as in an isness that God is in himself [*denne in einer isticheit, daz got in im selber ist*]" (DW 1: 197,4–5/TP 268; trans. mod.).[35] Although it seems natural to place God on the left side of the copula, as I have done here, we would come much closer to Heidegger's sense if we were to place God on the right: "as in an isness that is God in himself," that is, as in an isness that "ises" God, that "lets" God "be" in himself, that brings him into his own. Whatever the case may be, the idea that the Godhead, as *wesen*, *isticheit*, or "*weselîche isticheit*" (DW 1: 19,1/Walshe 70 Pr. 1 ["Intravit Iesus in templum"]), lets God the Father and the other Persons of the Trinity be (in the sense of bringing them forth) is quite compatible with Eckhart's thought. It is also remarkable that Heidegger traces the notion of transitive being back to Eckhart, for it plays an important role in Heidegger's own thought as well, so much so that his student Käte Oltmanns was willing to divert from the manuscript when she was editing GA 63, changing "intransitive" to "transitive": "Being—transitive: to be factical life!" (8/5).[36]

3. Käte Oltmanns

To turn back to the late 1920s, the strongest piece of evidence for Heidegger's interest in Eckhart during this period does not come from what he wrote, but from Oltmanns herself. Starting in Winter Semester 1926–27, Oltmanns (who would later marry another student of Heidegger's, Walter Bröcker) began studying with Heidegger. She would remain in his inner circle of exemplary students, and attend nearly all of his seminars up through 1934, the year she completed her dissertation under his directorship on

"Die Philosophie des Meister Ekkehart."[37] (The topic of the dissertation, incidentally, was suggested by Heidegger himself, after she had rejected his initial proposal that she write on Francisco Suárez.)[38] Much could be said of Oltmann's dissertation, more than I can treat here.[39] It should be noted, however, that she received the highest grade possible, and that Heidegger had nothing but positive things to say about her work in his evaluation (which I have reproduced and translated in §7 of Appendix One, below). Instead of analyzing Oltmanns's dissertation, I would like to discuss an assignment Heidegger gave her for a session of his Winter Semester 1927–28 Schelling seminar, namely, to prepare and deliver a presentation on Eckhart.[40]

In this presentation, which she titled "Wesenheit, Dasein und Grund bei Meister Eckehart" (Essentiality, Existence, and Ground in Meister Eckehart), and which I have translated in full in Appendix Two, Oltmanns begins by noting the linguistic creativity of Eckhart's German and Latin writings. She then proceeds to show how the problem of ground appears in connection with the problem of the being of God. Similarly to Heidegger's comments in the *Basic Problems of Phenomenology*, she explains that Eckhart's notion of the Godhead precedes all distinction, be it between essence and existence, between *actus* and *potentia,* or even between Father, Son, and Holy Ghost. She then demonstrates that, when, in texts such as the *Opus tripartitum*, Eckhart operates under the conception that only God really *is* and that creatures are nothing in themselves,

> Eckehart decisively moves beyond the approach of antiquity and Christianity according to which being = being-present-at-hand = being-created or being-produced, where an *analogia attributionis* can be posited between the being of God and the being of creatures as between the being of the uncreated creator and the being of the created that is derived from it. (192)

In other words, Oltmanns shows how Eckhart's understanding of being in terms of ground is not metaphysical, that is, is not conceived as the mere being of beings. She then discusses the vexed problem of analogy, and attempts to reconcile the *Opus tripartitum* with Eckhart's early Parisian Questions, where God's intellect seems to take priority over his being. Nevertheless, Oltmanns maintains that Eckhart is still thinking of God's "way of being [*Seinsart*]" when he thinks of God as *intelligere* (193). In other words, we could say that Eckhart is still motivated by the question of being, even when he does not use the language of being, just as Heidegger is still motivated by the question of being, even when he does not use such language, but attempts rather to think of being as *Walten,* as *Anwesen,* as *Ereignis,* etc.

Before concluding with a comparison of Eckhart and Schelling, Oltmanns discusses Eckhart's psychology (in the ancient sense): how the Son comes to be born in the soul and how we appropriate our oneness with the Godhead. Despite the fact that Eckhart's psychology at times resembles that of Scholasticism, with its division into the powers of memory, reason, and will, there is another dimension of the soul that is uncreated, not just *like* God, but sharing with God *one and the same ground*: "The soul and the Godhead are thus, in their ground, one and unseparated, and therefore the ground of the soul is uncreatable and untouched by any creature" (194). This ground exceeds the faculties of "understanding and will," and even lies beyond anything the Persons are capable of arriving at (194). For the human being, however, unity with this ground is only *in potentia* until "the human being turns away from external things and directs himself solely to his own essence" (193). Here we see Oltmanns's understanding of the supra-volitional character of the spark of the soul and of the Godhead, as well as her understanding of the role of detachment in making our implicit oneness with the Godhead explicit. While much more could be said of Oltmanns's work, it is manifest that, along with Heidegger's independent interest in Eckhart during these years, he had in Oltmanns a student and conversation partner with a vast understanding of Eckhart's corpus, both the Latin and German works, and even of the contemporaneous state of Eckhart scholarship and philology.

4. Nishitani Keiji

Although Oltmanns would remain in contact with Heidegger for the remainder of Heidegger's life, she did not remain active in academia or in publishing after defending her dissertation in 1934. However, just three years later, Heidegger would find another interlocutor nearly as steeped in Eckhart as his former student. This was the Japanese philosopher and scholar of religion Nishitani Keiji, who had received a grant from the Japanese Ministry of Education to conduct research in Freiburg for two years (1937–39). Nishitani began attending Heidegger's seminars (and presumably his lecture courses as well), and the two would eventually grow close. For Heidegger's birthday in 1938, Nishitani gave him a copy of the first volume of D. T. Suzuki's *Essays in Zen Buddhism* (1927), which, incidentally, contains numerous references to Eckhart.[41] Shortly thereafter, Nishitani learned from Heidegger that he had already read Suzuki's book and was looking forward to discussing it. This in turn led to a standing invitation to visit Heidegger's home on Saturday afternoons to talk about Zen Buddhism. According to Nishitani, Heidegger took much from these conversations, and would even draw from them in his lectures (although Heidegger would remain silent about their source in Zen).[42]

It is safe to assume that their conversations extended beyond just Zen. Nishitani's deep interests in Jakob Böhme, Eckhart, Schelling, and Nietzsche would have appealed to Heidegger, and Nishitani had already written on topics such as the history of Western mysticism and the role of freedom in the later Schelling (whom he had also translated into Japanese).[43] Moreover, this was the period of Heidegger's intense engagement with Nietzsche, and Nishitani himself gave a presentation on Eckhart and Zarathustra in one of Heidegger's classes during Nishitani's sojourn in Freiburg. Not only was this presentation pivotal for the development of Nishitani's own thought.[44] It also received praise from Heidegger as a sensible point of comparison.[45] The reader will find the published version of Nishitani's text translated in Appendix Three, below, but I would like to say a few words about it here before proceeding with my analysis of Heidegger's relation to Eckhart.

A chasm seems to separate Eckhart's medieval theism from Nietzsche's modern atheism. However, if we are able to take a broader perspective, we will come to see that the deepest stratum of their respective philosophies is one and the same. Both philosophies, Nishitani argues, are grounded in a "radicalization of the dialectical movement of living" (212). By this he means that both are committed to an extreme affirmation of life only by way of its extreme negation. We cannot just deny the world of human affairs and live like saints in the woods on Zarathustra's mountain. We cannot, in Eckhart's language, merely become "united" (*vereinet*) with God. Rather, we must realize that "God is dead" (Nietzsche), that the God of our fathers—that any God which stands over against us—is no living God. We must negate this God and "break through" God to the ground of God which is our ground, where there is a single oneness (*ein einic ein*) that is always already at work, where I am God and God is I. Or in the words of Zarathustra: "Peak and abyss—they are now merged as one!" (212, 213). Only as a result of this utter negation can we truly affirm the childlike, "overflowing life" that surges through ourselves and through all things (212). It is at this point that Nishitani can declaim their companionship: Nietzsche and Eckhart "stand together in the blazing present moment of living's bottomless depths" (212).[46]

Many of these themes will reappear in Part Two of this book, including the relation between negation and affirmation and the contrast between oneness and unity. Suffice it to say here that Eckhart was a crucial philosopher for Nishitani, perhaps even the greatest Western counterpart to Nishitani's own philosophy of absolute emptiness. We will soon see that Eckhart played a similarly important role in Heidegger's thought.

5. Eckhart, Thinker of (the Analogy of) Being

Indeed, in the 1930s, as Heidegger becomes more overt about Eckhart's significance, Eckhart comes to stand out as an even more exceptional philosopher in Heidegger's corpus. Heidegger identifies Eckhart (along with Hegel) as a representative of the "deep and creative philosophical character" of German, the only language, according to Heidegger, on a par with Ancient Greek (GA 31: 51, n. 3/36, n. 2; see also MH/HA, 247/208). He calls Eckhart the first *German,* and not *modern,* philosopher, where German philosophy is distinguished by its proximity to the Greeks, especially Heraclitus and Parmenides, and by its "understanding of *Seyn*" (GA 39: 123/111, 133–34/118; GA 41: 98/98; EDP, 40/339).[47] And he notes that Eckhart is unique among the medievals in his approach to the *analogia entis*.

This last point is particularly worthy of development. In his Summer Semester 1931 lecture course on Aristotle, Heidegger returns to a problem addressed by Oltmanns, explaining that the *Seinsfrage* cannot be answered by way of the analogy of being, for the latter is but a "title for the most stringent aporia, the impasse in which ancient philosophy, and along with it all subsequent philosophy right up to today, is enmeshed." When the analogy of being was taken up in the Middle Ages, at issue was not, according to Heidegger, the question of being, but rather how to understand one's beliefs philosophically. How, if humans are finite and God is infinite, can we say of both that they *are*? *Are* they in exactly the same way (univocally), utterly differently (equivocally), or only in some sense or to some degree (analogically)? It was the last approach that allowed the medievals to "rescue . . . themselves from this dilemma," although what they provided was not "a solution but a formula." Everyone except Meister Eckhart, that is:

> Meister Eckhart—the only one who sought a solution—says "God 'is' not at all, because 'being' is a finite predicate and

absolutely cannot be said of God." (This was admittedly only a beginning which disappeared in Eckhart's later development, although it remained alive in his thinking in another respect.) (GA 33: 46–47/38)

Heidegger is here referring to two seemingly opposed positions in Eckhart's Latin writings. I will devote considerable attention to this topic in chapter 2. For now, let us note that the first position, developed most prominently in the early Parisian Questions, maintains, ostensibly, that God is best understood, not as being (*esse*), but as understanding (*intelligere*). It was this position that would later lead Heidegger to declare, in a letter to Bernhard Welte, that Eckhart's thought should be exempted from the charge that the history of metaphysics is but a history of the oblivion of being.[48]

The second position (which led to the apparent "disappearance" of the first) comes from Eckhart's *Opus tripartitum*, which, as we already learned from Gadamer and Oltmanns, develops the idea that being is God (*esse est deus*). Heidegger, apparently following Martin Grabmann's edition of the Parisian Questions (Grabmann, 86), thought that the second position marks a later period in Eckhart's development, although this chronology has recently been called into question.[49] What is important, however, is something that Heidegger recognizes in this quote too, namely, that there is a certain continuity between the two positions (the beginning which "remained alive in Eckhart's thinking in another respect"). The continuity may be seen in Eckhart's anti-Thomistic doctrine of analogy, according to which whatever is in one analogate cannot belong essentially in the other. Health, for instance, would belong essentially only in the animal, not in urine or diet. What we call a healthy urine or diet shares nothing, other than the name, with the health of the animal. When we apply this to God and creation, the mode of thinking remains the same across Eckhart's two positions (even if the content differs). If we wish to call God understanding, then he must have nothing in common with the creatures that one attempts to relate to him analogically. Thus, he has no being. If we call God being, in contrast, then creatures, insofar as they are taken as anything other than being, are nothing. There is no hierarchy of being, no more and less being. There is being, or there is not. It comes as little surprise, then, that Heidegger would turn to Eckhart when he was developing a critique of the metaphysical basis of analogy, as Gadamer again relates in another reflection on Heidegger's philosophical trajectory.[50]

6. *Gelassenheit* and the Will

In the 1940s, as Heidegger endeavored to extricate himself from the willfulness of the metaphysical tradition (in which his own thought appears for a time to have been ensconced), he invoked Eckhart several times throughout his writings. In an elliptical note from around 1940, he brings Eckhart together with Nietzsche, as Nishitani had done just two years prior. The note concerns justice: "*Nietzsche's* thought of '*justice*' and 'Christian' metaphysics. *Cf. justice and the just man in Meister Eckhart;—iustitia and certitudo.*" While Heidegger may seem to intend a comparison here, the following line speaks in favor of a contrast: " 'Justice'—its concealed essence: the totality of the truth of beings as such, insofar as being is the will to power as unconditioned subjectivity" (GA 50: 83/63; trans. mod.). For, however ambiguous the status of the will in Eckhart may be, his understanding of justice, according to which those who are just become justice itself, can hardly be labeled a subjective voluntarism. In his sixth German sermon ("Iusti vivent in aeternum"), for example, Eckhart declares bluntly: "The just have no will at all" (DW 1: 102,12–13/Walshe 329).[51] Such willlessness involves, among other things, becoming released (*gelâzen*) from *self*-love and directing one's love toward God (or more properly, the Godhead), who one thereby comes to be—or better: whose oneness with the soul is thereby *appropriated*.[52] At this point one may live as God, *without a why*.

Heidegger develops this last-mentioned theme, on life without why, in a recently published collection of what look like poems but what he prefers to call *Winke* or hints. In a *Wink* titled *Thinking* (and comprised entirely of trochees in the original German), which Heidegger sent to his brother Fritz in December 1945 (DLA HS.2014.0069.00012), we read:

> Thinking is dwelling-near,
> is quiet thanks.
>
> Thinking is noble protecting,
> is the bold bend.
>
> In a path of obscure signs,
> Turns between nothingness and being.
>
> Thinking is never shrinking
> from evil, in the face of agony.

> Thinking is without seizing and grasping,
> is a frank questioning.
>
> Thinking is letting-be-said,
> is the cool drink
>
> On the course, where gently are cleared
> lights without number,
>
> Roses without why, that poetize,
> greeting river and valley.
>
> Thinking remains this freeing of all,
> a modeless call,
>
> that they be mortal, that they be:
> for the sake of healing.[53]

Not only are there many Eckhartian dimensions at play in this composition, such as nobility, letting something be said rather than saying it of one's own volition,[54] a wayless or modeless call, and, of course, groundlessness. There is also, immediately following the composition, a quote from Eckhart's Sermon 5b "In hoc apparuit" (along with one from his baroque poetic successor Angelus Silesius). Heidegger writes, as though to himself:

> for an elucidation of "*Thinking*" / cf. Angelus Silesius, *Cherubinischer Wandersmann* I, 289: / "Without Why. / The rose is without why; it blooms because it blooms; it does not heed itself, asks not if one does see it." // cf. on this Meister Eckhart (Pfeiffer, Predigt 13, S. 66.5f.) / "Out of this inmost ground, all your works should be wrought without why. I say truly, as long as you do works for the sake of heaven or God or eternal bliss, from without, you are at fault." (GA 81: 187; Eckhart translation from Walshe, 110; cf. DW 1: 90,11–91,2 Pr. 5b)

This passage confirms Heidegger's awareness of the importance of living without why for Eckhart. To be sure, Heidegger would have been acquainted with this theme already in the late 1910s, when he read the two-volume war book *Deutscher Weltberuf* (1918) by Paul Natorp. In a chapter on

"German Faith" devoted to Meister Eckhart, Natorp quotes from the very same Eckhart sermon: "*life lives from out of its own ground and wells up from out of its own* [aus seinem Eigenen]; thus it lives without why, insofar as it lives *itself.*" This becomes, in Heidegger's first lecture course as Husserl's assistant (1919): "Lived experiences [*Erlebnisse*] are events of appropriation [*Er-eignisse*] insofar as they live from out of one's own [*aus dem Eigenen*] and life lives only in this way."[55]

It would nevertheless take Heidegger many years to aver the profound significance of this doctrine. Only in his 1955–56 lecture course *The Principle of Reason* will he set out the stakes. There he again takes up Silesius's distich on the rose without why, this time pointing to its ethical relevance, that is, its relevance for how to live and how to *be*: "What is unsaid in [Silesius's] saying—and everything depends on this—. . . says that humans, in the concealed grounds of their essential being, first truly are when in their own way they are like the rose—without why" (GA 10: 57–58/37; trans. mod.). Although Heidegger does not pursue this matter, his comment does reveal that it did not altogether elude him when he read texts such as Eckhart's *Die rede der underscheidunge* (Counsels on Discernment) and Suso's *Little Book of Truth*, which was written in defense of Eckhart.[56] Heidegger also ascribes great relevance to Eckhartian *mysticism*: "The entire saying [of Silesius] is so astoundingly clear and neatly constructed that one is inclined to get the idea that the most extreme sharpness and depth of thought belong to genuine and great mysticism. This is also true. Meister Eckhart proves it" (GA 10: 56/36–37; trans. mod.). Indeed, earlier in the lecture, Heidegger appears to grant mysticism a place alongside poetizing and thinking as ways out of metaphysics (GA 10: 54/35).[57]

Such would not seem to be the case in the first "Country Path Conversation," however, where Heidegger's thinking of *Gelassenheit* (releasement) as an indispensable alternative to the willfulness of Western metaphysics receives its most substantial treatment. In this dialogue, which Heidegger composed in the mid-1940s, the Scholar—one of the three interlocutors, alongside the Researcher and the Sage—asserts that Eckhart's conception of *Gelassenheit* is "thought of still within the domain of the will," as "the casting-off of sinful selfishness and the letting-go [*Fahrenlassen*] of self-will in favor of the divine will" (GA 77: 109/70). Now this should seem puzzling, not least because of Heidegger's praise of Eckhart elsewhere. Any close—indeed any casual—reader of Eckhart ought to know that the will is precisely a faculty that Eckhart strives not just to deemphasize in the human, but even occasionally to deny altogether in the Godhead. To take just two examples, one from a famous sermon that Heidegger doubtless read early on and from which he would later quote, namely "Beati pauperes spiritu," and another from "In hoc apparuit," which speaks of the *emergence* of the will in the Godhead:

> These people say that a poor man is one who wants nothing and they explain it this way: A man should so live that he never does his own will in anything, but should strive to do the dearest will of God. . . . They are much admired by those who know no better, but I say that they are asses with no understanding of God's truth . . . for a poor man is one who wills nothing and desires nothing. . . . [T]he poor man is not he who wants to fulfil the will of God but he who lives in such a way as to be free of his own will and of God's will, as he was when he was not. (DW 2: 490,1–4, 490,7–8, 492,2, 499,1–3/Walshe 421, 423 Pr. 52)

> Go right out of yourself for God's sake, and God will go right out of *Himself* for your sake! When these two have gone out, what is left is one and simple. In this One the Father bears His Son in the inmost source. Out of that the Holy Ghost blossoms forth, and *then* there arises in God a will which belongs to the soul. (DW 1: 93,6–94,2/Walshe 110 Pr. 5b)[58]

While the Scholar's comment is not false if considered in light of select passages from *Die rede der underscheidunge* which Heidegger marked up in his personal copies of this text (some of which he copied out), or in light of passages relating to *Gelassenheit* in the likes of Tauler, Luther, and Böhme,[59] it hardly epitomizes Eckhart's thought as a whole. One could, of course, stress that Heidegger's viewpoint in the first "Country Path Conversation" is confined to this text. However, there are several problems with such an approach. First, while Heidegger was composing the dialogue in the Upper Danube Valley as the end of the war was approaching, in addition to Bernhart's translation of *Die rede der underscheidunge* he also had available the copy of Pfeiffer's edition, which his wife Elfride—who herself had an abiding interest in Eckhart—had given to him as a birthday present in 1917.[60] Indeed, he even cites from this edition in his notes for the conversation (GA 77: 158/103). Second, he also would have had access to dozens of texts by and about Eckhart in the library of the nearby Benedictine archabbey of Beuron, where Heidegger appears to have actually lectured on the first "Country Path Conversation" in April and May 1945.[61] Third, the edition in which Bernhart's translation appears also contains two sermons (of eight total) that challenge the relegation of Eckhartian *Gelassenheit* to the domain of the will.[62] Finally, even more problematic is the fact that Heidegger allowed the critique of Eckhart to stand when he republished an edited portion of the dialogue in 1959 (G1, 33–34/61–62), well after he had read other texts of Eckhart that clearly place his thought outside the domain of the will.

Thus, when faced with the peculiar charge against Eckhart in the first "Country Path Conversation," one ought to begin, not by charging *Heidegger* with poor scholarship or, worse, self-serving deception, but by asking, *Are there other passages in Heidegger's corpus that suggest otherwise?* We have seen that there are. *Despite the easy objections one can make, might the Scholar have a point?* He does, but only to a certain extent, and Heidegger is not one to shirk the hard labor of unearthing an author's most authentic and concealed thoughts. *Why, then, would Heidegger write a dialogue in which Eckhart is characterized thus? Is it perhaps because, for Heidegger,* Gelassenheit *is primarily about thinking, whereas for Eckhart it is primarily about a way of being?* Yet thinking and ways of being are not radically separate for Heidegger, nor, ultimately, for Eckhart. *Well, then, perhaps because he wishes to distance himself from Eckhart, who is a little too close for comfort?* Yet Heidegger does not hesitate to acknowledge Eckhart's influence elsewhere. *Perhaps, finally, because Heidegger wants to provoke us, his readers, into thinking more deeply about his relation to the Meister?*

If we pay attention to the context in which this statement is made, the last seems to be the most plausible explanation. The Scholar does, after all, count Eckhart among the "old masters of *thought*," not of piety or spirituality or theology or philosophy. And to the Scholar's accusation, the Sage replies that Eckhart is someone "[f]rom whom, *all the same*, many good things can be learned" (GA 77: 109/70; emphases added). It is also important to note that the Scholar says releasement *can* be thought from within the domain of the will, as occurs with Eckhart. This is certainly true. Eckhart sometimes thinks *Gelassenheit* in this way. Yet it *need not* be thought in this way, nor, indeed, is it always thought this way in Eckhart, as Heidegger was (at times) well aware.[63] Was the Scholar? He'd hardly be deserving of the name if he were ignorant of this other, iconoclastic Eckhart. But maybe Heidegger intends to critique the captious character of contemporary scholarship, those who would insist on the letter rather than the spirit, the surface rather than the depths, the smoking gun rather than the situation that brought one to fire it. Perhaps the Scholar should be renamed the Pedant.

Instead of entertaining such possibilities, nearly every commentator on this passage has done with Heidegger what many have done with Plato: they have attributed—admittedly with varying degrees of subtlety—the character's position (in this case the Scholar's) to the author himself (in this case Heidegger).[64] This is especially surprising in the case of the first "Country Path Conversation," not only because readers of Heidegger tend to be more attentive to the literary character of Plato's dialogues, but because it is the Sage who, at least initially and superficially, seems to stand in for Heidegger's thought, not the Scholar. At any rate, the Eckhartian strain of releasement will only grow stronger in Heidegger's own thought over the coming months and years.

7. Poverty

After the Allied bombings of Freiburg in November 1944, during which much of the city center was destroyed, Heidegger fled to his hometown of Meßkirch.[65] Meßkirch was then bombed in February 1945. In March, Heidegger joined around ten professors and twenty students[66] of Freiburg University who had taken refuge in the thirteenth-century castle Wildenstein in Leibertingen, not far from Meßkirch and the Benedictine archabbey of Beuron. (The abbey, which also served as a meeting place for the faculty and as a place of refuge, is also called Erzabtei St. Martin—named, like Heidegger, after Saint Martin of Tours). In this area Heidegger would reside safely until June, apparently spending this unusual summer semester lecturing on the essence of thinking in the first "Country Path Conversation," as well as on Hölderlin's poem on the river Ister, now called the Donau, which is actually visible from the high location of the castle. So too is the sheepfold where Heidegger's paternal grandfather (also named Martin) was born in 1803. This was the year of some of Hölderlin's greatest hymns, including "Patmos"—the island on which the Apocalypse was revealed to John the Evangelist. Heidegger himself found fate in such coincidences:

> It was perhaps inevitable that the poet Hölderlin should become the determining influence on the critical thought of one whose grandfather was born at the very time when the "Ister Hymn"

and the poem "Remembrance" were written—born according to the records, "*in ovili*" (that is to say, in a sheepfold on a farm), which lies near the bank of the river in the valley of the Upper Danube, beneath the lofty crags. Nothing is chance in the unseen history of poetic discourse. All is destiny.[67]

On June 27, 1945, three days after a party had brought the semester to a close, Heidegger gave a lecture of sorts—more of a sermon, actually—in a forester's lodge across the valley, where, unlike the other professors, who stayed at Wildenstein, Heidegger had in large part been living with his lover and former student Princess Margot von Sachsen-Meiningen. The lecture bore the title "Armut" (Poverty). In it, Heidegger glosses a line from Hölderlin: "For us, everything is concentrated upon the spiritual, we have become poor in order to become rich" (AR, 5/3). Along with the strong and explicit Hölderlinian resonance, there is also a strong and implicit resonance with Eckhart, not least in its homiletic character. (One thinks, for example, of Eckhart's own celebrated sermon on poverty, Pr. 52 ["Beati pauperes spiritu"]). Indeed, Werner Beierwaltes has written that "Heidegger's own path of thought is hardly thinkable without its proximity to Eckhart's radically 'liberating' movement in *Gelassenheit*. . . . This holds in like manner for [the lecture] 'Poverty.' "[68] Two moments stand out in particular to support the Eckhart connection.

The first pertains to Heidegger's striking employment of an old metaphor. He notes that the human stands in a relation to being, but that this relation is not of a subject opposed to an object. Being is rather that which encompasses and sustains all things, including the human being. It "is" (transitively) all things in the sense of letting them be. Only when we experience this will we experience the spirit of which Hölderlin sings. His dictum, "everything is concentrated upon the spiritual,"

> now means: a concentration comes about [*ereignet sich*], i.e., a gathering upon the relationship of beyng to our essence, a relationship which is the center, the midpoint, that is everywhere as the midpoint of a circle whose periphery is nowhere. (AR, 7/6; trans. mod.)

This explosive geometrical figure has a long history. It was first used in the pseudo-Hermetic collection of definitions of God titled *The Book of Twenty-Four Philosophers*. The second definition understands God as an "infinite sphere whose center is everywhere and whose circumference is nowhere."[69] Later, figures such as Nicholas of Cusa, Giordano Bruno, and Blaise Pascal would apply it to the universe.[70] Now, while Cusa or Pascal may be Heidegger's source,[71] Eckhart seems more likely. For Eckhart avails himself of this metaphor not with respect to the cosmos, but with respect to God, and a note in Heidegger's collection of materials containing "Poverty" reveals that he too had God in mind when he adapted it: "What is going on with the image of a circle whose center is everywhere, yet whose circumference is nowhere—what kind of image of the highest being, of God himself is being used?" (GA 73.1: 712).[72]

There is also a noteworthy philosophical parallel in the way Eckhart interprets the image. He combines it with the third definition ("God is completely in whatever belongs to him") in order to convey the idea that God, as the ground of each thing, is wholly present in each thing, no matter how small or insignificant. Yet, as we know from Aristotle, the soul too has the ability to become all things. It can transcend multiplicity, corporeality, and temporality and reach out to anything, no matter how far or great. It can bring all things back to their unity in God, by seeing God in all things. As Elizabeth Brient puts it: "Thus if the manifest, creative God is figured as a sphere emanating infinitely outwards, the human intellect may be viewed as an inverse, infinitely contracting, sphere which channels all things back into an absolutely unified center."[73] This is because, at their core, there is one and the same ground for God and the soul. While their sameness is of course not the sameness of being and the human essence, Heidegger's gloss may nonetheless be viewed as a transformation of that Parmenidean-Eckhartian current running throughout his corpus. It also points back to his earlier appropriation of Eckhart from around 1916–19, where he was interested in finding a site for the manifestation of the divine. At issue in "Poverty" is, admittedly, being, but this is based on Heidegger's interpretation of Hölderlin's interest in the divine,[74] and there is at any rate a similar intention: "That upon which everything is gathered and from which everything comes about, everything that has come to be and will come to be, is 'the spiritual.'" (GA 73.1: 872).[75]

In order for the soul to be an infinite sphere, it must detach itself from all guises of limitation. It must become poor in order to become rich. Here we come to the second allusion to Eckhart in Heidegger's lecture. Inversions of wealth and poverty abound in the Gospels, and Eckhart draws on them frequently. So do many others, of course, even Hölderlin. But Heidegger's wording is unmistakably Eckhartian:

> Wahrhaft arm seyn besagt: so seyn, daß wir nichts entbehren, es sey denn das Unnötige.

> To be truly poor means to be so that one is deprived of nothing except what is not needed. (AR, 8/6)

Compare this with a passage from Eckhart's *Die rede der underscheidunge*:

> Dér mensche ist wærlîche arm von geiste, der allez daz wol enbern mac, daz niht nôt enist.

> That human being is truly poor in spirit who can well be deprived of everything that is not needed. (DW 5: 300,1–2/ES 282, §23; trans. mod.)[76]

Indeed, Heidegger even takes up the idea of perpetual impoverishment:

> Poverty is the mourning joyfulness [*trauernde Freude*] of never beyng sufficiently poor. In this reticent restiveness lies poverty's releasement [*Gelassenheit*] (AR, 10/8; trans. mod.).[77]

This too can be compared with *Die rede der underscheidunge*, where Eckhart likewise connects the notion of becoming ever poorer with releasement. As one reads in Heidegger's personal copy of Diederichs's edition of Eckhart, which contains the following underlining in lead pencil:

> (D)u solt wissen, das sich nie kein mensch so vil geliess in disem leben, er fünde sich danocht mer zelassen. (8; cf. DW 5: 196,7–8, §4)

> You should know that no one has ever released themselves so much in this life that there was nothing left of themselves to release." (Davies, 7; trans. mod.)[78]

When Heidegger lectured on poverty National Socialism was at an end. The fate of Germany, and Heidegger's own fate, hung in the balance. Heidegger could not have known what was to come, but there is an unmistakable sense in his lecture that an era had come to a close. It is telling that he chose to mark this closure with an appeal to *Gelassenheit*. For this

aps more than any other, will mark the remainder of his *Denkweg*.
s ever, will continue to accompany him.

8. Practical Apriori

An especially important citation of Eckhart (also from *Die rede der underscheidunge*) can be found in Heidegger's 1949 lecture "The Turning":

> Apart from first cultivating himself within this essential space [of the human essence in its relation to being] and taking up a dwelling therein, the human is not capable of anything essential within the dispensation now reigning. In considering this, we attend to a saying of Meister Eckhart and think it from its ground. It runs: "Those who are not of great essence [*wesen*], whatever work they effect, nothing will come of it." (GA 79: 70/66)[79]

In other words, to do something essential, which for Heidegger involves the kind of *thinking* that "is needed by the essence of being so as to guard it in its truth," one must be prepared. For Eckhart this means being of great essence. For Heidegger this entails tracing a path along which we may come to have an experience that will in turn enable us to consider the essence of being as worthy of thought and then guard it as such (GA 79: 70/76). What is at stake, Heidegger goes on to explain, is similar to what we saw in his 1916 notes on Eckhart: we must prepare a site for the articulation of being. Doing so is "authentic action," which Heidegger endeavors to understand not as separate from thinking, but *as* a kind of thinking (GA 79: 71/67). Such thinking-action is more primordial than knowledge (at least in any traditional sense of the term). It is what Eckhart might call, during one his more oxymoronic moments, an "unknown-knowing."[80] Here we see an example of what, in the introduction, I called a practical apriori, which I will develop in subsequent chapters.

In a letter to Arendt from 1950, Heidegger notes the difficulty with trying to develop a practical apriori that is at the same time a kind of thinking. He cites Eckhart's Commentary on John for support:

> [T]hinking is a very strict craft, even when the results bear no traces of the labor involved in it. . . . I am constantly pondering whether there is still a way to keep two things together and inconspicuously present: first that to thinking belongs the

longest and strictest craft [*Handwerk*]; and then that thinking is itself acting [*Handeln*], in that it lends a hand to [*an die Hand geht*] the essence of beyng. Meister Eckhart says at one point in his commentary on John: ipsa cogitatio . . . spirat ignem amoris [thinking itself . . . breathes the fire of love]. (MH/HA, 111–12/90–91; trans. mod.)[81]

9. Eckhart in Heidegger's Late Thought

Heidegger will again cite Eckhart's Commentary on John, together with Latin and German sermons of the Meister, in notes on being and God recorded no earlier than 1956 (GA 73.2: 995–96). Here and in the previous quotation, Heidegger cites from the Stuttgart critical edition, portions of which he and his brother Fritz—another great admirer of Eckhart—made a joint effort to obtain.[82] Although Heidegger does not provide much of an interpretation in these notes, his comments before and after the quotations are critical of the Scholastic, ontotheological approach to God, which can indeed be found in some of the passages he reproduces from Eckhart.[83] In chapter 2 I will address the matter of ontotheology in Eckhart's Latin writings. Here, however, I would like to note only that the quotations pertain to the reduplicative way in which created things may be said either to be God or to be nothing. *Insofar as something is common,* it is God; *insofar as it is particular,* taken in itself, it is not. Indeed, considered in themselves, creatures are nothing, for being belongs only to God (LW 4: 24/TP 208, no. 23, S. IV,1, "Ex ipso, per ipsum et in ipso"). Thus, in saying that being is God, Eckhart is saying that beings, insofar as they *are,* are God. Yet this is merely one restricted way in which to take them. It does not diminish the fact that "[e]very created being smacks of the shadow of nothingness" (LW 3: 17/ES 128, no. 20, In Ioh.).

This points to a possible difference in Eckhart's and Heidegger's understanding of "things." For Eckhart, the thing is either nothing in itself or that which "becomes pure God to you." Even if Heidegger, like Eckhart, sometimes says that only being "is" (GA 79: 74–75/70–71),[84] the thing for Heidegger "is" not just any thing, either nothing or God, but this singular, unique thing which gathers earth and sky, divinities and mortals into a mutual belonging.

And yet Heidegger did turn to Eckhart in order to think the relation between thing and world. In two fascicles titled "Zum Weltbegriff" (On the Concept of World) and "Der Meister Eckehart" from a collection of unpublished notes (which also must have been composed in or after 1956), Heidegger copies out several passages from Eckhart (and from what is now considered to be Pseudo-Eckhart) with headings pertaining to this theme. After citing a passage in which Eckhart preaches the need to become like a desert to ourselves and to all things (Büttner 2nd ed., 1, 99),[85] Heidegger writes down the following quote, which shows how the detached person can come to see the world as but a gift and unfolding of God's presence:

> God looked upon himself and beheld at the same time *himself* and *all things*. And yet he was not therefore something manifold, as things are now in their distinction, but rather he remained a singular. For even if creatures are now something manifold, in God they are nevertheless but *one* glance. In the presence of himself [*bei sich selbst*], God is always but a single-one [*ein Einig-Eines*]. And they—and especially the rational creature—will behold this clearly when they turn back into their first origin: there one sees God in no other way than as onefold in essence, and yet threefold in persons, and manifold in his works! Thus all creatures have their being in God, and the essence that they have, God gives it to them with his presence [*Gegenwart*]. ("Von dem Zorne der Seele und von ihrer rechten Stätte," in Büttner 2nd ed., 1, 190)

Other notes in the fascicles deal with the soul as a sort of world, with reason's breakthrough to the Godhead, with poverty of spirit, with the Trinity, and with the status of *Ereignis* (the event) as *Er-"eignen"* (en-"owning") in Eckhart. The reader may consult §3 of Appendix One, below, for all of the Eckhart-quotations on which Heidegger relies.

It is not only terms such as *Anwesen* (presencing), *Ereignis,* and *Gelassenheit* that Heidegger finds prefigured in Eckhart's work. Even *Gestell* (enframing, com-position) has an Eckhartian provenance for Heidegger. In a series of reflections written around 1972–73 and expanded in the years to follow,[86] Heidegger notes that Eckhart coined the term *Gestellnis* to translate the Latin *forma*.[87] Eckhart of course did not use it in the sense of contemporary enframing. Yet neither did he use it to describe the substantial being of an entity. Rather, on Heidegger's reading, Eckhart understood it as "the gathering and setting out of presencing [*Anwesen*] into what presences [*das Anwesende*] (*materia*)" (GA 81: 286). This resembles the ways in which Heidegger himself uses *Gestell* and *Gestellung* to translate the Greek words *thesis, poiēsis,* and *morphē* in his essays "On the Origin of the Work of Art" (GA 5: Zusatz/Addendum) and "On the Essence and Concept of *Physis*" (GA 9: 276/211).[88] Although *Gestell* in this sense foreshadows enframing, there are still moments of letting and gathering that differ from the willful imposition we find in the age of planetary technology. Whether or not Heidegger had Eckhart in mind when he was writing these essays, what we see in his late reflection on *Gestellnis* is another instance in which Heidegger traces his own key concepts back to Eckhart. Even though he employs these concepts differently (as he will with *Gestellnis*),[89] Heidegger nevertheless places himself within the lineage of his Dominican forebear, and thereby calls on his readers to delve deeper into these connections.

Such a call can be distinctly heard in the correspondence between Heidegger and the theologian Bernhard Welte. I mentioned above that, in one of his letters to Welte, Heidegger acknowledged Eckhart's extrametaphysical significance, that is, his ability to think outside the forgetfulness of being that beleaguered philosophy from Plato to Nietzsche. What I did not mention was that, later in the letter, Heidegger writes that "[a] more extensive presentation of the 'problem of being' in Thomas Aquinas and Meister Eckhart would be necessary. Or is there already such a presentation?" (MH/BW, 30) It is unknown whether Heidegger and Welte discussed this matter. Years later, though, in November 1975, Welte told Heidegger that he was thinking about writing a book based on his current lecture course on Meister Eckhart, to which Heidegger replied eagerly and encouragingly in March, just a couple months before his (Heidegger's) own death (MH/BW, 41, 46).[90] It is as though Heidegger had wanted someone to take up and develop his own elliptical remarks on Eckhart, to complete the project on Eckhartian mysticism that he had merely announced in 1916, to "save"[91] Eckhart from the obfuscations of metaphysics and the machinations of technology. Heidegger the man did not live long enough to do so himself, nor to appreciate the work of those following in his wake.[92] But Heidegger's deconstruction of metaphysics, his frequent references to Eckhart, and his intimations of ways in which that master of letters and life might be read otherwise than metaphysically, for the sake of a new beginning—all this has struck a path on which we may begin to think Eckhart anew. Perhaps only now are we ready for him.

PART TWO

Introduction

Hardly any figure throughout history has been interpreted in as many different ways as Meister Eckhart. Indeed, it has become a common trope to preface one's study on Eckhart with references to the disparate "Eckharts" that have been resurrected since his death in 1328. Eckhart has been appropriated by beatified disciples, orthodox and heterodox Catholics, Protestant reformers, Buddhists, postmodern theologians, New Age spiritualists, baroque theosophists, German idealists, Neokantians, phenomenologists, Marxists, Jungian psychoanalysts, philosophers of the Kabbalah, and Nazi propagandists. Nishitani Keiji and others have brought Eckhart together with such an ulikely figure as Nietzsche, who for his part cites Eckhart approvingly.[1] John Cage's controversial *4'33"* has been traced back to his interest in Eckhartian silence, and Cage himself wrote a poem linking Eckhart to artist Marcel Duchamp.[2] Hitler's "chief ideologue" Alfred Rosenberg was a great admirer of Eckhart,[3] but, judging from several of his poems, so was Paul Celan.[4] After Franz von Baader read some of Eckhart's works to Hegel in Berlin, Hegel is reported to have been "so enthusiastic that the next day he held an entire lecture on Eckhart and at the end said: 'There we have it—just what we wanted.'"[5] And yet only a few decades later, Hegel's enemy Arthur Schopenhauer could write that, basically, Buddha, Eckhart, and he (Schopenhauer) teach the same thing.[6] Ernst Bloch and Hermann Ley found in Eckhart a leftist critique of otherworldliness, church hierarchy, and feudalism,[7] while, as we have seen, Heidegger recognized the authenticity of Eckhart's understanding of being. How could a single author open up so many interpretive possibilities?

There are many reasons for these diverse interpretations of Eckhart. Some of Eckhart's works remained incomplete. Others were unavailable to certain audiences, and some are no longer extant. Eckhart himself drew on various, and in some cases incompatible traditions, including Aristotelianism, Neoplatonism, illuminationism, Dionysianism, Albertinism, and the so-called *Frauenmystik* (female mysticism) of the thirteenth and early fourteenth centuries. He was acquainted with the works of Muslim philosophers such as Avicenna and Averroes, and in his Latin works he cites the Jewish sage Moses Maimonides more than any other non-Christian philosopher except Aristotle.[8] He wrote in Latin within the context of High Scholasticism, but he also preached in Middle High German to confreres, laymen, nuns, and Beguines.[9] At times he provides rational arguments for his positions. At others he calls on his reader or congregation first to experience, or better, to *be* the truth. For, with regard to certain topics, "if you are unlike this truth of which we want to speak, you cannot understand me" (DW 2: 487/ ES 199 Pr. 52 ["Beati pauperes spiritu"]).[10] Such a condition readily lends itself to miscomprehension.

Moreover, the hortatory character of his writings is profuse with stylistic devices that are deployed for the purpose of both deconstruction and cultivation: shattering congealed interpretations and fostering awareness of something not fully open to traditional modes of argumentation. Even if Eckhart does provide guidelines for how we can make strides toward attaining such awareness, it is not apparent that we can know in advance what it would look like, nor when exactly we will have achieved it. One can—and probably will—err.

Depending on one's familiarity or unfamiliarity with various figures or traditions influential on Eckhart, one will naturally be inclined to interpret him tendentiously, to point up similarities while obscuring differences, or at least occluding other possibilities. A similar problem presents itself in the other direction, depending on one's familiarity or unfamiliarity with various figures or traditions Eckhart influenced. In this study on Heidegger and Eckhart, I will naturally read Eckhart in a somewhat Heideggerian vein. This is not necessarily a bad thing, though. Perhaps Heidegger's own thought will let us catch sight of something previously unseen in Eckhart's.

I take as my point of departure a claim made by Reiner Schürmann, one of the best of the Heideggerian interpreters of Eckhart. Indeed, this approach has warrant to the extent that Schürmann's interpretation was inspired (and perhaps even approved) by Heidegger himself during their personal exchanges.[11] Although Schürmann has gained prominence in the last couple of decades as a brilliant thinker in his own right, comparatively little has been written on his reading of Eckhart—this despite the fact that it was from his studies of Eckhart that Schürmann came to develop many of his central ideas. Moreover, none of the commentaries devotes much attention to the simple, radical claim Schürmann makes:

> It is probably possible to reproduce Eckhart's experience of being, but only on one condition: "He who wants to understand my teaching of releasement must himself be perfectly released." An attitude is required for thinking to succeed. We propose to define mysticism as this reciprocity between existence and thought: to think of *being* as *releasement* one must first of all have a released existence.[12]

For Eckhart, and, as I will later argue, for Heidegger too, thinking is dependent on a practical apriori (or what in the general introduction I called a "mystical foundation"). To think being at its most basic level, I must act in terms of the very way in which being is to be thought. I must *do* something before I can understand. This "doing" should not, however, be treated as utterly separate from thinking, but rather as a more practical valence of the essential *activity* of thinking. What, then, must I do? For Eckhart, I must release myself. Doing so will enable me to understand that being, at its core, is not static, is not something that could be possessed as an object or conceived as an idea. Nor is it simply the infinite perfection of this-worldly categories. What, then, is it? It "is" releasement. But even this simple answer does not suffice. It withdraws from definition and declarative discourse. To quote Schürmann again: "What Meister Eckhart understands by 'being' will remain unintelligible as long as the meaning of being is not experienced and verified in the course of releasement."[13]

This is not to say that Eckhart remains silent. He endeavors again and again to convey his understanding of being. And he even uses the language of philosophy to do so. Yet this "speculative mysticism" is not just an alternative language to that of metaphysics in its various guises. It is designed to cultivate us for releasement (*gelâzenheit*). Eckhart's work not only issues a demand. It prepares us to fulfill it.

The following material on Eckhart will be divided into three chapters. Chapter 2 will examine the two ostensibly incompatible claims in Eckhart's Latin writings that I mentioned in the previous chapter, namely, that God is most properly to be understood in terms of understanding rather than being, and that being is God. As we saw, the first claim led Heidegger to acknowledge Eckhart's uniqueness as a thinker of being, whereas the second helped Heidegger to critique analogical reasoning. It is true, at least according to the traditional chronology of Eckhart's texts, that the first claim recedes as Eckhart develops the second; however, as Heidegger himself saw in 1931, "it remained alive in his thinking in another respect" (GA 33: 47/38). My chief aim in chapter 2 is to show how Eckhart's approach in these Latin writings involves a deconstructive preparation for releasement that is more discursively oriented—though by no means exclusively so—than the explosive, extradiscursive strategies of the German writings I will examine later in Part Two.

Chapter 3 argues that the essence of being and the human being, the way in which they "hold sway," is, at bottom, an identical letting-be that is always already operative, yet for the most part covered over. Releasement is at once the condition for understanding this and the content of that which is understood. It is what we are in our essence, what being itself is, and what we need to do—better, what we need to allow to happen—to understand it.

In chapter 4, I return to the question of method. I argue that, beyond his deconstructive endeavors, Eckhart deploys such strategies as dialectic, paradox, and deliberate mistranslation in order to cultivate his listeners and readers for the experience of releasement. All of this will prepare us to trace the Eckhartian connection between being, thinking, and method in Heidegger's thought in Part Three.

2

Thinking, Being, and the Problem of Ontotheology in Eckhart's Latin Writings

Ever since Parmenides, the connection between thinking and being has been a central issue in philosophy, and we know that, at philosophy's "end," Heidegger never stopped meditating on it.[1] This connection has taken many forms over the past two and a half millennia. Hegel prioritized thinking over being. The early German Romantics did the opposite. Parmenides himself identified thinking and being as the same, as did philosophers such as Aristotle and Thomas Aquinas when they were treating of God, even if they understood the human intellect to depend on sensation for its knowledge, and thus to be secondary in relation to what *is*. Although, following on Plato's "good beyond being," there were several Neoplatonic and medieval thinkers who conceived of God as in some sense beyond being, it appears that none, other than Meister Eckhart, maintained that this was due to God's understanding (*intelligere*). This distinguishes Eckhart from his contemporaries, and indeed marks an important revolution within the Scholasticism of his day.[2] One might even go so far as to say that, with this move, Eckhart anticipated modern subjectivity and German idealism,[3] if not, as Hermann Ley has claimed, atheist materialism.[4]

However this may be, it is curious that, in what until recently had been considered to be a later work,[5] Eckhart appears to espouse a contrary view: not that God's understanding takes priority over his being, but that *esse est deus*, being is God. What was said to represent "the first and most vigorous critique of ontotheology, more than six centuries before Heidegger" (MAP, 7),[6] appears to suffer a relapse. For what is the statement that being is God if not a classic case of ontotheology?

As seen in chapter 1, Heidegger was actually acquainted with this problem in Eckhart interpretation, and he recognized that it had something to do with the problem of analogy in ancient and medieval thought. While other theologians merely found refuge in an analogical treatment of the enigmatic relation between the being of God and the being of creatures, it was, in Heidegger's view, Eckhart and Eckhart alone who saw this as an impasse and wagered to circumvent it:

> Meister Eckhart—the only one who sought a solution—says "God 'is' not at all, because 'being' is a finite predicate and absolutely cannot be said of God." (This was admittedly only a beginning which disappeared in Eckhart's later development, although it remained alive in his thinking in another respect.) (GA 33: 46–47/38)

Here, Heidegger suggests that, even when Eckhart turned toward a seemingly more ontotheological approach, something of his iconoclasm persevered. Regarding precisely how and to what extent, Heidegger says nothing.

This chapter ventures to speak where Heidegger kept silent. After situating Eckhart's thought within the context of his Scholastic training and activity, I will examine the texts that are most representative of Eckhart's dual approach to God: his intellectualist, "meontological"[7] approach in the first of his 1302–03 Parisian Questions, and his analogical, ontological approach in his *Opus tripartitum*. I argue that the differences between these approaches are not as stark as they may initially appear. Not only do both rest on Eckhart's peculiar doctrine of analogy. Both serve to dismantle the ontotheological architecture. Indeed, rather than an intellectualist alternative to ontotheology, Eckhart's First Parisian Question presents a meticulously crafted dialectic designed to explode rational distinctions. Rather than a traditional account of God as the highest being, Eckhart's *Opus tripartitum* obliterates hierarchies with its appeal to treat all being as God. Both approaches contribute to an appreciation of Eckhart's principal concern—the basic unity of the ground of the soul and the Godhead in *gelâzenheit*—but neither one alone, nor indeed both together, suffices for unfolding its deepest implications. For that, we will have to turn to some of Eckhart's most radical German writings in chapter 3.

1. Eckhart the Scholastic, and His 1302–03 Parisian Questions

Although Eckhart is well known today as a mystic and less so as a philosopher, his relation to Scholasticism has yet to receive the attention it deserves, especially among philosophers. Not only did Eckhart study in Cologne—perhaps directly under Albert the Great—and at the University of Paris during the controversial period surrounding the condemnations of 1277.[8] He also held the external Dominican chair of theology at the University of Paris twice, from 1302–03 and from 1311–13, an honor shared only by Thomas Aquinas. After serving as vicar for the Dominican master general in Strasbourg from 1313–23/24, Eckhart returned to the Dominican House in Cologne. He stayed there until Spring 1327, when, having recently defended himself against the charge of heresy,[9] he left for Avignon to defend his teaching before the Papal Court. Due to his death in January 1328, a trial was never conducted. This did not, however, prevent Pope John XXII from issuing a papal edict condemning twenty-eight propositions. In addition to the German sermons and treatises for which he has rightly become famous, Eckhart also commented on the *Sentences* of Peter Lombard in 1293–94, engaged in academic disputations, and wrote Latin sermons, biblical commentaries, and prologues for a planned, though never completed, masterwork entitled the *Opus tripartitum* or "Three-Part Work," which was also to feature a thousand or more propositions divided into fourteen treatises, as well as questions modeled on Aquinas's *Summa theologiae*. It was within the milieu of High Scholasticism that Eckhart cut his teeth. And it was within the milieu of High Scholasticism, not altogether outside it, that Eckhart began to think beyond it. Thus, to understand properly the trajectory and uniqueness of Eckhart's thought, we cannot overlook his Latin accomplishments.

The first text I will be discussing comes from Eckhart's 1302–03 Parisian Questions.[10] Only two of these *quaestiones disputatae* survive under Eckhart's name, along with a recently discovered fragment from another that may date from the same period.[11] The first (which will be my main focus) is on "Whether Being and Understanding Are the Same in God." The second concerns "Whether the Understanding of an Angel, as an Action, Is Its Being." There is also a record of arguments Eckhart made for the priority of the intellect over the will in a disputed question of the Franciscan master Gonsalvus Hispanus, which is preserved under the title, "Whether Praising God in Heaven Is Nobler than Loving Him on Earth," and included as the Third Parisian Question in Eckhart's *Latin Writings*. Despite the numbering in the critical edition, there is good reason to believe these three questions were composed in reverse order, although this will be of little concern to me here.[12]

Scholars have interpreted the significance of these Questions in strikingly different ways. Not only are they "among the most famous texts of medieval thought ever produced";[13] they also represent "probably the most contested chapter of [Eckhart's] thought."[14] On one side are those who dismiss them as merely theological, Scholastic exercises, irrelevant to understanding his thought. Heribert Fischer, for instance, maintains that "[t]hese questions must initially be left out of consideration when one addresses Eckhart's philosophical thought, because in them one finds questions of a theological sort that, due to their Scholastic and more incidental nature, do not without further ado permit inferences as to how they fit into the entirety of Eckhart's corpus."[15] Such a position, however, overlooks the numerous correspondences with Eckhart's German and Latin sermons (such as in Prr. 9, 69, 70, 71; and SS. XI,1, XI,2, XXIX).

On the other side are those who think that these questions are of pivotal importance. Thus, the editors of *Maître Eckhart à Paris* speak of them as "the principal axis of Eckhart's entire theology" and "as the irreplaceable key for his entire thought, including and above all for what one calls his mysticism" (MAP, 7). Yet there are many aspects of Eckhart's thought that these questions alone do not allow us to understand, such as the ineffable desert of the Godhead, the spark of the soul, the practical apriori of releasement, and the verbal character of being (*wesen* in Middle High German).

I am therefore inclined to take a more moderate view. These questions clearly have great philosophical import. Moreover, there are similarities between these questions and Eckhart's other writings that invite comparison. Nevertheless, even if these questions serve as an excellent starting point for understanding Eckhart's thought, there are moments in his other writings that surpass what Eckhart is trying to do here, moments to which we will return later. For now, let us turn simply to the first of the Parisian Questions.

2. *Deus Est Intelligere*

At first blush, Eckhart's First Parisian Question divides readily into three parts, not least because of his own adverbs of number (*Primo, Secundo, Tertio*). First, Eckhart adduces arguments from Aquinas affirming the identity of being and understanding in God, where being nonetheless takes rational precedence (nos. 1–2). Second, Eckhart provides his own argument for such identity (no. 3). Third, Eckhart challenges this position by arguing instead for the primacy of God's understanding (nos. 4–12).

The problem with this ordering is that it obfuscates a number of crucial moments that have addled commentators for decades—when, that is, they have even bothered to address them.[16] Before suggesting an alternate structure for the Question and unfolding its implications, I will identify and examine sixteen such moments. As much as possible, I will follow the progression of Eckhart's text. My aim here is to expose Eckhart's meticulously crafted, explosive methodology.

(1) To the question, whether being and understanding are the same in God, Eckhart begins by answering not only *with* Aquinas that they are the same in reality (*re*), but also, *beyond* him, that they may be conceptually (*ratione*) as well (LW 5: 37, no. 1). He then proceeds to recount several of Aquinas's arguments for a real identity.

For Aquinas, there is no real difference between God's being and his understanding, even though we may conceive of that identity in different ways, according to which being comes to assume a rational precedence. To take Eckhart's first argument for divine identity, drawn from Aquinas's *Summa contra gentiles* (I, ch. 45): "since understanding is an immanent act, and whatever is in the first is the first, therefore God is his very understanding and is also his being" (LW 5: 37, no. 1). Aquinas's version, though more developed, essentially says the same. He points out that, unlike heating, where heat is transferred from one object to another, understanding remains within the one who understands. When I understand that this book is on the table, my understanding does not leave me for the object understood. Nor is the book in any way changed by my understanding something about it. Having already established that God's essence (*essentia*) is his being (*esse*), Aquinas can now say that whatever is in God is his essence. Consequently, inasmuch as God understands, this understanding must not be anything that is really different from God. That is to say, the distinction between God's being and God's understanding does not exist *in re* for Aquinas, but only *in ratione*. It is a distinction of reason. As he puts it in the *Summa theologiae* (I.26.2), "But in God being and understanding do not differ in reality [*secundum rem*], but only by reason of the understanding [*secundum intelligentiae rationem*]." The fact that Eckhart initially inflates Aquinas's position, then glosses it faithfully, and in just a few moments will appear to reject it brusquely, should give one pause. We will have occasion to return to this peculiar circumstance below.

(2) After presenting five more proofs from Aquinas in favor of the real identity of being and understanding in God, all of which rely on the conception of God as first and simple, Eckhart proposes a proof of his own, which he says he has employed elsewhere (LW 5: 39, no. 3). His proof runs as follows: Although the terms *human* and *rational* are convertible, it does

not follow that each automatically entails the other. The term *human* brings along with it the notion of rationality, but not vice versa. In other words, the term *human* is contained within the set of rational beings, but it does not exhaust that set. Likewise with regard to being. Living, understanding, and acting are all convertible with being. For example, when I speak of life I am speaking of being insofar as it is self-moving. However, even though they all entail being, the term *being* does not entail them in this way. For it exceeds them in scope. To the extent that being is perfect, however, it contains everything else within it, and nothing needs to be superadded to it to explain how, through it, all things are what they are. Such is God's being. Thus, Eckhart says, we must see that "through his very being, God works all things, both within his divinity and without in creatures, each in their own way; and thus in God being itself is <understanding> itself, since by this being he works and understands" (LW 5: 40, no. 3).[17]

The difficulty here, which does not concern Eckhart's proof per se, is that it is not entirely clear where else he had presented it. Although there have been some reasonable guesses,[18] we need not conclude that it represents an earlier phase in his development.[19] Perhaps Eckhart is perfectly willing to present seemingly incompatible arguments side by side. This is, after all, precisely what occurs in the Question under discussion. Why he would do so is a question I will endeavor to answer.

(3) Despite his initial response, in none of these seven arguments—the six from Aquinas and the one of his own—does Eckhart explain how the identity of being and understanding in God is both real *and* rational.[20] Alone, they would suggest he is in complete agreement with Aquinas.

(4) Eckhart next presents exegeses and arguments that appear to run counter to Aquinas and to his own position. Instead of God's being, God's understanding comes to take precedence. Yet because there is no explicit refutation of the former, no *Sed contra*,[21] it will be necessary to ask whether, in this case too, appearances are deceiving.

(5) Eckhart introduces these interpretations and arguments in favor of God's understanding with a sudden and surprising remark, which I must first present in Latin:

> Tertio ostendo quod non ita videtur mihi modo, ut quia sit, ideo intelligat, sed quia intelligit, ideo est, ita quod deus est intellectus et intelligere et est ipsum intelligere fundamentum ipsius esse. (LW 5: 40, no. 4)

For much hinges on how we translate *non ita mihi modo . . . sed*. Ought we to follow most commentators?

> Third, I declare that it is *not my present opinion* that God understands because he is, *but rather* that he is because he understands. God is an intellect and understanding, and his understanding itself is the ground of his being.[22]

Or is Loris Sturlese right?

> Third, I indicate that I am of the opinion *not only* that God thinks because he is, *but* that he is because he thinks . . .[23]

In other words, is *modo* an adverb of time (at present, now, recently) or a modal adverb together with *non* (not only)? If the latter, then perhaps we should be even more explicit than Sturlese: "I am of the opinion *not only* that God understands because he is, *but also* that he is because he understands." Rather than a change of perspective or a radical break with Aquinas,[24] Eckhart's arguments would represent a complementary, and perhaps transformative, approach to God. And even if we were to follow the standard translation, Eckhart would not be saying here that God has no being whatsoever; rather his claim would simply be that God's being is secondary in relation to his understanding.

Eckhart's initial support for the preeminence of understanding in God is exegetical. Four more difficulties present themselves here.

(6) Eckhart begins by citing John 1:1, "In the beginning was the word, and the word was with God, and God was the word." In a unique interpretation[25] that must have provoked a few scoffs—or perhaps chuckles—from some of his confreres, Eckhart points out that John does not say, "In the beginning was a being, and God was a being," but rather, "in the beginning was the word." This is crucial, because words are not of the order of being. They are of the order of the intellect, "wherein . . . neither being [*esse*] nor a being [*ens*] is mixed" (LW 5: 40, no. 4).

Eckhart next cites Jesus's claim in John 14:6, "I am the truth" (and not, we might add, "I am being"). Like the word, truth pertains to the intellect. Drawing on Dietrich of Freiberg's theory of relation, Eckhart explains, oddly, that truth involves a relation whose *real* categorial being depends *entirely* on the soul (and thus on the intellect) (LW 5: 40–41, no. 4).[26]

Now, whether or not these readings are plausible in and of themselves, they clearly fly in the face of the Augustinian reading of Exodus 3:14 as "I am being." Eckhart has a way of responding to this objection, as we will see, yet he does not address obvious counterexamples, such as the ones that Gonsalvus Hispanus poses in the Third Parisian Question, and that Eckhart himself cites elsewhere: "Amen, amen I say to you, before Abraham was made, I am" (John 8:58); "he alone is" (Job 23:13).[27]

(7) Moreover, neither in his reading of John 1:1 nor in that of John 14:6 does Eckhart question the copula and the incongruities it presents: "In the beginning *was* the word," "I *am* the truth."

(8) In another exegetical feat, Eckhart attempts to elide John 1:3 with the fourth proposition of the pseudo-Aristotelian *Liber de Causis*. In the Vulgate, one reads: *omnia per ipsum facta sunt*. Now, one would naturally interpret *sunt* as the helping verb in the passive construction *facta sunt*, that is, "are made": "Through him all things are made." Eckhart, however, proposes that we read the verb *to be* in an absolute sense: "All things made by him *are*." Or, in Eckhart's gloss: "To those things made, being itself comes along afterwards" (LW 5: 41, no. 4).[28] Createdness belongs essentially and above all to being, not to the intellect. As Proposition Four of the *Liber de Causis* puts it, "the first of things created is being."[29] Since God, as creator, is not created, being cannot belong to God.

But, one might object, what about Sirach 24:14: "From the beginning and before the world I [Wisdom] was created [*ab initio et ante saecula creata sum*]"? Doesn't this mean that creation, and thus being, is present within God before the creation of the world/being? Again, Eckhart proposes alternative readings. One reading would interpret *creata* as *genita* (engendered), which would enable us to maintain a stricter connection between creation and being (though it would still leave open the status of the *sum*). Another would take *creata* as an adjective of *saecula*, rather than in a perfect passive construction with *sum*. The verse would then read: "From the beginning and before the created world, I *am*." Wisdom would thus belong to God prior to any sort of generation or creation. It would signify God as intellect. What is striking about this second possibility, however, is that it parallels the absolute use of "to be" in Eckhart's reading of John 1:3, except that here it is applied to wisdom in God or God as wisdom rather than to creatures. We could of course say that, in the case of wisdom, "am" would not mean (created) being, but intellect and intellection. Yet Eckhart does not say this. He merely concludes that "God, who is the creator and not creatable, is intellect and understanding and not a being or being" (LW 5: 41, no. 4). If

Eckhart were really concerned with divesting God of all being, one would think that he would have avoided such a striking parallelism, or at least accounted for it somehow, especially given the proximity of the two glosses.

(9) Additionally, we should note that, in his explanation of John 1:3, Eckhart writes that "being has the *ratio* of creatability *first of all* [*primo*]" (LW 5: 41, no. 4; my emphasis), not that it has this *exclusively*.

Still more difficulties with the traditional division of Eckhart's First Parisian Question can be found among his three assumptions and four arguments in favor of God as understanding.[30]

(10) The first assumption, which is based on the premise that the workings of nature are workings of an understanding, and again on John 1:1, is that understanding is superior to being. Although Eckhart asserts his position quite strongly against those who would rank being above living and understanding ("But I believe the complete opposite"), he does not conclude bluntly that God is neither *esse* nor *ens*, as we saw above and will see again (LW 5: 42–43, nos. 5–6).[31] Instead, being is simply of a lower grade in comparison with understanding.

(11) Second, Eckhart now assumes that understanding and being are in fact of different orders. He turns to the human soul to develop this. Images in the soul cannot have being, for they are what enable us to know beings. If an image in the soul did have being, we would need another image to know it, but if that image also had being, we would need yet another image, and so on to infinity; we would be driven ever farther from the first being we were trying to understand. "Thus," Eckhart concludes, "those things that belong to the intellect are as such non-beings" (LW 5: 44, no. 7). The upshot of this is that we are able to think of things that cannot exist in actuality, indeed that God cannot even make to exist in actuality: "We are able to conceive [*Intelligimus*] what God cannot do, as for instance when we conceive of fire without conceiving of its heat; God, however, cannot make fire that does not heat" (LW 5: 44, no. 7). While it is not altogether clear what is going on here,[32] Eckhart seems to want to contrast the human intellect with the intellect of God. Yet Eckhart's claim here need not imply a certain superiority of human intellection over divine production. For example, would it really be better to be able to think of fire without heat than to be able to make hot fire just by the act of thinking it? Perhaps God cannot do what we can because what we can do is a sign of our imperfection. Perhaps God's thought always also brings along with it an act of creation. Perhaps, finally, this is because God's intellect is not dissociated from being in the way ours must be.[33]

Eckhart acknowledges that there is a problem here. For, right away, he makes a third assumption: that here the *imaginatio* or "power of representation" *deficit* (LW 5: 44, no. 8). We can read this claim in two ways. On the one hand, it may refer to the human being. When it comes to God, our imagination *falls short*.[34] We cannot rationally separate God's understanding from his being in the way we can rationally separate the form of fire from its ability to heat.[35] On the other hand (and perhaps at the same time?), it may refer to God. When it comes to God, there is *no* power of representation *at all*, for God does not need to extract phantasms from sensible things for his knowledge. We should accordingly not think of the human intellect as of a piece with God's (thus, we should not see a trace of Eckhart's doctrine of the spark of the soul here), for Eckhart goes on to say that, as our intellect is to beings, so beings are to God. Whereas we depend on beings for our knowledge, beings depend on God's knowledge as their cause. Even though Eckhart says that this means God is not being, God's intellectual nonbeing would not be the same as our intellectual nonbeing; it would not be "below beings [*sub ente*]" but rather would be "above being itself [*super ipsum esse*] and [would be] . . . complete understanding" (LW 5: 44, no. 8). Far from strengthening the notion that God is sheer understanding, however, and despite Eckhart's appeal to "complete understanding," reading Eckhart's assumptions shows only that God's intellect is not like our own. His relation to being may therefore be different.

Among Eckhart's four arguments, we find further difficulties with an exclusive ascription of understanding to God. Following the work of Stephan Grotz ("Meister Eckharts Pariser Quaestio I"), I count five additional moments of attenuation.

(12) Having established that "God is intellect and understanding [*intellectus et intelligere*] and that the latter is itself the foundation of his being" (LW 5: 40, no. 4), and indeed of "all being [*omnis esse*]" (LW 5: 45, no. 8), Eckhart seems to back off from his position. In an informal aside to his audience, he says, and again I must quote the Latin first: "Et si tu intelligere velis vocare esse, placet mihi" (LW 5: 45, no. 8). Here too, a decision about translation can make all the difference. Let's begin again with the standard reading: "Of course if you wish to call understanding being I do not mind." This rendering is quite plausible in light of what follows: "Nevertheless I say that if there is anything in God you want to call being, it belongs to him through his understanding" (Maurer, 48; trans. mod.). Yet might it be the case that, rather than simply tolerating such a designation, Eckhart would actually be *pleased* by it (*placet mihi*)?

The next three enigmatic moments in Eckhart's arguments for God's understanding come up in his gloss of Exodus 3:14, where God says (in the translation of the Vulgate): *Ego sum qui sum*, "I am who I am."

(13) Eckhart begins by saying that a principle can never be the same as that whose principle it is (*principium nunquam est principiatum*) (LW 5: 45, no. 9). As the point is to the line, so is God to the being of creatures. The point is the principle of the line, that is, it is only on the basis of the point that lines can be at all;[36] God is the principle of being of creatures, that is, it is only on the basis of God that creatures can be at all. Just as the point clearly cannot be the same as the line, so God cannot be the same as the being of that which he creates. If, as Eckhart says earlier, "nothing is formally in the cause and that which is caused, if the cause is a true cause" (LW 5: 45, no. 8), then we must conclude that God, as the creator of being, cannot himself *be*. Eckhart's view of analogy leads to the same conclusion. Just as a true cause must differ radically from that which it causes, one thing being compared by an analogy must differ radically from the other. Only on one side may the analogical term inhere properly or, as Eckhart puts it, "formally": "in those things which are spoken of analogically, what is in one analogate is not formally in the other, as only health is in the animal formally, while there is no more health in a diet or urine than there is in a stone. Since therefore everything caused is, formally, a being, God will not, formally, be a being" (LW 5: 46, no. 11). Aside from the peculiarity of Eckhart's position on analogy and "true causality," there would be little problem if we left it at that. God, as the creative principle, would differ utterly from that which he creates, from that whose principle he is, and from that to which he is analogically compared.

Let's pay closer attention to what's really going on here, though. Eckhart explains that "[n]othing that is in the creature is in God except insofar as it is in its cause, and it is not there formally" (LW 5: 45, no. 9). In other words, even if, in its primary sense, being belongs to creatures, there is still some sense in which being is "in God," as the line must in some sense be contained in the point as the principle of the line. In the next argument, Eckhart will speak of virtual (*in virtute*) containment. Here, he instead invokes the phrase *puritas essendi* or "purity of being" to describe this relation: "And therefore since being belongs to creatures, it is not in God except insofar as it is in its cause, and therefore in God there is not being but rather purity of being" (LW 5: 45, no. 9). Again there are two possible readings here. *Puritas essendi* could mean purity *from* being, which would serve to distinguish God from the limited, categorially determinable sense of being that is characteristic of creatures. Yet if it *only* meant purity from being,[37] then it would be hard to make sense of Eckhart's discussion of containment, of "being-in." In other words, regardless of how it is defined, if being is in God, God is not free of all being.[38] We must, then, read *puritas essendi* as *also* referring to a higher sense *of* being. Given the ever-shifting semantics of Eckhart's terms and registers, both senses should be borne in mind as we proceed.

To explain what he means by *puritas essendi*, Eckhart offers a remarkable interpretation of Exodus 3:14 that is unique among the many glosses of this passage throughout his corpus. He also, for once, actually pays attention to the story line.[39] We read:

> Just as, when someone wishing to remain hidden and nameless is asked at night, "Who are you?," he responds "I am who I am," so the Lord, wishing to indicate that the purity of being is in himself, said "I am who I am." He did not simply say "I am," but added "who I am." Being therefore does not belong to God, unless you call such purity being. (LW 5: 45, no. 9)

Note again that Eckhart speaks of the purity of being that is *in* God. He does not say: "God is pure of being" or "God is without being."

(14) Eckhart is also willing to use the term *being* for God here, so long as it is not taken in the sense of created being. *Use whatever term you want*, he's saying, *just make sure you think about what you're doing*.

(15) Eckhart's exegesis reflects the hesitation that we have seen again and again throughout the First Parisian Question. Yet we are not only dealing with the classic problem of naming God; God himself appears to hesitate. He at once describes himself and refuses to provide Moses with his proper name. He *is,* yet he is who he is. There is here a purity *of* being, but one that should not be mistaken for the properly nameable, definite being of creatures. There is thus here a purity *from* being *as well*. What we have is a sort of dialectic that strains traditional reason. Eckhart explains how we should interpret this dialectic in the last issue I would like to discuss, which concerns the role of negation in God and, as I will argue, in Eckhart's text in particular.

(16) Eckhart's final argument for the priority of understanding in God draws on Aristotle's *De Anima* (418b, 429a). Eckhart begins with the statement: "So also I say that being does not belong to God and that he is not a being, but is something higher than a being" (LW 5: 47, no. 12).

Then, following Aristotle, he notes that, as vision must be devoid of all color in order to be able to see all color, so the understanding must not be of the same sort as natural forms (*non esse formarum naturalium*) in order to be able to understand all of them. What Eckhart says next appears to be incomplete. In the critical edition, the editor has accordingly rendered it thus, interpolating the putatively missing words in angled brackets:

> sic etiam ego <nego> ipsi deo ipsum esse et talia, ut sic causa omnis esse et omnia praehabeat, ut sicut non negatur deo quod suum est, sic negetur eidem <quod suum non est>. (LW 5: 48, no. 12)

In the standard translation, which I have slightly modified in order to render *esse* as "being" rather than as "existence," we read:

> So also I deny being itself and suchlike of God so that he may be the cause of all being and precontain all things. Thus, as I do not deny to God anything that is his, so I do deny to him what is not his. (Maurer, 50)

Now, Grotz has recently called into question the plausibility of the second interpolation (viz., "quod suum non est" or "what is not his").[40] On the standard reading, Eckhart would be saying that he is not negating what is proper to God (that he is, above all, *understanding*), but rather what is not (that he is *being*). Although this resembles what Eckhart says of accidents earlier in the Question ("Unde non nego accidentibus quod suum est, nec volo eis conceder quod suum non est" [LW 5: 47, no. 11]), saying this of God is, frankly, banal. And it also obfuscates the point of Eckhart's subsequent remark, which is precisely to explain that, when it comes to God, negations bespeak elevated affirmations: "According to the first book of [*De Fide Orthodoxa* by John of] *Damascus*, such negations have a superabundance of affirmation in God" (LW 5: 48, no. 12). Negating being of God would accordingly amount to elevating it in him. It would thus be a kind of affirmation. His being would not, to be sure, resemble the finite, created, categorially determinable being of creatures. God would be higher than any particular being (*altius ente*). And yet he would still be being, albeit of a higher sort, one that is able to create beings and the kind of being proper to them. Eckhart's elliptical sentence could therefore be read intelligibly without the second interpolation:

So also I <negate> of God himself being itself and such things, so that he may be the cause of all being and precontain all things; thus just as I do not negate of God what is his, so do I negate it of him.

We might even extend Grotz's reasoning to the first interpolation. Grammatically, we need a verb, but it does not necessarily have to be *negare*. Verbs such as *assignare, ascribere,* or *attribuere* could work:

So also I <assign/ascribe/attribute> being itself and such things to God himself . . .

In his 1927 edition, Ephrem Longpré, who discovered Eckhart's Parisian Questions at around the same time as Martin Grabmann did, interpolates *non nego* (Longpré, 78).[41] We would thus have:

So also I <do not negate> of God himself being itself and such things . . .

Whether we use a verb such as *attribuo* or follow Longpré's *non nego*, it is noteworthy that the first words of this sentence mirror those of the beginning of the paragraph: *Sic etiam dico quod deo non convenit esse nec est ens* ("So also I say that being does not belong to God and that he is not a being"), on the one hand, and *Sic etiam ego <attribuo/non nego> ipsi deo ipsum esse et talia* ("So also I <attribute to/do not negate of> God himself being itself and such things"), on the other. A parallelism thus suggests itself. Whereas the first denies that being belongs to God, the second would affirm it. Rather than an *either/or*, Eckhart's First Parisian Question would present us with a *both/and*: both negation and affirmation, both being and nonbeing, both being and understanding.

What is interesting about reading Eckhart's First Parisian Question as presenting us with a *both/and* rather than an *either/or* is that it not only allows us to make sense of the numerous ambiguities on the microlevel, but also helps us to explain them on the macrolevel. Let us return to Eckhart's initial response to the question of whether being and understanding are the same in God: "It is *to be said* that they are the same in reality, and perhaps in reality and conceptually" (LW 5: 37, no. 1; emphasis added). As the Question proceeds, Eckhart admittedly never *says* that they are the same conceptually. Yet what he does is far more significant. He *performs* the impossibility of a strict rational separation. We are confronted with arguments for the priority of being, and we are confronted with arguments for the priority of understanding. Heeding the plethora of ambiguities that pervade the Question, it becomes clear that neither reigns supreme. And both collapse in Eckhart's penultimate words, where neither the term *intelligere* nor the term *esse*—nor even the copula—is used (*exsistere* appears for the first time instead): "For I say that God, existing as the root and cause of all things, precontains them in purity, plenitude, and perfection, in a more abundant and extensive fashion." "And this," Eckhart concludes, "is what he meant when he said: 'I am who I am'" (LW 5: 48, no. 12).

Instead of a three part sequential structure, I propose that Eckhart's text be read dialectically, in four: First is Eckhart's initial response to the question of whether being and understanding are the same in God (LW 5: 37, no. 1, line 4). Second are the arguments in favor of identity, including Eckhart's (LW 5: 37, no. 1, line 5 through LW 5: 40, no. 3). Third is the material seemingly in favor of understanding (LW 5: 40, no. 4 through LW 5: 48, no. 12, line 2, stopping at *intelligat*). Fourth and last is Eckhart's explanation of the method deployed in the Question, as well as a conclusion that circles back to his initial response (LW 5: 48, no. 12, line 2, beginning with *sic etiam*, to the end).

What we learn is that a conceptual distinction between God's being and God's understanding is impossible. Rather than providing strictly rational arguments for this, Eckhart forces us into a dialectic. He puts our thinking in motion. In the end, there is less a resolution than the need to move to a different sphere, where the *both/and* shifts into a *neither/nor*: neither Thomistic being *nor* the Anaxagorian-Aristotelian understanding. What, then? The most obvious candidate in Eckhart's Latin works is found in the *Opus tripartitum*, where God is said to be being (*deus est esse*) and being is said to be God (*esse est deus*). In what follows, I will discuss this position briefly, pointing out how it too fails to reach Eckhart's most subversive and, for Heideggerian thought at least, most important ideas. And yet, still shrouded in the language of metaphysics, it nonetheless serves to rend the fabric of ontotheology.

3. *Esse Est Deus*

Eckhart's claim in the First Parisian Question that God is understanding, and even more his paradoxical juxtaposition of God as both being and understanding, tempers one's fervor for an ontotheological God. God is not one being among others. As understanding, he may be the cause of all beings, but, as we saw, a true cause shares nothing with that of which it is a cause. God therefore cannot be *a* being. And yet Eckhart still deploys the language of perfection and causality. God is still perfect *in comparison with* beings. God is still *their* cause. In other words, God is still understood *by way of* beings, and not on his own terms. We affirm God by negating that with which we are most familiar: beings as substantial, finite, and categorially determinable (as well as caused/created). Eckhart does, to be sure, achieve more than this: not only does he take this classic negative theological approach to God; he also affirms and denies the very same predicates of God, thereby disrupting our reliance on the traditional ways to God, including the *via negativa*. The danger still looms, however, that Eckhart's approach relies too much on superficial experience, and that God would merely be the maximization, purification, or flip side of that experience.

Eckhart takes the opposite approach in the *Opus tripartitum*. Rather than God as nothingness and creatures as being, we have being as God and creatures as nothingness. Among the many texts extant from Eckhart's incomplete opus, the Prologues and the *Sermons and Lectures on Ecclesiasticus* provide some of the clearest expositions of this alternate perspective. I will discuss these two sets of texts in what follows, making occasional reference to Eckhart's 1326 Cologne defense[42] and to his only surviving New Testament commentary from the *Opus tripartitum*, namely, the Commentary on John, which was "most certainly" written after the early Parisian Questions of 1302–03.[43] According to Loris Sturlese, it is highly probable that the *Sermons and Lectures on Ecclesiasticus* were composed after the First Parisian Question though before Eckhart's second stay in Paris, thus between 1302–03 and 1311. The second sermon may have been delivered in 1302, however, and at any rate Eckhart decided to include the whole text as a portion of the *Opus tripartitum*, whose Prologues, it should be noted, were likely penned *before* the Questions of Eckhart's first Paris regency.[44] In other words, on the basis of the latest paleographical research, one may no longer speak of a strict chronological-biographical development between the early Parisian Questions and the *Opus tripartitum*. Whether there is a radical doctrinal divergence between the two texts remains to be seen.

To begin, let us take a well-known example from the *Sermons and Lectures on Ecclesiasticus*. In what has been described as "[t]he fundamental text of Eckhart's doctrine of analogy"[45]—a text that, it should be noted, was cited in the introduction to the edition of the Parisian Questions that

Heidegger used (Grabmann, 61)—Eckhart writes: "Analogous things are not distinguished according to things, nor through the differences of things, but 'according to the modes [of being]' of one and the same simple thing" (LW 2: 280/TP 178, no. 52, In Eccli.). To elucidate this, he uses the same example as he had in the First Parisian Question, only now he supplements it with a common example from medieval semiotics:

> For example, the one and the same health that is in an animal is that (and no other) which is in the diet and the urine [of the animal] in such a way that there is no more health in the diet and urine than there is in a stone. Urine is said to be "healthy" only because it signifies the health, the same in number, which is in the animal, just as a circular wreath which has nothing of wine in it [signifies] wine. (LW 2: 280–81/TP 178, no. 52, In Eccli.)

So far, there is little difference from what we saw previously. What is truly capable of health is the animal; only in the animal is health present "formally," as Eckhart puts it in the First Parisian Question (LW 5: 46, no. 11). Everything else we call healthy only signifies the health that properly belongs to the animal. There is nothing intrinsically healthy (or unhealthy) about urine or diets.

While, in the First Parisian Question, Eckhart viewed being as formally inhering in that which is caused, and therefore as absent in God insofar as he is the cause—unless, that is, God is conceived as *puritas essendi*—Eckhart now reverses his perspective:

> Being [*Ens . . . sive esse*] and every perfection, especially general ones such as being, oneness, goodness, light, justice, and so forth, are used to describe God and creatures in an analogical way. It follows from this that goodness and justice and the like [in creatures] have their goodness totally from something outside to which they are analogically ordered, namely, God. (LW 2: 281/ TP 178, no. 52, In Eccli.; trans. mod.)

Here, in the second lecture of his *Sermons and Lectures on Ecclesiasticus*, it is God to whom being (and all the other transcendentals) belongs formally. Consequently, on the basis of Eckhart's doctrine of " 'extrinsic analogy,' or the analogy of formal opposition" (as Bernard McGinn puts it in TP, 200, n. 215), we must conclude that beings intrinsically share nothing with God as that to which they are analogically related. They have no independent share in being, truth, goodness, justice, and so on. In themselves, they are "nothing, for what is outside the First Cause, that is, God, is outside being [*esse*] (God is being [*deus est esse*])" (LW 2: 277/TP 177, no. 49, In Eccli.; trans. mod.).

To deny any and all being in creatures may sound as implausible as denying any and all being in God. Yet it is noteworthy that, among the Eckhartian propositions condemned in the papal bull *In agro dominico*, it was not the putative intellectualist stance of the Parisian Questions that provoked the ire of the pope and the doctors of sacred theology, at least not insofar as God was understood as intellect.[46] Rather, it was precisely the utter nothingness of creatures that smacked of heresy. As the twenty-sixth article of *In agro dominico* puts it, echoing Eckhart's fourth German sermon: "All creatures are one pure nothing. I do not say that they are a little something or anything, but that they are pure nothing" (LW 5: 599/ES 80, Acta #65; cf. DW 1: 69,7–70,1/TP 250 Pr. 4 ["Omne datum optimum"]). What Eckhart's inquisitors missed, however, are the words *in se* and *inquantum*. Eckhart is nearly always careful to specify that, when he says creatures are nothing, he is treating them *in themselves* or *insofar as* they are utterly separate from God. Since, from the perspective of the *Sermons and Lectures on Ecclesiasticus*, God is being, that which, in itself, is considered not to be God must, in itself, be considered not to be being. Considered in this way, it is therefore nothing in itself: "[E]very created being radically and positively possesses being, life, and wisdom from and in God, not in itself as a created being" (LW 2: 282/TP 178, no. 53, In Eccli.; trans. mod.). Indeed, apart from God, even a conceptual inherence of being in creatures is impossible: "[B]eing is not fixed and does not inhere or have its source in [every being and everything that belongs to the number of beings], nor does it remain when the superior is absent, even if only conceptually" (LW 2: 274/TP 175, no. 45, In Eccli.; trans. mod.).

More surprising than the nothingness of creatures qua independent is the divinity of creatures *insofar as* they are related to or taken in God. "To clarify the objections brought against me," Eckhart explained in his 1326 defense at Cologne, "three things must be kept in mind. The first is that the words 'insofar as,' that is, a reduplication, exclude from the term in question everything that is other or foreign to it even according to reason" (LW 5: 277/ES 72, nos. 80–81, Acta #48). When we see creatures *as* being, we ignore altogether that which, in them, would be nothing. Considered *as* being, creatures are considered *as* God. For being, as Eckhart puts it in the Prologues of the *Opus tripartitum*, is God (*esse est deus*).

This has consequences for human action. If the first things to bear in mind are the ubiquitous reduplicative modifiers throughout Eckhart's writings,

> The second is that the good man and goodness are one. The good man insofar as he is good signifies goodness alone, just as something white signifies only the quality of whiteness. These two things, being good and goodness, are univocally one in the Father, Son and Holy Spirit. They are analogically one in God and in us considered as good. (LW 5: 278/ES 73, no. 82, Acta #48)

Here, the distinction between univocity and analogy may seem to mark a recursion to Thomism, according to which any resemblance to God would be deficient in comparison with God himself, even if God's glory would be reflected through that verisimilitude. Yet when we take into account Eckhart's distinctive doctrine of analogy, it holds that, *insofar as* we are good, we *are* goodness itself, "not less than it."[47] We thus become *one with* the goodness of the Father. The distinction between univocity and analogy collapses (except, perhaps, to the extent that our goodness would be "begotten" and not innate, but even on this point Eckhart appears to vacillate).[48] Practically, what this means is that we should detach ourselves from everything independent, that is, from everything insofar as it is taken to be independent from God. To the extent that we do so, we become one with God. Eckhart's teaching of detachment and releasement is anticipated here.

Even if the First Parisian Question and the *Opus tripartitum* both rest on Eckhart's doctrine of analogy, and differ simply on the basis of the perspective one takes on the respective analogates, isn't the position of the *Opus tripartitum* still ontotheological? Ultimately, this is hard to deny. After all, could there be a better translation of ontotheology into Latin than by *deus est esse* or, a fortiori, *esse est deus*? The copula is the logos holding together *esse* (*on,* being) and *deus* (*theos,* God). And yet, as we heard from Heidegger himself, some of Eckhart's thinking in the First Parisian Question persisted in what he took to be a later work. Let's accordingly draw some distinctions.

In his essay "Hegel's Concept of Experience," Heidegger explains ontotheology as follows:

> Aristotle calls this science he characterized (the science which inspects beings as beings) "first philosophy." However, not only does it observe beings [*das Seiende*] in their beingness [*Seiendheit*], but it also, at the same time, observes that being which corresponds purely to beingness, the highest being. This particular

being, *to theion*, the divine, is also called—in a strange ambiguity—"being" itself [*"das Sein"*]. As ontology, first philosophy is also the theology of true beings.... The science of beings as such is intrinsically onto-theological. (GA 5: 195/146)

Heidegger provides further clarification in a late essay on Kant:

The twofold question, What are beings? asks on the one hand, What are (in general) beings? The question asks on the other hand, What (which one) is the (ultimate) being?

Obviously, the twofold quality of the question about beings must result from the way the being of beings manifests itself. Being manifests itself in the character of that which we call ground. Beings in general are the ground in the sense of the foundation upon which any further consideration of beings takes place. That which is the highest being is the ground in the sense of that which allows all beings to come into being. (GA 9: 449–50/340)

According to Heidegger, ontotheology asks not just about the being of beings, but (1) about the highest being that (2) is somehow the ground of those beings. Both moments are problematized in Eckhart's *Opus tripartitum*.

First, God is not the *highest* being, since there is no being other than God. The hunger creatures feel for God as being is never more or less satiated: "There is no greater and less, prior and posterior in these things" (LW 2: 287/TP 180, no. 58, In Eccli.). Insofar as creatures are being, they are God. Insofar as they are not, they are nothing. There is no middle ground. Eckhart is not asking about how God, as a being, relates to beings, to which one might answer that God is the highest of all beings. God is not being in this sense. Rather, Eckhart is asking about the nature of being itself. The answer he gives in the Prologues (and espouses under the title "God is being" in the *Sermons and Lectures on Ecclesiasticus*) is that being is God. Here, the first characteristic of ontotheology identified by Heidegger is diminished.

Second, Eckhart hints at withdrawing the need for a ground altogether, as he does explicitly in other works to be examined in chapter 3:

Take the example of someone who is said to run for the sake of running. He always eats up the road as he runs; nonetheless he always hungers for it, because he runs for running and loves the road itself. Thus, he loves what he loves for itself—love for love's sake. (LW 2: 287–88/TP 181, no. 59, In Eccli.)

One thinks here of Eckhart's appeal to live as in the abyss (*abgrunt*) of the Godhead, working without reason (*sunder warumbe*), like a horse prancing on a heath (Pr. 5b, "In hoc apparuit," and Pr. 12, "Qui audit me"). Only, in the latter case, hunger and desire would be released as well. Or, as Eckhart puts it in his *Commentary on John*: "What is without principle lives in the proper sense, for everything that has the principle of its operation from another insofar as it is other does not live in the proper sense" (LW 3: 16/ES 128, no. 19). The task for good or just people would be to divest themselves of tasks, to *be* that which, in them, is not merely united (*vereinet*) with God, but is one (*ein*) with God (DW 1: 197,9/TP 269 Pr. 12 ["Qui audit me"]). It is only by means of such a practical apriori that they will be able to know justice (and hence God) (LW 3: 13–14/ES 126–27, no. 15, In Ioh.). As we will see with respect to releasement in chapter 3, knowledge does not merely involve tracing things back to their ground. It also involves becoming the ground or, better, the *abgrunt sunder warumbe* (abyss without why). Eckhart, along with every other thinker ranging from "Plato and Aristotle to Nietzsche," may not have asked after "the ground of the unity of the onto-theological essence of metaphysics" (GA 5: 195/146–47); yet what Heidegger calls Eckhart's remarkable "solution" to the medieval problem of analogy, which, as we have seen, remains vital even in the *Opus tripartitum*, was not completely entangled in the ontotheological essence of metaphysics. Even in his Latin works, Eckhart was able to think otherwise than ontotheologically.

Still, there is little doubt that the *Sermons and Lectures on Ecclesiasticus* and the Prologues of the *Opus tripartitum* are, for the most part, insufficient when compared with the more radical moments of the German writings. In the material surrounding the discussion of analogy in the second lecture on Ecclesiasticus from which I quoted previously, Eckhart still speaks of God as "First Cause," "Final Cause," "the End," "the Last," "the First," "end and beginning," "First Act," and "the Prime Mover" (LW 2: 278–79, 283–286/ TP 177, 179–80, nos. 50, 55–57, In Eccli.). God is still, quoting Aquinas, "The First Intellect and the First Intelligible" (LW 2: 280/TP 178, no. 51, In Eccli.). Eckhart delares that "negation has no place at all in God himself," and he deprecates becoming (*fieri*) as the province of nondivine causes, whereas God, as that which is steadfast, confers being (LW 2: 289, 276/TP 181, 176, nos. 60, 48, In Eccli.). And even though Eckhart denies being to creatures in themselves, thereby obliterating hierarchical distinctions, he still slips into the language of rank, speaking of God as "the superior" and "the Supreme" and quoting Augustine on God as "the highest being [*summe esse*]" (LW 2: 273–74, 281/TP 175, 178, nos. 44–45, 52, In Eccli.; trans. mod.). Similar tropes are to be found in the Prologues, where "the being of everything is immediately from the first and universal cause of all things," that is, God qua creator, "the first and last, the beginning and the end" (LW 1,2: 26–27, 37/Maurer 83, 92, nos. 8, 20, Prol. gen. [rec. L]; trans. mod.).[49] Let us therefore turn to some of Eckhart's German writings to see how the seeds of Eckhart's alternative to ontotheology come into their own.

3

Become Who You Are

The Oneness of Thinking and Being as Releasement in Eckhart's German Writings

> Jn GOtt wird nichts erkandt: Er ist ein Einig Ein.
> Was man in Jhm erkennt / das muß man selber seyn.
>
> In God nought e'er is known, Forever one is He.
> What we in Him e'er know, Ourselves must grow and be.
>
> —Angelus Silesius

Thinking and Being. Allow me to begin with some clarifications. When I use the word *thinking* in what follows, I mean to refer to the multifaceted, essential activity of human beings that allows them to unfold what they always already are implicitly in their essential unity with being. Heidegger's opening reflections in the "Letter on 'Humanism'" may serve as a guideline:

> [T]he essence of action is accomplishment. To accomplish [*Vollbringen*] means to unfold something into the fullness of its essence [*Wesens*], to lead it forth into this fullness—*producere*. Therefore only what already is can really be accomplished. But what "is" above all is being. Thinking accomplishes the relation of being to the essence of the human being. (GA 9: 313/239)[1]

When I use the word *being* in what follows, I have in mind the Middle High German *wesen*, which Eckhart at times uses to characterize God beyond multiplicity, God as One, the Godhead. The following words by Reiner Schürmann may serve as a guideline:

> Two of the several German words translated as "being" in [Eckhart's] writings refer directly to the ontological difference. The

one, *iht*, is a noun usually translated as "something"; it designates any entity whatsoever, including God. The other, *wesen*, is a verb. It can be translated as "essentializing" or "unfolding," and it designates the Godhead as well as the mind's identification with the Godhead.[2]

My thesis is that, implicitly, the essential activity of the human being is ultimately identical with the essential activity of being, and that, explicitly, such activity is what allows the human being to appropriate or own up to this identity. This identical activity of the human being and of being may be glossed with the term *abegescheidenheit* (Middle High German for *detachment*) or, more properly, as I will explain below, with the term *gelâzenheit* (Middle High German for *releasement*).

I doubt Heidegger would ever go so far as to say that thinking, "as the distinctive characteristic of the human," is identical to being; being and the human being (as characterized by thinking), are, to be sure, the "same," but by this Heidegger means that they are delivered over and belong to one another through the event of appropriation (*Er-eignis*), which *lets* them so belong (*gehörenlassen*), not that they are utterly identical (GA 11: 38/30; trans. mod.). Or, as Heidegger continues in the "Letter on 'Humanism,'" without invoking the language of *Ereignis*: "Thinking brings this relation to being solely as something handed over to thought itself from being. . . . Thinking . . . lets itself [*läßt sich*] be claimed by being so that it can say the truth of being. Thinking accomplishes this letting [*Lassen*]" (GA 9: 313/239).

Eckhart, however, at his most extreme, will say that I can come to realize, through detachment or releasement, that I am, not similar to, but absolutely identical, sheer *oneness*, with the God beyond distinction: that fathomless abyss before grounds and reasons, before the Trinity and creation, to which Eckhart gives the name *Godhead*. On this level, then, I would be just as primordial, just as abyssal, just as crucial as being itself. In the unified relation between being and the human, it would not, as the later Heidegger thought, chiefly come down to being (GA 9: 333–34/254).

Eckhart uses various terms to describe the relata of this unity (or rather non-relata, for relation implies at least two), and he does not always explicate it in the same way. Nor, for that matter, does he explicate how exactly we can come to appropriate it. Sometimes he speaks of the power of the intellect in the soul, sometimes of that which lies beyond the intellect (such as the spark of the soul, the little castle, the ground of both God and the soul). Sometimes he speaks of a unity through activity, sometimes he dismisses not just activity, but all potentiality for it as well. Sometimes he speaks of an operative unity that is always already the case, sometimes he speaks of a unity that is to be achieved. And sometimes he speaks of the need for detachment from possessiveness, which might suggest asceticism, but for Eckhart is much more a matter of intentional comportment toward things. Although the connection between these different senses is not self-evident, they are not necessarily incompatible. They may even be organized according to their degrees of radicality as facets of the thoughtful activity of *abegescheidenheit/gelâzenheit*. What we would then have would be grades of detachment or releasement, which would themselves obtain (1) with respect to our external comportment, (2) with respect to our internal comportment or comportment toward ourselves, and (3) with respect to God himself. These grades may accordingly be arranged along three paths ascending to the same summit, or, better, three trails descending into the same abyss:

(1) The human being's detachment or releasement (i) *from* things; (ii) from essences; (iii) from the Son as image of the Father and exemplar of creatures; (iv) from the Father as Person of the Trinity; (v) from the Godhead as *a* being at all; (vi) from the Godhead as the potential cause of the Trinity, which would still be intelligible as the counterpart of an actual cause; and then—and here the language of detachment is insufficient—releasement (vii) *to* the Godhead as itself detached *from* all, and yet at the same time as the abyssal (and therefore causally unintelligible) releasement (letting-be, letting-emerge) *of* all; (viii) to the Trinity in its non-causal relation to the Godhead, and so on until we are back at things.

(2) The human being's detachment or releasement (i) from corporeality; (ii) from the powers of the soul, including discursive reason; (iii) from intellection; (iv) from the soul as image of God; (v) from the soul as Son of God; (vi) from the soul as at all involved in distinction, even that of the Trinity; and then releasement (vii) *to* the soul as absolutely one with the abyssal detachment and releasement of the Godhead, (viii) to the soul as released (here in the sense of issued forth) from its identity with the Godhead into Trinitarian distinction and (ix) Sonship, and so on until we are back at corporeality.

(3) God's own detachment or releasement (i) from his relation to creation; (ii) from his relation to the other Persons of the Trinity; (iii) from himself as the potential source of the Trinity; and then releasement (iv) *to* "his"—and here we should question ownership and masculinity as much as everything else—detached/released hovering in the desert of indistinction;

(v) to the non-causal, event-like emergence or welling up into the Trinity; (vi) to the welling forth into creation.³

What I wish to draw from the foregoing is that releasement is at once the condition for attaining union with God and that which is revealed in such attainment: namely, that God and the soul are always already one in releasement. This cannot be thought, however, let alone rationally seized on, without the broader activity of thinking, which involves all these different facets of releasement. Insofar as unfolding the being of the Godhead requires a more practical valence of thinking (namely, detachment *from*) for its accomplishment, we may speak, with Reiner Schürmann, of a practical apriori in Eckhart (with the caveat that we not fall back into the traditional chasm between theory and praxis). To unfold being as letting-be, I must let be. I cannot understand being without undertaking the thoughtful activity of letting-be. And what is revealed thereby? That the essence of being and of my being is letting-be. Using a different terminology: to understand the truth of which Eckhart speaks, I must *be* the truth. That is to say, I must become who I am, I must own up to and live in accordance with my essence as releasement. I must *be* released: "if we are to hear God's word, we must be wholly *gelâzen*" (DW 1: 193,6–7/Davies 175–76 Pr. 12 ["Qui audit me"]).⁴

As we will see in Part Three, I take it that this structure—that of letting-be to understand being and the human being as letting-be, or, put formally, of doing X to understand being and the human being as X—together with Eckhart's methods for teaching and preaching it, were some of the most fruitful aspects of Eckhartian thought developed by Heidegger. Indeed, they will provide us with a way in which to read several key stretches along Heidegger's path of thought. This chapter will accordingly examine the structure of releasement in Eckhart, and the next his methods for cultivating it.

I believe it possible to develop the structure of releasement from a variety of Eckhart's texts. Since, however, we lack proof positive of whether Heidegger had studied them all as closely as he did the works of Aristotle, Kant, or Hölderlin, for example, I will narrow my horizon by concentrating, with two exceptions, on authentic Middle High German texts by Eckhart that Heidegger cited or read (Prr. 5b, 9, 32, 52, 69, 73, 83, 100, 101, 102, 103, 104; RdU; BgT).⁵ The first exception is a sermon that Heidegger read but that has a disputed legacy, namely the eighty-second text in Jostes's 1895 edition, which deals with the kingdom of God and the three deaths of the soul. While many Eckhart scholars have argued in favor of its authenticity, it was recently published in the critical edition (German sermon 117) as a text of dubious origin.⁶ Whatever the case may be (and it does not seem to me that the case is closed yet), this sermon is one of the most radical that Eckhart (or perhaps one of his followers) ever wrote.⁷ Heidegger himself cites it in his lecture "Das Ding"; he made marginal notes in his personal copy of Büttner's edition of this sermon; and he even wrote an index in this copy with the entry "Soul and God," which includes a reference to the sermon.⁸

The second exception is a text that most scholars consider genuine but that Heidegger did not necessarily read, namely *Von abegescheidenheit* (On Detachment).⁹ It will be important for us in what follows, though, because it is the only text in which *abegescheidenheit* (or, in one of the manuscripts, *gelâzenheit*) is used to describe God himself, which resonates with Heidegger's own ideas about the essence of being as letting. Additionally, on the philological level, Heidegger does cite from the third tractate in Pfeiffer's edition, which includes passages from or closely resembling *On Detachment*.¹⁰ Given Heidegger's interest in Eckhartian detachment in the second half of the 1910s and his citations of many other texts in Pfeiffer's edition, it seems quite likely that Heidegger would have read the version of *On Detachment* found therein.¹¹

I will accordingly draw on German sermon 117 and *On Detachment* in what follows. However, before turning to these and other texts to unfold the identity of thinking and being in *gelâzenheit*, I would first like to provide a preliminary definition of *gelâzenheit* by contrasting it with potentially misleading valences of *abegescheidenheit*. This approach will also furnish some orientation for what I hope to accomplish in the remainder of the chapter.

1. *Gelâzenheit* versus *Abegescheidenheit*

Although Eckhart uses the nominalized past participle *gelâzenheit* only once in the critical edition (DW 5: 283,8/ES 277, RdU, §21),¹² the verb *lâzen* and its cognates can be found throughout his German texts. They often appear as synonymous with *abegescheidenheit* and its cognates. (Incidentally, Eckhart may well have coined both words.)¹³ As we saw in the previous chapters, in contrast to other medieval thinkers who held that created things have a genuine, albeit deficient, share in being, Eckhart maintains that created things are, in themselves, characterized either by being (in which case God is not) or, as is more often the case, by nothingness. In the latter scenario, the only things that can properly be said to exist are therefore

God and that uncreated aspect of the human soul that is one with God.[14] Consequently, any attachment to created things, any sense of possessiveness over them, amounts to possessing what *is not*. For Eckhart this means being preoccupied with, indeed being possessed by, nothingness. Such possession prohibits explicit union with God, who is opposite of nothingness.[15] We must therefore divest ourselves of all possessiveness over things if we are to unite with our divine origin.

However, detachment only conveys one aspect of *gelâzenheit* (or two if it is considered to be a *habitus*). When taken superficially, it has at least six connotations that stand opposed to the phenomenon Eckhart is invoking.

First, detachment may suggest ecstatic removal or having "cut away" (*abe-gescheiden*) from things. Yet *gelâzenheit* is not ecstatic. Eckhart does not advocate fleeing this world to attain union in the beyond. Rather, union is to be accomplished and lived out as one engages with the world.[16]

The second reason as to why the term *detachment* is insufficient is that it may evoke a temporary break from the world. Although Eckhart does speak of the momentary character of *gelâzenheit* (DW 1: 202,11–203,1/ TP 270 Pr. 12 ["Qui audit me"]), this must be understood, not as a temporary break, but as that which exceeds and encompasses all of time, and as that which ought to be maintained and carried out within time (DW 4: 1136,438–1138,469/Davies 250 Pr. 117 ["Ze dem êrsten suochet daz rîche gotes"]; cf. DW 3: 484,14–486,2/TP 340 Pr. 86 ["Intravit Iesus in quoddam castellum, etc."]).

Third, detachment may suggest being impervious to things. Yet *gelâzenheit* lets things be as they truly are. Unlike Stoic *apatheia*, *gelâzenheit* does not harden itself against things and emotions. It releases itself *to* them, allowing them to "become pure God to you" (DW 4: 488,136/Davies 228 Pr. 103 ["Cum factus esset Iesus annorum duodecim"]).

Fourth, detachment may suggest a task to be accomplished. Yet *gelâzenheit* is without reason or goal. Eckhart does admonish us to detach ourselves, but, inasmuch as this is still taken as something to be accomplished, we are not yet released. The truly released person lives without reason, without a why (DW 1: 90,3–92,6/ES 183–84 Pr. 5b ["In hoc apparuit"]).

Fifth, *abegescheidenheit* and its root verb *scheiden* or *gescheiden* are most readily understood *ex negativo*, as detachment *from* something already given, as cutting something off that is already there. Even though, as we will see, Eckhart does use *abegescheidenheit* as a positive description of God, and even though it does have the positive valences of a *habitus* and of uniting us with him, this term hardly conveys what God as *abegescheiden* and what such dispositional unity would amount to. To be sure, *gelâzenheit* and its root verb *lâzen* also bear the same negative aspects, but they also better allow for the inverse: not only releasement *from,* but also releasement *to,* not only letting *go* and leaving *behind,* but letting *be* and letting *prevail* and letting *emerge.*

Finally, detachment may imply that there is already something in existence from which we must detach ourselves. Yet *gelâzenheit* is at once an implicit, originary state and something to unfold explicitly.[17]

Drawing on these distinctions, we may accordingly define *gelâzenheit* as *the state of being in which we have come to recognize our primordial unity with the divinity and in which we live out this unity aimlessly and with equanimity in all our thoughts and activities, letting all things be as having proceeded from out of the very letting-be of the identical source of God and the soul.* It is precisely such a state that Eckhart tries to cultivate in his teaching and preaching.

2. The Soul's Way of Releasement

As Ueda Shizuteru noted in 1965, Eckhart really speaks about only one thing, the relation between God and the soul, although he explicates this relation sometimes from the side of God, and sometimes from that of the soul.[18] I will begin with the soul, though much about God will be revealed along the way.

In order to unite with God, a necessary, though not sufficient, step is to leave off from created things, which, as we have seen, are for Eckhart nothing at all in and of themselves. When we attach ourselves to things as though they had independent worth, we attach ourselves to what *is not* apart from God—we attach ourselves to nothingness. We therefore fail to own up to that which truly and solely *is*: God and the part of soul that is one with him. We must, Eckhart preaches, accordingly hold ourselves free of the nothing. Still more must we spiritually annihilate all creatureliness, characterized as it is by temporality, multiplicity, and corporeality, by separateness from the pure and simple One that is God: "[Y]ou should be of pure heart, for only that heart is pure which has annihilated everything that is created" (DW 1: 88,7/ES 182–83 Pr. 5b ["In hoc apparuit"]).[19] *Spiritually,* because Eckhart is not advocating physical asceticism or isolation, and works are of little to no concern to him.[20] Rather, he is attempting to turn us toward what he calls *the inner man,* which is as distinct from *the outer man* of the senses and of the world as is heaven from earth.[21]

The inner man is not one creature among others. Insofar as the self contains traces of creaturely distinction, it, like creatures, must also be released. In fact, in the *Rede der underscheidunge*, Eckhart suggests that what is at issue is not really things at all, but rather how we comport ourselves toward them (DW 5: 192,8–193,2/Davies 6, §3). To facilitate a proper comportment, we must leave off from our own self-will. To the extent that we do so, to that extent is God *compelled* to enter in and will for us just what he wills for himself.[22] Indeed, God's very being is dependent on it:

> When I leave off from my own self [*mich ane lâze*], then he must of necessity will for me everything that he wills for himself. . . . And if God did not do this, then by the truth which God is, he would not be just nor would he be God (which of course he is by nature).

Such divestiture does, admittedly, involve the will: I must give up my will for the sake of God's will. In this regard, the Scholar in Heidegger's first "Country Path Conversation" is correct to charge Eckhart with failing to escape the domain of the will. However, even without turning to any other passages in Eckhart, it is not hard to see that here Eckhart seems to be describing an ontological condition rather than a facultative voluntarism.[23] This should make us question the degree to which Eckhart's God can really be grasped under the banner of the will. And voiding our own self-will is just the beginning.

Start, Eckhart says, by releasing yourself (*lâz dich!*) (DW 5: 193,3/ Davies 6, RdU, §3), and you will have released all things:

> Those who seek peace in external things . . . proceed like someone who has lost their way: the further they go, the more lost they become. But what then should they do? First of all, they should release themselves [*sich selber lâzen*], and then they will have released all things [*alliu dinc gelâzen*]. (DW 5: 193,5–194,4/ Davies 6, RdU, §3; trans. mod.)

But what else is there to *lâzen*, if releasing ourselves suffices to unite us with God, *einez in dem einen*, where everything manifold is "unmanifolded"—if it suffices to retain God's presence in all we do? (DW 5: 202,3–203,10/ Davies 9, RdU, §6).

It is not just our personal features that must be left behind. It is not just our will and all natural powers of the soul that must be left behind. We must also leave behind intellect (*vernünfticheit*) both as distinct from natural reason and as image and Son of God. It is not surprising that commentators such as Kurt Flasch have endeavored to understand Eckhart's description of the aspect of the soul that is one with God in terms of the interpretation of the Aristotelian active intellect developed by the school of Albert the Great.[24] Nor is it surprising that others have endeavored to do so in terms of the Aristotelian passive intellect.[25] There are indeed parallels, such as what we saw in some of the Latin works discussed in chapter 2 and what one finds in Pr. 69 ("Modicum et iam non videbitis me"), where Eckhart says that the intellect "is like nothing," "is active and seeking in itself," "is pure and uncompounded," and "becomes detached [*abescheidet*] from here and now" (DW 3: 169,2–4/Walshe 235).[26] And Eckhart himself speaks of the intellect not just as an undifferentiated "image" of God (DW 3: 169,4–5/ Walshe 235), not just as Son of God or as the place where God bears his Son in my soul, but as that which "breaks through" beyond God to the ground of God and to the source of goodness and truth:

> Intellect peeps in and breaks through [*durchbrichet*] every corner of the Godhead. . . . [I]t breaks into [*brichet in*] the ground whence goodness and truth proceed, and seizes it *in principio*, in the beginning where goodness and truth are just coming out. . . . But its sister, the will, is well satisfied with God as He is good. But intellect strips all this off and enters in and breaks through to the roots, where the Son wells up and the Holy Ghost blossoms forth. (DW 3: 178,3–180,2/Walshe 237; trans. mod.)

There are at least six problems with these interpretations, however:

(1) Notice that, in this passage, the intellect only goes in one direction: it breaks through to the ground, but it is not described as *that ground* itself.

(2) What the intellect unveils is the beginning of truth and goodness. This beginning therefore still remains tied to such truth and goodness, if only in the sense of containing them *in potentia*. Potentiality, as we will see later on, must also be released.

(3) With regard to the soul's ground as an empty passive intellect that may be filled in by God's graceful birthing of his Son, this may well hold for certain aspects of the soul. As for its *ground*, there can be no distinction between God's acting and my becoming.

(4) In fact, elsewhere Eckhart calls into question the very idea that the ground of God and the soul could be active (although it is not, for all that, passive).

(5) In other sermons, Eckhart also maintains the insufficiency of intellect, knowledge, and reason in describing the identical ground of God and the soul.[27]

(6) Finally, if, as argued in chapter 2, *intellectus* fails ultimately to capture God's way of being, then it should also fail to capture the soul's oneness with that being.

We must, then, leave off from the intellect if we are to reach the ground of the soul and of God, or, as Eckhart (or one of his disciples) preaches in German sermon 117 ("Ze dem êrsten suochet daz rîche gotes"), if we are to reach the kingdom of God that is also my kingdom. It is to this sermon that I would like to turn now.

In his sermon on the kingdom of God and the soul, Eckhart begins by recalling Jesus's imperative to seek God's kingdom (Luke 12:31; Matthew 6:33). Eckhart explains that this kingdom signifies on the one hand God's perfect being (*wesen*), and on the other hand God's kingdom in the soul. Although Eckhart commences with a discussion of God and the Trinity, before turning to the soul, let us continue with our discussion of the soul's steps of releasement, before turning to God's own releasement.

"[I]n order to come to know [*bekennen*] the nobility of God and the nobility of the soul," we must fulfill the ancient Delphic imperative and come to know ourselves, as Eckhart suggests in his misleading translation of Song of Solomon 1:8: "Do you not know yourself, most beautiful of women? Go out then and follow in the footsteps of your lord" (DW 4: 1110,203–207/Davies 241). (*Misleading*, because context would suggest "you yourself do not know," namely, the question I had just posed to you, not "you do not know yourself." We will return to Eckhart's peculiar translation choices in chapter 4.) At any rate, in order to come to know ourselves, Eckhart preaches that there must be a threefold exodus from the soul's threefold being. The soul must go out (1) from its being qua creature; (2) from the being it has in "the personal Word of the Trinity"; and (3) from the being it has in "the fruitful nature that is active in the Father, who is the origin of all creatures" (DW 4: 1110,210–1110,213/Davies 241; trans. mod.). I will address each of these in turn.

(1) To an extent, the first exodus resembles what we have already seen. At issue is not so much detachment from things (a necessary, but by no means sufficient condition), but letting go of oneself. Eckhart does amp up the rhetoric and declaim against those who become attached to their external observances and esteem themselves in their practices. It matters not whether such practices be of a devotional or ascetic nature: "these people

do not follow God if they do not release themselves [*sich niht enlâzent*]" (DW 4: 1113,233–1114,234/Davies 242; trans. mod.). Eckhart also shows how such can hold even of the virtues of the soul. One's self may become particularly attached to such virtues and thus become a particular self in this attachment. Thus, if we are truly to abandon the self and unite with God, we must raise ourselves above the virtues, for God himself is above the virtues. And Eckhart proceeds to cast these thoughts in the mold of the *mors mystica* tradition (being dead to the self and creatures).[28] Nevertheless, it is only when he comes to promote the abandonment of God that something new comes to light for our trajectory.

Apparently, fully dying to our createdness necessitates dying to our God. "For the fact that God is called God comes from creatures" (DW 4: 1121,297/Davies 244). How so? The word *God* is essentially indexed to what he, the creator, creates. "God" is the creator. If we annihilate creatures in spirit, God qua creator must be annihilated too. Conversely, if we still have God, then we still have creatures, or at least that which stands in an inextricable relation to them as their counterpart.[29] We must moreover be so dead to God that we neither know nor are aware of him, and so dead to him that there would be no place whatsoever in us, no creaturely site, for God to enter and live (DW 4: 1119,284–86/Davies 244). For both would presumably still entail an opposition between the soul and God, counterparts between knower and known, subject and object, agent and patient. We are better off "leaving God to himself [*im selber lâze*]" and abandoning any fixation on his creaturely connection to the things of this world (DW 4: 1121,298–99/Davies 245). Only in this way may we be as "empty of ourselves as we were before we existed" (DW 4: 1111,217–18/Davies 242).

In this first fatal exodus, then, the soul leaves itself, all things, and God ("lâzen, daz si ist," "lâzen sich und alliu dinc," "got verliesen"; DW 4: 1118,274–76, 1120,291/Davies 244–45). And yet, says Eckhart, this death is but "the *smallest* death" (DW 4: 1121,300/Davies 245; emphasis added).

(2) Having left behind its creatureliness, the soul must now leave behind its uncreated image within the Godhead. Here, the soul accomplishes its second going-out, its second spiritual death. The first death, Eckhart now explains, brought the soul to its being as an uncreated divine image, or rather to *the* uncreated divine image of the Father as personified by the Son, where all creatures are pre-contained as by a "blueprint [*exemplâr*]" (DW 4: 1123,312/Davies 245). Yet here too the soul encounters "distinction and multiplicity," for "the Persons are distinct [*in underscheide*] from one another." To reach the One God, the soul must go through the Son,

as Jesus says in John 14:6: "No one comes to the Father except through me" (DW 4: 1125,325–26/Davies 246). For most exegetes, the Son is more than a mere escort here. We remain with the Son even as he leads us to the Father. For Eckhart, however, the Son is but a forecourt of the house of God: "Now the soul should not remain in him but rather must pass through him. . . . If the soul is to enter in again, she must leave [*verliesen*] the Son behind" (DW 4: 1125,326, 1126,334–35/Davies 246). This accordingly means "leaving behind the identity [or similarity, *die glicheit verliesen*]" between Father and Son, between God and soul (DW 4: 1128,345/Davies 246). *Glicheit* requires two, but the soul is after oneness, and not just the acceptable Christian oneness according to which everything that is in God is God.[30] Consequently, the soul must die a "divine death," that is, it must die to its uncreated Sonship. Only in this way does it "break through [*durchbrichet*]" to the Godhead (DW 4: 1123,317 and 322/Davies 245–46).

It may seem that the process of *releasement from* is now complete. The soul, at this stage, has left off from creatures, from its creaturely being, from God as the creator, from its own uncreated being, from the Son, from its Sonship, from multiplicity, and even from identity (inasmuch as the latter has multiplicity at its foundation). What else is left, then? To what else can it die? Isn't oneness enough?

The question ultimately comes down to whether, in abandoning its createdness and its uncreated image, the soul has sufficiently abandoned multiplicity. In the first death, the soul left God the Creator behind, a god who acts on his creation, a god who is understood only in relation to that which he creates. In the second, the soul left the distinction of the Trinity behind. Yet here too there is a danger that resembles the need to die to the creator God. For it is still possible, even having abandoned the Trinity, to think of the Godhead as the potential cause of the Trinity, as the potency for Trinitarian emanation that awaits self-actualization—in short, as an expectant parent. This too must be released.

(3) In its third exodus, the soul must die to all divine activity. Eckhart initially explains this in terms of Thomist metaphysics, which he will endeavor to undermine:

> [A]ll masters are agreed that God the Father comprehends his essence where he is the origin of the eternal Word and of all creatures. The masters make a distinction between being [*wesene*,

or the Latin *esse*] and essence [*natûre*, or the Latin *essentia*]. Where being is active being in the Father, it is also essence. Therefore the distinction is a logical one. And therefore where God is active, all creatures peer out from him in search of possibility [*mügelicheit*]. (DW 4: 1129,357–62/Davies 247)

According to this interpretation, there is no real difference between God and the Word/Son/exemplar-of-all-creatures that he pre-contains. We can only parse them logically. In reality, God's being is tied inextricably to, indeed *is,* his essence, where he actuates the Word and creation. Thus, God's being is still understood *in terms of that essence.* His connection to the Word and to creatures *as their source* still smacks of multiplicity.

Yet neither the reciprocity between being and essence, nor that between potentiality and actuality, will satisfy the soul's search for oneness. Not only must the soul leave behind God as active if it "is to enter the divine essentiality where God is free of all his work"; additionally, "this highest image" of God must also "die" with it (DW 4: 1129,366–1130,369/Davies 247). Although it is not obvious what Eckhart means here, I take him to be saying that the soul must also die to God as potentiality for activity,[31] just as, as Eckhart will say later on in the sermon, the soul must die to itself as a potential recipient from God—for the Godhead does not act.[32] It must, in other words, escape the metaphysical binary of potentiality and actuality, lest it fail to know the oneness that it seeks and the oneness that it fundamentally *is.*

Paradoxically, such knowledge and seeking must also be abandoned in the third, most extreme death of the soul. As Eckhart writes, summarizing the soul's trajectory so far,

> Now when the soul has gone out from its created being [*wesens*] and from the uncreated being in which it finds itself in the eternal image, and has entered the divine essence [*natûre*] where it cannot comprehend [*enbegrîfet*] the kingdom of God and where it knows [*bekennet*] that no creature can enter the kingdom of God, then the soul discovers itself, goes its own way and never seeks God; and thus it dies its highest death. In this death the soul loses all its desire, all its images, all understanding [*verstantnisse*] and form and is stripped of its being. . . . It finds that it is itself that same thing which it had sought without success. (DW 4: 1130,374–79, 1132,389–91/Davies 247–48; trans. mod.)

In addition to the binaries of being and essence and of potentiality and activity, Eckhart undermines two further metaphysical categories here, namely, those of (i) knowledge and (ii) searching for grounds or reasons (*Gründe*).

(i) First, knowledge is no longer a product of reason, but a matter of realizing, not so much in the sense of bringing about as in the sense of owning up to, making real *for oneself*, that which one already is: "I have occasionally said, as I do again now, that I already have all that I ever shall possess in eternity. . . . [T]he more the soul departs from [*sich . . . scheidet von*] . . . multiplicity, the more the kingdom of God is *uncovered* in her" (DW 4: 1133,403–409/Davies 249; emphasis added). And this realization occurs only on the basis of what I am calling the broader activity of thinking, which harbors a practical apriori. Understanding is, in other words, contingent on thoughtful activity. As Eckhart preaches:

> O noble soul, consider your nobility! For until you have entirely released [*enlæzest*] yourself and cast yourself into the fathomless ocean of the Godhead [*gruntlôsen mer der gotheit*], you cannot know [*bekennen*] this [third] divine death. (DW 4: 1131,384–86/Davies 248; trans. mod.)

(ii) The second metaphysical category Eckhart undermines here is that of searching for grounds. This can easily be tied to the first category if we recall the famous opening of Aristotle's *Metaphysics*: "All humans desire by nature to know." For Eckhart, knowledge—if one can still speak of knowledge here—of the Godhead/oneself only transpires in the act of detachment. We cannot find it if we search for it as something we lack, or as something outside of ourselves to be grasped or won. It is more an explicit mode of being than a possession, which is no doubt one of the reasons Eckhart elsewhere speaks of it as an "unknowing" or, oxymoronically, as an "unknown-knowing [*unbekante bekantnisse*]" (Prr. 101–104). In order to appropriate it, we must abandon our inborn desire for it, since the latter presupposes the distinction of inside and outside, lacking and having. Moreover, tracing things back to their cause in God does not suffice, since the Godhead, with which we are always operatively, if not thematically, one, is not such a cause. The ground of the soul and of God is no ordinary ground; it is bottomless, abyssal, fathomless (*gruntlôs*). To grasp such a "ground" is extremely difficult. In fact, if knowledge means tracing things back to their firm grounds, it is by definition unknowable. This does not, however, mean that it cannot be thought and described from out of the experience of oneness. Eckhart endeavors to do so in a plethora of ways, such as with the metaphors of "hovering" and "ocean" in this sermon. Elsewhere he privileges the terms *abyss* and *nothingness*.[33] I propose that one of the best—or at least one of the most fecund and influential—terms to describe such an unfathomable groundless ground of God and the soul, and to do so otherwise than metaphysically, is to describe it as *gelâzenheit*. I will undertake to do so in what follows.

3. The Godhead's Generative Releasement

As far as I am aware, the only time that Eckhart comes close to defining God as *gelâzenheit* is when, in the tractate *On Detachment*, he uses the related term *abegescheidenheit*.[34] What is even more striking about this tractate is that union is to be appropriated via the same (virtue of) *abegescheidenheit* on the part of the human being.

At the beginning of the tractate, Eckhart relates that he has mined the depths of scripture and philosophy to unearth what the best virtue is for the human to unite with God, to become, "by grace," "that which God is by nature, and with which man can come most of all to resemble [*glîchest*] that image which he was in God, and between which and God there was no distinction [*underscheit*] before ever God made created things" (DW 5: 401,1–4/ES 285). We know that Eckhart will wish to push beyond being a mere image in God, even if it be that of the images precontained in God before creation. It is also questionable whether grace is an appropriate term to describe the human being's *dei-formatio*. For, as we saw in the third death, God does not work and the soul does not receive. I will return to this in a moment. In any event, what Eckhart says he discovered is that only pure detachment, *lûteriu abegescheidenheit*, suffices, as all other virtues are directed at creatures, whereas *abegescheidenheit* holds itself aloof. Moreover, unlike love, which compels me to love God, detachment compels God to love me. This is because God, like all things, wants to rest in "the natural state that is proper to him," and the natural state proper to him is "oneness and purity, which comes from [his] detachment [*abegescheidenheit*]" (DW 5: 403,3–4/ES 286; trans. mod.). Yet it is not as though God were waiting for me to do something for him to go out and make a change.

God's *abegescheidenheit* keeps to itself even as it allows for all things. It is the original *epochē*:

> [D]etachment [*abegescheidenheit*] and humility are in God, so far as we can speak of virtues as present in God. Now you must know that it was loving humility that brought God to abase himself into human nature; yet when he became man, detachment remained immovable in itself as it was when he created the kingdoms of heaven and earth. (DW 5: 407,7–408,2/ES 287; cf. DW 5: 413,5–14,1/ES 288)

If the language of compulsion seems perverse here, in a sense it is, and not just because God is supposed to be above such constraint. What is really perverse about it is that there is ultimately no change in God, nor, ultimately, as we saw above, in our fundamental ontological status. When Eckhart speaks of compulsion, then, I think it is best understood as an "explosive metaphor"[35] deployed to set us on the path of releasement. And this path, as we have seen, does not lead to an ontological change in the human being, but to an awareness of who we are. *On Detachment* still speaks of a unity through grace, of becoming one with God *to the extent possible*, and in this sense does not go far enough.[36] What the tractate does give us, however, are two things no other text does with the same degree of clarity and explicitness: (1) God is himself called *abegescheiden* here; and (2) if I wish to unite with the detached God (or better: to own up to my always already operative, though implicit oneness with the *abegescheidene* God), I must become detached myself:

> It is from his immovable detachment [*abegescheidenheit*] that God is God, and it is from his detachment that he has his purity and his simplicity and his unchangeability. And if a human being is to become equal with God, insofar as a creature can have equality with God, that must happen through detachment [*abegescheidenheit*]. (DW 5: 412,4–8/ES 288; trans. mod.)

If, to know the truth, we must be the truth, and if the truth is God's detachment, then, in order to know God's detachment, we must be detached. What we have here is thus have the formal structure of the identity between thinking (as the broad, essential activity of the human being) and being (as the way of being of both the Godhead and the ground of the soul).

The problem with the term *abegescheidenheit*, however, is that it is too negative, as we saw above in §1. No single translation of *abegescheidenheit* seems to capture the three crucial aspects of Eckhart's basic insight: the fundamental way of being of the Godhead and the soul, the way in which we can come to appropriate this, and, although I have not discussed this extensively, the comportmental consequences of such appropriation. However, although hardly a translation, at least in the way in which we normally understand this word, the term *gelâzenheit* does seem to harbor valences of all three senses, as do its French and English counterparts *délaissement* and *releasement*. It is at once releasement *of,* releasement *from,* and releasement *to.* Moreover, the German prefix *ge-*, unlike the Latinate *dé-* and *re-*, which imply intensive force, even conveys the sense of gathering these different modes of letting together, as a *Gebirge* is a range of mountains gathered together or a *Gespräch* is a gathering of language in conversation. It is no accident that *Gelassenheit* became the preferred term of Eckhart's successors.[37] And it is also no accident, I take it, that one of the manuscripts of *On Detachment* (N4) employs both terms throughout the treatise in a manner similar to the way in which one finds them being used synonymously in Eckhart's indubitably authentic text *Rede der underscheidunge*.[38] While the latter speaks of "true detachment or . . . releasement [*wârer abegescheidenheit oder . . . gelâzenheit*]" with respect to human activity (DW 5: 283,8/ ES 277, §21; trans. mod.), MS N4 uses *gelâzenheit* for God's way of being, too.[39] Here are few examples for comparison:

Table 3.1. Human *abegescheidenheit/gelâzenheit*

Critical Edition	MS N4
"Sô lobe ich abegescheidenheit vür alle minne" (DW 5: 402,3).	"Ich lobe aber die tugent der lvtern abgescheidenheit vnd der gantzen gelassenheit fur sie alle vnd zu dem ersten fur alle minne vnd das zu dem ersten" (DW 5: 402, n. 3).
"And yet I praise detachment above all love" (ES, 286).	"However, I praise the virtue of pure detachment and complete releasement above all else; and first before all love and that first of all."

Table 3.2. Divine *abegescheidenheit/gelâzenheit*

Critical Edition	MS N4
"Des antwürte ich alsô und spriche, daz in gote ist abegescheidenheit und dêmüeticeit, als verre wir tugende von gote gesprechen mügen. Nû solt dû wizzen, daz diu minnebære dêmüeticheit got dâ zuo brâhte, daz er sich neigete in menschlîche natûre, und stuont abegescheidenheit unbewegelich in ir selber, dô er mensche wart" (DW 5: 407,7–408,1).	"Die antwort wie wol in got alle tugent sint Minne diemut abgescheidenheit etc. So pracht in doch allein minne vnd die diemutikeit dar zu das er sich von erpermde neigte in menschliche nature vnd stvnde also in im die abgescheidenheit vnd die gelassenheit in ir selber stille" (DW 5: 407, n. 7).
"To this I answer and say that detachment and humility are in God, so far as we can speak of virtues as present in God. Now you must know that it was loving humility that brought God to abase himself into human nature; yet when he became man, detachment remained immovable in itself as it was when he created the kingdoms of heaven and earth" (ES, 287).	"The answer is that although all the virtues (love, humility, detachment, etc.) are in God, only love and humility brought him to abase himself into human nature, and [yet] detachment and releasement thereby remained in him in their same stillness."

Table 3.3. Union in and through *abegescheidenheit/gelâzenheit*

Critical Edition	MS N4
"Nû maht dû vrâgen, waz abegescheidenheit sî, wan si als gar edel an ir selber ist? Hie solt dû wizzen, daz rehtiu abegescheidenheit niht anders enist, wan daz der geist alsô unbewegelich stande gegen allen zuovellen liebes und leides, êren, schanden und lasters als ein blîgîn berc unbewegelich ist gegen einem kleinen winde. Disiu unbewegelîchiu abegescheidenheit bringet den menschen in die grœste glîcheit mit gote" (DW 5: 411,11–412,4).	"Nû mochst du vrâgen, was ist abgescheidenheit vnd gelassenheit, seit si als gar edel an ir selber ist? Du solt wizzen, daz rehtiu abgescheidenheit vnd gelassenheit . . ." (DW 5: 412, nn. 11–12).

> "Now you may ask what detachment is since it is in itself so excellent. Here you should know that true detachment is nothing else than for the spirit to stand as immovable against whatever may chance to it of joy and sorrow, honor, shame and disgrace, as a mountain of lead stands before a little breath of wind. This immovable detachment brings a man into the greatest equality with God."

> "Now you may ask what detachment and releasement are since they are in themselves so excellent. You should know that true detachment and releasement..."

The valences of releasement *from* things and releasement *to* God and things in *gelâzenheit* should be clear enough from the foregoing. While detachment harbors the negative sense of releasement *from* and the positive sense of releasement *to* the Godhead, it lacks the valence of releasement *to* things, that is, *letting* them become sheer God to you. More significantly, we do not find in it the valence of releasement *of,* by which I mean *the verbal (as opposed to substantive), non-causal, neither active nor passive, generative way of being of the Godhead and the soul.*

The Godhead/ground-of-the-soul does not decide to produce the Trinity or create the world at some point in time. Such genesis is always already *happening.* It is not something the Godhead is *doing,* nor is it something the Godhead is *suffering.* It lies before such distinctions, which is why evental and middle-voiced verbs are better suited to describe it than is the language of substance metaphysics. Genesis should be thought, not in the sense of the first book of the Pentateuch, but in its radical, middle-voiced sense as *gignesthai,* becoming, where we have neither an active subject nor a passive recipient. *Releasement of* describes the state of having always already let the Trinity and world emerge, having always already let them be. The Godhead's *wesen* is at once intransitive (its way of being) and transitive (the way it "ises" or lets the world be in its own way of being). What we have here, to quote Reiner Schürmann on the significance of Neoplatonic henology, "is the very movement of *nasci,* or *phyein,* of coming-to-presence, in all that there is. It is the *phainesthai,* the appearance as such, in all phenomena. It is their origin in the sense of pure *oriri,* showing-forth."[40] When all things become pure God to you in the movement of releasement *to* things, what becomes manifest is this very releasement *of* things in the ground of God and the soul. You behold and release yourself to the constellation of divine presencing in phenomena, while also bearing in mind their abyssal, never-fully-present source.

Here, thinking has unfolded its identity with being. The essential activity of the human being has laid bare its identity with the essential activity of being. It has released itself to understand and live out its essential oneness with being as releasement. It has learned to become what it is.

4

Eckhart's Strategies for Cultivating Releasement

The preceding chapter has revealed that *gelâzenheit* (releasement) in Eckhart is ultimately neither voluntarist nor intellectualist. Eckhart's approach to union with God is ultimately neither Franciscan (with the general focus on will) nor Dominican (with the general focus on the intellect). While it is *in part* true that *gelâzenheit* involves divesting oneself of one's will in order to carry out the will of God, it is not the case that *gelâzenheit* remains stuck within the domain of the will. As we saw in chapter 1, Eckhart says that those who would give up their will in order to fulfill God's will "are asses with no understanding of God's truth." This volitional moment, then, is, at best, only one facet of *gelâzenheit*. Moreover, although Eckhart often suggests that *gelâzenheit* (or those terms that pertain to, or are used synonymously with, *gelâzenheit*, such as *abegescheidenheit*) is a matter for the intellect, there are moments where not only discursive reason but even intellection seems insufficient to measure up to this experience, an experience that lies at the basis not only of understanding Eckhart's thought, but also, according to Eckhart, of becoming one with, or rather realizing that one is already fundamentally one with, God.[1]

Thus, Eckhart demands that we move beyond not only the will but also discursive reason and the intellect if we are to have a proper experience of *gelâzenheit*. As he repeatedly emphasizes, one cannot understand his thought unless one has become *gelâzen*. But if this is so, and if *gelâzenheit* is essential for becoming one with God, then how are we to make sense of Eckhart's very claims about it? One possibility would be to say that Eckhart is simply laying out an epistemological criterion, and that all he is doing is describing an experience retrospectively. In other words, Eckhart did not know about *gelâzenheit* until he himself had become released. Yet, unlike other mystics, Eckhart rarely speaks about himself in his sermons and treatises. Furthermore, such an interpretation would amount to ignoring the hortatory character of Eckhart's thought, as well as just how important *gelâzenheit* is, a pure moment of which would make the agony of hell seem trivial, indeed a joy and blessing, as he says at one point (DW 1: 200,17–201,1/Walshe 297 Pr. 12 ["Qui audit me"]). Therefore, if Eckhart cannot use reason to convince us of the significance of *gelâzenheit*, nor provide proofs or a sure series of steps for achieving it; if, furthermore, he cannot *make* us have this experience, nor *will* its emergence—then he must resort to other means.

Three of these means will be examined: Eckhart's dialectical logic (§1), his paradoxical and seemingly heretical statements (§2), and his ostensibly deliberate mistranslations of the Vulgate into Middle High German (§3). I argue that these means are strategies Eckhart employs in order to cultivate *gelâzenheit*. My concern here is more to examine how these strategies relate to releasement than to offer an extensive treatment of Eckhart's extradiscursive methodology as such, which in any case has received substantial treatment in the secondary literature.[2] My analysis here will accordingly be much briefer than in the previous two chapters, and I will take the liberty of citing from across Eckhart's corpus, rather than confining myself to the Middle High German texts that Heidegger himself cited or excerpted.

If chapter 3 sought to demonstrate an interconnection between being and method on the experiential level (releasing ourselves to understand being as releasement), this chapter seeks to examine this interconnection on the strategic level (the need to employ devices that will better address, convey, enable, and correspond to the happening of releasement than traditional metaphysical discourse). Both levels are crucial to Eckhart's teaching, and both will factor into my analysis of Heidegger's works in Part Three.

1. Dialectical Logic

One strategy Eckhart uses to cultivate releasement is to employ what one might call a dialectical logic. Rather than establishing premises and deducing conclusions therefrom, Eckhart attempts to cultivate a different kind of awareness that would "grasp God in the ocean of his groundlessness," which the intellect is incapable of accomplishing (DW 1: 123,2–3/Walshe 369 Pr. 7 ["Populi eius"]; trans. mod.). Eckhart does so by showing how we may say of certain things that, when considered in different ways, they both *are* and *are not* X, and that they *are* X the more they *are not* X or *are not* X the more they *are* X. In other words, as Bernard McGinn explains it, dialectical language involves "(a) predicating determinations (e.g., God is distinct); (b) simultaneously predicating opposed determinations (e.g., God is distinct and God is indistinct); and (c) predicating a necessary mutual relationship between the opposed determinations (e.g., God is distinct the more indistinct he is)."[3] This does not, strictly speaking, violate the principle of noncontradiction. What it does is expose the inadequacy of language when it comes to certain topics. Eckhart thinks that this is a proper procedure not only for addressing what, in the strict sense, cannot be spoken of or named simply (DW 3: 221,6–222,10/TP 322–23 Pr. 71 ["Surrexit autem Saulus de terra"]), but also for provoking us to detach ourselves and to appropriate the way of being of *gelâzenheit*. This is most apparent when Eckhart speaks about God.

Although Eckhart uses many terms dialectically in order to convey his ideas about God, including *distinction* and its opposite, as well as the transcendentals (being, one, true, good), I would like to examine a passage from German Sermon 71 ("Surrexit autem Saulus de terra"), where Eckhart suggests that any predication of God whatsoever is insufficient. What is remarkable about this passage is that he does so dialectically, both in terms of *what* is predicated, and by the very fact *that* he is predicating. Eckhart writes, "God is a nothing and he is a something. Whatever is something is also nothing [*Got ist ein niht, und got ist ein iht. Swaz iht ist, daz ist ouch niht*]" (DW 3: 223,1–2/TP 323). While the second statement ("whatever is something is also nothing") does pertain to creatures—which, as independent, are nothing, though, as being of God, are something—it also applies to God as Eckhart conceives of him. Eckhart does not go on to explain this quite as clearly as he does when he speaks of the distinct indistinctness or the indistinct distinctness of God in his Latin commentary on the Book of Wisdom.[4] Nevertheless, there is something similar going on here within the homiletic context. As mentioned in previous chapters, Eckhart holds that created things are, in themselves, nothing. God, therefore, insofar as he is not the nothingness of created things, can be called a something. But God is not some particular thing among many; "he is neither this nor that" (DW 3: 223,6/TP 323). In other words, God is nothing, no thing. Further, the more God is nothing, the more he is something. Taken from the perspective of indistinction, the more indistinct he is in being nothing, that is, in not being something that could be compared with or even distinguished from created things, the more he is distinct as something other than the nothingness of those things. Inversely, the more he is something, the more he is nothing. Taken from the perspective of distinction, the more distinct he is in being distinguished from created things as something, the more he is indistinct as nothing, that is, as no particular thing at all.

Thus, we may refer to God as both something and nothing. Taken separately, neither of these predications is definitive. For each may be qualified by the other. Taken together, they stand in contradiction. Is there some higher term, then, that could account for both and be more fitting when attributed to God?

Eckhart does not seem to think so. In fact, toward the end of the sermon, he sums up his analysis by declaring, again dialectically, that, "One must take God as a mode without mode [*wîse âne wîse*] and being without being [*wesen âne wesen*], because he has no mode" (DW 3: 231,1–2/TP 325; trans. mod.). Like negative theology, Eckhart's dialectical logic attempts to gesture at the enigmatic essence of the divinity via nontraditional argumentation. It also exposes the inadequacy of language and traditional logic when it comes to explaining God and other themes like the divine ground of the soul.[5] But Eckhart's intention is neither merely indicative nor merely negative. Although he does not have a third term that would mediate between something and nothing, raising them up to a higher plane, he does think that dialectics is one way he can prepare us to achieve a more proper state of awareness and being. If there is a kind of *Aufhebung* in Eckhart's thought, it is not conceptual, but rather something that he calls on us to experience.

There is a strategic dimension to Eckhart's dialectical logic. By deliberately employing putatively contradictory language, Eckhart aims to confuse us, to disrupt our reliance on reason and our engrained modes of discourse. Having become aware of the insufficiency of language and traditional logic, we may now let go of our attachment to these modes of operation. Since the divine ground of the soul is also described dialectically; and since, like God, it is "neither this nor that" and "is free of all names" (DW 1: 39,4–40,2/ ES 180 Pr. 2 ["Intravit Iesus in quoddam castellum"])—such detachment opens up the possibility for thinking of ourselves no longer as separate from God, but as one with him, or rather for appropriating this ever-operative identity and living it out, without a why, in all aspects of our existence (DW 1: 90,3–92,6/ES 183–84 Pr. 5b ["In hoc apparuit"]). Only when we have released ourselves and let this overwhelming oneness sweep over us will we understand God, being without being.

2. Paradox

The second strategy I would like to examine is when Eckhart attempts to shock his audience with blatantly paradoxical statements that often sound heretical on first impression. One of the most famous of these is from German Sermon 52 ("Beati pauperes spiritu"), when Eckhart proclaims: "*Her umbe sô biten wir got, daz wir gotes ledic werden*" (DW 2: 493,7–8). In English, "So therefore let us pray to God that we may become void of God" (ES, 200; trans. mod.).[6] For purposes of clarification, I would first like to separate analytically the theoretical content of this prayer from its hortatory function, even though, according to Eckhart, there is a sense in which experience must precede properly understanding such content.

Eckhart explains that God, "insofar as he possesses himself in the mode and according to the property of his persons," cannot "peek" into what Eckhart calls the desert that is at once the divine ground of the soul and the Godhead or divinity beyond the Trinity (DW 1: 43,3–5/ES 181 Pr. 2 ["Intravit Iesus in quoddam castellum"]; trans. mod.).[7] Here in this desert, there is no distinction. God and we are one and the same. Likewise, insofar as we take God as distinct from the Godhead, we cannot peek into that desert. We must therefore strive to move beyond God as separate from Christ and from the Holy Spirit, and as separate from our most proper essence. We do this not only for our own benefit, but for the sake of God as well. Letting go of God in this way is, in fact, the "highest and ultimate thing which a human being can release [*gelâzen*]" (DW 1: 196,6–7/ Walshe 296 Pr. 12 ["Qui audit me"]; trans. mod.). Only from out of this experience can we truly become *gelâzen*. It is in this sense that Eckhart is praying to be void of God.

All the same, we should not overlook the fact that Eckhart is praying *to God* for this to happen. He is not saying that we can simply will it to be so, or even follow a series of steps that would result necessarily in *gelâzenheit*. To be sure, we must release ourselves *from* misconstrued interpretations of God and ourselves. Yet we cannot accomplish this alone, at least not if we think of ourselves as overcoming a lack or achieving something new of our own volition. Although God is ultimately not an agent, as we saw in chapter 3, Eckhart appears to speak of him in this manner to disrupt the confidence we place in our faculties. Thus, praying to God for releasement from God suggests that God must withdraw to some extent of his own accord for *gelâzenheit* to become explicit. We must open ourselves up to *letting* him do so, just as we must release ourselves *to* this ineffable desert of the Godhead, letting ourselves be overtaken *by* it. Here, in a profound, though ultimately insufficient, reversal, *gelâzenheit* would mean being-let just as much as it means letting-be.

Like his dialectical logic, Eckhart's contradictory prayer provokes us into questioning received dogmas and rational argumentation. But it also suggests that we are not fully in control when it comes to *gelâzenheit*. Indeed, rather than simply providing reasons to support his position, Eckhart *prays* that we may be void of God. Or rather he includes us as subjects of the prayer: "Thus *we* pray God to be void of God." Having attempted to release ourselves from God, Eckhart invites us to join him in praying that God release himself from us.

3. Translation

The last of the provocative strategies I would like to examine is when Eckhart takes passages from the Vulgate and translates them into the vernacular in widely, indeed wildly, divergent ways.[8] For instance, in his twelfth German sermon ("Qui audit me"), he alludes to Luke 14:26, which, in Eckhart's Vulgate, reads: "*si quis venit ad me et non odit . . . animam suam non potest esse meus discipulus* [if someone comes to me and does not hate his own life and soul, he cannot be my disciple]." Eckhart renders this as follows: "*nieman enhœret mîn wort noch mîne lêre, er enhabe denne sich selben gelâzen* [no one hears my word or my teaching unless he has released himself]" (DW 1: 193,5–6/TP 267; trans. mod.). Now, although this may seem suspect, if indeed he means for it to be a translation,[9] Eckhart believes that exegesis ought to reveal what lies hidden under the letter of the text and can be brought to correspond to that which is proven philosophically (LW 1: 454–56/ES 95, nos. 4–7, In Gen. II). This seems to be the case with this passage. No one can receive the word of God and thereby achieve blessedness unless one has divested oneself of possessiveness and has come to experience, indeed to correspond to, the indistinct oneness that is proper to the divine ground of God and the soul. Insofar as one hates something, one remains attached to it, indeed possessed by it. And since attachment involves taking something as distinct from God (rather than as of God or as nothing in itself), Jesus must not mean that we have to focus on our souls as objects of hatred in order to be his disciple. Instead, he means that we have to let go of everything that distinguishes us from God—our possessions, our families, our bodies, even our particular souls. Only in this way may we become aware of our oneness with the divinity and hear the word of God.

But there is more going on here than simple exegesis. There is a performative element to this translation that is intended to provoke us. Eckhart does not just want us to understand the true import of Christ's message. He wants us to live it. As with Eckhart's other two strategies, rendering the passage from Luke in this way shocks us into reevaluating our commonplace interpretations of God and our role in the world. This particular translation also challenges us to question the way in which we relate to mundane things. We are compelled to ask: *Does our hatred of something keep us fixated on it, at the expense of comporting ourselves with* gelâzenheit? *Are we overly concerned with our affairs or with ourselves?*

Moreover, Eckhart's translation strategy enables him to emphasize what is of utmost importance, especially when a passage might be interpreted in a way that would inhibit carrying this out. God must divest himself of his own being if he is to enter into the "abyss of his Godhead [*abgrunt sîner gotheit*]" (DW 1: 194,5/Walshe 296 Pr. 12 ["Qui audit me"]; trans. mod.). So too must we release ourselves from our stubborn, possessive preoccupation with mundane things, indeed from our own selves to the extent that we think we are ultimately separate from that unfathomable ground. Even in his translations, Eckhart exhorts us to see that nothing is more essential than to enter into and to live from out of this ground.

※

Rather than exclusively employing reason to convince us of the truth of his claims, or even trying to persuade us into believing them, Eckhart attempts to cultivate us for the experience of *gelâzenheit*. As soil must be broken up in preparation for planting, so too must our habits and expectations be broken up if we are to become released. Eckhart's provocative strategies are designed to till the land and plant the seed of *gelâzenheit*, but only if we let it grow may we truly reap its fruits.

PART THREE

Introduction

As demonstrated in chapter 1, Heidegger turns to Eckhart again and again to address or corroborate his interpretations of the most wide-ranging topics: from Scholasticism to mysticism, from thing to world, from being to the human being, from the principle of sufficient reason to living without why. Each of these topics would doubtless merit a chapter unto itself. While we will have occasion to return to some of them, my main concern in Part Three is to examine how the Eckhartian connections among being, thinking, and method play out at three stages of Heidegger's thought. Here I will first provide justification for my focus and periodization, before describing the chapters to follow.

In earlier chapters, I frequently revealed my debt to Reiner Schürmann for suggestions he makes in his works on Eckhart and Heidegger, and here I must do so again. The next three chapters can be understood as an attempt to think through and develop the following sentences from Schürmann's *Heidegger on Being and Acting*:

> Thinking is a consequent inasmuch as it does not arise without preparation. On this crucial point—still more than on the two topics of *Gelassenheit*, "releasement," and of *Anwesen* understood as a verb, as "presencing"—Heidegger belongs to the tradition initiated by Meister Eckhart. . . . To understand poverty [for Eckhart] one must be poor. To understand detachment one must be detached. In Heidegger, to understand the turn, one must oneself turn about. To understand authentic temporality, one must exist authentically. To understand the directionality, *Sinn*, of being, one must become *besinnlich,* meditative. To understand the fourfold's play without why, one must live without why. To understand the primordial leap (*Ur-sprung*) which is the originary, one must take a leap.[1]

Schürmann suggests in this passage that Heidegger's fundamental concerns mirror what we saw in Eckhart: not only that, in order to understand being, one must *do* something (even if that activity is not separate from a broader conception of thinking), but also that what one does turns out to reveal being as the same as what one does. Schürmann unfortunately does not fully explicate such sameness between thinking (with its dependence on a practical apriori) and being in Heidegger, just as he did not fully explicate the oneness of the ground of the soul and the Godhead as *gelâzenheit* in his earlier work on Eckhart. As with his work on Eckhart, his discussions of Heidegger also lack treatment of the philosopher's modus operandi. This part of the book therefore endeavors to follow up on Schürmann's suggestion that Heidegger's greatest debt to Eckhart lies in the dependence of thinking on a sort of activity. It also shows how method in Heidegger involves not just a practical apriori, but also extradiscursive strategies for encouraging and facilitating the connection between being and thinking.[2]

"Method" may not be the best term to describe Heidegger's mode of operation, nor, for that matter, Eckhart's, especially not if one thinks of Descartes's *Discourse on the Method*, with its appeals to knowledge, clarity, and distinctness, the exclusion of doubt, and the division of difficulties into parts, beginning with the simplest and advancing step by step from there. For Eckhart, as for Heidegger, the activity of essential thinking (though not, of course, of all thinking) is essentially uncertain, hazy, doubt-ridden, comprehensive, involving the whole (including oneself), and so on. Moreover, neither Eckhart nor Heidegger attempts to provide a clear-cut approach to truth. Knowing truth is something that requires us to enact and truthfully *be* the truth we are, yet there are no sure steps we can take or definite prescriptions we can follow to accomplish this. All Eckhart and Heidegger can do is help us along. It is thus no wonder that Heidegger opposes the term *method* at several points in his career.[3]

Still, there are moments when Heidegger himself uses the term positively or approves of it conditionally. I do not just mean during his ostensibly more scientific period in and around *Being and Time*, where method designates the primary sense of phenomenology, and where Heidegger deploys the method of formal indication (SZ, §7; GA 29/30: §70). During a conversation with a Buddhist monk in 1963, later taken up in the famous *Spiegel* interview (GA 16: 675/328), Heidegger declared that a new method was *precisely* what thinking needed today:

> The task that is posed to thought today, as I understand it, is in one way new: namely, that it requires an entirely new method

of thinking. This method can only be attained in the direct conversation between one human being and another, through long practice, and through an exercise, in some measure an exercise of seeing in thought; that is, this way of thinking can initially be carried out only by a few human beings, but then, indirectly, can be conveyed to others by means of different areas of education. (GA 16: 589)

Earlier, in his Summer Semester 1942–43 lecture course on Parmenides, Heidegger endeavors to understand method, not "in the sense of a procedure with the aid of which man undertakes an assault on objects with his investigations and research," but rather, with the Greeks, as

> to-be-on-the-way, namely on a way not thought of as a "method" man devises but a way that already exists, arising from the very things themselves, as they show themselves through and through. The Greek *hē methodos* does not refer to the "procedure" of an inquiry but rather is this inquiry itself as remaining-on-the-way. (GA 54: 87/59)

To an extent, the way I am using the term *method*, namely as involving a practical apriori, concurs with this description. That is, what the practical apriori reveals is that which is always already the case, that which we already are. It reveals the path we are always already treading, even if for the most part like sleepwalkers.

Regarding my appeal to method as involving extradiscursive strategies, however, one might retort that all of Heidegger's writing is but a thoughtful response to being-on-the-way, that there are no intentional or premeditated strategies, only ever-varied attempts to think what being itself gives to be thought. To this I would reply that Heidegger endeavors through his writing and, as I will show, especially through his teaching, not just to respond and correspond to being, but to awaken the thinker in each of us and to set us on the path of thinking.[4] As preaching was essential to who Eckhart was as a thinker, so teaching was for Heidegger. Now, although this pedagogic dimension of his thought hardly resembles method in the Cartesian or scientific sense, there are still certain extradiscursive modes of operation that Heidegger develops and deploys to help us identify and follow our pregiven itinerary. It is not just the "inquiry itself as remaining-on-the-way" that I would like to call method in Heidegger, but the strategic-pedagogic dimension of that inquiry as well.

I will accordingly narrow my focus in Part Three to texts by Heidegger that, in addition to a treatment of the practical aprori as it pertains to understanding being, also bear a strong pedagogic bent. While Heidegger's pedagogic strategies are by no means absent in his texts written for publication—nor even in the esoteric writings not intended for publication during his lifetime—they are more fully on display in those written for presentation. Moreover, the exoteric, public character of the latter lends itself more readily to comparison with strategies that Eckhart develops in his sermons.

In contrast to my analysis of Eckhart, each of the following three chapters on Heidegger will speak to both aspects of method outlined above. It was possible to examine Eckhart's thought more or less as a whole in Part Two, even if I loosely divided that thought according to language (Latin in chapter 2, Middle High German in chapters 3 and 4) and theme (the connection between being and method as strategy in chapters 2 and 4, the connection between being and method as practical apriori in chapter 3). Such a procedure was justified, or rather necessitated, by the uncertain chronology of many of Eckhart's texts, and by the fact that the earliest extant complete texts stem from a period of his life that the ancients would have called flourishing. Although there are problems of chronology beleaguering certain texts by Heidegger, many of the texts I will be discussing bear comparatively exact dates and stem clearly from different phases of Heidegger's development. Even if one wishes to see Heidegger's thought as a single path, or to show how the earlier work anticipates the later or how the later helps us make sense of the earlier, one can hardly read a text from 1962 as though it had been written in 1926 (even if the title of the former, "Time and Being," appears to be a mere inversion as well), much less one from 1973 as though it had been written in 1915. Diachronic consideration cannot be neglected.

My analysis will concentrate mostly on texts from Fall 1928 through Summer 1945. Although I believe that it is possible to find the connection between being and method (in the two senses I specified above) as early as 1919 in Heidegger,[5] and continuing up through *Being and Time*;[6] and although there are developments with regard to this connection post-1945 that would merit consideration in a study devoted solely to Heidegger—the advantage to confining ourselves to this time frame is that it will allow us to see formal and methodological similarities among texts before, during, and after Heidegger's so-called turn while also highlighting certain radical dissimilarities in content, and this within a relatively short time span (seventeen years) of Heidegger's six-plus decades of philosophical activity.

This focus will also still permit a rather detailed discussion of *Gelassenheit* or "releasement" in Heidegger, which is of course the most prominent and conspicuous term Heidegger takes from Eckhart. We will examine the roles that *Gelassenheit* and action play within the more transcendental framework of 1928–30 (chapter 5), the increasing significance of concepts ostensibly antithetical to *Gelassenheit* such as the will and violence in 1935 (chapter 6), and the status of *Gelassenheit* vis-à-vis the will from the non-transcendental perspective of the open-region and the appropriative event in 1945 (chapter 7). We will see that, regardless of whether Heidegger is promoting asserting one's will to understand being in terms of the will or, like Eckhart, letting-be to understand being in terms of letting-be, the same formal connection between being and method is in play, and Heidegger is constantly at pains to push language to the limits in order to attune his readers to this connection.

Chapter 5 examines two lecture courses Heidegger held at the University of Freiburg after assuming Husserl's chair in 1928: the Winter Semester 1928–29 lecture course *Einleitung in die Philosophie*, and the Winter Semester 1929–30 lecture course *The Fundamental Concepts of Metaphysics*. Regarding the former, we will see that, implicitly, each of us always already philosophizes, which means that each of us always already lets the difference between being and beings be through our fundamental way of being: transcendence. The task of Heidegger's introduction to philosophy is to awaken this in us, to allow us to take over our inner philosopher and make it explicit. We—Heidegger's students or rather those who would philosophize along with him—must, however, *let* this happen. Only in the explicit "letting happen of transcendence as philosophizing" do we become who we are. Only when we "let happen" do we come to understand ourselves as a letting happen of being. Only here do we take on our "primordial *Gelassenheit*" (GA 27: 401).

I argue, in particular, that this letting is best understood in terms of the middle voice, before the emergence of metaphysical binaries such as activity/passivity and subjectivity/objectivity. Heidegger's oscillation between the language of activity and the seemingly passive language of letting-be in this course, and especially in the 1929–30 course, is rather a methodological strategy for attuning us to the premetaphysical domain of releasement than an unwelcome inconsistency or an unrecognized contradiction in Heidegger's thought. Although I do touch on Heidegger's extradiscursive strategies for helping awaken us to our essence in my discussion of *Einleitung in die Philosophie*, it is particularly in my discussion of *The Fundamental Concepts of Metaphysics* that we will see Heidegger at his methodological, Eckhartian best.

Chapter 6 turns to what might seem to be Heidegger's least Eckhartian period. In the speeches of the rectorship (1933–34) and in the *Introduction to Metaphysics* (1935), Heidegger comes to adopt astoundingly militarist, violent, and voluntarist language to describe both being itself (which, given the transcendental framework of the years surrounding *Being and Time*, was only barely broached) and the human being. Although such language could hardly be more remote from Eckhart, I argue that Heidegger still deploys the same method as he had in the writings of 1928–30. The difference is that, rather than interpreting the connection between being and the human being in terms of letting, Heidegger instead interprets it in terms of violence. To understand being as violent, we must exercise violence. Only in doing so can we own up to our essential reciprocity with the violence of being.

Chapter 7 takes up the first "Country Path Conversation," i.e., Heidegger's quasi-Platonic dialogue "*Agchibasiē*: A Triadic Conversation on a Country Path between a Scientist, a Scholar, and a Guide," where both thinking, or the essence of the human being, and being itself are understood in terms of releasement. Although there is no published record of the public-pedagogic character of this text, I discovered an unpublished typescript by Heidegger, as well as an unpublished report by one of his students, which reveal that Heidegger probably lectured on or with this text in 1945. Thus, it is not just the dialogic dimension to this text that bears a pedagogic character (recreating the event of learning in written form, as it were). It also appears to have been used within a pedagogic context, and perhaps even composed with this context in mind.

5

The Middle Voice of Releasement in Heidegger's Lecture Courses, 1928–30

> *Gnothi seauton*: know yourself, i.e., know what you are, and be as you have come to know yourself. This self-knowledge, as knowledge of the humanness in the human, i.e., of the essence of the human, is philosophy.
>
> —Heidegger, GA 27: 11–12

It has become commonplace to characterize Heidegger's development as a turn away from the active, voluntarist resoluteness of *Being and Time* and the writings of the rectorship to the passive, submissive releasement of his later works.[1] However, the term *Gelassenheit* (releasement) appears more than a hundred times throughout Heidegger's corpus, from as early as August 1919 (GA 60: 309/235)[2] all the way up to January 1976 (GA 81: 319), the year of Heidegger's death.[3] Passages from the late 1920s and the 1930s challenge any univocal prioritization of activity in this period, and, as we will see in chapter 7, those from the mid-1940s and beyond challenge any univocal prioritization of passivity. *Gelassenheit* in Heidegger must be understood not in terms of the active or passive voices, but in terms of the middle voice, even though there are many different senses of *Gelassenheit* in play throughout his corpus. After briefly explaining the middle voice in §1 of this chapter, I will argue for the medial or middle-voiced character of some of these different senses[4] in §2 by interpreting a little-studied, and as yet untranslated, text written shortly after *Being and Time*, namely, Heidegger's 1928–29 lecture course *Einleitung in die Philosophie* (Introduction to Philosophy).[5] We will see that, in order to appropriate and understand the fundamental, middle-voiced letting-be that is characteristic of Dasein as such, Dasein must let be in a middle-voiced fashion as well. It must expressly let be the letting-be that it is, which means nothing other than explicitly philosophizing from out of the philosophizing that implicitly defines it. This is something Heidegger can neither force to come about nor prove without his and our own engagement of letting-be, although he can help "*let* philosophy transpire in us" (GA 27: 4; emphasis added). I will broach some of the ways Heidegger endeavors to do so throughout my discussion of releasement in this course; however, given the much more prominent role accorded to extradiscursive methodology in Heidegger's lecture course from the following year (*The Fundamental Concepts of Metaphysics*, 1929–30), I will reserve the bulk of my discussion of Heidegger's strategies for §3. This final section will examine the tension between middle-voiced letting-be and activity in *The Fundamental Concepts of Metaphysics*, arguing that, as in *Einleitung in die Philosophie*, letting-be must ultimately take priority.

1. The Middle Voice

In the active voice, a subject does something to an object (*I hit the car*). In the passive voice, something is done to a subject by an object (*I was hit by the car*). Notice that, in these two examples, that which is hit plays no part in what is expressed by the main verb. Hitting, it would seem, is something that is only either done or suffered. Yet if we pay attention to everyday language, another possibility suggests itself. When we say, *There was an accident*, we are describing an event in which subject and object are implicated, in which neither one is entirely active or entirely passive. In languages such as Ancient Greek, there is a third grammatical voice for such phenomena, referred to as the middle voice. I cannot delve into the intricacies of this voice here,[6] nor into the interesting ways it has been appropriated philosophically, above all in the twentieth and twenty-first centuries,[7] but it is not hard to see that an appreciation of this voice (as well as of its traces in modern languages) would be invaluable for thinking through and beyond modern subjectivity.

Heidegger, one of the greatest critics of such subjectivity, was well aware of the significance of this grammatical structure. He invokes it many times throughout his corpus, most famously with regard to the Greek verb *apophainesthai* in §7 of *Being and Time*.[8] He also draws on and develops new linguistic devices to convey a middle-voiced understanding of being and our relationship to it, prior to the bifurcation into subjectivity and objectivity. These include impersonal expressions such as "it worlds" (1915)[9] and "it values" (1919) (GA 56/57: §10, and 73/61); cognate nominatives such as "temporality temporalizes" (1927) (SZ, 328/314), "world worlds" (1936) (GA 5: 30/23), "being 'ises'" (1941) (GA 70: 66 and 69), and "the thing things" (1949) (GA 79: 13/12, 17/16); and, not least, words derived from *Lassen* such as *Gelassenheit*.

2. The Middle Voice of *Gelassenheit* in *Einleitung in die Philosophie*

Scholars have already discussed the role of middle-voiced phenomena in *Being and Time* and in Heidegger's book on Kant, where the term *Gelassenheit* does not appear.[10] However, just after *Being and Time* (1927) and one year before the publication of the Kant book (1929), Heidegger inaugurated his return to Freiburg in 1928 not with the so-called Inaugural Address, "What Is Metaphysics?," but with an introduction to philosophy (*Einleitung in die Philosophie*). Here, in contrast to the seemingly active, voluntarist language of resoluteness for which Heidegger's work of this period has been criticized[11]—whether rightly or wrongly—he draws heavily on the language of letting and releasement, employing it in three important senses.

First, Heidegger uses the language of releasement in 1928–29 to describe the implicit, primordial happening of Dasein, from which several layers of operative, though still implicit, "letting" emerge. Before any practical or theoretical comportment toward beings, Heidegger explains that there is a prior projection of the ontological constitution of beings, on which basis one may then relate to beings in particular ways. This projection is not an everyday, ontic activity, but a "primal action [*Urhandlung*] of Dasein" (GA 27: 199). Lest this primal action be interpreted voluntaristically or couched in terms of agency, Heidegger writes that it is "nothing other than the . . . *letting*-be [*Sein*lassen] of beings" (GA 27: 199; cf. 183–84). Such letting-be transcends, goes out beyond, every relation to beings, and "yet it lies in every comportment to beings" (GA 27: 206; cf. 180, 207–10). It is a primal happening of transcendence that is neither sheer activity nor sheer passivity, but middle voiced, which is perhaps one of the reasons why Heidegger is at pains throughout this course not to let one term take precedence. (We will see a similar oscillation with regard to *The Fundamental Concepts of Metaphysics* in §3, below.) This primal happening is also transcendental, insofar as it grounds the possibility for, and belongs to, any relation to beings (GA 27: 210). As Heidegger puts it in terms of Dasein:

This being, which, not without reason, we call Da-sein, lets [*läßt*], insofar as it exists, i.e., lets in and through its being [*Sein*], something like a "there" [*"Da"*] first be. . . . The "there": a sphere of manifestation, on the basis of which present things can first of all become manifest, i.e., be discovered. (GA 27: 136; cf. 129–30, 138)

This brings us to the second sense of the middle-voiced character of releasement. For Heidegger also describes the more ontic relations to beings in terms of middle-voiced letting-be. It is on the basis of the primordial projection of being that we are able to encounter or be addressed by entities within the world as meaningful. While it may seem that turning our attention to beings is an activity or form of spontaneity, Heidegger contends that it is, rather, "in its genuine essence precisely a letting-encounter [*Begegnen-lassen*]," which he glosses as both "a peculiar passivity" and "in a certain way spontaneity, but one which, in terms of intentionality, has the character of taking-in, of receptivity" (GA 27: 74).[12] Here, letting-encounter is best understood medially, as at once letting ourselves be encountered and letting ourselves encounter, in between, or rather before the separation into subject and object. In a brilliant phenomenological analysis of a piece of chalk and our communal relation to it,[13] Heidegger shows how, prior to interacting with the chalk, prior to taking interest or being uninterested in it, we must let it lie there as it is; there must be a prior "letting-lie [*Liegen-lassen*]" and "letting-be [*Seinlassen*]" that, again, is not passive, but a "'doing' of the highest and most originary sort" (GA 27: 101–103; cf. 108).[14] This is all before any objectification of the chalk into something merely present-at-hand (GA 27: 184–86). Though Heidegger does not pursue this in the lecture course, having decided methodologically to bracket the distinction between the ready-to-hand and the present-at-hand (GA 27: 111–12), we might draw from Heidegger's other phenomenological analyses and take his example one step farther. When I do take up the chalk, not as an object of scientific analysis, but as something to write with, I must give myself over to it. When I write on the blackboard, I am not a subject acting on an object; rather, in the act of writing, neither I nor the chalk nor my students are radically separate from the event that is transpiring. There is, in other words, a middle-voiced character to ready-to-hand involvement in general.

It is only with the third sense of letting-be that Heidegger uses the word *Gelassenheit*, even though he retrospectively connects it with the first, most primordial sense of letting-be. Inasmuch as Dasein through its transcendence implicitly projects or lets be the open realm in which beings may be encountered, Dasein implicitly philosophizes. "Human Dasein as such philosophizes; to exist means to philosophize" (GA 27: 214).[15] Inasmuch as this is made thematic through philosophical questioning, Dasein explicitly becomes what it is. It takes on its essence. As Heidegger writes,

> If transcendence comprises the basic essence of human Dasein in general, then, in explicit transcending, nothing less happens than that the Dasein who essentially transcends becomes essential in the explicit letting-happen [*Geschehenlassen*] of transcendence. This becoming-essential of Dasein in explicit transcending, the explicit questioning about being as such, is nothing other than philosophizing. (GA 27: 213; cf. 214, 218)

For the most part, it is not in terms of activity or passivity that Heidegger describes such explicit questioning, but in terms of letting. The proper stance for letting such transcendence happen is, Heidegger writes, "a peculiar releasement [*Gelassenheit*], in which beings in themselves come to word" (GA 27: 214; cf. 180, 199) and in which being itself becomes questionworthy (GA 27: 214–17). He then goes on to say that this peculiar releasement not only stems from the "originary action [*ursprünglichen Handeln*]" of transcendence, as one might expect; it moreover "is nothing other" than that originary action (GA 27: 214). The philosophical task, then, is to let such transcendence show itself of its own accord. As this originary transcendence is middle voiced, so must be our philosophical approach to it. Recalling the middle-voiced language of *apophainesthai* in *Being and Time*, Heidegger says that, "[Transcendence] is 'to show itself,' not like a present-at-hand, describable painting, but rather to bring transcendence into a phenomenon, to bring it to show itself, means first of all to let it form itself [*sich bilden lassen*] in the ground of its essence" (GA 27: 395). To let something show itself of itself is not to force it into appearance, nor simply to wait passively for it to do so, but to bring or help it along, to participate in, but not to determine, the process, the middle-voiced *happening*, of its self-revelation. Here, "In the letting happen of transcendence as philosophizing, lies the originary releasement [*ursprüngliche Gelassenheit*] of Dasein" (GA 27: 401).

One must, in other words, let be to understand and exist in accordance with the primordial projection of being as letting-be. Although the focus here is on the way in which Dasein projects being rather than on being itself and the human being's implication in it (cf. chapter 7, below),[16] Heidegger nevertheless operates with the same formal structure as we saw in Eckhart and as we will continue to see throughout Heidegger's career: to understand the letting-be that we fundamentally *are* before any particular action we undertake or any particular thing we undergo, we must fulfill the imperative to let be. And fulfilling this imperative is itself neither active nor passive, but middle voiced, just as the releasement at the heart of transcendence is middle voiced. Such middle-voiced letting-be continues to play an important role in Heidegger's lecture course of the following year, although its tension with action is even more acute.

3. To Act or To Let Be? The Status of Philosophy in *The Fundamental Concepts of Metaphysics*

The relationship between acting and letting-be in Heidegger's 1929–30 lecture course, *The Fundamental Concepts of Metaphysics: World, Finitude, Solitude*, is ostensibly vague, if not confused. This holds especially true for the way in which Heidegger describes philosophy. On the one hand, nowhere else in the 1920s does Heidegger's discourse come to focus so centrally on activity as proper to philosophy than in the 1929–30 lecture course. Indeed, the emphasis is at times so pronounced that one may be led to conclude that it already intimates Heidegger's subsequent Nazi political commitments, as found, one might argue further, in the Rectoral Address and subsequent speeches, where Heidegger stresses decision and action, and calls on the German people to assert and will itself (or simply to will the absolute will of the *Führer*). We shall have occasion to examine this more voluntaristic, even violent language in chapter 6. Here, however, it should be noted that such a reading moves too quickly, and fails to appreciate the subtleties of Heidegger's arguments. For, on the other hand, Heidegger also speaks of a requisite *Gelassenheit,* a releasement or letting-be that is "decisive in all our methodological considerations," many if not all of which concern the essence of philosophy (GA 29/30: 137/91). Furthermore, we first have to ask whether Heidegger's very ambiguity concerning activity and letting-be might not also serve a methodological function, such as we saw in *Einleitung in die Philosophie*. That is to say, before dismissing Heidegger's claims on account of their apparent inconsistency, we should first consider whether Heidegger did not in fact intend to present his arguments in such a manner—or rather whether the matter itself did not in fact demand this of him.

The following section will accordingly be divided into two parts. I will first provide an explanation for the frequent oscillation between action and letting-be in Heidegger's lecture course, in light of his various characterizations of genuine philosophizing. Then, I will argue that these characterizations do not resemble those of an unreflective, headstrong willfulness. Rather, such features can be properly understood only from out of an experience and conception of middle-voiced letting-be. This experience must itself undergird what Heidegger calls "essential action [*wesentlichen Handeln*]" (GA 29/30: 244/163).

(1) Although Heidegger does not make the distinction between activity and letting-be thematic in the lecture course, it is not as if he were unaware of such a tension, or even of its importance for the trajectory of the course. On the contrary, I take it that the putative contradiction between these two terms stems from what Heidegger at one point describes as the task of the lecture course: to "cause [the principle of noncontradiction] to shatter [or become unsettled, *erschüttern*] in its very foundations" (GA 29/30: 110/61). He accomplishes this most conspicuously with his analyses of animality and the fundamental attunement of boredom, wherein he contends, for example, that the animal does and does not have world, or that attunements are both there and not there (GA 29/30: 293–94/199–200, 91/60). As we saw with Eckhart in chapter 4, Heidegger is not trying to turn himself into a plant here, as Aristotle said of those who would violate the principle of noncontradiction. Rather, he is pointing toward a domain that precedes the rules of logic and discursive reason. As he puts it in *Einleitung in die Philosophie*, the overemphasis on rational provability has occluded all immediate intuition of what lies in front of us (GA 27: 70). In the language of 1929–30 course, it has blocked the "*releasement* [Gelassenheit] *of our free, everyday perspective*" (GA 29/30: 137/91).

While Heidegger's apparent contradictions throughout *The Fundamental Concepts of Metaphysics* would be anathema to the common understanding, which insists on progress in philosophy as well as obtaining results, Heidegger maintains that the kinds of questions that philosophy must ask are essentially ambiguous and, with respect to progress, "fruitless," even "hopeless" (GA 29/30: 276/187, 31/21; cf. GA 27: 50–51, 223–24). These questions of philosophy, which ask after the whole and thereby necessarily bring the questioner him- or herself into question, are terrifying, but it is precisely the task of philosophy to hold Dasein out into such terror (GA 29/30: 36/24, 31/21; cf. 407/281, and GA 27: 223–27). Furthermore, these questions, along with the "comprehensive concepts" (*Inbegriffe*) belonging to them, must remain unsettled and without definitive answer, if by answer we mean conveying a fact in an immediately apprehensible way (GA 29/30: 273/185; cf. 303/207). This is because it is the responsibility of the individual to undertake a transformation in his or her Dasein in each case. Philosophy, then, cannot be taught and, as I will discuss below, must remain merely preparatory (GA 29/30: 18/12–13; cf. GA 27: 220, and GA 80.1: 345).

What is more, the essence of philosophy has a distinctive kind of knowing that lies between certainty and uncertainty, indeed a sort of knowing wherein one does not know whether one is actually philosophizing or not (GA 29/30: 28–29/19; cf. GA 27: 5 and 50–51). One is here reminded of Eckhart's emphasis on "unknown-knowing," as well as his discussion of the spiritual poverty of knowing in German Sermon 52 ("Beati pauperes spiritu"). For Heidegger as for Eckhart, such "knowing" is not like learning a new fact. It must be acquired over time. Heidegger says in the lecture course that it is something "we first grow into through philosophizing" (GA 29/30: 28/19). If this sounds circular (philosophy is a certain kind of knowledge one obtains only through philosophizing), it should. For philosophy is, Heidegger maintains, intrinsically circular, even vertiginous (GA 29/30: 266–67/179). This sort of uncertainty results in "everything . . . begin[ning] to vacillate" in a kind of "turbulence" (GA 29/30: 28–29/19).

Precisely because of these characteristics of philosophy, then, Heidegger is forced to present his position in nontraditional ways, prime examples of which include contradictory assertions and deliberately circular argumentation. This is further accentuated, though less obviously, by Heidegger's terminological inconsistencies regarding the relation between the human and the animal. Rather than employing different terms to describe the distinctions essential to each, Heidegger uses the same terms, sometimes clarifying the distinctions, sometimes leaving it up to the audience to do so, sometimes even recanting their scope or tenability.[17]

It should be no surprise, then, that in view of the distinctive way in which he describes philosophy, Heidegger's language would here, in this lecture course perhaps more than all others, fluctuate so perplexingly between activity and letting-be. For by using seemingly contradictory terms to describe the same undertakings, and by doing so in an inconsistent manner, Heidegger is attempting to disrupt our ordinary conceptions and way of being, so that we may thereby be cast into the vortex that philosophy essentially is, and undergo a fundamental transformation in our Dasein.

(2) Nevertheless, despite these reflections, I still think it is possible to maintain that some form of letting-be must precede activity. While one can,

of course, conceive of letting-be itself as an activity (and indeed Heidegger seems to do so at a number of points), there are different kinds of activity, or, to follow Heidegger's lead, within letting-be there is and there is not activity. If this is too confounding, then another, perhaps better way to think of such activity is to think of it as a middle-voiced phenomenon, preceding or outside the distinctions between subject and object or between activity and passivity, such as we saw above with regard to primal action in *Einleitung in die Philosophie*. To reveal the precedence of this middle-voiced letting-be, I will examine just two features of philosophy as Heidegger develops it in the 1929–30 lecture course: philosophy's rootedness in fundamental attunements, and its irrevocably preparatory status. While a broader analysis would prove useful in a more thoroughgoing study of this lecture course, I will focus on these two because of Heidegger's contention that all philosophy emerges from out of being gripped by a fundamental attunement (GA 29/30: 9/7), and therefore ultimately has to be understood by means of such a source; and because Heidegger's discussion of the essentially preparatory character of philosophy speaks both *against* unreflective action and *for* a sort of action that would be grounded in a more fundamental letting-be.

At the end of his preliminary assessment of attunements, Heidegger concludes, "If we have understood our task, then we must now see to it that we do not suddenly start to deliberate [*verhandeln*] *about* attunements again or even *about* awakening [an attunement], but inasmuch as this awakening is an acting, we must *act* [*handeln*] in accordance with it" (GA 29/30: 103/68). On the basis of this passage, it might seem as though Heidegger would proceed simply to engage in the activity of what he calls awakening an attunement. If being attuned is "the *fundamental way in which Dasein is as Dasein*," and indeed "first gives us the possibility of grasping the Da-sein of man as such," then it appears that all we would have to do is make the attunement explicit so that we can examine its various dimensions and thereby understand who and what we are (GA 29/30: 101/67, 123/82).

This approach, however, is problematic for two reasons. First, like the transformation that each individual must undergo in his or her Dasein in each case, "Awakening is a matter for each individual human being" as well (GA 29/30: 510/351). As with Eckhart's essential inability to force *gelâzenheit*, this means that neither Heidegger nor philosophy as such can willfully effectuate or awaken an attunement. On the contrary, since an attunement is in a sense always already awake inasmuch as it is persistently at work coloring and shaping our lives, philosophy can be characterized as "*letting it be awake, guarding against it falling asleep*"; or, better still, as making room for the particular individual to *let* it become awake for him or her, to avoid counteracting it, to "*let* [*it*] *resonate*," thus "letting Da-sein be as it is, or can be, as Da-sein" (GA 29/30: 118/79, 122/82, 103/68). For, at one point in the lecture course, Heidegger wonders whether he and his audience have not actually entered the attunement of profound boredom, but then he says that it is enough for them to have simply arrived at a more conspicuous "*receptivity*" for it (GA 29/30: 239/160).

This brings us to the second point, concerning the preparatory character of philosophy. After having arrived at a definition of the fundamental attunement of profound boredom, which is said to bring beings as a whole before Dasein and to open up the moment for essential action, Heidegger cautions that this definition should not be conceived as a fixed, readily translatable determination of essence, but rather must be seen as preparation for seeing the profound boredom that prevails in "*our* Dasein," in yours and mine here and now (GA 29/30: 233/155). It should, Heidegger hopes, be taken as an interpretation that has moved beyond itself, one that has brought us to "the brink of the attunement to be interpreted" (GA 29/30: 230/153–54; trans. mod.), but one that cannot alone make the transition into this attunement. "Only individual action itself," Heidegger writes, "can dislodge us from this brink of possibility [that is intrinsic to philosophy] into actuality, and this is the *moment of vision [Augenblick]*" (GA 29/30: 257/173). Although philosophy will seek to do more than simply make room for the awakening of attunements, Heidegger says that "*what philosophy deals with only discloses itself at all within and from out of a transformation of human Dasein*" (GA 29/30: 423/292). Thus, philosophy's proper concerns are themselves grounded in such a transformation,[18] even though philosophy can contribute to, though not independently bring about, its occurrence. However, while for philosophy this contribution occurs only though a vigilance that lets be, it now seems as though Heidegger wished to say that the transition into attunement itself occurs by means of an *action* on the part of the individual, and not, as we saw earlier, a letting-be. Does this merely amount to one of many inconsistencies on Heidegger's part (be they intentional or not), or might there be another way in which to understand such action?

It is essential to note that, in this passage referring to action, Heidegger speaks of the "moment of vision."[19] Before spelling out the positive implications of this, let us first compare the moment of vision with the activity of "contemporary man." Unlike what transpires in the moment of vision, it seems that "contemporary man" can be characterized by "abruptness," "haste to react," and intransigency when it comes to letting a fundamental attunement like boredom arise (GA 29/30: 248/166, 131/87). In fact, Heidegger worries that the problem with the contemporary situation is that "we are always already undertaking too much" (GA 29/30: 122/82). In addition to preparing individuals to undergo a transformation in their Dasein, the task of philosophy is to articulate what "Dasein wishes to speak about in this fundamental attunement [of profound boredom]—bring it to that word which is not simply a matter of gossip, but the word that addresses us and summons us to action and to being" (GA 29/30: 249/167). Since it is precisely this word that contemporary man seeks to suppress through such hastiness, we can infer that the action for which philosophy prepares us will not be hasty, reactive, or driven by a fervent desire to undertake everything. Rather, philosophy will prepare us to become who we are in the moment of vision, which is what Heidegger seems to mean when he speaks of "essential action" (GA 29/30: 227/151).

In contrast to the activity of contemporary man, there appear to be at least five dimensions of letting-be underpinning the essential action involved in the moment of vision. These include not counteracting attunements, not being opposed to them, awaiting them, comporting oneself in a questioning manner, and taking on a burden in order to be free. Because the moment of vision is opened up only by a disclosure of beings as a whole and of Dasein as arranged amid those beings (GA 29/30: 223–24/149), which, for its part, comes to pass in an exemplary way only from out of a fundamental attunement (GA 29/30: 410–11/283), such action can properly take place only when one has become attuned in the manner of a fundamental attunement. Now, this attunement comes to the fore "only," Heidegger writes, "if we do not counteract [*entgegenhandeln*] it" (GA 29/30: 240/160). He explains that this involves something *neither passive nor active,* but is prior to such a distinction. Foreshadowing the role of *Warten* in the first "Country Path Conversation" (see chapter 7, below), he says it involves a sort of "*waiting*" that "*is directed out toward an essential questioning of Dasein itself*" (GA 29/30: 240/161). That is, in order for beings even to come before us as a whole through a fundamental attunement, our comportment must be one of *questioning*. Such comportment does not strive to "produce" a fundamental attunement, but stands at the ready for it to sweep over us (GA 29/30: 199/132).[20] Heidegger associates such a stance with both "letting" an attunement come to affect us, and with not being opposed to it (GA 29/30: 199/132, 233/155).

Furthermore, even at the level of the revelation of beings as a whole there must be a form of letting-be. When beings as a whole become manifest to us through a fundamental attunement, thereby preparing us for the moment of vision, we stand within a domain "over which the individual person, the public individual subject, no longer has any power" (GA 29/30: 205–206/136). That is to say, at this point we do not merely have a capacity to act that we can choose to exercise or not. For, when beings are revealed as a whole, they are also refused to us *in a telling way*; that is to say, their refusal is simultaneously "a *calling,* is that which properly makes possible the Dasein in me" (GA 29/30: 216/143). The latter lacks determinate content in a way that is "disturbing," but, Heidegger says, we cannot "eliminate" this "if we are at all in a position to let this attunement . . . oscillate in us over the entire expanse of its oscillation" (GA 29/30: 216/144). Rather, in order for this telling refusal to occur we must be open to hear such a call, and allow what is revealed in the attunement to manifest itself and affect us in such a way that it guides us toward the moment of vision.

Regarding letting-be and freedom, Heidegger explains that we can be free only when we liberate the Dasein in ourselves. This means taking over our essence as our "ownmost burden," "*letting it become essential*" (GA 29/30: 248/166; trans. mod.).[21] This in turn involves, among other things, allowing an attunement to "be overpowering" or "oppressing." For, on the one hand, it is precisely by being overpowered in this manner that we are brought before ourselves to act freely in the moment of vision (GA 29/30: 204–205/136). On the other hand, without such oppressiveness we cannot engage in essential action, which is why Heidegger thinks that contemporary Dasein, despite all of its bustling activity, does not act in an *essential* manner (GA 29/30: 205/136).

When we take into consideration these various dimensions of letting-be, it becomes clear that Heidegger is not advocating reckless or even simply immediate, unreflective action. On the contrary, such action is what Heidegger explicitly argues *against* in a number of passages. While Heidegger's terminological ambiguity concerning the relation between activity and letting-be can be conceived as part and parcel of his methodological aims in the lecture course, more can be said about this relation as it pertains both to philosophy and to essential action. We have seen that philosophy is a preparatory undertaking that must allow for, though never determine, Dasein's letting an attunement pervade it in each case. Moreover, the sort of activity involved in the moment of vision cannot be understood without accounting for the moments of middle-voiced letting-be that both *precede* and *facilitate* it. Thus, although Heidegger's language does fluctuate between activity and letting-be, there can be neither genuine philosophy nor proper, authentic activity unless an element of letting-be supports and sustains them both. As Heidegger writes just one year later: "letting-be, *a questioning releasement* [*Seinlassen,* fragende Gelassenheit]," is the "fundamental attunement of philosophizing from out of the essence of the human" (GA 83: 81).

6

Violent Thinking and Being in Heidegger's *Introduction to Metaphysics*, 1935

> The true is not for everyman, but only for the strong.
>
> —Heidegger, GA 40: 142/148

One gets the feeling, in reading texts such as *Einleitung in die Philosophie* and *The Fundamental Concepts of Metaphysics*, that Heidegger's thought could have taken a radically different course. Rather than an emphatic embrace of the will, he could have emphasized letting-be. Rather than self-assertion and its paradoxical counterpart—deference to the *Führer*—he could have sooner developed a critique of a regime that sought little else than to *not* let beings be. Rather than violence, Heidegger could have promoted releasement.

But things turned out differently. In texts such as his 1930 course on Kant's practical philosophy, his speeches during the rectorate (1933–34), and his 1935 *Introduction to Metaphysics*, Heidegger's voluntarist, violent rhetoric reaches a pitch nearly without parallel in the history of serious philosophy:

> [W]illing from the ground of essence . . . determines the fundamental philosophical stance, and thus the content of philosophy. (GA 31: 303/205)

> The self-assertion of the German university is the original, common will to its essence. . . . The will to the essence of the German university is the will to science as the will to the historical, spiritual mission of the German people as a people that knows itself in its state. Science and German fate must come to power at *the same time* in the will to essence [*Wesenswillen*]. (GA 16: 108/109)

> Beings as a whole, as the prevailing [*Walten*], are the overwhelming [*das Überwältigende*]. . . . The human being is the one who does violence [*der Gewalt-tätige*] not in addition to and aside from other qualities, but solely in the sense that from the ground up and in his doing violence, he uses violence against the over-whelming. (GA 40: 159/167; trans. mod.)

The few glimmers of *Gelassenheit* in the first half of the 1930s only barely peek though the grim mantle of such violent voluntarism.[1] While they should not be ignored, they hardly exemplify the aim of Heidegger's thought during this period, even if they were pointing to the single star toward which Heidegger later believed he had always been heading. Just as Heidegger's thought in 1928–30 should not be viewed solely in light of what was to follow, so should Heidegger's thought in 1930–35 be taken on its own terms. However reprehensible, Heidegger's violent voluntarism should be given its due.

In what follows, I will endeavor to do so by focusing on just one text, "arguably Heidegger's major work of the 1930s":[2] the notorious *Introduction to Metaphysics*, first held as a lecture course at the University of Freiburg in Summer Semester 1935 and then published on Heidegger's own initiative in 1953. Although this course, "one of Heidegger's finest and most crucial,"[3] was reworked for publication, he sought to distinguish subsequent insertions by square brackets. Where he failed to do so, the editor of the *Gesamtausgabe* version of his text (GA 40) silently corrected him on the basis of a comparison of the published version with the original manuscript.[4] Unless otherwise specified, I will only cite nonbracketed material, since Heidegger's later insertions occasionally obscure the idiosyncrasy of his discourse in the 1930s by recasting it in terms of his later thinking of releasement.[5] This recasting may go a long way to confirming how important *Gelassenheit* is for Heidegger. It does not, for all that, help us to understand what is really going on in Heidegger's text. For here, rather than as letting-be, the essence of being and of the human being is interpreted in terms of willfulness, struggle, and violence. And yet, although the *content* of Heidegger's discussion could hardly be more remote from Eckhart, by no means is it in *form*. The method remains the same. We will find both a practical apriori that will reveal being and the human being to be the same as that activity, and extradiscursive strategies deployed to awaken us to this connection. As in chapter 5, I will not delve into Heidegger's modus operandi, but will only flag a few moments in which his discourse runs off the track of rational argumentation.

Heidegger begins his lecture course with a fundamental question, indeed with what is here called *the* fundamental question of philosophizing: Why are there beings rather than nothing? After much vacillation, repetition, and retraction—all strategically designed to awaken us to this untimely, ultimately unanswerable question and to make us feel its weight—Heidegger poses an even more fundamental question. This question, he explains, does not lie prior to the other, but rather, like the fire of a hearth, illumines the space in which it may appear (GA 40: 45/46). This question is the *Vor-frage* of the *Grundfrage*. It asks about being.

Heidegger then investigates the grammar, etymology, and essence of being, before turning to four ways in which being has historically been demarcated: from becoming, from appearance, from thinking, and from obligation. It is only with the third demarcation, which is said to take precedence over the other three (GA 40: 124/128–29, 127/131–32), that we may fully appreciate Heidegger's conception of the essential reciprocity between the human being and being itself in this lecture course. As we saw in chapter 5, this reciprocity will be understandable only on the basis of a practical apriori on the part of the human being, which will show being to be the same as that which the human being does. However, rather than letting be to understand the essence of the human being (and being itself) as letting-be, here we must perpetrate a sort of violence to understand being (and the human being) as itself violent. For here being prevails (*waltet*) as violence (*Gewalt*), as overwhelming power (*das Überwältigende*), and, to use a middle-voiced cognate nominative, as prevailing itself: *Das Sein waltet als Walten, das Walten waltet*. And here the human being is ultimately also characterized by violence. The human is essentially *gewalt-tätig*.

Heidegger unfolds this violent reciprocity between being and the human being through an interpretation—an avowedly violent interpretation (more on this below)—of the second choral ode from Sophocles's *Antigone*, the so-called Ode to Man, although he anticipates it at several points earlier on in the lecture course, not just with the language of violence, but also with that of willing, venturing, struggling, attacking, ripping, and wresting. I will begin by recounting a few of these earlier discussions, before turning to his interpretation of the ode itself.

From nearly the beginning of the lecture course, Heidegger takes the ancient Greek word *physis* as his point of departure for an interpretation of being. Far from "nature" as opposed to artifice or spirit, Heidegger would instead have us understand *physis* as a unique, originary emergence of being, on the basis of which—and only on the basis of which—beings and all other occurrences may be encountered and experienced. "*Physis* is being itself," writes Heidegger. It is—and here we have our first, albeit most innocuous description of what will become increasingly violent—nothing other than *Walten*: the prevailing, that which *holds sway* (GA 40: 16–17/16; trans. mod.).[6]

Heidegger then glosses this ontological *Walten* in terms of another Greek word: *polemos*. That which primordially prevails does so as strife and struggle. It holds together rest and movement in a strife-ridden, counterturning unity. However, in order for a world of relations to open up *for us,* we ourselves—or rather the poets, thinkers, and statesmen—must venture to tame it. We must *bewältigen* the "noch unbewältigt überwältigende . . . Gewalten des Waltenden" (*dominate* the "not-yet dominated, overpowering . . . violent forces of the prevailing") (GA 40: 66–67/67–69; trans. mod.). How do we do so? Not, as in *Einleitung in die Philosophie*, by letting be, but rather by struggling against it ourselves. A world must be "erkämpft" from "ursprünglicher Kampf" ("attained through struggle against originary struggle") (GA 40: 66/67–68; trans. mod.).[7] Here we already see a certain reciprocity between what being does (as *Kampf*, as *Walten*) and what we must do to open it up (*kämpfen, bewältigen*).

Heidegger also draws on the language of resoluteness, the will, and self-assertion from his 1933 Rectoral Address to explain the bellicose comportment we must adopt toward being.[8] In a discussion of the distinction between being and semblance, he explains that the Greeks had to wrest being from beings through a "creative self-assertion" (GA 40: 113/116). Oedipus, for example, not only stands for "the human being who meets his downfall"; Oedipus also embodies "that form of Greek existence [*Dasein*] in which this existence's fundamental passion ventures into what is wildest and most far-flung: the passion for the unveiling of being, that is, the struggle over being itself" (GA 40: 114/118; trans. mod.). Heidegger notes that, even in his own times, there is a "concealed will" that wants science to be more than a mere valet of the people. This, however, "requires that one first found and truly build a fundamental relation to the being of beings as a whole" (GA 40: 114/118; trans. mod.). Again, what is at issue here is not letting-be, much less an originary *Gelassenheit*; rather, being must be ripped out (*entrissen*) of concealment, semblance, and nonbeing (GA 40: 89/91, 113/115-16, 118/121).[9] Even Heidegger's typical prioritization of questioning is folded back into a primal "*willing*-to-know" that amounts to nothing less than resoluteness (GA 40: 14–15/14–15, 23/23).

Before turning to Heidegger's interpretation of the first stasimon of *Antigone*, a few words are in order about that to which it is supposed to attest, namely, the relationship between thinking and being in the extant fragments of Parmenides. Among his many creative translations of Parmenides—translations as jolting and idiosyncratic as Eckhart's in chapter 4—one in particular stands out for our purposes. It is of Parmenides's famous line: *to gar auto noein estin te kai einai,* which Heidegger renders as "belonging together reciprocally are apprehending and being." Heidegger mentions this line alongside Eckhart as crucial for his thought (MH/KJ, 181–82/172), and in this lecture course, he calls it the "guiding sentence of Western philosophy" (GA 40: 154/161–62; trans. mod.). Although, given his lifelong predilection for the word *Denken* (thinking), one might suppose Heidegger would use it as a translation of *noein* here, he instead relegates thinking to the activity of a subject that *determines* being, such as one finds in Kant and German idealism (GA 40: 145/152). By 1935, Heidegger had turned away from the Kantian valences of his earlier thought toward a privileging of being itself (GA 40: 148/155). The word *thinking* would therefore be misleading by this definition. Here, he accordingly uses the word *Vernehmen* (apprehending), which, interestingly enough, bears a degree of letting in Heidegger's initial description of it. As this description is full of Eckhartian word plays, it is worth citing in full:

> *Noein* means to apprehend, *nous* means apprehending, in a double sense that intrinsically belongs together. On the one hand, to apprehend [*Vernehmen*] means to take in [*hin-nehmen*], to let something come to oneself [*zukommen lassen*]—namely, what shows itself, what appears. On the other hand, to apprehend means to interrogate [*vernehmen*] a witness, to call him to account [*vornehmen*], and thus to comprehend [*aufnehmen*] the state of affairs, to determine and set fast how things are going [*fest-stellen, wie es mit der Sache bestellt ist*] and how things stand. Apprehending in this double sense denotes a process of letting things come to oneself [*das auf einen Zukommenlassen*] in which one does not simply take things in [*hingenommen*], but rather takes up a position [*Aufnahmestellung*] vis-à-vis that which shows itself. (GA 40: 146/153; trans. mod.)

Despite the degree of letting here, which is not altogether absent at other points in the lecture course, Heidegger's subsequent explanation of the second valence of *Vernehmen* gives us a better idea as to the direction in which we will be heading. It is military activity that will teach us what philosophy is all about: "When troops take up a position to receive the enemy, then they *want* [or *will*] to meet the enemy that is coming toward them, and meet him in such a way that they *at least* bring him to a halt, a stand" (GA 40: 146–47/153; emphases added). Although *Vernehmen* does not determine being here, it still relates to it in a violent manner. Like troops, it must bring being to a stand for the sake of confrontation and seizure. This is because it belongs in an essentially violent unity with violent being itself, as Heidegger's exegesis of Sophocles will make plain: "Where being holds sway [*waltet*], apprehending holds sway too and happens too, as belonging to being" (GA 40: 147/154; trans. mod.).

Although I have said little about the human being so far, by *Vernehmen* Heidegger no doubt means to refer to the essential character of the human being in the latter's relation with being. Indeed, Heidegger says it is on the basis of being that the human being (as *Vernehmung*) is determined in Parmenides's line, although we do not yet know how exactly this is so. It is for this reason that Heidegger turns to Sophocles's *Antigone*, where the relation between *Sein* and *Dasein* is brought to word and "authentically founded" (GA 40: 153/161).

After presenting a translation of the chorus, Heidegger begins his interpretation by pulling out the guiding thread not just of the ode, nor even solely of the tragedy as a whole, but of the essence of being and the human being as such. The mystery of this thread may be unraveled in a single Greek word: *deinos,* which Heidegger translates uniquely as *unheimlich,* meaning uncanny or, literally, un-home-like. "Manifold is the uncanny," begins the chorus in Heidegger's rendering, "yet nothing / uncannier than man bestirs itself, rising up beyond him" (GA 40: 158/165). Heidegger proceeds to explain how this word bears a twofold, yet unified sense, with one side pertaining to being, the other to the human being. In the former sense, it signifies

> the terrible in the sense of the overwhelming sway [*überwältigenden Waltens*], which induces panicked fear, true anxiety, as well as collected, inwardly reverberating, reticent awe. The violent, the overwhelming [*Das Gewaltige, das Überwältigende*] is the essential character of the sway [*Waltens*] itself. (GA 40: 159/166)

Here, being itself is clearly understood as overwhelming violence.

However much the aspect of "collected, inwardly reverberating, reticent awe" may resemble *Gelassenheit* (at least in its more modern valence of calm composure), this possibility becomes obscured by the way in which

Heidegger explains the second sense of *deinos,* which concerns the human being. Here, the human being is also understood in terms of violence, a violence that is moreover essentially *active*:

> But on the other hand, *deinon* means the violent [*das Gewaltige*] in the sense of one who needs to use violence [*Gewalt braucht*]—and does not just have violence at his disposal, but is violence-doing [*gewalt-tätig*], insofar as using violence [*Gewaltbrauchen*] is the basic trait not just of his doing, but of his Dasein. (GA 40: 159/167)

Like being, the human being is essentially violent: "[F]rom the ground up and in his doing violence, he uses violence against the over-whelming [*in seiner Gewalt-tätigkeit gegen das Über-wältigende Gewalt braucht*]." Indeed, inasmuch as the human being is both exposed to the overwhelming violence of being and is himself a perpetrator of violence *against* being, the human being is the most uncanny of all (GA 40: 159/167).

Such uncanniness is only revealed in the human being's very attempt to master being—and, like Oedipus, in his tragic failure to do so (GA 40: 161/169, 166/174). We thus have a practical apriori regarding the revelation of the essence of the human being: in exercising violence (*Gewalt brauchen*) against the violence of the overwhelming (*Gewalt des Überwältigenden*), the human being falters, and comes to see himself as the most uncanny. As we saw above, this uncanniness is, in Heidegger's interpretation of the ode in 1935, inextricably bound up with violence. The human being comes to see himself as essentially violent by way of his very activity of violence. Only in this way may he own up to who he is. But is there also a practical apriori with respect to the revelation of being itself?

One would expect so, given the connection that Heidegger himself draws between violence and being as uncanny. And Heidegger does in fact grant this, although here it is not just the philosopher or thinker who must engage in praxis in order for truth to show itself; here, poets, builders, and statesmen are involved as well. We accordingly have several layers of revelatory violence, several practical aprioris. Two passages support this. The first pertains to the *singulare tantum* of *das Seiende,* beings as such, and thereby points toward being (*das Sein*), if indirectly. It names all the above-mentioned roles. The second is more clearly about being, although it refers more explicitly to artists (as practitioners of originary *technē,* which Heidegger translates as *Wissen* or knowing). However, Heidegger mentions questioning and the passion of knowing, which hearken back to his earlier discussion of philosophy. And *technē*, at least in the Rectoral Address, holds for the activity of statesmen just as much as it does for philosophers and poets. Moreover, Heidegger says that *technē* characterizes the basic feature of *deinon*, which we know is the basic feature of human being as such. To get a better idea for the connection between the human practical apriori of violence and the violence of being (or beings as such), I will cite these two passages in full, placing words derived from *Walten* in square brackets:

> The violence-doing [*Gewalttätigkeit*] of poetic saying, of thoughtful projection, of constructive building, of state-creating action, is not an application of faculties that the human being has, but is a disciplining and disposing of the violent forces [*Gewalten*] by virtue of which beings disclose themselves as such, insofar as the human being enters into them. This disclosedness of beings is the violence [*Gewalt*] that humanity has to conquer [*bewältigen*] in order to be itself first of all, that is, to be historical in doing violence [*Gewalt-tätigkeit*] in the midst of beings. (GA 40: 166/175)

> Thus *technē* characterizes the *deinon*, the violence-doing [*das Gewalttätige*], in its basic trait; for to do violence [*Gewalt-tätigkeit*] is to need to use violence against the over-whelming [*Gewaltbrauchen gegen das Über-wältigende*]: the knowing struggle to set being, which was formerly closed off, into what appears as beings. (GA 40: 168–69/178; trans. mod.)

What we have, then, is, first, an *experiential* practical apriori: using violence against the violence of the overwhelming to unlock the closure of being and the human being. There is also, second, a *poetic* (in the Greek sense of *poiēsis* or making) practical apriori, which is at least as important as the experiential practical apriori: using violence against the violence of the overwhelming in such a way that the latter's violence is, for a time, contained (both held and held in check) in a work. (*At least as important*—because it is not altogether clear which is more foundational, the experiential or the poetic practical apriori. Must we first experience being in order to shape it in the work, or must the work first shape any possible experience of being? Heidegger suggests both possibilities in the lecture course, without clearly demarcating them, and without fully clarifying which, if either, has precedence.) This poetic practical apriori applies to statesmen as much as it does to sculptors, to poets as much as to thinkers (GA 40: 200/213).

Third, there is the violence of "authentic interpretation." To open up the truth of the violent experience or shaping of being, which cannot be found solely on the surface of Sophocles's ode, the interpreter must first exert violence on the text.

> The authentic interpretation must show what does not stand there in the words and nevertheless is said. For this, the interpretation must necessarily use violence [*Gewalt brauchen*]. What is authentic is to be sought where nothing further can be found by scientific exegesis. (GA 40: 180/171; cf. SZ, 327/312, and GA 3: XVII/xx, 202/141)

Violence is foundational for the praxis of genuine interpretation. Thus, alongside experiential and poetic practical aprioris, there is a violent *interpretive* practical apriori as well.

Regardless of the rank of these practical aprioris, each is essentially violent, and each reveals being and the human being to be essentially violent. This truth, the truth of being's violence, is not for the weak or poor in spirit. Whoever wants to understand this truth must be, not detached or released, but *strong*, that is to say, *violent*. Only through violence may the human being be who he is.

And yet, at the end of his interpretation of the ode, Heidegger reintroduces the language of letting:

> The uncanniest (the human being) is what it is, because from the ground up, it deals with and conserves the familiar only in order to break out of it and to let [*lassen*] what overwhelms it break in. . . . In willing the unprecedented, the violence-doer casts aside all help. For such a one, disaster is the deepest and broadest yes to the overwhelming. In the shattering of the wrought work, in knowing that the work is unfit and a *sarma* (dungheap), the violence-doer leaves [*überläßt*] the overwhelming to its fittingness. (GA 40: 172/182)

Although the language of letting still stands in jarring parallel with that of violence and the will here, it is nonetheless significant. For it suggests that at least two levels of letting must be operative even amid the human's essential violence. The human being must let being prevail as the overwhelming. He must let being enter in if he is to violently shape it into a work. Yet he must also let his work shatter before the overwhelming power of being. In order to let being be, he must let it be overpowering, and this means letting it overpower his creations, his customs, and his thoughts.

When we connect these two levels of letting with other hints of releasement in the lecture course, such as with the letting that is involved in *Vernehmen* or when being is said to "let emerge" and "let appear,"[10] Heidegger's later self-interpretation becomes more convincing.[11] He was not entirely wrong to see currents of releasement in the violent voluntarism of his 1935 lecture course. Still, these were hardly subterranean waters holding up the foundation of *Walten,* at least not overtly. They were more like countercurrents running against the flow of his text and times.

※

Over the next ten years, the tension between willfulness and releasement will continue to play itself out in Heidegger's corpus. As Heidegger is aligning himself with, but also critiquing, Schelling and Nietzsche in the second half of the 1930s, the language of letting returns, indeed the language of *Gelassenheit* itself, but it returns in conjunction with forceful and sometimes voluntaristic language. In the *Contributions to Philosophy* (1936–38), for example, Heidegger writes that

> [e]very *projection* is storm, felicity, verve, moment. Every *carrying out* is releasement [*Gelassenheit*], persistence, renunciation. . . . Neither of the two happens without co-determination through the other, and both always on account of the necessity of a sheltering. (GA 65: 391/309; trans. mod.; cf. GA 16: 330, and GA 66: 137/117)

Heidegger also continues to use the language of the will, even as distances himself from it. For example, he links the fundamental attunements of shock and restraint by means of the former's "own most proper 'will,'" which is in turn connected to the renunciation of mere subjective willing (GA 65: 15/14). In other words, as Bret Davis explains, what is required in the *Contributions* is the sort of willing not to will that is but *preliminary* for genuine *Gelassenheit* in the first "Country Path Conversation."[12] Being, for its part, will also be understood both in terms of the will *and* in terms of releasement.¹³

In the first half of the 1940s, however, the language of violence and the will subsides considerably as Heidegger's debt to Eckhart becomes more manifest. In texts such as *The Event* (1941–42), *Hölderlin's Hymn "The Ister"* (Summer Semester 1942), and especially "Anmerkungen I" (begun in Summer 1942), Heidegger starts to understand both being and the human being in terms of releasement, which he connects with other Eckhartian terms such as *Abgeschiedenheit* (detachment), *Wesung* (essencing), *Inständigkeit* (devout and steadfast indwelling), *Armut* (poverty), and *Ruhe* (rest, tranquility).¹⁴ The content, and not just the form, of the interconnection between being, thinking, and method in Heidegger's work comes to be more and more Eckhartian. It culminates in the first "Country Path Conversation."

7

Releasement as the Essence of Thinking and Being in Heidegger's First "Country Path Conversation," 1945

> "Released" and "Releasement" [*"Gelassen" und "Gelassenheit"*]—now no longer to be conceived primarily from the perspective of human comportment, but from out of the appropriative event [*Ereignis*].
>
> —Heidegger, GA 97: 295

By the end of World War II, subject to incessant bombings and surrounded by rubble, Heidegger comes to see that willful violence and violent willfulness, far from providing access to the truth of being, are precisely what obstructs it. The will is inextricably bound up with representation and objectification, and no amount of violence will allow us to break through our fixations to reach being itself. Instead, everything comes down to *letting-be*.

But it is not just we who let be. Being lets be as well. Whereas, in the 1928–29 *Einleitung in die Philosophie*, Heidegger's understanding of releasement was oriented to Dasein's transcendence, releasement must now also be thought in relation to being itself. Indeed, as I will show, releasement best names the way in which being appropriates the human being, allowing them to belong to one another in a manner that is not quite Eckhart's oneness, but is still in line with the sameness of *noein* and *einai*, thinking and being, that Heidegger never tired of pondering. And yet, as we saw in the previous two chapters, we cannot understand and own up to this sameness unless we act in accordance with it. Being must allow (*zulassen*), occasion (*veranlassen*), and admit (*einlassen*) us, but we too must let ourselves get involved with (*sich einlassen auf*) being by leaving off (*ablassen*) and letting ourselves loose (*loslassen*) from violence and the will. We must let being prevail (*walten lassen*) if we are to understand that being itself prevails as letting (*als Lassen waltet*). One way in which to interpret the gathering of all these valences of letting, and still more besides, is as *Ge-lassenheit*.[1]

My main focus, in what follows, will be on the first of several *Gespräche* (dialogues or conversations)[2] Heidegger wrote in 1945 in various towns of the Upper Danube Valley such as Hausen im Tal and his birthplace of Meßkirch. It bears the title "*Agchibasiē*: A Triadic Conversation on a Country Path between a Scientist, a Scholar, and a Guide," although Heidegger would himself refer to it simply as the *Gelassenheit Feldweggespräch* (the country path conversation on releasement) (GA 73.2: 1254, 1258). As he relates in a letter from April 4, 1945, Heidegger composed the majority of this dialogue in just two weeks:

> Think, in the last fourteen days, despite being unable to sleep and working at half my strength, I was suddenly taken by storm, and with complete wakefulness I wrote down a "*Gespräch*," which I hope to complete within the next few days. (MH/HF, 101–102)[3]

He relates further that he has been thinking about Plato's *Phaedo*, without, however, desiring to imitate him.[4] Indeed, only now, he says, does he actually understand him. "And everything is a unique necessity of pure, free saying" (MH/HF, 102).[5]

Judging by a date at the end of the published version of the dialogue (April 7, 1945), Heidegger was in fact to complete it within a few days of his letter. Over the next two months, he then appears to have used this text as a basis for lectures at the Benedictine Archabbey of Beuron, which is within easy cycling distance of Meßkirch.[6] For, in the Marbach archives, there is a three-page typescript summarizing the trajectory of the dialogue in four sections dated April 18, April 30, May 22, and May 29.[7] At the top of the typescript, one reads, in lead pencil, Heidegger's name, the timespan (Winter 1944–45, possibly the date of composition, or more likely of the ideas for the composition), and the location (Beuron). I could not determine the hand, nor who produced the typescript, but it is perhaps worth noting that, on two separate occasions in April, Heidegger says that his brother Fritz was typing up the dialogue for him (MH/EH, 235/188; MH/HF, 102).[8]

There is at present no way to prove that Heidegger composed this dialogue with the purpose of teaching in mind; however, it is quite plausible that he did, given that a small portion of the Freiburg philosophy department fled to Beuron and the nearby castle of Wildenstein at the end of March to hold a final summer semester under the Third Reich, and that Heidegger had been aware, and was involved in the planning, of the location of this semester before he began composing the dialogue. Moreover, a later, unpublished recollection by Hermine Lossmann (who was one of the student's there) proves that Heidegger was at least talking about themes that appear in his text. She quotes Heidegger almost verbatim:

> Heidegger, who had found refuge with the princess Leiningen [*sic*, should be 'Meiningen'] at Castle Werenwag (on the other side of the valley), sometimes came over to a seminar in the large hall of the Castle [Wildenstein]. On one occasion . . . the others came back laughing after the session. 'You missed out today, he spoke about the night as seamstress of the stars without seam and hem [*Nacht als Näherin der Sterne ohne Naht und Saum*]!' The evening before, in semidarkness, we had, as we did so often, recited [Christian] Morgenstern-poems from memory, among them also 'Die Nähe.' "[9]

As Heidegger writes at the end of the dialogue:

> GUIDE: For the child in the human, the night [*Nacht*] remains the seamstress [*Näherin*] who brings near [*nähert*], so that one star next to the other [*Stern bei Stern*] gleams in silent light.
>
> SCHOLAR: She joins the lights together without seam or hem [*ohne Naht und Saum*] or yarn.
>
> SCIENTIST: The night is the seamstress who in sewing brings near [*Die Nacht ist die Näherin, die nähernd näht*]. . . . (GA 77: 156–57/102)

At any rate, Heidegger's text teems with extradiscursive strategies that do not so much teach us facts as guide us along the path of thought. These include circular argumentation, unorthodox translation, neologisms, paradox, oxymoron, and the proliferation of words sharing the same root. What is especially striking about the form of this text is that it enables us both to follow the path in our thinking and to observe the interlocutors traversing it throughout their conversation. As in chapters 5 and 6, I will signal several of these extradiscursive moments during the course of my analysis.

Heidegger's dialogue is closely related to another text on *Gelassenheit*. In 1955, the mayor of Meßkirch asked Heidegger to deliver an address in honor of the composer Conradin Kreutzer's 175th birthday. Heidegger agreed on the condition that he be the one to select the theme.[10] He chose to discuss the role of releasement in the atomic age.[11] Four years later, he published his address, together with a truncated and retitled version of the first "Country Path Conversation," in a short volume with the one-word title: *Gelassenheit*.[12] Although the thoughts of the dialogue provide the philosophical foundation for the memorial address, the address serves as an excellent entry point into the themes of the dialogue. It is presumably for this reason that Heidegger placed the memorial address first in his volume.

I will accordingly begin with a brief discussion of the memorial address, focusing on the distinction Heidegger draws between the violence of calculative thinking and the releasement of meditative thinking (§1). Yet the latter is not as easy to achieve as Heidegger presents it in the address. For, however postmetaphysical our epoch may seem, the metaphysical problems of the will and representational thinking still pervade our activity and discourse. I will therefore turn next to the first "Country Path Conversation" to show how we must first work through these problems if we are truly to think with releasement (§§2–3). Thereafter, I will discuss the interlocutors' topological presentation of being as *die Gegnet* (the open-region) (§4), before addressing the way in which we should understand it, as well as ourselves, in terms of middle-voiced *Gelassenheit* (§5). I will conclude with some reflections on how the middle voice of *Gelassenheit* and the open-region connect both to Heidegger's lifelong effort to understand the sameness of thinking and being and to Eckhart's conception of the Godhead (§6).

1. From Calculative to Meditative Thinking

In his 1955 memorial address, Heidegger distinguishes between two types of thinking. The first he calls "calculative thinking" (G1, 13/46). This mode of thinking has come to dominate the planet and is often taken to be the only legitimate way in which to relate to things. Indeed, it imposes not just *how* to relate to things, but what they fundamentally *are*. It holds that *what is* is what can appear as calculable, orderable, and, ultimately, manipulable (G1, 18/50–51; cf. GA 77: 11/7). To be sure, this kind of thinking, which has its roots in the Greek understanding of *technē*, is indispensable; we cannot do away with it, just as we cannot do away with technology (G1,

12/45–46, 22/53). However, Heidegger worries that calculative thinking has come to take precedence over other modes of comportment, with the result that there may come a time in which we know of no other way to relate to things (G1, 25/56). For it is already the case that the world shows up as "an object upon which calculative thinking sets its attacks" (G1, 18/50; trans. mod.). Such attacks threaten not just nature as such, which "becomes a single, gigantic gas station" (G1, 18/50; trans. mod.), but our autochthony, our rootedness to the land (*Bodenständigkeit*) (G1, 16/48–49), indeed our very essence (G1, 20/52, 23/54). If we really are uprooted, though, if we are no longer capable of dwelling on the sacred earth of the homeland, is there any hope left for us? And what is our essence, if not to use reason to better our lot?

The second mode of thinking Heidegger identifies is called "meditative thinking" or "meditative contemplation" (G1, 13/46). He describes this type of thinking in several ways, chief of which is that it "contemplates the sense that prevails [*waltet*] in everything that is" (G1, 13/46; trans. mod.). Two things should be noted: first, although Heidegger uses the language of *Walten* here, as he does in the first "Country Path Conversation," it is not to be thought of as violent. Instead, Heidegger will connect it with being's unfolding as a kind of letting-be. Second, meditative thinking does not mark a rupture in the human essence, but is rather "the most proper feature of the human" (G1, 25/56; trans. mod.). What the human *is* most fundamentally is a "*thinking*, i.e., *meditating* being" (G1, 13–14/47). The problem is that we have grown too comfortable with our reliance on calculative thinking and the technological apparatus it has produced. We no longer see who we are. We even flee from it (G1, 12/45). Heidegger nevertheless calls on us to resist the claims that technology relentlessly makes on us in all facets of our lives. We must try to save ourselves not just from the destruction of the earth, but from what Heidegger believes to be "a far greater danger": the annihilation of our essence (G1, 25/56; cf. GA 77: 18–22/11–14). Only by doing so may we find a new autochthony, a new "ground and soil" in which "the creating of lasting works could strike new root" (G1, 26/57; trans. mod.). How are we to do this, though, and what is the connection to *Gelassenheit*?

One answer Heidegger gives in his commemorative address is that we can relate to technology differently. We can say both yes and no to the demands it makes on us. We can make use of technology without letting it exclusively dictate our relation to things. We can let technology be what it is, and see that what comes under its sway need "not attack what is most intimate and proper about us" (G1, 22/54; trans. mod.). Such a stance Heidegger calls "releasement toward things [*Gelassenheit zu den Dingen*]" (G1, 23/54).

Two problems present themselves here. First, releasement is not *just* an ontical affair. Only from out of a more fundamental releasement, one in which we essentially belong to being as itself a form of releasement—only from out of such sameness may we develop a properly released comportment toward things. Second, developing a stance of releasement is easier said than done. It is not as if we could simply will things to be otherwise. Nor could we simply will a change of heart. For willfulness is one of the primary characteristics of the technological worldview. That said, some degree of willfulness might be required in order to first transform the will, before convalescing from it altogether. The first "Country Path Conversation" deals with precisely these two problems, which I will address in reverse order; for only in letting go of the will may we let being be. And only in letting being be may we come to understand being, and ourselves, as letting-be.

2. The Problem of the Will

At the beginning of the Third Reich, Heidegger failed to properly interrogate the voluntarism that seized his work and placed him center stage in university politics. By the end of the regime, he would come to see the problem of the will as one of the most question-worthy, and most recalcitrant, matters for modern thought. Today's age is an age of willfulness, and yet meditative thinking, the thinking that most defines who we are and ought to be, is supposed to be free of willfulness. Don't we have to employ the will to get beyond it? But can we really will not to will?

Heidegger's first "Country Path Conversation" takes the form of a dialogue between a researcher or scientist (*Forscher*), a scholar (*Gelehrte*), and a sage or guide (*Weise*) during an evening stroll through a forest.[13] The principal focus of the exchange is the essence of thinking, which turns into a question concerning the essence of the human being and of being as such. However, after a number of apparent detours and dead ends—at once literal and metaphorical—we come to see that this question cannot be posed without addressing the status of the will. Frustrated by the seeming lack of progress on their walk and in their talk, the Scholar eventually asks the Sage what it is he "really wants [*wollen*]." The Sage replies: "What I really want . . . is non-willing [*Nicht-Wollen*]" (GA 77: 51/33; trans. mod.).

But is this possible, the Researcher wonders? "Can one," he asks, "then [want or] will non-willing? With such willing, after all, willing is merely increased" (GA 77: 51/33).

The Sage is aware of this problem. In fact, the other interlocutors and he go on to discuss a variety of ways in which non-willing seems to reinforce, rather than to transcend, the will. For instance, under the category of what one might call resisting the will, fall the activities of "refusing," "opposing," and "forbidding." An example of this kind would be saying, *I will not do what you want me to do*. Here I am still willing (GA 77: 76–77/48). It just so happens that my will is in opposition to another's. Another category of non-willing would be "suspending" the will. "Abhorring," "forgoing," and "renouncing" would all belong to this category. Here, too, however, all we find is simply another variety of willing (GA 77: 78/49). For, attempting to suspend the will is but an asceticism that remains dependent on the will for its very existence. There is nothing positive about such suspension. It merely defines itself by what it strives *not* to be. The task is rather to get beyond everything willful and will-bound (GA 77: 79/50). Only in doing so can we reach "the positive essence of thinking" (GA 77: 72/45).

There is, to be sure, something ambiguous about the term *non-willing*. On the one hand, it falls prey to the paradoxes just mentioned, wherein we simply affirm the very thing beyond which we are attempting to go. On the other hand, it is "supposed to give us a preview of the positive essence of thinking" (GA 77: 72/45). While it will turn out that, as the Scholar surmises, "thinking essentially has nothing to do with willing" (GA 77: 65/41), some volitional preparation may be requisite if we are to move beyond the will into meditative thinking. The Researcher comes to this conclusion later on in the conversation:

> You [the Sage] want a non-willing in the sense of a renouncing of willing, so that *through this renouncing* we can let ourselves engage in [*uns einlassen*]—or at least prepare ourselves for an engagement in—the sought-for essence of that thinking which is not a willing. (GA 77: 107/69; trans. mod.; emphasis added)

Still later, he says:

> Releasement [*Gelassenheit*], as the releasing of oneself [*Sichloslassen*] from transcendental representing, is in fact a refraining from the willing of a horizon. This refraining also no longer comes from

> a willing unless a trace of willing is required to occasion the letting-oneself-into [*Veranlassen zum Sicheinlassen*] a belonging to the open-region—a trace which, however, vanishes in the letting-oneself-into, and is completely extinguished in authentic releasement. (GA 77: 142–43/92)

Despite these concessions, we might still wonder how we could ever move beyond the will, if all the problems with attempting to do so really are as irresolvable as they appeared a moment ago. Simply granting that a trace of will might be necessary in order to begin to let myself loose from transcendental representation does not explain how I actually get out of the dilemma with which we were faced earlier. To ask it again: How can I will myself beyond the will? For even if I renounce my will, even if I look away from it, don't I need the will to do this? And how exactly would this result in me transcending the will altogether? How, moreover, could I ever know if had done so?

The resolution of these difficulties lies not so much in providing answers, but in beginning to see that there is something misleading about the kinds of answers these questions demand. The first is practical. What sort of *activity* must I undertake in order to get beyond the will? The second is epistemological. What are the criteria for *knowing* (in advance) that this will work? Yet what if activity, at least as something carried out by the will, and knowledge, as what determines that with respect to which the will is supposed to act, were the problems? What if meditative thinking were not a simple act that one could perform at will? And what if there were something essentially uncertain about it? Something out of our control? Before examining these issues explicitly, it should prove helpful to first look at how traditional thinking has been defined. For only in understanding our tradition will we be able to move beyond it, or rather to what is more originary.

3. Horizonal-Transcendental Thinking

During the course of the conversation, the interlocutors come to realize that their inquiry into the essence of thinking has transformed into an inquiry into the essence of the human (GA 77: 91/58). This inquiry, however, should not be conceived as a study of the being of the human, that is, as anthropology (GA 77: 102/65–66, 105/68). Rather, the interlocutors come to see that it is only in looking away from the human that one can come to understand the human. While this may sound illogical, there is a good reason for it. Throughout their exchange, it becomes clear to the interlocutors that thinking, as it has come to be defined and experienced in the West, is horizonal-transcendental. That is to say, thinking involves furnishing a "circle of vision" (GA 77: 83/53) or "horizon" in which, "from the outward view that is delimited by it, the outward look of objects comes to encounter us" (GA 77: 113/73). In other words, it projects a horizon of intelligibility upon things, enabling us to experience those things as in each case particular instantiations of the general form or "outward look" proper to each. Only in doing so do we even experience individual things. For instance, when I look outside my window and think I am perceiving a tree, I am in fact perceiving more than just this particular object in front of me. I am perceiving at the same time the "treeness" of the tree. I am looking beyond, I am *transcending*, the particular object toward its form. It is the already projected *horizon* that enables the tree to be a tree for me, to be seen *as* an individual tree, *as* an instance of a class (GA 77: 87/55; cf. GA 40: 86/89). (Whence the locution *horizonal-transcendental*.) Without such a horizon, I would never be able to speak about—moreover I would never even be able to perceive—trees.

It might seem that, in projecting such a horizon, we produce it, and that, beholden to this horizon, we simply represent, we simply set before our gaze (*vor-stellen*), something like treeness so that we can experience individual trees. This would amount to a kind of transcendental idealism, albeit one grounded, the Scholar points out, in the Greek understanding of *technē* (GA 77: 86/55). In fact, what is being described here as horizonal-transcendental thinking is but a variation on the traditional theme of the human being as a rational animal (GA 77: 88/56).

However, although it may seem that we alone create the horizon, the Sage is careful to note that "[t]he horizon goes out beyond us and our capability." In order properly to understand it, we would need to examine it "in itself and in its own relation to us and to objects," not "from us and from objects" (GA 77: 88/56; cf. GA 77: 111/72). Put differently, we would need to think the horizon in and of itself, not as we relate to it. We must beware thinking of this as yet another horizon, though. For what, then, would be its horizon? In order to avoid an infinite regress, it will be necessary to think of that which enables horizons not as itself horizonal, not as merely "the side turned toward us of a surrounding open," but as the surrounding open in itself, or what the Scholar, apparently drawing on a Middle High German word still in use in certain South German dialects, terms "the open-region [*die Gegnet*]" (GA 77: 112–14/72–74; cf. GA 77: 121/78).[14]

4. The Open-Region

Even though none of the interlocutors calls it this, we may understand the open-region as another, more topological valence of what Heidegger names with the terms *Ereignis* (appropriative event), *Sein* (being), and *Seyn* (beyng).[15] As Heidegger himself writes in a collection of notes on *Ereignis*, here using the third-person singular of the verb *gegnen*, "Beyng regions [*Seyn gegnet*]" (GA 73.1: 23).[16] Many passages throughout the conversation indicate as much, such as when the open-region is described in terms of being as primordial *logos* (gathering), *physis* (letting arise), and *a-lētheia* (truth as unveiling while holding itself back). The Sage says, "The open-region is the abiding expanse which, *gathering* all, opens itself so that in it the open is held and halted, *letting* each thing *arise*." To this the Researcher replies in terms of truth as unconcealment: "the open-region *draws itself back*, goes away from us, rather than coming to encounter us" as a horizon would (GA 77: 114/74; emphases added). Like being, "the open-region is presumably that which essentially occurs in *concealment*"; it is "the essential occurring [*Wesung*] of truth" (GA 77: 144/93). It is said to "prevail" (GA 77: 113/73) and "eventuate [*sich ereignet*]" (GA 77: 142/92; trans. mod.). Most significantly for our concerns, it is glossed above all in terms of letting, which I will discuss in the next section.

From the human perspective, such a region can be thought, just not represented; for it is what first grants any sort of representation. Throughout the conversation, we learn that the best we can do is to *let* ourselves engage in waiting. Such waiting, however, does not await anything in particular, since that would objectify it, and the open-region is unobjectifiable. Nor is it even directed toward the future, awaiting *something* to come. Rather, when we partake in intransitive waiting, "waiting lets itself be involved in the open itself," an openness that is in fact granted by the open-region (GA 77: 116/75). This, however, is only possible when we think, which gets glossed as "a coming-into-nearness to the far" (GA 77: 116/75). When we think genuinely, then, we are coming near to the open-region by holding ourselves open to and within the openness furnished by it, but also preserving the unrepresentable, indescribable farness and excess of such a region. But there is something circular about all of this, since thinking itself is said to require waiting. A similar circularity, which is not necessarily vicious, but perhaps simply a way of attuning us to that preobjective, prerepresentational region wherein we essentially, if for the most part inconspicuously, belong, can be found in the interlocutors' discussion of *Gelassenheit*.

5. *Gelassenheit*

Moving away from the horizon in order to understand what enables it is connected with the claim made earlier that, in order to understand the human essence, we must look away from the human. Indeed, we must look away from the very question concerning the essence of the human. "It could be the case," the Sage reflects, "not only that the determination of the human essence does not originate in a question about the human, but that it does not originate from a question at all, precisely for the reason that this determination cannot be obtained from the human" (GA 77: 103/66). How is it possible to determine something without first posing questions about what is to be determined? Haven't thinkers always questioned first?

Even though the Sage does want to move beyond the traditional and still prevalent notion of the human as *animal rationale,* he does not think that this definition was arrived at through human invention:

> RESEARCHER: So you mean that what the thinkers say, for example, about the essence of the human, is not put forward and worked out by them?
>
> SAGE: The essential determination of the human is an event [*Geschehnis*] that the thinkers do not make, but rather only express. (GA 77: 89/57; trans. mod.)

What the Sage is suggesting here is that we alone do not determine the essence of who we are. Such determination exceeds us. We belong to it more than it belongs to us. Once we realize that defining the human essence is not entirely up to us, and that the horizon within which this might transpire is not something we simply project, there emerges the possibility that "the relationship [between the human and the horizon] which gives itself to be known in the horizonal essence of the human, could in its time manifest itself more originally" (GA 77: 89/57). This would require that the heretofore predominant notion of the human essence be "eliminated," or, as Heidegger would have put it earlier in his career, deconstructed (*destruiert*) (GA 77: 89/57). Once this has been accomplished—or at least once the traditional definition of the human essence has become unsettled (*erschüttert*)—there may transpire an "event,"[17] something may come to pass, that would reveal a more primordial essence of the human.

That said, some preparation is required in order for us to be appropriated into such an event, and there is a sense in which we must already be admitted (*eingelassen*) into authentic releasement (*Gelassenheit*) if we are to be let loose (*losgelassen*) from horizonal-transcendental thinking (GA 77: 121/79).[18] Such releasement is, after all, our essence; it is just an essence of which we are, traditionally and for the most part, unaware. Although it requires preparation and some sort of activity on our part, transitioning out of the will into our more primordial essence and relation to the open-region stands in stark contrast to the appeal to willful activity and epistemological certainty that was mentioned earlier. It requires that we *be let* just as much as it requires that we *let be*. Any activity still operative in authentic *Gelassenheit* is an *enabled* activity. Conversely, Heidegger is careful to note that this does not mean we must submit passively to some higher power. Such submission would be but a "deferred willing."[19] Leaving things up to God's will, for instance, doesn't get us beyond the domain of the will. Doing so just transposes one will onto another. (It is for this reason that the Scholar charges Eckhart with voluntarism. See §6 of chapter 1, above.) So the task would be to find some mode of being that would be neither entirely active nor entirely passive, neither something certain that we can simply perform whenever we want or will, nor something accidental that we simply undergo (G1, 25/56). This comportment is *Gelassenheit*, which is described as at once a "reception [*Empfängnis*]" (GA 77: 144/94)[20] and "perhaps . . . a higher activity than that found in all the deeds of the world and in all the machinations of the realms of mankind" (GA 77: 108/70; trans. mod.). The latter claim is objected to in the 1945 version of the conversation, since this "higher activity is in fact not an activity." In the 1959 version, "activity" is changed to "doing" (G1, 33/61; trans. mod.), to which it is still replied that it would not be something active as opposed to something passive, but would be something that "lies . . . outside the distinction between passivity and activity" (GA 77: 109/70). In other words, like *Gelassenheit* in *Einleitung in die Philosophie*, it would be middle voiced.

The doing that is proper to *Gelassenheit* thus involves and demands both a letting-be and a being-let, a preparation and a being prepared. Such paradoxical interchange becomes apparent when the interlocutors begin to discuss *Gelassenheit* proper toward the end of the conversation. Although the language of letting pervades the conversation,[21] it is not really until their exchange on and through *Gelassenheit* that we see just how important such language is.

Following Friedrich-Wilhelm von Herrmann, I believe we can identify five different aspects of letting that are at work in the fully developed notion of *Gelassenheit*:[22]

1. allowing (*Zulassen*) or occasioning (*Veranlassen*);
2. ceasing (*Ablassen*), letting loose (*Loslassen*), or letting go (*Fahrenlassen*);
3. letting oneself into, engage in, or become involved with (*Sicheinlassen*);
4. letting prevail (*Waltenlassen*); and
5. remaining released or delivered over to (*Überlassenbleiben*).[23]

We might begin to understand these terms by saying that the open-region allows us, or occasions the possibility for us, to cease relying upon the will, such that we can let ourselves loose from it. This in turn enables us to let ourselves become involved with or engaged in the open-region and to let ourselves correspond to it, as well as to the way in which it prevails. Once this has come to pass, we may come to realize that it has always already let us (and indeed all things) be, and we may remain released or delivered over to it as that "in relation to [or toward] which releasement [that is, our essence] is what it is [*in der Gegnet, zu der die Gelassenheit ist, was sie ist*]" (GA 77: 118/77).[24]

However, although I have rendered these terms actively and passively, and could just as well switch some of them around—for instance, I could say that the open-region must permit us to do these things, but I could also say that we must permit the open-region to do so by preparing ourselves for it—they should be thought always in both senses, or rather in the middle voice, whenever possible. This is most conspicuous with the phrase *sich einlassen auf* and with the term *Gelassenheit*. I can only let myself become involved with the open-region if the open-region has permitted me entrance (*mich eingelassen*, has let me in). All *Sicheinlassen* is, in other words, an *eingelassenes Sicheinlassen*. Yet we should not think of this as occurring diachronically. Thus, rather than speaking of *Gelassenheit* as the state of having been released or as the state of having released oneself, it would be better to think of it as a middle-voiced event in which both the open-region and we are implicated; an event that is always already happening within the time of our life, but one of which we are for the most part oblivious; an event, finally, in which all of these aspects of letting are gathered together as one (*Ge-lassenheit*).

This is not to say that our essence may not be forgotten, though. Indeed, the historical strand of Heidegger's thought would suggest the possibility that we could even lose our essence altogether, as Heidegger feared in the memorial address. Whatever the case may be, the danger still remains that we, by accepting unquestioningly the claims that the technological worldview makes upon us, will fail to recognize and to correspond to our essence as implicated in the letting-be of the open-region. Yet we cannot force an awareness of this. When the interlocutors begin to discuss *Gelassenheit*, they note that we cannot simply awaken this ultimate fundamental attunement.[25] Rather, the best we can do is to attempt to remain awake for it, such that we may be released into (an awareness of) it. This occurs through waiting, the essence of which is said to be *Gelassenheit* (GA 77: 123/80). In such releasement, "thinking transforms itself from such [horizonal-transcendental] representing into waiting upon the open-region." Yet such releasement—and consequently such waiting and such thinking—itself comes from the open-region, to which we belong essentially. For the non-horizonal-transcendental thinking proper to waiting "rests in the fact that . . . the open-region enregions releasement in itself [*die Gegnet die Gelassenheit in sich . . . vergegnet*]" (GA 77: 122/80–81). We are moving in a circle again. We have to wait to become released, so that we may think in accord with our essence ("waiting upon the open-region") (GA 77: 122/79), letting ourselves come into the nearness of the far, which is nothing other than the meditative thinking that was discussed earlier. This state of waiting is also referred to as a sort of "suspension" between "yes and no," between our essential appropriation to the open-region and our everyday expropriation from it, between what we fundamentally (*existentially*) are and the way we tend to experience and take this up today (how we *existentielly* interpret it) (GA 77: 123/80). In the earlier version of the conversation, the interlocutors conclude that this waiting is "no suspension at all," since it is "rather a restful resting," whereas the later version does not deny that it is such. At any rate, waiting, and consequently thinking and *Gelassenheit*, involves remaining between belonging and not belonging, between being near to, yet far from, the open-region.

Finally, it is important to note that Heidegger interprets the open-region in terms of middle-voiced releasement as well: "The open-region is the abiding expanse which, gathering all, opens itself [or is opened, *sich öffnet*]" (GA 77: 114/74). It is what "lets all things belong to one another"

(GA 77: 125/81). He also deploys cognate nominative structures as he had done much earlier in his career: "the world, insofar as it worlds,[26] gathers everything, each to the other, and lets everything return to itself in its own resting in the selfsame" (GA 77: 149/98).[27] Later, in 1969, Heidegger even says that "the deepest meaning of being is *letting*" (GA 15: 363/59). Just as with our own proper comportment toward the open-region, the sense of "letting" at play in these various descriptions is neither passive nor active, but a letting-happen that occurs before there are agents and patients, subjects and objects.

6. Implications

We may draw out several implications from the foregoing. First, although it is quite plausible to understand *Gelassenheit* as including all of the valences of letting that are discussed in the dialogue, we may also understand it in a more particular sense, that is, as the gathering of the essence of the human being and of being (or the open-region) itself. In this sense, it would be even less active or passive than those preliminary steps requisite for becoming attuned to our essence. For, these steps still bear stronger valences of either passivity or activity depending on the context and historical situation in which we find ourselves. The practical apriori of letting-go may still bear a trace of will-laden activity. *Gelassenheit*, as the essence of the human, however, is our free, open relation to being, which is more originary than any particular activity we undertake or any particular thing we suffer. Freedom here is not the ability to act according to the moral law. Here, "Freedom has nothing to do with the will" (GA 73.1: 731).[28] Freedom is a prior, middle-voiced play space in which this or that may take place. It is what holds sway, what, to use Heideggerian language, essences or eventuates. Here there are neither subjects nor objects. There is only the event from which they issue and in which they are implicated. The middle voice of *Gelassenheit* is precisely one way in which to express such an event.

Second, the human's relation to being is one of sameness. Like Parmenides, Heidegger constantly endeavors throughout his corpus to understand the sameness of thinking and being, even if the way in which that relation is described changes over time. Now, if it is true that the language of releasement is a fitting way to describe the essence of the human and of being, if, at their core, being and thinking are the same in *Gelassenheit*, then the way we relate to being cannot be as to an object standing over against us. Nor can the task simply be to divest ourselves of all traces of agency so that being may act upon us as passive recipients. There is no outside of being. Being is not an otherworldly deity to entrap and compel or to beseech and receive from. At stake is rather attuning ourselves to this relation and finding fitting words to describe it. Since this relation is neither subjective nor objective, neither active nor passive, the metaphysical language that we inherited above all from Aristotle and that became rigidified in modernity, the language which divides the world into subject and predicate, agent and patient, and which foists the semantic weight of the verb onto the subject of the sentence—that language cannot suffice.[29] Other linguistic resources nonetheless remain, even if just under the surface of our modern languages. Throughout his career, Heidegger, like Eckhart, drew on such resources, especially the middle voice of releasement, to think what underlies metaphysical binaries.

Finally, regarding Heidegger's relation to Eckhart, it becomes clear in the first "Country Path Conversation" that, again like Eckhart, Heidegger is able to understand the way in which the human being belongs to being itself in terms of *Gelassenheit*. "Letting," moreover, is not just a matter for human thought, but for being as well. Heidegger's open-region, as the non-representable, nonobjectifiable thither side of the horizon, also resembles the abyssal, desert-like character of Eckhart's Godhead. There is, furthermore, a belonging and not belonging to the open-region for Heidegger, and for Eckhart, we are in our essence one with the Godhead, and yet we are still ineluctably embodied, amid multiplicity, and subject to time. For both Eckhart and Heidegger, we must exercise restraint in the face of that which cannot be represented. We must allow the concealment of the Godhead and of the open-region to be, even as we allow that, at bottom, we essentially belong to them. Yet we cannot come to realize this without a practical apriori. For Heidegger, we have to let go of the will and let ourselves wait for the essence of thinking and being to show itself, which turns out to be *Gelassenheit* and only shows itself in *Gelassenheit*. For Eckhart, we have to be *gelâzen* in order to understand that letting-be characterizes the oneness of the Godhead and the ground of the soul. In both cases, the imperative of releasement is primary.

Conclusion

We began this book with the requirement that knowing the truth is dependent on action or a way of being. For Eckhart, the truth of being is the Godhead's generative releasement or letting-be (*gelâzenheit*). This releasement precedes and preserves not just the Trinity and the world, but even the dichotomies of activity and passivity, potentiality and actuality, and immanence and transcendence. Our mode of access to it therefore cannot be as to something outside of ourselves from which to receive illumination. Rather, we must realize that, at our core, we are more than just an image of God. We are more than just occasionally privileged to unite with him. Our ground and God's ground are in fact one ground. The spark of our soul is but a single oneness (*ein einic ein*) with the Godhead itself.

But how can we come to this realization? Eckhart does, admittedly, help us along. In both his Latin and Middle High German writings, he tries to cultivate us for releasement. Yet only if we act will we experience the truth of which he preaches. We must *let be* if we are to learn that thinking and being, or what we fundamentally are and what the Godhead fundamentally is, are one and the same *letting-be*.

When, later in his career, Heidegger contends that the essence of thinking is releasement (*Gelassenheit*), and that the deepest meaning of being is letting (*Lassen*), he is clearly indebted to Eckhart. But he owes much more to the Meister than might initially appear. Not only are thinking as releasement and being as letting-be in some sense the same for Heidegger; Heidegger also demands that we let be in order to own up to this. The fundamental mood is imperative.

This imperative character of Heidegger's thought, or what I have also been calling the "practical apriori," extends beyond the language of releasement. When, for example, Heidegger conceives of being and the human being in terms of violence, he still demands that we exercise violence against being in order to understand it, and ourselves, as violent. Thus, even when the content of Heidegger's discourse couldn't seem farther from that of Eckhart's, he still remains formally in line with his Dominican predecessor.

Throughout the course of this study we have seen many other parallels between Eckhart and Heidegger, such as their similar deployment of extradiscursive linguistic strategies, their understanding of being as verbal and event-like, and the importance they accord to living without a reason why, to name but a few. The secondary aim of this book was to reconstruct Heidegger's relation to Eckhart, and it has revealed these parallels to be more than coincidental. Heidegger has no problem ranking Eckhart among the few great thinkers of the West. At this point, scholars should have no problem ranking Eckhart among those who were most influential on Heidegger.

Despite this influence, there are of course divergences between their projects, as one would expect from any genuine philosophical confrontation. I have mostly refrained from discussing the divergences in this book. Two, however, call for further reflection. Although I cannot analyze them in any detail here, I would nevertheless like to conclude by addressing (1) the status of history in Eckhart and Heidegger, and (2) the problem of anti-Semitism in Heidegger's *Black Notebooks*.

(1) If each great thinker is motivated by one fundamental experience, then we can say that Eckhart was motivated by the fundamental experience of infinite oneness—a oneness beyond corporeality, beyond multiplicity, beyond limitation, and, ultimately, beyond time. There is, to be sure, an abyssal aspect of the ground of God and the soul for Eckhart. The Godhead withdraws from all attempts to bring it to presence. It cannot be understood by the metaphysical categories of activity, potentiality, causality, subjectivity, substance, or nature. In this respect it resembles Heidegger's conception of being. And yet Eckhart would never say that, without the spark of the human soul, the Godhead would cease to be, as Heidegger sometimes suggests of being without Dasein.[1] (Without creatures, there would be no Triune "God," but God the Father is of little concern to Eckhart.) The oneness of the Godhead and of the spark of the soul endures eternally.

Heidegger, in contrast, is so profoundly affected by the experience of human finitude that infinite being comes to appear to him as a delusion. "Being itself," he writes, "is essentially finite" (GA 9: 120/95). In the 1930s, as his hopes for power are shattered and the desert grows all about him, Heidegger inscribes not just finitude, but even division, in being itself.[2] Being comes to have a history.

The interplay of concealment and unconcealment certainly characterizes Eckhart's Godhead. But Eckhart was too close a reader of Maimonides to accept a God rent asunder. Perhaps the most significant difference between Eckhart's and Heidegger's thought, then, lies in their understanding of the temporality of being (and consequently of the human being). It is no wonder that the thought of history is absent in Eckhart. If Husserl forgot history,[3] Eckhart appears to have never heard of it.

And yet, when Heidegger is engaged with and engaged in Eckhartian thought, his own work tends toward a non-epochal or infra-historical sense of being. Even though the meaning of the beingness of beings changes across time, being itself, or beyng (*Seyn*), as that which underlies these shifts, does not.

How to reconcile these two positions? Is being historical, finite, and temporally riven, or is Heidegger trying to uncover a sense of being that is *always* at work, even if it has long been forgotten? Another monograph would be required to figure out which of these alternatives is ultimately the case for Heidegger. The Eckhartian strand of Heidegger's thinking nevertheless makes it a pressing question for future study.

(2) If there were still lingering doubts at the start of this decade, the 2014 publication of many of Heidegger's *Black Notebooks* has revealed that it is no longer possible to deny the existence of anti-Semitic passages in Heidegger's corpus. When Heidegger accuses the Jews of "uprooting . . . all beings from being" owing to their "*emphatically calculative giftedness*" (GA 96: 56/44, 243/191), he is accusing them of distorting the proper way in which to understand and relate to being. When Heidegger privileges the Germans for their unique and genuine relation to being, and interprets such Jewish distortion as a threat to that relation, it is not hard to see that some form of anti-Semitism is at work here. How we should understand the significance of such passages within the context of Heidegger's philosophy as a whole, however, is still far from clear.[4]

I am inclined to think that such passages are an indication of a certain failure of Heidegger's to acknowledge and live up to his own avowed insights. I believe one could reach this conclusion by way of what may appear to be an unlikely and circuitous route: that of Heidegger's relation to Eckhart. As we have seen, Eckhart influences Heidegger in profound ways. Yet Heidegger fails to discuss and develop the ethical consequences of the distinctive methodology that both he and Eckhart employ. Both Eckhart and Heidegger try to understand ethics more fundamentally as a way of life rather than as a set of rules to follow or results to achieve. For Eckhart, this means "living without why," without any significant distinctions between oneself and others or between oneself and things. Everything should "become pure God to you." The spark of the soul in me is absolutely one, not just with the Godhead, but with the spark of the soul in you. Thus, Eckhart's ethics is open to everyone. Heidegger's ethics, in contrast, especially during the Third Reich, is at times too entangled in questions about what it means to be a historical people or *Volk*. Even though Heidegger's anti-Semitism is not rooted in racial biology, and even though Heidegger's reading of Eckhart differs markedly from the ways in which other Germans were reading him under National Socialism, Heidegger's preoccupation with the German *Volk* nevertheless led him to assign questionable roles to various peoples, including the Jews. In this regard he failed to follow through on the Eckhartian, an-archic undercurrent in his thought. In this regard his thought remained, at least for a time, "metaphysical."[5]

Indeed, even later, as Heidegger came to suspect that life *sine principio* might represent the *sine qua non* of authentic existence, he shrank back from pursuing it (GA 10: 57–58/38). Had Heidegger followed through in his reading of Eckhart from the beginning, rather than shirking its ethical implications, he may have escaped such sweeping, contentious gestures. He did not. Yet this does not mean that his thought should be dismissed wholesale, as some are proposing today. Rather, it would be fruitful for future research, not just to work out Eckhart's an-archic ethics—no small feat in and of itself—but to reconsider Heidegger's thought in light of its Eckhartian underpinnings and its failure, for a time, to stay true to those underpinnings.

※

This is not to say, however, that the master of letters and life did not impact the way Heidegger himself lived. And he certainly did not fail to impact the way Heidegger died. Bernhard Welte relates that, in January 1976, he visited Heidegger at his home in Freiburg. During their conversation, Heidegger, knowing that death was near, surprised Welte by asking whether he would deliver the eulogy at Heidegger's burial in their shared hometown of Meßkirch.[6] Welte reports that they spoke "above all and urgently"[7] about Eckhart:

> Heidegger was long acquainted with Meister Eckhart. During the course of our conversation, he thus asked about *Abgeschieden-*

heit in Meister Eckhart's sense, posing a question that was at once careful and certain of its path. The theme had a concealed currency in this remarkable hour.

(This is because *Abgeschiedenheit* means not just detachment, but departedness, in the sense of parting with this life. Welte continues:)

> The Eckhartian thought that God is like the nothing also hovered in the room. These Eckhartian thoughts were now brought into connection with the homelike character of the homeland and also into connection with the nearness of death; thus the hour formed the realm in which, in a special way, heaven and earth, mortals and immortals, belonged together. The gathering of the fourfold lived in that evening hour and was gathered around him whom death was already beckoning.[8]

There is no other figure in Heidegger's corpus who received so much praise, yet to whom Heidegger devoted so little interpretive attention—and I say this despite the deep affinities I have attempted to unearth in this book. Heidegger's interest in Eckhart was not scholastic. It was, in the end, and not just in the end, a matter of life and death.

Appendix One

Materials on Heidegger's Relation to Eckhart

1. Editions of Eckhart Consulted, Owned, or Referenced by Heidegger

The following editions by Bernhart, Bindschedler, Büttner (1 vol. ed.), Diederichs, and Kunisch were in Heidegger's library at the time of his death in 1976.[1] Of these, Heidegger wrote in his copies of Bernhart, Büttner (1 vol. ed.), and Diederichs (see §4, below), and he cites from Bernhart and Diederichs (see §3, below). Heidegger recalls in a letter to Hannah Arendt that his wife Elfride, who had herself written a note on Eckhart and Duns Scotus in Heidegger's copy of Bindschedler (see p. 237, n. 60, below), had given him Pfeiffer's edition for his birthday in 1917 (MH/HA, 247/208). This copy of Pfeiffer, which, other than a dedication from Elfride ("Geschenk von Elfride: Zum 26.IX.17 und fürs Leben," "Gift from Elfride: for the 26th of September 1917 and for life"), contains no markings, can still be found in the Heidegger family library on Filibachstraße in Freiburg containing some of Heidegger's books. Heidegger's copy of Grabmann's edition was at one point located in this library as well, although it was not there on July 12, 2016.[2] In addition to Pfeiffer's and Grabmann's editions, Heidegger cites from Büttner (2nd ed.), Jostes's edition, and from Volumes 3 and 4 of the Latin works (and perhaps Volume 1 of the German works) of the Stuttgart critical edition. He also cites quotations by Eckhart from the Grimm dictionary and from Käte Oltmanns's book on Eckhart (see §3, below). Heidegger's references to Daniels's and Denifle's editions are much more elliptical.[3]

Bernhart, Joseph, ed. and trans. *Meister Eckhart* (*Deutsche Mystiker*, Vol. 3). Kempten: Kösel, 1914.

Bindschedler, Maria, ed. and trans. Meister Eckhart, *Vom mystischen Leben: Eine Auswahl aus seinen deutschen Predigten*. Klosterberg: Schwabe, 1951.

Büttner, Herman, ed. and trans. *Meister Eckeharts Schriften und Predigten*. 2nd ed. Vol. 1. Jena: Eugen Diederichs, 1921. 1st edition of Vol. 1 published in 1903.[4]

Büttner, Herman, ed. and trans. *Meister Eckehart Schriften*. Jena: Eugen Diederichs, 1938. Reprint of the 1934, one volume edition.

Daniels, Augustinus, ed. *Eine lateinische Rechtfertigungsschrift des Meister Eckhart*. With a foreword by Clemens Baeumker. Münster i. W.: Aschendorff, 1923.

Denifle, Heinrich, ed. "Meister Eckharts lateinische Schriften und die Grundanschauung seiner Lehre." *Archiv für Literatur und Kirchengeschichte des Mittelalters* 2 (1886): 417–652, 673–87.

Diederichs, Ernst, ed. *Meister Eckharts Reden der Unterscheidung*. Bonn: A. Marcus and E. Weber, 1925. Anastatic reprint of the 1913 edition.

Grabmann, Martin, ed. *Neuaufgefundene Pariser Quaestionen Meister Eckharts und ihre Stellung in seinem geistigen Entwicklungsgange: Untersuchungen und Texte*. Munich: Verlag der Bayerischen Akademie der Wissenschaften in Kommission des Verlags R. Oldenbourg, 1927.

Jostes, Franz, ed. *Meister Eckhart und seine Jünger: Ungedruckte Texte zur deutschen Mystik*. Freiburg, Switzerland: Universitätsbuchhandlung, 1895.

Kunisch, Hermann, ed. and trans. *Ein Textbuch aus der altdeutschen Mystik: Eckhart, Tauler, Seuse*. Hamburg: Rowohlt, 1958.

Meister Eckhart, *Die deutschen und lateinischen Werke*. Herausgegeben im Auftrag der deutschen Forschungsgemeinschaft. Stuttgart: Kohlhammer, 1936–.

Pfeiffer, Franz, ed. *Meister Eckhart*. Vol. 2 of *Deutsche Mystiker des vierzehnten Jahrhunderts*. Third, unchanged edition. Göttingen: Vandenhoeck u. Ruprecht, 1914. Anastatic reprint of the 1857 edition.

2. Locations of Heidegger's References to Eckhart and Pseudo-Eckhart

As is fairly common in references to Eckhart, especially in German texts, Heidegger writes Eckhart's name in different ways: Eckhart, Eckehardt, Eckehart, Eckart, Eckhard, Ekkhart, Ekkehart. I have always used the spelling

"Eckhart," but, when citing other texts, I have left the alternate spellings as they are found there. François Jaran and Christophe Perrin, editors of *The Heidegger Concordance*, include references only under "Eckhart" and "Eckehart" in the *Gesamtausgabe* volumes published up to 2013, that is, neither Heidegger's correspondence nor works and notes not yet or not to be included in the *Gesamtausgabe*. What follows may accordingly be considered as a supplement to their work. I have also ordered the references chronologically, and provided references to English translations when they exist. I only provide references when Heidegger mentions or quotes Eckhart, not when he may be alluding to him or paraphrasing or modifying a quote. (See chapter 1, above, for some allusions and paraphrases.) By references to Pseudo-Eckhart, I mean references to texts that are no longer considered to be authentic or whose authenticity is still a matter of significant dispute. For more details, see my introduction to §3, below.

1915 KT 22/34, GA 1: 218/34. **1916** GA 1: 402, n. 2/187, n. 4, 415/49;[5] "Ursinn der Geistigkeit in ihrer zentralen Lebendigkeit" (Original Sense of Spirituality in its Central Vitality), in Kisiel, "Notes for a Work," 327, nn. 33–37 (Heidegger's German) and 319 (Kisiel's English translation).[6] **1917** GA 60: 315–18/239–41. **September 1918** GA 60: 336/254. **April 17, 1919** MH/EH, 93/61–62. **September 1, 1919** MH/EH, 97/64. **Winter Semester 1919–20** GA 58: 61–62/47–48. **Summer Semester 1927** GA 24: 127–28/90–91; unpublished note for *Die Grundprobleme der Phänomenologie* (DLA 75.7054). **Summer Semester 1928** GA 26: 56/45. **Summer Semester 1930** GA 31: 6/4, 51, n. 3/36 n. 2. **Summer Semester 1931** GA 33: 46–47/38. **January 29, 1934** Evaluation of Käte Oltmanns' dissertation on Eckhart (UAF B 42/2457) (see §7, below). **February 15, 1934** Report that Heidegger and Martin Honecker had agreed to award Käte Oltmanns's dissertation the best grade possible ("I. Prädikat") (UAF B 42/2457). **February 28, 1934** Notes on Käte Oltmanns's oral examination (UAF B 42/2457) (see §8, below). **Summer Semester 1934** GA 84.1: 338. **August 11, 1934** MH/ER, 223–24.[7] **Winter Semester 1934–35** GA 39: 123/111, 133–34/118. **Winter Semester 1935–36** GA 41: 98/98. **April 8, 1936, or before**[8] Preparatory note for the lecture "Europa und die deutsche Philosophie" (DLA 75.7072/23); EDP, 40/339. **Summer Semester 1936** GA 42: 54/31, 203–204/117. **Winter Semester 1938–39** GA 46: 213/176. **1938–39** GA 95: 428/334. **Late 1930s–40s** GA 81: 187. **Around August 1940 or after** GA 50: 83/63. **Between 1940 and 1955**[9] GA 76: 11. **1943**

GA 75: 282. **Between 1944 and April 7, 1945**[10] GA 77: 109/70 (cf. the entry under "1959," below), 158/103. **November 30, 1945** GA 16: 406. **September 13, 1946** Loose sheet appended to a letter to Fritz Heidegger (DLA HS.2014.0069.00013). **1948** GA 97: 436, 470, 478. **"1949/50 (May)"** GA 98: 211, 240. **August 12, 1949** MH/KJ, 181–82/172. **1949** GA 13: 89/35; GA 79: 15–16/14–15, 70/66; "Notizen über das 'Ding'" (DLA 75.7305,3); an unpublished, undated note contained as the first page of several bundles of notes for the third division of *Sein und Zeit*, available under the misleading title "'Logik. Die Frage nach der Wahrheit.' Dr. T." (DLA 75.7051), and undoubtedly to be included among Heidegger's preparatory notes for the lecture "Das Ding." **June 27, 1950** MH/HA, 112/90–91. **December 21, 1951** Letter to Fritz Heidegger (DLA HS.2014.0069.00018). **Summer Semester 1952** GA 8: 153/149. **Around 1955–56** Unpublished note for the lecture course *Der Satz vom Grund* (DLA 57.7314,2). **Winter Semester 1955–56** GA 10: 56/37. **March 3, 1956** Letter to Fritz Heidegger (DLA HS.2014.0069.00021). **December 20, 1956** Letter to Fritz Heidegger (DLA HS.2014.0069.00021). **Probably around 1956 or later**[11] GA 73.2: 922. **In or after 1956** GA 73.2: 995–96; an unpublished collection of notes with the titles "Zum Weltbegriff" and "Der Meister Eckehart" (DLA 75.7305,9). **1959** G1, 33–34 (= GA 13: 42)/61–62 (cf. the first entry under "Between 1944 and 7 April 1945," above). **February 29, 1968** MH/BW, 29–30. **March 2, 1968** Letter to Fritz Heidegger (DLA HS.2014.0069.00027). **September 8, 1968** GA 15: 325/34. **January 11, 1972** Letter to Fritz Heidegger (DLA HS.2014.0069.00028). **Around 1972–73 or later** GA 81: 286. **March 14, 1974** MH/HA, 247/208. **March 28, 1976** MH/BW, 46.

3. Heidegger's Citations of Eckhart and Pseudo-Eckhart

Unless otherwise indicated, I first reproduce Heidegger's citations of Eckhart/Pseudo-Eckhart and Eckhart/Pseudo-Eckhart's texts as they are found in Heidegger's corpus. I then provide a translation. Afterward, when appropriate, I indicate the likely source and pagination of Heidegger's quote. When Heidegger paraphrases Eckhart or uses Bernhart's or Büttner's modern German translation of Eckhart's Middle High German, I provide Eckhart's original. When possible, I refer to where Heidegger's citation can be found in the Stuttgart critical edition of Eckhart's writings. With the exception of RdU, none of the German tractates (nor the "Liber positionum") cited by Heidegger from Pfeiffer's edition can be found in the critical edition of Eckhart's writings, as they are no longer considered to have been composed by Eckhart himself. Büttner's translation into modern German, "Vom Zorne der Seele und von ihrer rechten Stätte" (On the Wrath of the Soul and Its Proper Site), which Heidegger cites three times, derives from inauthentic Middle High German material that is large part available scattered throughout Pfeiffer's edition.[12] Büttner's translation, "Vom Schauen Gottes und von Seligkeit" (On Beholding God and on Blessedness), which stems from Preger's edition, is also spurious and cannot be found in the critical edition. The only other text of uncertain authenticity cited by Heidegger is the eighty-second text of Jostes's 1895 edition of Eckhart (recently published as Pr. 117, "Zu dem êrsten suochet daz rîche gotes," in the critical edition); see the introduction to chapter 3, above, for more details.

1916

GA 1: 415/49 ("Der Zeitbegriff in der Geschichtswissenschaft" ["The Concept of Time in the Science of History"]): "*Motto*: 'Zeit ist das, was sich *wandelt* und *mannigfaltigt*, Ewigkeit hält sich einfach.' Meister Eckhart." "Motto: Time is what changes and diversifies itself, eternity remains simple.—Meister Eckhart." Pfeiffer, 170,8–11 (Pr. LII): "Ein alter meister sprichet, das diu sêle ist gemachet mitene zwischen einem unde zwein. Daz ein ist diu êwikeit, diu sich alle zît aleine heldet und einvar ist. Daz zwei daz ist diu zît, diu sich wandelt unde manicvaldeget." Walshe, 275: "An old master says the soul is created in the middle between one and two. The one is eternity, which maintains itself ever alone and without variation. The two is time, which is changeable and given to multiplication." Cf. DW 2: 133,1–134,1 Pr. 32 ("Consideravit semitas domus suae"). Heidegger later references "The Concept of Time in the Science of History," in GA 64: 19, n. 3/12, n. **, and SZ, 419, n. 4/398, n. 5.

"Ursinn der Geistigkeit in ihrer zentralen Lebendigkeit" ("Original Sense of Spirituality in Its Central Vitality"), in Kisiel, "Notes for a Work," 319 (Kisiel's English translation)/327, n. 33 (Heidegger's German):[13] "Cf. Meister Eckhart: 'Since no one can give form to God, so likewise can one give no form to the soul' (Pfeiffer 1857: 394, 10f.)." "Vgl. Meister Eckhart: Wan als gote niemen keine gestalt geben mag, alsô mac man ouch der sêle keine gestalt geben." Pfeiffer, 394,10–11 (Tractate III, "Von der sêle werdikeit und eigenschaft"). Cf. Löser 330,14–16.

"Ursinn der Geistigkeit in ihrer zentralen Lebendigkeit" ("Original Sense of Spirituality in Its Central Vitality"), in Kisiel, "Notes for a Work," 319/327, n. 34: "But cf. 'the true visionaries of God' and the twenty-four signs by which they become known (Pfeiffer 1857: 476, 29f.): [Sign 1] If you do not have the right love, all other gifts are of little or no help to you at all (Pfeiffer 1857: 476, 40). [Sign 13] They do not become deceived by some false light nor by the sight of creatures: they let all things stand on their own (Pfeiffer 1857: 477, 28). [Sign 17] They have few words and much life (Pfeiffer 1857: 477, 36)." "Vgl. aber 'die gerehten anschouwer gotes' und die 24 zeichen, daran sie erkannt werden. 1. habet ir niht rehte minne, sô hilfet ez iu wênic oder nihtes niht. 13. Sie enwerdent niht betrogen von deheinem valschen liehte noch von schouwe der crêatûre: sie lâzent alliu dinc ûf sich selber stân. 17. sie habent wenic wort unde vil lebens." Pfeiffer, 476,29–32; 426,40–477,1; 477,28–30, 36 (Tractate VII, "Diu zeichen eines wârhaften grundes").

"Ursinn der Geistigkeit in ihrer zentralen Lebendigkeit" ("Original Sense of Spirituality in Its Central Vitality"), in Kisiel, "Notes for a Work," 319/327, n. 35: "For God's birth in the soul, it is, among other things, necessary 'that the spirit elevate reason and sees, since seeing is the most delightful and most noble work, which the soul can achieve' (Pfeiffer 1857: 479, 4f.). 'God's birth in the soul is nothing else than a unique divine contact in a unique heavenly way, where God entices the spirit out of the storms of creaturely unrest into His still unity, so that God may communicate Himself in His divine quality' (Pfeiffer 1857: 479, 10f.). 'The Father thus conveys His word to the soul and the soul, again in the word, conveys itself to the Father. Let us nurture this eternal play in God, so help us God' (Pfeiffer 1857: 479, 25f.)." "Für Gottes Gebärde in der Seele ist es u.a. notwendig 'daz der geist die vernunft ûf hebe unde sehe, wan sehen ist daz lustlîchest werc unde daz edelst, daz diu sêle geleisten mac.' 'Gotes gebûrt in der sêle ist niht anders denne ein sunderlîchez götelîchez berüeren in einer sunderlîchen himelischen wîse, dâ got dem geiste locket ûz dem gestürme crêatûrliche unruowe in sîne stille einekeit, dâ sich got dem geiste gemeinen mac nâch sîner götlîchen eigenschaft.' 'Alsô treit der vater sîn wort in die sêle, sô treit sich diu sêle in dem worte wider in den vater. Daz wir diss spils êwichlîche in gote pflegen, des helf uns got.'" Pfeiffer, 479,4–6, 10–14, 25–28 (Tractate VIII, "Von der geburt des êwigen wortes in der sêle").

"Ursinn der Geistigkeit in ihrer zentralen Lebendigkeit" ("Original Sense of Spirituality in Its Central Vitality"), in Kisiel, "Notes for a Work," 319/327, n. 36: "At what place and in what power is the Eternal Word born? (Pfeiffer 1857: 480, 19f.) This question is the topic of many beautiful words by the great teachers and saints: 1. In the reason—for it is most like God. 2. In the will—for it is the free power of the soul. 3. In the *spark of the soul*, for it is most immediately God. 4. In the *concealment of the heart*, for this is God at his most mysterious. 5. In the most intimate essence of the soul—where all the powers of the soul are first born *in a divine taste*, [which manifests] each power in its essence (Pfeiffer 1857: 480, 29): —*reason* as the highest power by which the soul engages in the divine Good. —*free will* as a power that savours the divine good known to you by reason. —*divine spark* as the light of divine equality, which at all times bends toward God (Pfeiffer 1857: 480, 32). —*concealment of the heart* as a concentration of all divine gifts in the innermost essence of the soul, like a bottomless spring of all divine goods (Pfeiffer 1857: 480, 34f.)." "An welcher Stätte und in welcher Kraft wird eigentlichst das ewige Wort geboren? Darüber manige schoene [rede] bei meister und heiligen: 1. in der vernunft—denn sie ist gote am gleichsten. 2. im willen—denn er ist freie Kraft der Seele. 3. im *Seelenfunken*, er ist Gott am nächsten. 4. in der *Verborgenheit des Gemütes*, denn diese ist Gott am geheimsten. 5. in dem aller Innersten des Wesens der Seele—welches geboren werden alle Kräfte der Seele *in einem göttlichen Geschmack*, eine jegliche Kraft in ihrem Wesen. —die *Vernunft* höchste Kraft, mit der die Seele ein Eingreifen hat in das göttliche Guot. —*freier Wille* ein smackendiu kraft götlichen guotes, daz ir diu vernunft gewîset hât. —*göttlicher Funke*: lieht götlicher glicheit, daz sich alle zît ûf got neiget. —*Verborgenheit des Gemütes* ist als ein samenunge alles götlichen gâben in dem innersten Wesen der Seele, daz ist als ein grüntloser brunne alles götlichen guotes." Pfeiffer, 480,19–36 (Tractate VIII, "Von der geburt des êwigen wortes in der sêle").

"Ursinn der Geistigkeit in ihrer zentralen Lebendigkeit" ("Original Sense of Spirituality in its Central Vitality"), in Kisiel, "Notes for a Work," 319/327, n. 37: "Does the spirit know that God is at work within it? (Pfeiffer 1857: 480, 39f.). —There are signs 'with sensuous features' that are found in humans (Pfeiffer 1857: 481, 2). —In the birthing process, 'the spirit is estranged from all the marks of creatures and now stands in a pure vision of the first truth' (Pfeiffer 1857: 481, 6f.)." "Hat nun der geist ein Wissen davon, daß Gott in ihm wirkt? —es gibt merke, die im Menschen sind 'mit sinnelichem gemerke' —in der Geburt wird 'der geist entfremedet allem gemerke der crêatûren unde stât in einem blôzen anschowen der êrsten wârheit.' " Pfeiffer, 480,39–40, 481,2–3, 6–8 (Tractate VIII, "Von der geburt des êwigen wortes in der sêle").

Summer Semester 1927

GA 24: 127–28/90–91 (*Die Grundprobleme der Phänomenologie* [*The Basic Problems of Phenomenology*]): "Daher spricht Meister Eckhart meist von dem 'überwesentlichen Wesen,' d. h. ihn interessiert nicht eigentlich Gott—Gott ist für ihn noch ein vorläufiger Gegenstand—, sondern die Gottheit. Wenn Meister Eckhart 'Gott' sagt, meint er Gottheit, nicht deus, sondern die deitas, nicht das ens, sondern die essentia, nicht die Natur, sondern was über die Natur, d. h. das Wesen ist, das Wesen, dem man noch gleichsam jede Existenzbestimmung absprechen, jede additio existentiae fernhalten muß. Daher sagt er auch: 'Spräche man von Gott er ist, das wäre hinzugelegt.' Das ist die deutsche Übersetzung von: es wäre eine additio entis, wie Thomas sagt. 'So ist Gott im selben Sinne nicht und ist nicht dem Begriffe aller Kreaturen.' So ist Gott für sich selbst sein Nicht, d. h. er ist als das allgemeinste Wesen, als die reinste noch unbestimmte Möglichkeit alles Möglichen, das reine Nichts. Er ist das Nichts gegenüber dem Begriffe aller Kreatur, gegenüber allem bestimmten Möglichen und Verwirklichten." "Meister Eckhart speaks mostly of the 'superessential essence'; that is to say, what interests him is not, strictly speaking, God—God is still a provisional object for him—but Godhead. When Meister Eckhart says 'God' he means Godhead, not deus but deitas, not ens but essentia, not nature but what is above nature, the essence—the essence to which, as it were, every existential determination must still be refused, from which every additio existentiae must be kept at a distance. Hence he also says: 'Spräche man von Gott er ist, das wäre hinzugelegt.' 'If it were said of God that he is, that would be added on.' Meister Eckhart's expression 'das wäre hinzugelegt' is the German translation, using Thomas' phrase, of: it would be an additio entis. 'So ist Gott im selben Sinne nicht und ist nicht dem Begriffe aller Kreaturen.' Thus God is for himself his 'not'; that is to say, he is the most universal being, the purest indeterminate possibility of everything possible, pure nothing. He is the nothing over against the concept of every creature, over against every determinate possible and actualized being." The first quote can be found in Pfeiffer, 318,12–16 (Pr. XCIX): "Swenne aber alliu bilde der sêle abegescheiden werdent unde si alleine schouwet daz einig ein, sô vindet daz blôze wesen der sêle daz blôze formelôse wesen gotlîcher einkeit, daz dâ ist ein überwesende wesen, lîdende, ligende in ime selben." Walshe, 462: "But when all images are detached from the soul and she sees nothing but the one alone, then the naked essence of the soul finds the naked, formless essence of divine unity, which is superessential being, passive, reposing in itself." Cf. DW 3: 437,13–438,1 (Pr. 83, "Renouamini spiritu"). The second quote can be found in Pfeiffer, 659,17–18 ("Liber positionum," no. 106): "Sprêche man: er ist, daz wêre zuo geleit." The third quote can be found in Pfeiffer, 506,30–31 (Tractate XI, "Von der übervart der gotheit," §2): "Sô ist got ime selben sîn niht und ist niht deme begriffe aller crêatûren." Evans, 1, 360: "But God is to himself his aught and naught to the mind of any creature."[14]

Summer Semester 1930

GA 31: 6 (*Vom Wesen der menschlichen Freiheit* [*The Essence of Human Freedom*]): "Freiheit ist das Freisein von. . . . Daz dinc ist vrî daz dà an nihte hanget und an deme ouch niht enhanget." "Freedom is being free from. . . . That thing is free which depends on nothing and on which nothing depends either."[15] Pfeiffer, 379,7–8 (Tractate I, "Von den XII nutzen unsers herren lîchames").

Late 1930s–1940s

GA 81: 187 ("Aus der Erfahrung des Denkens" ["From the Experience of Thinking"], following a poem entitled *Denken* ["Thinking"]): "zur Erläuterung von '*Denken*' / vgl. Angelus Silesius, Cherubinischer Wandersmann I, 289: / 'Ohn Warum / Die Ros' ist ohn Warum; sie blühet, weil sie blühet, sie acht't nicht ihrer selbst, fragt nicht, ob man sie siehet.' // vgl. dazu Meister Eckhart (Pfeiffer, Predigt 13, S. 66.5f.) / 'Uzer diesem inrestem Grunde solt du würken alliu dîniu werc sunder warumbe. . . . al die wîle dû dîniu werc wirkest umbe himelrîche oder umbe got oder umbe dîn êwige sêlikeit von ûzen zuo, sô ist dir wêrlich unreht.'" "For an elucidation of '*Thinking*' / cf. Angelus Silesius, *Cherubinischer Wandersmann* I, 289: / 'Without Why / The Rose is without why; it blooms because it blooms; it does not heed itself, asks not if one does see it.' / cf. on this Meister Eckhart (Pfeiffer, Sermon 13, p. 66,5f.) / 'Out of this inmost ground, all your works should be wrought without Why. . . . [A]s long as you do works for the sake of heaven or God or eternal bliss, from without, you are at fault' [Walshe, 110]." Pfeiffer, 66,5–7 (Pr. XIII). Cf. DW 1: 90,12–91,2 (Pr. 5b, "In hoc apparuit").

August 1940 or after

GA 76: 11 ("Einige Leitgedanken über das Entstehen und Vergehen der Metaphysik" ["Some Guiding Thoughts on the Emergence and Decay of Metaphysics"], in a section entitled *Metaphysik und Christentum* ["Metaphysics and Christianity"]): "Vgl. Augustinus, Confessiones, lib. VII. Cap. 9. N. 13. / Dicit se in libris Platonis legisse 'in principio erat verbum' et magnam partem huius . . . :[16] capituli Johannis. / Vgl. Meister Eckhart, Prooemium zu Expositio Sancti Evangelii secundum Ioannem." "Cf. Augustine, *Confessions*, Book VII, Chapter 9, Section Number 13. / 'In the seventh book of the *Confessions* Augustine says that he read "In the beginning was the Word" and a large part of this first chapter of John in the works of Plato' [ES, 123]. / Cf. Meister Eckhart, 'Prooemium zu Expositio Sancti Evangelii secundum Ioannem.' " LW 3: 4, no. 2 (In Ioh.).

Between 1944 and April 7, 1945[17]

GA 77: 158/103 (trans. mod.): (Supplements to "*Agchibasiē*," under the heading *Vom Lassen der Dinge* ["On Letting Go of Things"]): " 'Wo ich für mich nichts will, da will statt meiner Gott / Eckhart, Reden der Unterweisung (n. 1)." " 'Where I will nothing for myself, there wills instead my God' / Eckhart, *Counsels on Discernment* (n. 1)." Bernhart, 77. Cf. Davies, 4, and DW 5: 187,6–7 (RdU, §1): "Alsô in allen dingen, dâ ich mir niht enwil, dâ wil mir got."

GA 77: 158/103 (Supplements to "*Agchibasiē*," under the heading *Vom Lassen der Dinge* ["On Letting Go of Things"]): " 'Denn wer seinen Willen, wer sich selber läßt, der hat die ganze Welt gelassen, so gut als ob sie sein freies Eigen wäre, und er sie zu voller Gewalt besessen hätte. Alles, was du ausdrücklich nicht begehrst, des hast du dich begeben, hast es gelassen um Gott. '*Selig sind die Armen im Geist*,' hat unser Herr gesagt, es bedeutet: die arm sind an Wollen' (n. 3, S. 79)." " 'For whoever has let go of his own will and of himself, has let go of the whole world as truly as if it were his free property, as if he possessed it with full power of authority. Everything that you expressly do not desire—that you have forsaken and let go of for the sake of God. '*Blessed are the poor in spirit*,' our Lord has said; and this means: those who are poor in will' (n. 3, p. 79)." Bernhart, 79. Cf. Davies, 6–7, and DW 5: 195,4–8 (RdU, §3): "wan, der sînen willen und sich selber læzet, der hât alliu dinc gelâzen als wærlîche, als sie sîn vrî eigen wæren und sie besezzen hæte in ganzem gewalte. Wan, daz dû niht enwilt begern, daz hâst dû allez übergeben und gelâzen durch got. Dar umbe sprach unser herre: 'sælic sint die armen des geistes,' daz ist des willen."

GA 77: 158/103 (Supplements to "*Agchibasiē*," under the heading *Vom Lassen der Dinge* ["On Letting Go of Things"]): " 'Soweit du selber ausgehst aus den Dingen, genau so weit, keinen Schritt weniger oder mehr, geht Gott ein mit allem, was sein ist.' (n. 4, S. 80)." " 'As far as you yourself go out of all things, just this far—not one step less or more—does God go in with all that is His.' (n. 4, p. 80)." Bernhart, 80. Cf. Davies, 7, and DW 5: 197,2–3 (RdU, §4): "als vil dû ûzgâst aller dinge, als vil, noch minner noch mêr, gât got în mit allem dem sînen."

GA 77: 158/103 (Supplements to "*Agchibasiē*," under the heading *Von großem Wesen sein* ["Being of Great Essence"]): " 'Daß Gott groß werde in uns.' (n. 5, S. 81)." " 'May God become great in us' (n. 5, p. 81)." Bernhart, 81, actually writes: "Darauf setze all dein Studieren, daß dir Gott groß werde." "Set all your efforts on God becoming great to you." Cf. ES, 251, and DW 5: 199,4–5 (RdU, §5): "Dar ûf setze al dîn studieren, daz dir got grôz werde."

GA 77: 158/103 (Supplements to "*Agchibasiē*," under the heading *Von großem Wesen sein* ["Being of Great Essence"]): " 'Niht gedenke heilikeit ze setzen ûf ein tuon: man sol heilikeit setzen ûf ein sîn.' " " 'Do not think that holiness is to be attributed to a manner of acting: one should attribute holiness to a manner of being.' " Pfeiffer, 546,22–23 (Tractate XVII). Cf. Davies, 7, and DW 5: 198,1–2 (RdU, §4).

1949

GA 79: 15/14 ("Das Ding" ["The Thing"]): "Das Gleiche wie mit dem Wort res geschieht mit dem der res entsprechenden Namen dinc; denn dinc heißt jegliches, was irgendwie ist. Demgemäß gebraucht der Meister Eckhart das Wort dinc sowohl für Gott als auch für die Seele. Gott ist ihm das 'hoehste und oberste dinc.' "[18] "The same thing that happens with the word *res* happens with the name corresponding to *res, dinc;* for *dinc* means every single thing that somehow is. Accordingly Meister Eckhart uses the word *dinc* as much for God as for the soul. God is to him the 'highest and most elevated thing.' " Pfeiffer, 169,9–11 (quote in l. 10) (Pr. LI): "Nû kumet sanctus Augustinus unde vellet in die rede unde sprichet: got ist etwaz hœhste und oberste dinc, daz gemeine ist aller gebrûchunge." Evans, 1, 133: "Then comes St Augustine with his dictum, God is something sovran, supreme, which is common to all partakers." Cf. DW 4: 275,36–37 (Pr. 100, "Et quaerebat videre Iesum, quis esset").

GA 79: 15/14 ("Das Ding" ["The Thing"]): "Die Seele ist ein 'grôz dinc.' Damit will dieser Meister des Denkens keineswegs sagen, Gott und die Seele seien dergleichen wie ein Felsblock, ein stofflicher Gegenstand; dinc ist hier der vorsichtige und enthaltsame Name für etwas, das überhaupt ist." "The soul is a 'great thing.' With this, this Master of thinking by no means wishes to say that God and the soul would be the same as a block of stone, a material object; *dinc* is here the careful and unassuming name for anything that is at all." Pfeiffer, 141,38–39 (quote in l. 39) (Pr. XLII): "Sît got die sêle alsô krefteklîche minnet, sô muoz diu sêle ein alze grôz dinc sîn." Evans, 1, 114: "But if God loves the soul so much the soul must be a most important thing." Cf. DW 3: 164,2 (Pr. 69, "Modicum et iam non videbitis me").

GA 79: 15/14–15 ("Das Ding" ["The Thing"]): "So sagt der Meister Eckhart nach einem Wort des Dionysius Areopagit [Hg.: vermutlich Augustinus gemeint]:[19] die minne ist der natur, das si den menschen wandelt in die dink, die er minnet." "Thus Meister Eckhart, following a saying of Dionysius the Areopagite, says: love is of such a nature that it changes man into the things he loves." Jostes, 92,14–15 (no. 82): "Also spricht sant Dyonisius, daz di minne ist der natur, daz si den menschen wandelt in die dink, die er minnet." Evans, 1, 273: "St. Dionysius says, it is the nature of love to change a man into that which he loves." Cf. DW 4: 1116,251–52 (Pr. 117, "Zu dem êrsten suochet daz rîche gotes").

GA 79: 70/66 ("Die Kehre" ["The Turn"]): "Damit aber das Menschenwesen achtsam werde auf das Wesen der Technik, damit zwischen Technik und Mensch hinsichtlich ihres Wesens sich ein Wesensverhältnis stifte, muß der neuzeitliche Mensch zuvor allererst einmal in die Weite seines Wesensraumes zurückfinden. Dieser Wesensraum des Menschenwesens aber empfängt seine ihn fügende Dimension einzig aus demjenigen Verhältnis, als welches die Wahrnis des Seyns selbst dem Wesen des Menschen als dem von ihm gebrauchten vereignet ist. Anders als so, daß nämlich der Mensch zuvor erst in seinem Wesensraum sich anbaut und darin Wohnung nimmt, vermag der Mensch nichts Wesenhaftes, innerhalb des jetzt waltenden Geschickes. Wir beachten, dies bedenkend, ein Wort des Meisters Eckhart, indem wir es aus seinem Grunde denken. Es lautet: 'die nitt von grossem Wesen sind, was werk die wirkend, da wirt nit us.' (Reden der Unterscheidung n. 4). / Das große Wesen des Menschen beruht darin, daß es dem Wesen des Seins zugehört. . . ." "But in order that the human essence would become attentive to the essence of technology, in order that an essential relationship would be founded between technology and the human in respect to their essences, the modern human must first of all find his way back into the breadth of his essential space. The dimension that joins together this essential space of the human essence is only received through that relationship by which the guardianship of beyng itself is brought into the ownership of the human essence as what is needed by it. Apart from first cultivating himself within this essential space and taking up a dwelling therein, the human is not capable of anything essential within the dispensation now reigning. In considering this, we attend to a saying of Meister Eckhart and think it from its ground. It runs: 'Those who are not of great essence, whatever work they effect, nothing will come of it.' / The great essence of the human lies in its belonging to the essence of being." Diederichs, 8. Cf. DW 5: 198,6–7 (RdU, §4), and Davies, 7: "Little comes from the works of those whose being is slight."

In his unpublished preparatory notes for "Das Ding" (DLA 75.7305,3), Heidegger cites Pfeiffer, 250,20–22 (Pr. LXXVII, "Faciamus hominem ad imaginem et similitudinem nostram"): "Die meister sprechen, waz nâture sî. Si ist ein dinc, daz wesen enpfâhen mac. Dar umbe einegete got die menschheit an sich unde niht einen menschen." Evans, 1, 195 (trans. mod.): "Philosophers define what nature is. It is the thing that being can receive. Hence God assumed manhood and not man."

May 1949–1950

GA 98: 211:

"Denken: ipsa cogitatio . . . spirat
ignem amoris.

das Denken selber   atmet duftend
das Feuer der Liebe

Meister Eckhart, In Joh., n. 509
(spirare: atmend duften als . . .)"

"Thinking: ipsa cogitatio . . . spirat ignem amoris.

thinking itself breathes, scenting,
the fire of love

Meister Eckhart, In Joh., n. 509
(spirare: breathing, to scent as . . .)"

LW 3: 440, no. 509 (In Ioh.): "Adhuc autem notandum quod omnem cogitationem sive meditationem semper consequitur amor et ipsa cogitatio sive meditatio spirat ignem amoris, secundum illud Psalmi: 'in meditatione mea exardescet ignis.'" "Yet moreover it is to be noted that love always follows thinking or meditation, and thinking itself or meditation breaths the fire of love, according to the Psalm [38:4]: 'in my meditation a fire will flare up.'"

June 27, 1950

MH/HA, 111–12/90–91 (trans. mod.): "Ich sinne ständig darüber nach, ob es noch einen Weg gibt, zwei Dinge zusammen und unscheinbar gegenwärtig zu halten: einmal daß zum Denken das längste und strengste Handwerk gehört; zum andern, daß das Denken in sich das Handeln ist, insofern es dem Wesen des Seyns an die Hand geht. Der Meister Eckhart sagt einmal in seinem Johanneskommentar: ipsa cogitatio . . . spirat ignem amoris. So weit mußten wir kommen." "I am constantly pondering whether there is still a way to keep two things together and inconspicuously present: first that to thinking belongs the longest and strictest craft; and then that thinking is in itself acting, in that it lends a hand to the essence of beyng. Meister Eckhart says at one point in his commentary on John: ipsa cogitatio . . . spirat ignem amoris. We had to come that far." LW 3: 440, no. 509 (In Ioh.). See the previous entry for the full quotation from Eckhart.

Around 1955–1956

In an unpublished note for the lecture course *Der Satz vom Grund* (*The Principle of Reason*) (DLA 57.7314,2), Heidegger cites from the Grimm dictionary entry on "abgründig": "abgründig, *immense profundus* . . . got hat ein vollkommen einsehen in sich selber und abgrundiges durchkennen sich selbs mit im selber. TAULER." The full entry reads: "abgründig, *immense profundus, unermeszlich tief*: got hat ein vollkommen einsehen in sich selber und abgrundiges durchkennen sich selbs mit im selber. TAULER *Leipz.* 1498, 5a; abgründige verzuckung. FISCHART *Garg.* 112a." "abyssal, *immense profundus,* immeasurably deep: God has a perfect insight into himself and abyssal thorough knowledge of himself by himself. TAULER *Leipz.* 1498, 5a; abyssal rapture FISCHART *Garg.* 112a." Although edited under Tauler's name in the fifteenth century, the quote actually comes from Eckhart. See DW 4: 350,87–351,88 (Pr. 101, "Dum medium silentium tenerent omnia"): "Sehet, got der vater hât ein volkomen însehen in sich selber und ein abgründic durchkennen sîn selbes mit im selber, niht mit keinem bilde." Walshe, 32: "God the Father has a perfect insight into Himself, profound and thorough knowledge of Himself by Himself, and not through any image."

In or after 1956

GA 73.2: 995 (in a section on *'Sein' und 'Gott'* [" 'Being' and 'God' "], *1. ens—esse*): "Omne ens et omne omnium esse ipse est. / Deus caritas est. Sermo VI, 1, n. 53, LW IV." LW 4: 51, no. 53 (S. VI,1, "Deus caritas est"). TP, 212 (trans. mod.): "He is every being and the whole being of all things."

GA 73.2: 995 (in a section on *'Sein' und 'Gott'* [" 'Being' and 'God' "], *1. ens—esse*): "Vgl. In Ioh. n. 103, LW III, Pr. LXXXVII / Hier umbe ist got ledic aller dinge und hier umbe ist er alliu dinc."[20] Walshe, 423: "Thus God is free of all things, and so He *is* all things." Pfeiffer, 282,30–31 (Pr. LXXXVII). Cf. DW 2: 497,5–6 (Pr. 52, "Beati pauperes spiritu, quoniam ipsorum est regnum caelorum"). LW 3: 88–89, no. 103 (In Ioh.): "Rursus: *in propria venit.* Notandum quod creatum omne, cum sit hoc aut hoc, distinctum quid, proprium est alicui generi, speciei vel singulari. Deus autem non est quid distinctum aut proprium alicui naturae, sed commune omnibus. Est enim extra et super omne genus. Probat hoc ipsum ens, effectus dei, quod non est in genere nec proprium alicui generi, sed commune omni generi. Deus ergo in hunc mundum veniens, creaturam assumens, factus homo, quasi de fastigio communis venit in propria. Et hoc est quod hic manifeste dicitur: 'erat lux vera quae illuminat omnem hominem,' utpote communis et superior omnibus; et sequitur: 'in mundo erat, et mundus' omne genus continens 'per ipsum factus est.' Et post concludit dicens: *in propria venit,* Ioh. 16: 'exivi a patre et veni in mundum'; Eccli. 24: 'ego ex ore altissimi prodii primogenita ante omnem creaturam'; et infra: 'exivi de paradiso,' scilicet divinitatis. 'Dixi: rigabo hortum meum, plantationem,' mundum scilicet creando." ES, 161–62: "Again, 'He came to his own.' Note that everything created, because it is a particular being, something distinct, belongs to some genus, species or individual thing. God is not anything distinct or proper to some nature, but is common to all. He is outside and above every genus. The proof of this is that being, God's effect, is not in a genus and does not belong to any genus, but is common to every genus. When God came into this world, assumed a created nature and was made man, it was as if he came to what is proper from the height of what is common. This is what the text clearly means, 'He was the true light that enlightens every man,' for this light is common and superior to all. There follows, 'He was in the world, and the world,' that which contains every genus, 'was made through him.' Finally, John concluded, 'He came to his own.' 'I came forth from the Father and have come into the world' (Jn. 16:28). 'I came out of the mouth of the Most High, the Firstborn before all creatures' (Si. 24:5); and below, 'I came forth from Paradise,' that is, divinity; 'I said, I will water my garden of plants,' that is, by creating the world (Si 24:41–42)."

GA 73.2: 995 (in a section on *'Sein' und 'Gott'* [" 'Being' and 'God' "], *1. ens—esse*): "Secundo nota quod omne commune, in quantum commune, deus, et omne non commune, in quantum non commune, deus non est, sed creatum est. / Sermo VI, 1, n. 53." LW 4: 52, no. 53 (S. VI,1, "Deus caritas est"). TP, 213: "Secondly, note that whatever is common insofar as it is common is God, and whatever is not common insofar as it is not common is not God, but is created."

GA 73.2: 995 (in a section on *'Sein' und 'Gott'* [" 'Being' and 'God' "], *1. ens—esse*): "got ist etwaz hœhste und oberste dinc, daz gemeine ist aller gebrûchunge. / Ib. Pr. LI, 169."[21] Evans, 1, 133: "God is something sovran, supreme, which is common to all partakers." Pfeiffer, 169,10–11 (Pr. LI). Cf. DW 4: 275,36–37 (Pr. 100, "Et quaerebat videre Iesum, quis esset").

GA 73.2: 995 (in a section on *'Sein' und 'Gott'* [" 'Being' and 'God' "], *1. ens—esse*): "Pr. LXXXIV: Got ist daz aller gemeineste. Kein dinc gemeinet sich von dem sînen, wan alle creâtûre von in selber niht ensint. Swaz sie gemeinent, daz habent sie von eime anderen."[22] Walshe, 343: "God shares Himself most of all. No thing shares of its own, for all creatures are nothing in themselves. Whatever they share, they have from another." Pfeiffer, 269,25–27 (Pr. LXXXIV). Cf. DW 1: 149,5–7 (Pr. 9, "Quasi stella matutina").

GA 73.2: 996 (in a section on *'Sein' und 'Gott'* [" 'Being' and 'God' "], *2. ens creatum*): "Nihil creatum dat suum. Item non dat omne sui. Item non dat se ipsum. / Sermo VI, 1, n. 55, LW IV." LW 4: 54, no. 55 (S. VI,1, "Deus caritas est"). TP, 213: "Nothing created gives its own, nor the whole of it, nor itself."

GA 73.2: 996 (in a section on *'Sein' und 'Gott'* [" 'Being' and 'God' "], *2. ens creatum*): "Omne enim creatum ratione nihili foedum est et dividit a deo | sicut nox a die, tenebrae a luce, nihil ab esse. Ubi dic quod nihil tam foedum quam nihil ipsum est. / Sermo, VI, 2, n. 57." LW 4: 57, no. 57 (S. VI,2, "In hoc apparuit gratia dei"). TP, 214 (trans. mod.): "Everything created is stained with nothingness and set apart from God, like night from day, darkness from light, nothingness from being. (Here remark that nothing is more offensive than nothingness itself.)"

GA 73.2: 996 (in a section on *'Sein' und 'Gott'* [" 'Being' and 'God' "], *2. ens creatum*): "In Ioh., n. 20, LW III: res enim omnis [creata] sapit umbram nihili. no. 74: in creaturis quae habent aliquid opaci, id est nihili, adiunctum."[23] LW 3: 17, no. 20 (In Ioh.). ES, 128: "Every created being smacks of the shadow of nothingness." LW 3: 62, no. 74 (In Ioh.). ES, 149: "in creatures that have something dark (i.e., nothingness) added to them."

GA 73.2: 996 (in a section on *'Sein' und 'Gott'* [" 'Being' and 'God' "], *4. Deus—esse*): "Esse autem a solo deo est, et ipse solus est esse. / Meister Eckhart, Sermo IV, 1, n. 23, LW IV." LW 4: 24, no. 23 (S. IV,1, "Ex ipso, per ipsum et in ipso"). TP, 208 (trans. mod.): "Being is from God alone, and he alone is being."

GA 73.2: 996 (in a section on *'Sein' und 'Gott'* [" 'Being' and 'God' "], *4. Deus—esse*): "extra deum nihil est, sicut nec extra esse quidquam esse potest. / Sermo XXIII, n. 222, LW IV." "Nothing is outside of God, just as there is not something that can be outside of being." LW 4: 207, no. 222 (S. XXIII, "Nemo potest dicere: dominus Iesus").

Also in or after 1956

In an unpublished collection of notes (DLA 75.7305,9), Heidegger copies out an Eckhart quote from Käte Oltmanns, *Meister Eckhart*, 68, who is herself citing from Pfeiffer's edition: "(Vernunft) ir genüeget als wenig an gote als an einem steine oder an eime boume. sie geruowet niemer, sie brichet in den grunt." Walshe, 237: "It [intellect/reason] is as little satisfied with God as with a stone or tree. It never rests; it bursts into the ground." Pfeiffer, 144,35–38 (Pr. XLII). Cf. DW 3: 179,3–5 (Pr. 69, "Modicum et iam non videbitis me").

In an unpublished collection of notes (DLA 75.7305,9), Heidegger copies out an Eckhart quote from the third of a group of four sermons in Büttner's edition that are gathered under the title "Von der ewigen Geburt" ("On the Eternal Birth"): "sei du deiner selbst und aller Dinge eine Wüste." Walshe, 52: "Be as a desert in respect of yourself and all things." Büttner 2nd ed., 1, 99. Cf. DW 4: 601,19–20 (Pr. 104, "In his, quae patris mei sunt, oportet me esse"): "habe dû dich dir selber und aller dinge wüeste."

In an unpublished collection of notes (DLA 75.7305,9), Heidegger copies out an Eckhart quote from the fourth of a group of four sermons in Büttner's edition that are gathered under the title "Von der ewigen Geburt" ("On the Eternal Birth"): "soll Gott *göttlich* in dir leuchten, dazu vermag kein natürliches Licht dich irgend zu fördern: es muß erst zu einem lauteren Nichts werden und sich selbst aufgeben, dann kann Gott mit seinem Lichte einstrahlen." "if God is to gleam in you *divinely*, no natural light can at all facilitate you in this: it must first become a sheer Nothing and give itself up, then God can shine in with his light." Büttner 2nd ed., 1, 103. Cf. Walshe, 56, and DW 4: 476,21–477,2 (Pr. 103: "Cum factus esset Iesus annorum duodecim"): "sol got götlîche in dir liuhten, dar envürdert dich dîn natiurlich lieht zemâle niht zuo, mêr: ez muoz ze einem lûtern nihte werden und sîn selbes ûzgân zemâle; und danne sô mac got îngân mit sînem liehte."

In an unpublished collection of notes (DLA 75.7305,9), Heidegger copies out an Eckhart quote from a sermon in Büttner's edition with the title "Von der Armut am Geiste" ("On the Poor in Spirit"): "Also sagen wir: der Mensch solle so arm stehn, daß er 'eine Stätte, darin Gott wirken möge' weder selber sei noch gar in sich habe! Solange der Mensch in sich Raum behält, solange behält er *Unterschiedenheit*. Darum eben bitte ich Gott, daß er mich Gottes quitt mache! Denn *das unseiende Sein* ist jenseits von Gott, jenseits von aller Unterschiedenheit: da war ich nur selber, da wollte ich mich selber, und schaute mich selber als den, der diesen *Menschen* gemacht hat! So bin ich denn die Ursache meiner selbst, nach meinem ewigen *und* nach meinem zeitlichen Wesen. Nur hierum bin ich geboren. Nach meiner ewigen Geburtsweise vermag ich auch nimmer zu sterben: Kraft meiner ewigen Geburtsweise bin ich von Ewigkeit her gewesen, und bin, und werde ewiglich bleiben! Nur was ich als *zeitliches* Wesen bin, das wird sterben und zu nichte werden; denn es gehört dem Tage an, darum muß es, wie die Zeit, verschwinden. In meiner Geburt wurden auch alle Dinge geboren: ich war zugleich meine *eigene* und *aller Dinge* Ursache. Und wollte ich: weder ich wäre, noch alle Dinge. Wäre aber ich nicht, so wäre auch Gott nicht.—Daß man dies verstehe, ist nicht erforderlich." "Thus we say: the human being should stand in such a poor manner that he neither himself is, nor even has in himself, 'a site in which God may work'! So long as the human being retains space in himself, so long does he retain *distinction*. Precisely therefore do I pray God to make me void of God! For the *nonexistent Being* is beyond God, beyond all distinction: there I was only myself, there I willed myself, and beheld myself as he who made this *human being*! Thus I am the cause of myself, according to my eternal *and* according to my temporal being. Only for this reason was I born. According to my eternal mode of birth I also can never die: by virtue of my eternal mode of birth I have been from eternity, and am, and will remain eternally! Only what I am as a *temporal* being will die and become nothing; for it belongs to the day, therefore it must, like time, disappear. In my birth all things were also born: I was at once my *own* cause and the cause *of all things*. And if I wanted: I would not be, nor would all things: Yet were I not, then God would not be either.—It is not necessary for one to understand this." Büttner 2nd ed., 1, 185. Cf. ES, 202–03, and DW 2: 502,4–504,3 (Pr. 52, "Beati pauperes spiritu"): "Alsô sagen wir, daz der mensche alsô arm sül sîn, daz er niht ensî noch enhabe deheine stat, dâ got inne müge würken. Dâ der mensche stat beheltet, dâ beheltet er underscheit. Her umbe sô bite ich got, daz er mich ledic mache gotes, wan mîn wesenlich wesen ist obe gote, alsô als wir got nemen begin der crêatûren; wan in dem selben wesene gotes, dâ got ist obe wesene und ob underscheide, dâ was ich selbe, dâ wolte ich mich selben und bekante mich selben ze machenne disen menschen. Her umbe sô bin ich mîn selbes sache nâch mînem wesene, daz êwic ist, und niht nâch mînem gewerdenne, daz zîtlich ist. Und her umbe sô bin ich ungeborn, und nâch mîner ungebornen wîse sô enmac ich niemer ersterben. Nâch mîner ungebornen wîse sô bin ich êwiclîche gewesen und bin nû und sol êwiclîche blîben. Daz ich bin nâch gebornheit, daz sol sterben und ze nihte werden, wan ez ist toetlich; her umbe sô muoz ez mit der zît verderben. In mîner geburt, dâ wurden alliu dinc geborn, und ich was sache mîn selbes und aller dinge; und hæte ich gewolt, ich enwære niht, noch alliu dinc enwæren niht; und enwære ich niht, sô enwære ouch 'got' niht. Daz got 'got' ist, des bin ich ein sache; enwære ich niht, sô enwære got niht 'got.' Diz ze wizzenne des enist niht nôt."

In an unpublished collection of notes (DLA 75.7305,9), Heidegger copies out an Eckhart quote from a text in Büttner's edition with the title

"Von dem Zorne der Seele und von ihrer rechten Stätte" ("On the Wrath of the Soul and Its Proper Site"): "Gott schaute sich selber an und erschaute zugleich *sich* und *alle Dinge*. Und doch war er darum nicht ein Mannigfaltiges, wie jetzt die Dinge es sind in ihrer Unterschiedenheit, sondern er blieb ein Einiges. Denn ob auch die Kreaturen jetzt ein Mannigfaltiges sind, in Gott sind sie doch nur *ein* Blick: Gott ist bei sich selber immer nur ein Einig-Eines. Und das werden sie—und besonders die vernünftige Kreatur— klar erschauen, wenn sie zurückkehren in ihrem ersten Ursprung: da schaut man Gott anders nicht denn einfaltig an Wesen, und doch dreifaltig an den Personen, und mannigfaltig an seinen Werken! Alle Kreaturen also haben ihr Sein in Gott, und das Wesen, das sie haben, gibt Gott ihnen mit seiner Gegenwart." "God looked upon himself and beheld at the same time *himself* and *all things*. And yet he was not therefore something manifold, as things are now in their distinction, but rather he remained a singular. For even if creatures are now something manifold, in God they are nevertheless but *one* glance. In the presence of himself, God is always but a single-one. And they—and especially the rational creature—will behold this clearly when they turn back into their first origin: there one sees God in no other way than as onefold in essence, and yet threefold in persons, and manifold in his works! Thus all creatures have their being in God, and the essence that they have, God gives it to them with his presence." Büttner 2nd ed., 1, 190.

In an unpublished collection of notes (DLA 75.7305,9), Heidegger copies out an Eckhart quote from a text in Büttner's edition with the title "Von dem Zorne der Seele und von ihrer rechten Stätte" ("On the Wrath of the Soul and Its Proper Site"): "'Denn er hat mich verwundet mit einem Blicke seines Auges!' Das ist die einende Kraft, die sich herergießt von diesem Punkte: so scheidet er die Seele von allem Erschaffenen und allen wandelbaren Dingen, in diesem Blicke zückt er sie zurück in den einen Punkt, dem sie nun geeint und ewiglich an ihm bestätigt wird. Bewußt bemerken aber wird man diesen Blick nur dann, wenn die Seele aller Bestimmtheit so bar ist, daß keinerlei Hinrichtung weder auf Tugend noch auf Untugend mehr in ihr ist. Nur was in diesem Zustande in sie fällt, von dem hat sie ein höchstes Erkennen. Darum senkt er gerade dann seinen Blick in sie, damit auch *sie ihn erkenne, wie er sie erkannt* und geliebt hat, ehe sie war. Das soll der Seele eine dringende Mahnung sein, aus ihrem Selbst und aus allen Dingen auszugehen. Wen dieser Blick nicht verwundet, der wird noch ward von Liebe jemals wund!" "'For he has wounded me with a glance of his eye!' That is the unifying power that pours itself out from this point: so does he separate the soul from everything created and from all transient things, in this glance he whips the soul back into the single point with which it is now unified and in which it is eternally confirmed. One only consciously takes note of this point when the soul is so void of all determinacy that there is no longer any directedness in it either to virtue or to vice. It has its highest knowledge only from what befalls it when it is in this state. For this reason he sinks his glance into the soul in order that *it* too *may know him as he has known it* and loved it, before it was. This should be an urgent admonition to the soul to go out of itself and all things. Whoever this glance does not wound is or was never wounded by love." Büttner 2nd ed., 1, 191–92.

In an unpublished collection of notes (DLA 75.7305,9), Heidegger copies out an Eckhart quote from a text in Büttner's edition with the title "Von dem Zorne der Seele und von ihrer rechten Stätte" ("On the Wrath of the Soul and Its Proper Site"): "den Anhauch der Einheit, in der alle Dinge still werden." "the whiff of unity, in which all things become still." Büttner 2nd ed., 1, 194.

In an unpublished collection of notes (DLA 75.7305,9), Heidegger copies out an Eckhart quote from a text in Büttner's edition with the title "Vom Schauen Gottes und von Seligkeit" ("On Beholding God and on Blessedness"): "Wo *Gleichheit* ist, da ist nicht *Einheit*, denn *gleich* ist eine 'Beraubung' der Einheit—und wo Einheit ist, da ist nicht Gleichheit, denn Gleichheit verbleibt in Unterschied und Vielheit. Wo es ein Gleichsein gibt, da kann es kein Einssein geben! Ich bin mir selber nicht *gleich,* ich bin *eins*: das eine und selbe, was ich bin." "Where there is *equality,* there is no *unity,* for *equal* is a 'theft' of unity—and where there is unity, there is no equality, for equality remains in distinction and multiplicity. Where there is an equalness, there can be no oneness! I am not *equal* to myself, I am *one*: the one and the same that I am." Büttner 2nd ed., 1, 203. Cf. Evans, 1, 410, and Preger, 1, 486 ("Tractat Eckhart's von dem Schauen Gottes durch die wirkende Vernunft"): "wa geleicheit ist, da ist kein einigkeit; wan geleich ist ein beraubung der einigkeit, und wa einikeit ist da ist kein geleicheit; wan geleicheit stet in unterscheit und vilheit. Wa geleicheit ist, da mag nicht einikeit sein. Ich pin mir selber nit geleich; in bin ein und das selb das ich pin."

In an unpublished collection of notes (DLA 75.7305,9), Heidegger copies out a Latin passage from Eckhart along with its translation by the editor Ernst Benz: "Dilectio enim, qua se diligunt pater et filius, est ipse spiritus sanctus. Diligunt enim spiritu sancto, sicut arbor floret floritione, floret flore." "Die Liebe nämlich, in der sich der Vater und der Sohn lieben, ist der Heilige Geist selbst. Sie lieben sich nämlich im Heiligen Geist, wie ein Baum blüht im Blühen, blüht in der Blüte." "The love, namely, in which the Father and the Son love each other, is the Holy Spirit itself. That is to say, they love each other in the Holy Spirit as a tree blooms in the blooming, blooms in the flowering." LW 4: 7, no. 5 (S. II,1, "Deus pacis et dilectionis erit vobiscum").

In an unpublished collection of notes (DLA 75.7305,9), Heidegger makes reference to LW 4: 57, no. 57 (S. VI,2, "In hoc apparuit gratia dei"): "Nota primo: *in hoc apparuit caritas* etc., quia secundum Augustinum maior gratia haec est etc. Secundo dic quod *misit in mundum* etc., quia in mundum cor mittit deus filium suum. Iuxta primum nota quod assumpsit naturam, non personam, de quo vide: 'verbum caro factum est'; iuxta secundum nota quod cor mundum est, quod cum nihilo nihil habet commune. / Ubi nota primo, quod deus verissime mittit, gignit unigenitum suum in anima munda et 'in ipso et per ipsum omnia,' se ipsum, Ioh. 14: 'ad eum veniemus' etc. Secundo, quare sic ait, aut quomodo anima munda; est autem munda nihil amans creatum. Omne enim creatum ratione nihili foedum est et dividit a deo, sicut nox a die, tenebrae a luce, nihil ab esse. Ubi dic quod nihil tam foedum quam nihil ipsum est." TP, 214 (trans. mod.): "The first point is that 'In this has love appeared,' because according to Augustine this is the greater grace. The second is that 'he sent his Son into the world,' because God sends his Son into a clean heart. On the first point note that the Son assumed human nature, not a human person (on which see the exegesis of 'The Word was made flesh' [Jn. 1:14]). On the second, note that a clean heart is one that has nothing in common with nothing. / The first thing to be noted is that God most truly sends and gives birth to his only-begotten Son in the pure soul, and 'in him and through him all things' (Rm. 11:36) [and] himself. 'We will come to him and make our abode with him' (Jn. 14:23). Second, why does he speak thus, or how does the soul become clean? It is clean when it loves nothing created. Everything created is stained with nothingness and set apart from God, like night from day, darkness from light, nothingness from being. (Here remark that nothing is more offensive than nothingness itself.)"

In an unpublished collection of notes (DLA 75.7305,9), Heidegger quotes from Pfeiffer, 166,11–12 (Pr. L, "Exivi a patre et veni in mundum"): "Werlt sprichet als vil als reine; er meinet die sêle."[24] Evans, 1, 130: "*World* meaning pure or virgin. He is referring to the soul."

February 29, 1968

MH/BW, 29–30: "Ich danke . . . besonders für Ihren Aufsatz 'Rückblick auf die Metaphysik.' . . . Ist der 'Hintergrund' bei Thomas wirklich ein gedachter Hinter*gedanke*? Dagegen 'folgt' bei Meister Eckhart wirklich ein neuer Schritt. Ein Satz wie *Sed etiam Deus* [sic, should be *dico*] *quod Deo non convenit esse nec est ens, sed est aliquid altius ente* (*Quaestio utrum in Deo sit idem esse et intelligere*—Grabmann, Abhandlungen der Bayerischen Akademie der Wissenschaften. Philosophisch-historische Klasse XXXII. Bd. 7. Abfolge,[25] S. 104) findet sich nach meiner Kenntnis nirgends. Dieser Satz sagt mehr als der Hinweis, daß das *esse* keine Gattung sei. / Aber Sie kennen gewiß diese Sachverhalte besser als ich. Mir scheint indes, was Sie Thomas von Aquin zuschreiben, gehört ausschließlich dem Meister Eckhart. . . . Nötig wäre eine ausführliche Darstellung des 'Seinsproblems' bei Thomas von Aquin und Meister Eckhart." "I thank you . . . especially for your essay 'Rückblick auf der Metaphysik' [Looking Back at Metaphysics]. . . . Is the 'background' in Thomas really thought as a background *thought*? In contrast, there really does 'follow' in Meister Eckhart a new step. A sentence like *Sed etiam Deus* [sic, should be *dico*], *quod Deo non convenit esse nec est ens, sed est aliquid altius ente* (*Quaestio utrum in Deo sit idem esse et intelligere*—Grabmann, Abhandlungen der Bayerischen Akademie der Wissenschaften. Philosophisch-historische Klasse, Vol. XXXII, 7th treatise, p. 104) can, as far as I know, be found nowhere else. This sentence says more than the indication that *esse* is not a genus. / Yet you are certainly more familiar with this state of affairs than I am. It appears to me however that what you ascribe to Thomas Aquinas belongs exclusively to Meister Eckhart. . . . A detailed presentation of the 'problem of being' in Thomas Aquinas and Meister Eckhart would be necessary." Grabmann, 104. Cf. LW 5: 47, no. 12 (Qu. Par. 1, "Utrum in deo sit idem esse et intelligere"). Maurer, 50 (trans. mod.): "I also assert that being does not belong to God, nor is he a being, but he is something loftier than a being."

4. Heidegger's Marginalia and Underlining in His Personal Copies of Eckhart

Heidegger marked up his copies of Bernhart's, Büttner's, and Diederichs's editions of Eckhart. These copies are located in the personal library of Friedrich-Wilhelm von Herrmann, emeritus professor at the University of Freiburg and Heidegger's assistant from 1972 until his death in 1976. In what follows, I will explain and cite Heidegger's marginalia and other markings, providing references to the critical edition when appropriate. I will not provide an English translation of what he marks up in Diederichs's Middle High German edition of RdU, nor a translation of the seven sections of Bernhart's translation of RdU that Heidegger frequently underlined, although I will transcribe and translate Heidegger's marginalia in these sections. However, for other passages that Heidegger marks up or to which he refers, I will provide English translations in the body of the text, as in §3, above.

Bernhart

On the title page, Heidegger wrote his name in black pen in the old, thick script he employed from around 1910 until mid-April 1919.[26] With red, green, yellow, and lead pencil, he underlined numerous words in §§1–7 of Bernhart's translation of RdU (pp. 76–88). After the respective underlined word or words, I will insert, in square brackets, the following abbreviations for the different colors: 'r' (red), 'g' (green), 'y' (yellow), and 'l' (lead). In personal conversations, Friedrich-Wilhelm von Herrmann explained that red often signifies very important, green important, and yellow critical reservations. Some of the underlining in lead pencil derives from von Herrmann. Given that it was impossible always to determine which stems from Heidegger and which from von Herrmann, I have included all underlining in lead pencil in the following. In square brackets, I will also explain Heidegger's marginalia and other markings, some of which are in black pen.

§1: "*Vom wahren Gehorsam.* / Wahrer und vollkommener Gehorsam ist eine Tugend vor [r] allen Tugenden, und kein großes Werk kann geschehen und vollbracht werden ohne [r] diese Tugend. Und so klein ein Geschäft auch sei und unbedeutend, es ist nützer getan in wahrem Gehorsam: es sei Messelesen oder -hören, beten, kontemplieren oder was du erdenken magst. Und nimm eine Arbeit, so gering du nur willst, es sei was immer, wahrer Gehorsam macht sie dir edler und besser. Gehorsam bewirkt in allweg das Beste an allen Dingen, ja Gehorsam geht nimmer fehl und versäumt auch nichts, es mag einer tun, was er will—wenn es nur aus wahrem Gehorsam kommt: denn er verabsäumt nichts Gutes. Gehorsam braucht nimmer Sorge zu haben, ihm gebricht es an keinem Gute. Wo immer der Mensch in Gehorsam aus [r] sich ausgeht [r], in denselben [r] muß hinwieder Gott notwendig eingehen [r]; denn wenn einer für sich selber nichts mehr will, für den muß Gott so [r] wollen wie für sich selber. Wenn ich meines Willens mich begeben habe in die Hand meines Obern und mir selber nichts mehr will, so muß Gott für mich wollen. Und soviel er dann mich außer acht ließe, soviel ließe er sich selber außer acht. Also kurz: Wo ich nicht selber will, da will statt meiner Gott. / Nun gib acht! Was will er da, wo ich [r] nicht [r] will [in between "ich" and "nicht" Heidegger drew a diagonal line in red pencil]. Worin ich mich *lasse,* darin muß er [r] mir notwendig alles das [r] wollen, was er [r] sich selber will, nicht weniger und nicht mehr, und in der nämlichen Weise [r], mit der er für sich will. Und täte Gott das nicht [g]: bei der Wahrheit, die doch Gott ist [g], so wäre er nicht gerecht und nicht Gott, was doch sein natürlich Wesen ist. Bei wahrem Gehorsam soll es kein 'ich will so oder so, dies oder das' geben, sondern ein unbedingtes Fahrenlassen des Deinigen. Und darum soll es in dem allerbesten Gebet, das der Mensch beten kann, nicht [g] heißen: 'Gib mir diese Tugend oder jene Weise,' oder 'Ja, Herr, gib mir dich selber oder ewiges Leben,' sondern allein: 'Herr, gib mir nur, was du [r] willst, und tue, Herr, was und wie du willst auf jede [r] Weise.' Das übertrifft jenes andere wie der Himmel die Erde. Und wenn man dies [r] Gebet also vollbringt, so hat man wohl gebetet. Denn so ist man in wahrem Gehorsam gänzlich eingegangen in Gott. Wie aber wahrer Gehorsam kein 'Ich will also' kennen soll, so soll man von ihm auch kein 'Ich will nicht [r]' vernehmen. Denn ein 'Ich will nicht' ist ein wahres Vergiften des Gehorsams. Wie Sankt Augustinus sagt: Den getreuen Diener Gottes gelüstet nicht, daß man ihm sage oder gebe, was er gern sähe oder hörte; denn sein erstes und höchstes Bemühen ist, zu hören, was Gott allermeist gefällt."

§2: "*Von dem allerkräftigen Gebet und dem allerhöchsten Werk.* / Das kräftigste Gebet, allmächtig fast, alle Dinge zu erwerben, und das erhabenste Werk von allen ist jenes, das da hervorgeht aus einem ledigen [r] Gemüt. Je lediger das ist, je kräftiger, würdiger, angelegentlicher, löblicher und vollkommener ist das Gebet und Werk. *Das ledige Gemüt vermag alle Dinge.* Was ist nun aber ein lediges Gemüt? Das [r] ist ein lediges Gemüt: das mit nichts beladen ist noch bewirrt noch an etwas gebunden noch je etwann das Seinige meint, sondern ganz und gar nur in den liebsten Willen Gottes versenkt ist und den seinigen aufgegeben hat. Der Mensch kann kein noch so verächtliches Werk tun, es schöpft hierinne Kraft und Wirkung. Also kräftiglich soll man beten, daß man alle seine Glieder und Kräfte, beide Augen und Ohren, Mund und alle Sinne dazu sammelt, und nicht eher soll man aufhören, als bis man fühlt, daß man sich nun vereine mit dem, den man gegenwärtig hält, das ist Gott."

§3: "*Von ungelassenen Leuten, die voll Eigenwillens sind.* / Da sagen die Leute oft: 'Ach ja, Herr, ich wollte gerne, ich stünde mit unserm Herrgott auch [r] so gut und hätte soviel Andacht und Friede mit Gott, wie andere [r] Leute haben, und daß ich's auch [r] so hätte und so [r] arm sein könnte.' Oder sie sagen: 'Mit mir wird's nimmer recht, ich sei denn da oder dort und tue so oder so, muß weg von daheim in Klause oder Kloster sein.' Wahrhaftig, an all dem bist du selber [r] schuld, und weiter nichts. Es ist nur dein Eigenwille [l]. Und wenn du's auch nicht weißt oder einsiehst: nimmer steht ein Unfriede [l] auf in dir, er komme denn vom Eigenwillen [l], ob man das nun merke oder nicht. Was wir [r] da meinen: der Mensch solle das eine [r] fliehen, das andere [r] suchen (als da sind andre Orte, andre Leute, andre Weise, andren Sinn oder neues Tun)—nicht [r] das ist schuld, daß die Weise [r] oder die Dinge dich hindern. Vielmehr: du selber [r] in den Dingen bist es, was dich hindert, denn du [r] hältst dich zu den Dingen nicht in der rechten Weise [l]. Darum fang zuallererst bei dir [r] selber an und *lasse dich* [r; Heidegger also drew a diagonal line in red pencil between "*lasse*" and "*dich*"]! Fürwahr, wenn du nicht zuerst dich selber [r] fliehst, so magst du fliehen wohin [r] du willst, du findest da nur Erschwerung und Unfrieden, es sei, was [r] es sei. Die Leute, die Frieden suchen an äußeren [r] Dingen, es sei an Orten oder Weisen oder Menschen oder Werken oder Heimatlosigkeit oder Armut und Verachtung—wie groß sich das auch ausnehme oder was [r] es sei, das ist doch alles nichts und gibt keinen Frieden. Sie suchen alles verkehrt, die so suchen: Je weiter weg sie wandern, je weniger finden sie, was sie suchen. Sie gehen wie einer, der den Weg verfehlt: Je weiter er geht, je mehr er irrt. [Heidegger drew a circle in red pencil in the right margin next to the line beginning with "einer, der" and ending with "je."] Ja, was soll er aber tun? Vor allem, er soll sich selber lassen [r], so hat er alle Dinge gelassen [l]. Wahrlich, ließe [l] ein Mensch ein Königreich, ja, die ganze Welt und behielte doch [g] sich [g; this word is also partially circled in green pencil] selber, so hätte er nichts [g] gelassen [l]. Gibt er aber sich selber [l] auf—er mag dann behalten [g] was [g] er will, es sei Reichtum oder Ehre oder was es sei, er hat doch *alles* aufgegeben. / Ein Heiliger bemerkt zu dem Wort, das Sankt Peter sprach: 'Sieh, Herr, wir haben alles verlassen'—und dabei hat er doch nichts verlassen als sein Netz und sein Schifflein—dieser Heilige sagt: Wer das Kleine willig [g] läßt, der läßt nicht dies allein, er läßt alles [g], was Weltmenschen je nur gewinnen, ja auch nur begehren können. Denn wer seinen [l] Willen [l] und sich [l] selber läßt [l], der hat alles gelassen [l], so eigentlich, als ob sie sein freies Eigen und er [g] ganz ihr Herr gewesen wäre. Denn wonach du kein [g] Begehren trägst, all dessen hast du dich begeben und es gelassen [l] um Gottes [Heidegger drew an "L"-shaped figure in red pencil in the right margin] willen [l]. Darum sprach unser Herr: Selig sind die Armen im Geiste, das ist dem Willen nach [r] Armen. Und hieran soll keiner zweifeln: Gäb es eine bessere Weise, unser Herr hätte sie genannt—wie er ja auch sagte: Wer mir nachfolgen will, der verleugne zuerst sich selbst! Daran ist alles gelegen. Wache über dich, und wo du dein Ich [r] am Werke spürst, da laß es [r; Heidegger also drew a diagonal line in red pencil between 'da' and 'laß es'] fahren—das ist das Allerbeste."

§4: "*Vom Segen der Gelassenheit, die man innerlich und äußerlich üben soll.* / Merke wohl, daß noch nie [r] ein Mensch im Leben sich so überwand, daß ihm nicht noch [r] etwas zu überwinden übrig [r] blieb. Der Leute sind wenig, die das recht wahrnehmen und darin [g] bestehen [g; Heidegger also drew a diagonal line in green pencil between "darin" and "bestehen"]. Es ist ein gerechter Tausch und Handel: soweit du [g] ausgehst [r, g] aus den Dingen und des Deinen dich begibst [l], soweit (nicht weniger und nicht mehr) geht Gott [g] ein [r] in dich [g] mit all dem Seinen. Damit heb an und das laß dich kosten alles, was du nur leisten kannst. So findest du wahren Frieden—und anders nicht. Die Menschen sollten nicht soviel nachdenken, was sie *tun* sollen, sie sollten aber bedenken, was sie [r] sind [r]. [In red pencil, Heidegger drew a vertical line and a red circle in the margin next to the preceding sentence.] Wären nur sie [r] selber gut und ihre Weise [r], so möchten ihre Werke [r] herrlich leuchten. Bist [r; Heidegger also drew a diagonal line in red pencil after "Bist"] du gerecht, so sind auch deine Werke gerecht. Denke nicht Heiligkeit zu gründen auf ein Tun: man soll Heiligkeit gründen auf ein Sein. Denn nicht die Werke [r] heiligen uns [r], sondern wir [r] sollen die Werke [r] heiligen. Denn wie heilig immer die Werke auch seien, so heiligen sie uns durchaus nicht, weil sie etwa von uns getan sind, vielmehr gilt: insoweit wir [r] wahres Sein und Wesen haben, insoweit heiligen wir auch all unser Tun, es sei Essen, Schlafen, Wachen oder was das sei.[27] [Heidegger drew a diagonal line in red pencil here.] Die nicht groß von Wesen sind—was die auch wirken mögen, daraus wird nichts. [Heidegger drew a diagonal line in red pencil here.] Hieran lerne, daß man allen Fleiß daran wenden soll, gut zu sein [r]: nicht so sehr, was [r] man tue oder welcher Art die Werke seien, sondern wie der Grund [r] der Werke sei."

§5: "*Bedenke, was das Wesen und den Grund gut mache.* / Die Ursache, an der es gelegen ist, daß eines Menschen Wesen und Seelengrund vollkommen gut sei, und aus der seine Werke ihre Güte empfangen, das ist dies:

daß des Menschen Gemüt <u>gänzlich</u> [r] <u>zu Gott</u> [r] gekehrt sei. [Heidegger drew a diagonal line in red pencil here.] Darauf setze all dein Studieren [Heidegger drew a diagonal line in green pencil here], <u>daß dir Gott groß werde</u> [g] und daß all dein Trachten und Bemühen ihm zugewandt sei in all deinem Tun und Lassen. Fürwahr, je mehr du <u>davon</u> [r] hast, je besser sind auch, welcher Art sie seien, deine Werke. Hafte Gott an, so hängt er dir alles Gute an. <u>Suche</u> [r] Gott, so <u>findest</u> [r] du Gott und alles Gute. Ja, in Wahrheit, du könntest in <u>solcher</u> [g] Meinung auf einen Stein treten, und es wäre heiliger getan, als wenn du, [Heidegger drew a diagonal line in green pencil here] das *Deinige* im Sinne [Heidegger drew a diagonal line in green pencil here], den Leib unseres Herrn nähmest, dein Trachten fern von ihm. Wer Gott anhaftet, dem haftet Gott an und alle Tugend. Und was vorher <u>du</u> [r] suchtest, das sucht <u>nun</u> [r] <u>dich</u> [r], und was vorher <u>du</u> [r] jagtest, das jagt nun <u>dich</u> [r], und was vorher du fliehen mochtest, das flieht nun dich. Darum, wer Gott anhaftet, dem haftet alles an, was göttlich ist, den <u>flieht</u> [r] alles, was anders ist und fremd."

§6: *"Von der Abgeschiedenheit und vom Gotthaben.* / Ich wurde gefragt: manche Leute zögen sich streng von den Menschen zurück und wären gerne allein und wären gerne in der Kirche, und daran läge ihr Friede—ob <u>das</u> [g] das Beste wäre. Da sagte ich: nein! Und wisse warum. Mit wem es recht bestellt ist, fürwahr, dem ist es an allen Orten und bei allen Leuten recht. Mit wem es aber <u>nicht</u> [g] recht steht, dem ist es <u>nicht</u> [g] recht, an <u>keinem</u> [g] Ort und bei <u>keinem</u> [g] Menschen. Mit wem es aber recht steht, der hat Gott in Wahrheit bei sich. Wer aber Gott recht so in Wahrheit hat, der hat ihn an <u>allen</u> [g] Orten und auf der Straße und bei allen Leuten geradeso wie in der Kirche oder in der Einöde oder in der Zelle. Wenn er ihn nur <u>recht</u> [g] hat und <u>ihn</u> [g] <u>allein</u> [g] hat, einen solchen Menschen kann nichts beirren. Warum? Da hat er Gott allein; wer aber in allen Dingen lauter nur Gott meint, der Mensch trägt Gott in alle seine Werke und an alle Orte. Und eines <u>solchen</u> [g] Menschen ganzes Tun wirkt schlechthin Gott; denn wer das Werk verursacht [in lead pencil, Heidegger crossed out "verur" in the word "verursachet" and wrote in the left margin: "? sachet u. im Wesen trägt"],[28] dessen ist das Werk eigentlicher und wahrhafter denn dessen, der es vollbringt. [In lead pencil, Heidegger crossed out "vollbringt" and wrote in the right margin: "<u>wirkt</u>."][29] Meinen wir nun Gott rein und allein, in Wahrheit, so muß <u>er</u> [g] unser Tun wirken, und an *seinen* Werken allen kann ihn nichts hindern, kein Ort und kein Vielerlei. So mag auch jener Mensch von nichts beirrt werden, denn er meint und sucht und läßt sich nichts genügen als nur Gott, der ja mit diesem Menschen durch seine Meinung sich einigt. Und wie Gott von keiner Mannigfaltigkeit zerstreut werden kann, so kann auch diesen Menschen nichts zerstreuen noch vermannigfaltigen, denn er ist eins in dem Einen, wo alle Mannigfaltigkeit Einheit ist und Unvermannigfaltigkeit. Der Mensch soll Gott erleben [In lead pencil, Heidegger crossed out the word *erleben* (to experience) and made a mark referring to the margin, where he wrote Eckhart's Middle High German: *nemen* (to grasp)] in allen Dingen und soll sein Gemüt gewöhnen, daß er allzeit Gott gegenwärtig habe in seinem Sinne, in Meinung und Minne. Hab acht, wie [g] du nach deinem Gotte trachtest, so du in der Kirche bist oder in der Zelle: dieses [g] selbe [g] Gemüt [g] behalte und trage es unter die Menge und in die Unruh und in eine fremde Welt. Und wie ich oft gesagt habe: wenn man nun von Gleichbleiben spricht, so ist nicht [g] gemeint, daß man alles Tun für gleich achten soll oder alle Stätten, alle Menschen. Das wäre gar unrecht: denn es ist ein besser Werk zu beten denn zu spinnen, und eine edlere Stätte die Kirche denn die Straße. Aber du sollst in deiner Arbeit das gleiche Gemüt [l] haben und die gleiche Treue [g] und den gleichen Ernst [g] zu deinem Gott. Traun, bliebest du in solcher [l] Gleichheit, so hinderte dich niemand daran, deinen Gott gegenwärtig zu haben. [Heidegger drew a diagonal line in lead pencil here.] Aber wem Gott nicht [g] so in der Wahrheit inne [g] ist [Heidegger drew a box in green pencil around "ist"], sondern fern [Heidegger drew a thick diagonal line in lead pencil in the right margin] so daß er stets Gott von draußen [l] holen [g, l; Heidegger also drew a box in lead pencil around "holen"] muß, von hier und von dort, und wer ihn in wechselnder [l] Weise sucht, an einem Tun, an Menschen oder Stätten, der hat [g] Gott nicht. Und dann kann es leicht geschehen, daß den Menschen etwas hindert, denn er hat Gott nicht inne und sucht nicht und minnt und meint nicht ihn allein. Und darum hindert ihn nicht nur böse [r, l] Gesellschaft, ihn hindert [r] auch die gute [l], und nicht allein die Straße, und nicht allein böses Wort und Werk, wahrlich auch gutes [l] Wort und Werk. Denn das Hindernis ist in [l] ihm, denn in [g] ihm sind nicht alle Dinge zu [g] Gott geworden; wäre ihm alles [r] Gott, so wäre ihm an allen [r] Orten und bei allen [r] Leuten gar recht und wohl, denn er hätte Gott inne [l], und den könnte ihm niemand rauben, wie niemand ihn in seinem Wirken hindern könnte. / Woran liegt nun dieses wahre [r, y] Gotthaben—daß man ihn wirklich [r, y] habe? [In the left margin next to the sentence "Woran liegt nun dieses wahre [r, y] Gotthaben—daß man ihn wirklich [r, y] habe?" Heidegger wrote an x in black pen. To the right of this sentence, he wrote a question mark in black pen. At the bottom of the page, also in black pen, he wrote: "i. S. v. [im Sinne von] gegenständlich Vorstellen. / diss war haben gotes, das man in warlich hab"].[30] / Dieses <u>wahre Gotthaben</u> [y] ist am <u>Gemüte</u> [g] gelegen [Heidegger drew a thick diagonal line in yellow pencil in the right margin] und an einer innigen und bewußten Hinwendung und <u>Strebung</u> [r] <u>zu</u> [r] Gott, nicht etwa an einem gleichmäßig stetigen <u>Denken</u> [g] an Gott; denn das wäre der Natur unmöglich zu erstreben und wäre auch gar schwer und nicht einmal das Allerbeste. Der Mensch soll nicht bloß einen gedachten Gott haben und es sich bei dem genug sein lassen—wenn der Gedanke vergeht, so vergeht auch der Gott. Vielmehr: man soll einen wesenhaften Gott haben, der hoch über den Gedanken der Menschen ist und aller Kreatur. Der Gott vergeht nicht, es kehre sich denn der Mensch freiwillig von ihm ab. Wer <u>Gott</u> [r] so im <u>Wesen</u> [r] <u>inne</u> [r] hat der erfaßt ihn <u>göttlich</u> [r], und dem leuchtet er in allen Dingen, denn alle Dinge kommen ihm dann göttlich vor, und aus allem auch erbildet sich ihm Gott. In ihm hat allzeit Gott die Augen offen, in ihm begibt sich eine stille Abkehr vom Äußeren und ein <u>Eindringen des gemeinten</u> [r] gegenwärtigen Gottes. [Heidegger drew a diagonal line in red pencil here, and then a horizontal line above following five words ("Geradeso, wie wenn einen hitzig dürstet"), which he then carried across the margin to the words "sich selber sind" (see below). There he drew another diagonal line in red pencil, thus demarcating this entire passage. In the left margin, he drew another diagonal line in red pencil.] Geradeso, wie wenn einen hitzig dürstet, so mit rechtem Durst; der mag wohl anderes tun als trinken und mag auch wohl anderer Dinge gedenken; aber was er auch tue oder bei wem er sei, in welchen Wünschen oder Gedanken oder welchem Tun: ihm vergeht doch das Bild des Trankes nicht, so lange der Durst währt. Und soviel größer der Durst ist, soviel mehr und inwendiger und lebhafter und dauernder ist das Bild des Trankes. Oder wer da hitzig ein Ding liebt mit ganzer Kraft, so daß ihn nichts anderes freut und ihm zu Herzen geht denn nur das Eine, so daß er dies nur will und gar nichts sonst: traun, <u>wo</u> [r] der Mensch auch ist oder bei <u>wem</u> [r], oder <u>was</u> [r] er beginnt oder vollbringt, so verlischt in ihm doch nimmer, was er <u>so</u> [r; underlined twice] liebt, und in allen Dingen findet er das Bild des Einen, und es ist ihm um so lebhafter zugegen, je mehr die Liebe tief und tiefer wird. Ein solcher Mensch sucht nicht die Ruhe auf, denn ihn beirrt ja keine Unruhe. Ein solcher Mensch ist um so mehr von Gott begnadet, als er alle Dinge göttlich[31] schätzt und höher als die Dinge an sich selber sind. [End of demarcated passage.] Freilich, dazu gehört Eifer und Hingabe und ein scharfes Achthaben auf unsere Inwendigkeit und ein wachsames, klares, begründetes Bewußtsein, wie das Gemüt sich zu stellen habe zu Sachen und Menschen. Und so etwas kann der Mensch nicht durch Fliehen lernen, indem er <u>vor</u> [r] den Dingen <u>flüchtet</u> [r] und sich in die Einsamkeit kehrt weg von der Außenheit, sondern er muß ein <u>innerliches</u> [l] Einsamsein lernen, wo oder bei wem er sei. Er muß lernen, <u>die Dinge</u> [r] zu durchbrechen, und seinen Gott *darin* ergreifen und es fertig bringen, in sich ihn wirksam herauszubilden, gerade so wie einer, der da will schreiben lernen.³² Fürwahr, soll er die Kunst verstehen, da muß er sich <u>viel</u> [r] und <u>oft</u> [r] in ihr <u>üben</u> [r], wie sauer und schwer es ihm auch werde und wie unmöglich es ihn dünke. [Heidegger drew a diagonal line in red pencil here.] <u>Will</u> [r] er nur fleißig <u>üben</u> [r] und <u>oft</u> [r], er lernt es und gewinnt die Kunst. [Heidegger drew a diagonal line in red pencil here.] Traun, zum ersten muß er an jeden Buchstaben einzeln denken und <u>den</u> [r] sich gar fest vorstellen. Darnach, wenn er die Kunst <u>inne</u> [r] hat, so wird er der Vorstellung gänzlich ledig und des Denkens an den Buchstaben, er schreibt frei und leicht dahin es seien Kleinigkeiten oder kühne [Heidegger drew a circle in red pencil in the left margin of the line beginning with "frei" and ending with "kühne"] Werke, die durch seine Kunst entstehen sollen. Ihm ist's genug, nur zu wissen, daß er jetzt seine Kunst zu üben habe. Und wenn er auch nicht stetig an sie denkt, ja was er auch denken mag, er schafft doch sein Werk durch seine Kunst. / Also soll auch der Mensch von Gottes Gegenwart leuchten ohne besondere Bemühung, vielmehr soll er die Dinge in ihrer wahren Gestalt sehen und ihrer gänzlich ledig bleiben. Da gehört vor allem ein Drandenken und ein bewußtes Einprägen dazu wie dem Schüler zu seiner Schreibkunst. Also soll der Mensch von Gottes Gegenwart durchdrungen, soll mit der Form seines geliebten Gottes durchformt³³ und in ihn eingewest sein, daß ihm seine Gegenwart leuchtet ohne alle Bemühung."

§7, p. 86: Heidegger underlined several words in red pencil in the following sentences. "Wir sollen uns alle Dinge auf eine <u>höhere</u> Art zu frommen machen, auf daß <u>sie seien</u>, was <u>wir</u> sind: was wir da sehen oder hören, wie fremd es uns sei oder wie ungleich. <u>Dann</u> erst steht es gut um uns und nicht eher. Und <u>darin</u> soll der Mensch gar nie zu Ende kommen, ohne Unterlaß soll er hierin wachsen und in einem wahren Zunehmen reicher werden."

§7, p. 87: Heidegger underlined two words in red pencil in the following sentence: "Weil nun aber der Mensch in diesem Leben nicht bestehen kann ohne Geschäftigkeit, die doch einmal des Menschen Teil ist und mannigfach von Art, darum soll der Mensch es lernen, seinen Gott zu besitzen in allem was geschieht, und unbeirrt zu bleiben bei <u>jedem</u> Werk, an <u>jedem</u> Ort."

On the front side of the final, cream-colored page, "4" is underlined, and a question mark is drawn next to it, in lead pencil in the following passage: "Im Herbst 1914 erscheint: / Deutsche Mystiker Band IV: / Johannes Tauler / Ausgewählte Predigten, / übersetzt von Prof. Dr. W. Oehl."

On the back side of the final, cream-colored page, Heidegger wrote: "Leere [emptiness] 147, 78." The relevant passage on p. 147 reads: "Noch ist ein anderes dem gleich. Kein Faß vermag zweierlei Trank in sich selber zu haben. Soll es Wein haben, man muß von Not das Wasser ausgießen—es muß leer und ledig werden. Darum: sollst du göttliche Freude empfangen, so mußt du von Not die Kreaturen ausgießen und auswerfen. / Darum spricht Sankt Augustinus: Giese aus, daß du erfüllt werdest! Verlerne die Liebe, auf daß du Liebe lernest! Kehre dich ab, auf daß du zugekehrt werdest. Kurz gesagt: Alles, was nehmen und empfänglich soll sein, das soll und muß leer sein." Cf. DW 5: 28,3–9 (BgT): "Noch ist ein anderz dem glîch: kein vaz enmac zweierleie trank in im gehaben. Sol ez wîn haben, man muoz von nôt wazzer ûzgiezen; daz vaz muoz blôz und îtel werden. Dar umbe, soltû götlîche vröude und got nemen, dû muost von nôt die crêatûren ûzgiezen. Sant Augustînus sprichet: 'giuz ûz, daz dû ervüllet werdest. Lerne niht minnen, daz dû lernest minnen. Kêre dich abe, daz dû zuo gekêret werdest.' Kürzlîche gesaget: allez, daz nemen sol und enpfenclich sîn, daz sol und muoz blôz sîn." Walshe, 534: "Another of the same kind: no vessel can hold two separate kinds of drink. If it is to contain wine, we must pour out the water; the vessel must be bare and empty. And so, if you would receive divine joy and God, you must pour away creatures. St. Augustine says, 'Pour out, that you may be filled. Learn not to love that you may learn to love. Turn away that you may be turned toward.' In short, to take in, to be receptive, a thing must be empty." The relevant passage on p. 78 reads: "Je lediger das ist, je kräftiger, würdiger, angelegentlicher, löblicher und vollkommener ist das Gebet und Werk. *Das ledige Gemüt vermag alle Dinge.* Was ist nun aber ein lediges Gemüt? Das ist ein lediges Gemüt: das mit nichts beladen ist noch bewirrt noch an etwas gebunden noch je etwann das Seinige meint, sondern ganz und gar nur in den liebsten Willen Gottes versenkt ist und den seinigen aufgegeben hat." Cf. DW 5: 190,5–12 (RdU, §2): "Ie lediger daz ist, ie daz gebet und daz werk kreftiger, wirdiger, nützer und lobelîcher und volkomener ist. Daz ledige gemüete vermac alliu dinc. / Waz ist ein ledic gemüete? / Daz ist ein ledic gemüete, daz mit nihte beworren enist noch zu nihte gebunden enist noch daz sîn bestez ze keiner wîse gebunden enhât noch des sînen niht enmeinet in deheinen dingen, dan alzemâle in dem liebesten willen gotes versunken ist und des sînen ûzgegangen ist." Walshe, 487: "The more bare it is, the more powerful, worthy, useful, praiseworthy and perfect the prayer and the work. A bare mind can do all things. What is a bare mind? / A bare mind is one which is worried by nothing and is tied to nothing, which has not bound its best part to any mode, does not seek its own in anything, that is fully immersed in God's dearest will and gone out of its own." For Heidegger's underlining, see the material reproduced from §2 of Bernhart, above.

Büttner, 1938 reprint of the one-volume edition of 1934

On the cover page Heidegger wrote his name in gray pen in Sütterlinschrift. He also wrote, in dark gray pen, "Juli [July] 1950."

P. 279: Heidegger drew an "x" in lead pencil next to the following line: "Nun ich sage: seine [Gottes] Gottheit hängt daran, daß er sich gemeinen muß"; the quote continues: "jeglichem Wesen, das für seine Güte empfänglich ist, und gemeinte er sich nicht, so wär er nicht Gott! Die Seele aber, die Gott lieben und der er sich gemeinen soll, die muß völlig entkleidet sein von Zeitlichkeit und allem Geschmack der Kreaturen, damit Gott ihr schmecke nach seinem Geschmack." "Now I say that his [God's] Godhead depends on making himself common to every being that is receptive to his goodness, and if he were not to make himself common, then he would not be God! But the soul, which is to love God and to which he is to make himself common, must be fully divested of temporality and every taste of creatures for God to taste it according to his own taste." Cf. Walshe, 371–71, and DW 3: 265,7–266,3 (Pr. 73, "Dilectus deo et hominibus"): "Und ich spriche, daz sîn gotheit hanget dar ane, daz er sich gemeinen müge allem dem, daz sîn enpfenclich ist; und engemeinete er sich niht, sô enwære er niht got. / Diu sêle, die got minnen sol und der er sich gemeinen sol, diu muoz sô gar entblœzet sîn von zîtlicheit und von allem gesmacke der crêatûren, daz got in ir smacke nâch sînem eigenen gesmacke."

P. 299: Heidegger drew an "x" in lead pencil next to the following sentences: "Und zwar wenn Gott in sich ein Wesender ist sonder Anfang, so ist er im Reich der Seele ein Wesender sonder Ende. Dermaßen, sagt ein Meister, ist Gott in der Seele, daß sein ganzes Gottsein auf ihr beruht." "And indeed if God in himself is an essencing without beginning, then in the kingdom of the soul he is an essencing without end. A master says that God is in the soul to such an extent that his entire divine being depends on it." Cf. Evans, 1, 271, and DW 4: 1103,10–11 (Pr. 117, "Ze dem êrsten suochet daz rîche gotes"): "Wan alsô als got ist in im wesenlîche sunder anvanc, alsô ist er in dem rîche der sêle wesenlîche sunder ende. / Alsô sprichet ein *meister*, daz got sî alsô in der sêle, rehte als ob alliu siniu gotheit an der sêle gelegen sî."

Inside of back cover: Heidegger wrote in lead pencil: "Becher [jar] 219." The relevant passage on that page reads: "Wär man imstande, einen Becher gänzlich zu entleeren und leer zu erhalten von allem, was füllen mag, auch von der Luft, kein Zweifel, der Becher vergäße ganz seiner Natur: die Leere trüg ihn empor bis an den Himmel. So trägt arm und leer sein aller Endlichkeit die Seele empor in Gott." "If one were in a position to empty a jar completely and to keep it empty of everything that could fill it, even of air, there is no doubt that the jar would entirely forget its nature: the emptiness would carry it up to heaven. So does being poor and empty of all finitude carry the soul up into God." Cf. Walshe, 535, and DW 5: 30,5–9 (BgT): "Möhte und künde der mensche einen becher zemâle îtel gemachen und îtel behalten von allem dem, daz vüllen mac, ouch luftes, âne zwîvel der becher verzige und vergæze aller sîner natûre, und îtelkeit trüege in ûf biz an den himel. Alsô treget blôz, arm und îtel aller crêatûren die sêle ûf ze gote."

Inside of back cover: Heidegger wrote in lead pencil: "Gottheit Gottes u. die Seele [God's Godhead and the soul] 279 / 299." See the quotes above.

Diederichs

P. 3: Heidegger wrote at the top in lead pencil: "Meister Eckhart, / Reden der Unterscheidung / hrg [herausgegeben] v. Ernst Diederichs / Bonn 1925 / anast [anastischer] Nd [Nachdruck] v. 1913."

P. 3: Heidegger drew a vertical line alongside the following sentence from Diederichs's introduction: "Die überschrift des traktats, der vor 1298 entstanden sein muss (vgl. dissertation, einleitung), findet sich noch in acht handschriften vor."

P. 3: Heidegger drew a vertical line alongside the following sentences from Diederichs's introduction: "Wie steht es nun mit der aufzeichnung der reden? Alle anzeichen sprechen dafür, dass der meister sie selbst niederge-schrieben hat, gibt"; the quote continues on p. 4: "sich doch an drei stellen der bearbeiter als mit dem redner identisch zu erkennen (9, 25; 39, 3. 20)."

P. 5: In lead pencil, Heidegger underlined the following words, and drew a circle next to them in the margin: "gehorsamy wirct alweg das aller best in allen dingen."

P. 7: Heidegger underlined the word *eygem* in lead pencil in the following sentence: "weistu es nit, oder dunckt dich es nit, nymer enstät ein unfrid in dir uff, es komme von eygem willen, man merck es oder man merck es nit."

Pp. 7–8: Although it has been erased, there are faint traces indicating that much of this section ("3. von ungelassenen lüten, die vol eigens willens sind") was underlined at one point.

P. 8: Heidegger underlined words in the following sentence in lead pencil: "(D)u solt wissen, das sich nie kein mensch so vil geliess in disem leben, er fünde sich danocht mer zelassen."

P. 8: Heidegger drew multiple vertical lines in lead pencil next to the following sentence: "die nitt von grossem wesen sind, was werck die wirckend, da wirt nit uss."

P. 10: Heidegger underlined the word *sachet* in green pencil, and drew a horizontal green line next to "dz werck eigentlicher und wårlicher, dann des, der da wircket" in the following sentence: "der mensch tregt got in allen sinen wercken und in allen stetten, und alle des menschen werck die wirckt got luterlich; wann wer das werck sachet, des ist dz werck eigentlicher und wårlicher, dann des, der da wircket das werck."

5. Summary of Eckhart's/Pseudo-Eckhart's Texts Read or Cited by Heidegger

German Works

- Prr. 5b ("In hoc apparuit"), 9 ("Quasi stella matutina"), 32 ("Consideravit semitas domus"), 52 ("Beati pauperes spiritu"), 69 ("Modicum et iam non videbitis me"), 73 ("Dilectus deo et hominibus"), 83 ("Renouamini spiritu"), 100 ("Et quaerebat videre Iesum, quis esset"), 101 ("Dum medium silentium tenerent omnia"),[34] 102 ("Ubi est, qui natus est rex Iudaeorum?"),

103 ("Cum factus esset Iesus annorum duodecim"), 104 ("In his, quae patris mei sunt, oportet me esse"), 117 ("Ze dem êrsten suochet daz rîche gotes").

- Sermons in Pfeiffer's edition not included in the critical edition: L ("Exivi a patre et veni in mundum"), LXXVII ("Faciamus hominem ad imaginem et similitudinem nostram").

- Texts translated into modern German in Büttner's edition and not included in the critical edition: "Von dem Zorne der Seele und von ihrer rechten Stätte," "Vom Schauen Gottes und von Seligkeit."

- Tractates: RdU, BgT.

- Tractates in Pfeiffer's edition not included in the critical edition:[35] I, "Von den XII nutzen unsers herren lîchames"; III, "Von der sêle werdikeit und eigenschaft"; VII, "Diu zeichen eines wârhaften grundes"; VIII, "Von der geburt des êwigen wortes in der sêle"; XI, "Von der übervart der gotheit."

- "Liber positionum" (Pfeiffer, Part IV) (not included in the critical edition).

Latin Works

- SS. II,1 ("Deus pacis et dilectionis erit vobiscum"), IV,1 ("Ex ipso, per ipsum et in ipso"), VI,1 ("Deus caritas est"), VI,2 ("In hoc apparuit gratia dei"), XXIII ("Nemo potest dicere: dominus Iesus").

- Qu. Par. 1 ("Utrum in deo sit idem esse et intelligere")

6. Reports on Heidegger's Relation to Eckhart

Hans-Georg Gadamer

In the following four passages, Gadamer recalls and reflects on the importance of Eckhart's *Opus tripartitum* for Heidegger. In a footnote to the second passage he refers to a 1924 edition of this text by Clemens Baeumker, without, however, providing any additional bibliographic information.[36] I have found no evidence to indicate that Baeumker edited portions of the *Opus tripartitum* in 1924 (the year of Baeumker's death), though he was the editor of the series *Beiträge zur Geschichte der Philosophie des Mittelalters* in 1923 when it featured an edition of Eckhart's defense at Cologne by Augustinus Daniels O.S.B. under the title *Eine lateinische Rechtfertigungsschrift des Meister Eckhart*. Baeumker only wrote a "much admired"[37] foreword for this edition and helped prepare it for publication. Much earlier (1886), an edition of related materials had appeared in the second volume of the *Archiv für Literatur und Kirchengeschichte des Mittelalters* under Heinrich Denifle's editorship, along with portions of the *Opus tripartitum*. Perhaps Gadamer is confusing these two editions, especially since both include discussions of analogy and of Eckhart's contention, mentioned by Gadamer, that *esse est deus* or "being is God." Moreover, at that time, both texts were crucial for appreciating Eckhart's scholastic activity and indeed his thought in general. At any rate, Gadamer's recollections provide additional insight into Heidegger's engagement with Eckhart during Heidegger's Marburg period.

- "Als der junge Heidegger seinen Weg suchte, vom Leben 'in und durch es hindurch' Sein zu denken, hat er eine Menge von Wegen versucht. Er hat den Neuplatonismus, wie es naheliegt, damals sehr stark ins Auge gefaßt. Er gab Vorlesungen über Augustinus, Vorlesungen über Plotin waren mindestens angekündigt, und ich habe selbst erlebt, mit welchem Enthusiasmus er 1923 die Veröffentlichung des *Opus tripartitum* von Meister Eckhart aufnahm. . . . Auf allen Wegen des frühen Heidegger stand offenkundig die Frage nach dem Wesen des Göttlichen. Von früh an meint aber 'Wesen' hier nicht die *essentia* im scholastischen Begriffssinne, sondern jenen Sinn, den Heidegger in unserem Bewußtsein zum Leben geweckt hat, demzufolge Wesen ein über jede begrenzte Gegenwart hinaus 'Anwesen' ist." "When the young Heidegger was seeking his path on which to think of being on the basis of life, 'in life, and all the way through it,' he tried a lot of paths. As one might expect, he took a hard look at Neoplatonism. He gave lecture courses on Augustine. Courses on Plotinus were at least announced. And I myself experienced the enthusiasm with which he greeted the 1923 publication of Meister Eckhart's *Opus tripartitum*. . . . Plainly, on all these paths of the early Heidegger there stood the question of the *Wesen* or nature of the divine. From early on *Wesen* no longer meant *essentia* in the sense of the Scholastic concept, but rather had that sense which Heidegger brought to life for us, and of which he made us aware, according to which *Wesen*, in exceeding any limited presence, is a presen*cing* or '*Anwesen*.'"[38]

- "Insbesondere spielte Meister Eckhart für Heidegger eine große Rolle. Damals (1924) war gerade das 'Opus tripartitum,' das lateinische Hauptwerk von Meister Eckhart,—neu ediert worden. Heidegger war ganz fasziniert davon, offenbar weil die Auflösung des Substanzbegriffes in der Anwendung auf Gott in die Richtung eines zeitlichen und verbalen Sinnes von Sein wies, wenn es da hieß: 'Esse est Deus.' Damals mag Heidegger in dem christlichen Mystiker einen geheimen Verbündeten geahnt haben."[39] "Meister Eckhart played a particularly great role for Heidegger. At that time (1924), the *Opus tripartitum*, Meister Eckhart's Latin magnum opus, had just been reedited. Heidegger was completely fascinated by it, evidently because the dissolution of the concept of substance in regards to God pointed in the direction of a temporal and verbal sense of being, when it was said that: 'Esse est Deus.' At that time, Heidegger may have suspected a secret ally in the Christian mystic."

- "Auch der junge Heidegger begann damals [d.h. in den frühen zwanziger Jahren]—es lag überhaupt in der Luft—, sich an Meister Eckhart zu orientieren, um die Frage nach dem 'Sein' stellen zu lernen, wo er im 'Opus tripartitum,' das 1924 herauskam, las: 'Deus est suum esse.'"[40] "Even the young Heidegger began at that time [i.e., in the early 1920s]—it simply was in the air—to orient himself toward Meister Eckhart, in order to learn to pose the question about 'being,' when in the 'Opus tripartitum,' which had come out in 1924, he read: 'Deus est suum esse.'"

- "Seine Interpretation der Phronesis als eines *allo eidos gnōseōs*, einer anderen Weise des Wissens, war geradezu eine Art von

Bestätigung für seine theoretischen und existenziellen Interessen. Das sprang auch auf die theoretische Philosophie, auf die Metaphysik über, sofern Heidegger in diesen Jahren [d.h. in den frühen zwanziger Jahren] in einer freilich noch nicht adäquat selbstbewußten Weise die 'berühmte Analogie,' wie er zu sagen pflegte, im Auge hatte. Das war das Element innerhalb der Aristotelischen Metaphysik, von dem aus er die systematische Ableitung aller Geltung aus einem Prinzip, dem transzendentalen Ego Husserls oder der Idee des Guten Platos, in gleicher Weise in Frage stellen konnte. Aus dem gleichen Interesse mußte ihn 1923 die Veröffentlichung des Opus tripartitum von Meister Eckhart begeistern." "His interpretation of *phronēsis* as *allo eidos gnōseōs,* another type of knowing, was actually a sort of confirmation of his own theoretical and existentiell interests. This extended to theoretical philosophy and metaphysics as well, inasmuch as Heidegger already had the 'famous analogy,' as he often called it, in view—although in those years [i.e., in the early 1920s] it was not yet thought out in a sufficiently self-conscious way. This was the basis within Aristotelian metaphysics from which Heidegger was able to put into question in a like manner the systematic derivation of all value from any one principle, be it Husserl's transcendental ego or Plato's idea of the Good. Because of this interest, the publication of the *Opus tripartitum* by Meister Eckhart in 1923 must have been an inspiration to him."[41]

Jean Guitton

In an article published in 1958, Guitton describes some of the books he saw during a visit to Heidegger's home: "La mystique est surtout présente sous la forme d'une vieille édition de Maître Eckhart, le théologien mystique, qui est là comme livre de chevet, dans une très vieille édition."[42] "Mysticism is present above all in the form of an old edition of Meister Eckhart, the mystical theologian, which is there as a bedside book in a very old edition."

Heinrich Heidegger

In a 2010 interview with Pierfrancesco Stagi, Heidegger's nephew Heinrich Heidegger reports: "In der heutigen Theologie taucht immer mehr das

Mystische auf, jene Erfahrungen, dass man in Gott eintauchen kann, ohne ein Wort darüber zu finden. Wie oft hat Martin Heidegger auf Meister Eckehart verwiesen."[43] "In contemporary theology the mystical comes to the surface more and more, those experiences of plunging into God without being able to find a single word for it. How often did Martin Heidegger make reference to Meister Eckehart!" Although Heinrich's comment could be taken to refer to his uncle's published writings, the personal nature of the interview seems to suggest that he had heard this from Heidegger himself.

Elisabeth Feist Hirsch

In a typescript containing recollections of her time studying under Heidegger in Marburg, Elisabeth Feist Hirsch writes, "Despite his Catholic upbringing, Heidegger's religious interests soon focused on Augustine, Eckhart, Luther and Kierkegaard. All of these theologians had experienced severe existential crises. . . . I do not know what Heidegger thought of the religious philosopher Rudolf Otto who was in Marburg at the time. In 1917 Otto had published the book The Holy which brought him immediate fame. Heidegger had read it. . . . Otto was like Heidegger a great admirer of Eckhart."[44]

Ōhashi Ryōsuke

Ōhashi Ryōsuke relays the following incident involving Nishitani Keiji and Heidegger: "Nishitani war 1938/39 zu einem Forschungsaufenthalt in Freiburg i. Br. . . . Nishitani legte bei Heidegger ein Referat über Nietzsche und Meister Eckhart vor, das nach seiner Rückkehr [nach Japan] unter dem Titel *Nietzsches Zarathustra und Meister Eckhart* [auf Japanisch] veröffentlicht wurde. Die Zusammenstellung von Nietzsche und Eckhart mußte damals etwas merkwürdig erschienen sein, aber Heidegger hielt, wie der Verfasser von Nishitani persönlich hörte, diese Zusammenstellung für sinnvoll. In diesem Aufsatz zeigt sich der Problemzusammenhang, in dem für Nishitani das Denken Heideggers steht: der europäische Nihilismus und die deutsche Mystik, noch bestimmter: das 'Nichts.' "[45] "Nishitani was in Freiburg i. Br. in 1938/39[46] for a research stay. . . . He presented a paper, in one of Heidegger's classes, on Nietzsche and Meister Eckhart, which, after his return [to Japan] was published [in Japanese] under the title 'Nietzsche's Zarathustra and Meister Eckhart.'[47] At that time, it must have appeared somewhat strange to bring Nietzsche and Eckhart together, although, as the author heard personally from Nishitani, Heidegger regarded it as sensible. In this essay, the context of problems in which, for Nishitani, Heidegger's thought stands becomes manifest: European nihilism and German mysticism, more precisely: the 'Nothing.' " Nishitani's 1938 essay is translated in Appendix Three, below.

Käte Oltmanns

In what Heidegger called her "excellent [*ausgezeichnet*]" dissertation on Meister Eckhart (MH/ER, 223–24), which was begun in Winter Semester 1927–28 on Heidegger's recommendation, submitted under Heidegger's directorship in 1934, and then published with Heidegger's approval in 1935, Oltmanns writes: "Diese Arbeit verdankt ihre Entstehung einer Anregung durch Herrn Professor Heidegger. Wieviel sie im ganzen der Philosophie Heideggers schuldet, kann jeder ermessen, der sich mit dieser beschäftigt hat; sie bildet so sehr die Voraussetzung dieser Arbeit, daß es nicht möglich war, im einzelnen auf Beziehungen hinzuweisen."[48] "This work owes its existence to a suggestion by Professor Heidegger. Anyone who has engaged with Heidegger's philosophy can appreciate how much this work as a whole is indebted to it; it forms the background of this work to such an extent that it was not possible to point out connections in particular instances."

Reiner Schürmann

On January 16, 1966, Schürmann sent Heidegger a letter, explaining that he was conducting doctoral research on the "unknown God in the thought of Meister Eckhart." He requested a meeting and posed two questions to Heidegger: "The first one concerns Eckhart's relevance to the situation in which thinking finds itself today: did he perhaps think being as self-sending, as only eventfully experienceable? Meister Eckhart's 'sole thought' is aimed at the unification of the 'separated soul' with God. Insofar as the soul lets all things be, it breaks through to the ground where the Godhead continually creates all things, and which in this breakthrough also becomes my ground. The unity is a unity of the 'fabric' in which God operates and I become— become son, that is. Being is thus thought as course of experience, and not represented as ontic 'standing reserve.' Closer to the soul than any created thing, the 'unknown God' is experienced in the event of words, beyond this and that, and for that reason, it always remains a 'nil of all things.' Might not Meister Eckhart's thinking help us along in a meditation directed at being which always withholds itself and, in this very withholding, addresses itself to us?"[49] After meeting with Heidegger on March 11, 1966, to discuss this and other issues, Schürmann wrote down his recollection of their conversation in the form of a letter that was never sent. Regarding Eckhart, Schürmann noted only that "Je ne vous dis pas ce qu'il a dit de Maître Eckhart et aussi de la scolastique, ce serait trop long." "I am not going to tell you what he said about Meister Eckhart and about scholasticism, for it would take too long."[50] Fortunately, in later publications, Schürmann relates what Heidegger said about Eckhart in this meeting (or perhaps others):[51] "Heidegger cite quelquefois Maître Eckhart, et en 1966 il nous confia avoir beaucoup lu ses sermons allemands lorsqu'il réfléchissait lui-même à l'être comme *Anwesen*."[52] "Heidegger sometimes cites Meister Eckhart, and in 1966, he confided to us that he often read his German sermons when he was himself reflecting on being as *Anwesen*." In Schürmann's own modified translation: "Heidegger sometimes quotes from Meister Eckhart, and we learned personally from him that he developed his understanding of being as *An-wesen* (a verb, not a noun) in the years in which he also read Meister Eckhart's sermons."[53]

Barbara von Wulffen

In a September 14, 2006, interview available on DVD in the Martin-Heidegger-Archiv der Stadt Meßkirch, Barbara von Wulffen (born 1936) recalls that Heidegger and her mother, Sophie Dorothee von Podewils (1909–1979), would read Eckhart together. Presumably she is referring to the 1950s, perhaps later.

Bernhard Welte

Welte recounts a conversation he had with Heidegger in mid-January 1976, four months prior to Heidegger's death: "Wir sprachen auch über die Vorlesung, die ich damals hielt, es war eine Vorlesung über Meister Eckhart, und so wieder ein religiöser Kontext. Mit Meister Eckhart war Heidegger auch seit langem vertraut. So fragte er im Laufe jenes Gespräches mit einer bedächtigen und ihres Weges sicheren Frage nach der Abgeschiedenheit im Sinne des Meister Eckhart. Das Thema hatte eine verborgene Aktualität in dieser merkwürdigen Stunde. Es schwebte auch der eckhartische Gedanke im Raum, daß Gott dem Nichts gleich sei. Diese eckhartischen Gedanken waren nun in den Zusammenhang des Heimatlichen der Heimat und auch in den Zusammenhang der Nähe des Todes gerückt, so bildete die Stunde den Bereich, in dem auf eine besondere Art Himmel und Erde zusammengehörten, Sterbliche und Unsterbliche. Das Gesammelte des Gevierts lebte in der abendlichen Stunde und war versammelt um den, dem der Tod schon winkte."[54] "We also spoke about a lecture course that I was holding at the time; it was a lecture course on Meister Eckhart, and thus a religious context again. Heidegger was long aquainted with Meister Eckhart. During the course of our conversation, he thus asked about *Abgeschiedenheit* [detachment, departedness] in Meister Eckhart's sense, posing a question that was at once careful and certain of its path. The theme had a concealed currency in this remarkable hour. The Eckhartian thought that God is like the nothing also hovered in the room. These Eckhartian thoughts were now brought into connection with the homelike character of the homeland and also into connection with the nearness of death; thus the hour formed the realm in which, in a special way, heaven and earth, mortals and immortals, belonged together. The gathering of the fourfold lived in that evening hour and was gathered around him whom death was already beckoning."

7. Heidegger's Evaluation of Käte Oltmanns's Dissertation on Eckhart

On January 29, 1934, Heidegger wrote the following evaluation of Käte Oltmanns's dissertation, for which he served as the director. I first reproduce the German typescript, which Heidegger signed and dated, as found in Oltmanns's file at the Universitätsarchiv Freiburg (B42/2457). Then I provide a translation.

Käte Oltmanns "Die Philosophie des Meisters Ekkehart"

Die vorliegende Arbeit ist aus einem Referat hervorgegangen, das die Verfasserin in meinen Marburger Übungen (Wintersemester 1927/28) über die Lehre des Meisters Ekkehart von der menschlichen Freiheit gehalten hat. Die überlegene Sicherheit, mit der die bisherigen Standorte und Richtungen der philosophischen Auslegungen des Meisters Ekkehart herausgestellt und grundsätzlich überwunden sind, konnte nur aus einem langjährigen Durchdenken und der wiederholten Überprüfung der Grundfragestellungen erwachsen.

Die bisherigen unter sich gegensätzlichen Auffassungen der Ekkehartschen Lehre entsprangen daraus, dass sie den Kern der Ekkehartschen Auffassungen vom Wesen des Seins verkannten, das in sich "dialektisch" ist. Die Vf. gebraucht diese überlieferte Kennzeichnung, um darzutun, dass die gegensätzlichen Bestimmungen, die Ekkehart dem Wesen Gottes, dem Wesen der Welt und dem Wesen des Menschen zuspricht, beide wahr und unwahr sind, jenachdem man sie in einer höheren Wesenseinheit zusammendenkt oder aber vereinzelt in gegenseitiger Ausschliesslichkeit ansetzt. Aber dieses "dialektische" Wesen des Seins kann erst begriffen werden, wenn klar erkannt ist, dass die ontologischen Grundbegriffe und bildlichen Umschreibungen von Seinsverhältnissen (Licht, Feuer, Bild) nicht dinghaft verstanden werden dürfen, dass vielmehr bei Ekkehart im Rahmen des mittelalterlichen Begriffs- und Sprachgebrauchs eine völlig neue Art des Fragens und Denkens durchbricht, die wir heute die existentielle nennen. In der klaren und folgerichtigen und eindringlichen Herausstellung des existentialen[55] Bedeutungsgehalts der Ekkehartschen Grundbegriffe besteht die Hauptleistung der Arbeit. Das sehr weit vorgetriebene Verständnis der Ekkehartschen Philosophie ermöglicht es, der genannten Arbeit einen sachgemässen und durchsichtigen Aufbau zu geben. Schliesslich muss angemerkt werden, dass die Sachinterpretation, deren Ergebnis ich für unanfechtbar halte, ganz neue innere Kennzeichen bereitstellt, um in der Frage der Echtheit oder Unechtheit des unter dem Namen des Meisters Ekkehart überlieferten Schrifttums eine ebenso besonnene wie entschiedene Stellungnahme vorzubereiten.

Die Arbeit ist im Ganzen eine ungewöhnliche und hervorragende Leistung.

Freiburg i. B. d. 29.I.34.

Heidegger

Käte Oltmanns "The Philosophy of Meister Ekkehart"

The present work arose from a presentation that the author gave on Meister Ekkehart's doctrine of human freedom in my Marburg tutorials (Winter Semester 1927/28).[56] The outstanding self-assurance with which the positions and directions of philosophical interpretations of Meister Ekkehart up to now are laid out and fundamentally overcome could only stem from many years of thinking through, and repeatedly examining, the fundamental issues.

The hitherto opposing conceptions of Ekkehart's doctrine emerged from a failure to recognize the core of Ekkehart's conceptions of the essence of being, which is, in itself, "dialectical." The author uses this traditional label to demonstrate that the opposing determinations Ekkehart makes of the essence of God, the essence of the world, and the essence of the human are both true and untrue, according to whether one thinks them together in a higher essential unity or individually in mutual exclusivity. But this "dialectical" essence of being can only first be grasped when one clearly recognizes that the fundamental ontological concepts and the imagistic paraphrases of the ontological relations (light, fire, image) ought not to be understood in terms of things; rather, in Ekkehart, a fully new way of questioning and thinking, which we today call existentiell, breaks through the framework of the conceptual and linguistic usage of the Middle Ages. The chief accomplishment of the work lies in laying out the existential[57] meaning of Ekkehart's basic concepts in a clear and consistent and penetrating manner. Advancing our understanding of Ekkehart's philosophy greatly, the author is able to give the mentioned work an appropriate and transparent structure. Finally it must be remarked that the objective interpretation, whose result I find to be indisputable, furnishes entirely new internal characteristics for preparing a response that is as sober as it is firm to the question concerning the authenticity or inauthenticity of the writings transmitted under the name Meister Ekkehart.

As a whole, the work is an uncommon and outstanding accomplishment.

Freiburg im Breisgau, January 29, 1934.

Heidegger

8. Heidegger's Notes on Käte Oltmanns's Oral Examination

On February 28, 1934, Käte Oltmanns's oral examination was held. All three referees (Heidegger for the major subject of philosophy, Walther Kolbe and Hermann Heimpel for the minor subjects of ancient and medieval history) awarded her the top grade ("I. Prädikat"), resulting in an overall grade of *summa cum laude*. Here I have transcribed Heidegger's notes from the examination, which can be found in Oltmanns's file at the Universitätsarchiv Freiburg (B42/2457). A translation follows.

> Die Kandidatin hat in ihrer Dissertation die Auslegung des Meisters Eckart unter dem Leitgedanken der "Dialektik" gestellt, ohne diesen Begriff selbst näher zu begründen. Frage: Ursprung u. Geschichte der "Dialektik" in den verschiedenen Stadien: Sophistik, Plato, Aristoteles, Schullogik—Kant. Die Durchführung dieses Nachweises im Zusammenhang mit Auslegungen (Plato, Parmenides, Sophistes; Aristoteles Met. Γ.[)] Erörterungen über Ursprung u. Sinn der abendländischen Logik u. deren Macht über die Entwicklungsgeschichte der Metaphysik: Kants Kritik der r. Vernunft im Lichte dieser Frage. Systematische Probleme der Ontologie; Unmöglichkeit der "Erkenntnistheorie."—Aufgrund des langjährigen Studiums u. der Teilnahme an den Übungen in selbstständigen Arbeiten zeigt die K. eine sichere u. ursprüngliche—nicht angelernte Beherrschung der Fragen. Eine gewisse Schwerfälligkeit aufgrund der Examenssituation ist für die Beurteilung unwesentlich.

> In her dissertation, the candidate placed her interpretation of Meister Eckart under the guiding idea of "dialectics," without justifying this concept itself more closely. Question: origin and history of "dialectics" in its various stages: Sophism, Plato, Aristotle, Scholastic logic—Kant. Carrying out this demonstration in connection with interpretations (Plato, *Parmenides, Sophist*; Aristotle *Metaphysics* Γ.[)] Discussions of the origin and sense of Western logic and its power over the history of the development of metaphysics: Kant's *Critique of Pure Reason* in light of this question. Systematic problems of ontology; impossibility of "epistemology."—On the basis of many years of study and participation in tutorials, the candidate shows, in her independent works, a confident and original—untaught mastery of the questions. A certain clumsiness owing to the situation of the examination is unessential for the evaluation.

Appendix Two

"Essentiality, Existence, and Ground in Meister Eckehart," by Käte Oltmanns

Here I offer the first English translation of Oltmanns's "Wesenheit, Dasein und Grund bei Meister Eckehart,"[1] which she presented on January 28, 1928, in Heidegger's seminar on Schelling's Philosophical Investigations into the Essence of Human Freedom. *See §3 of chapter 1, above, for discussion. All endnotes are mine.*

An investigation of philosophical concepts in Meister Eckehart is burdened with a unique difficulty, since the terminology in Eckehart's German writings, from which his concepts are in large part to be extrapolated, is not settled, but rather can be traced back mostly to non-univocal translations of Latin terms. It was believed that, by consulting his Latin writings, one could attain a surer guideline, yet even here there is such an elemental and independent force of philosophical questioning, for which the rigorous terminology of Scholasticism is no match, that, according to this measure, the same conceptual confusion predominates in the Latin writings too. On the other hand, it inures to the benefit of the German writings that, here, he not only translates, but creates freely from out of the language itself.

In Eckehart, the *problem of ground* [*Grund*] initially appears when he is determining the *being* [*Sein*] *of God*. A distinction is drawn in God between the Godhead and the Trinity or the Persons: Father, Son, and Holy Spirit. The Godhead is the ground in God or his essence, and this ground is, in and of itself, untouched by any acting and creating, as the abyss [*Abgrund*] and the stillness; everything comes from it and into it everything goes back. No individual determination is to be made of the Godhead, not even that it *is*, for it is everything at the same time, undistinguished and in unity; it lies before any severing of essence and existence or *actus* and *potentia*. The

Persons distinguish themselves from the Godhead by acting; indeed their initial function is to reveal the intrinsically unrevealed Godhead. Insofar as God knows himself, the Word or Son emerges, and God thus becomes the Father; they are not separate from one another, but remain in one another like the gleam in the light, and the love between them both is the Holy Spirit. However, as active, the three Persons are not to be opposed to the Godhead as *existentia* to *essentia*, but have all their capacity, as well as their existence, from the ground. The Trinity only *is* as long as something created *is*, for God as Trinity is at the same time the creator, and only as the creator is he to be marked off in his being from the Godhead. God only *is* as long as the world *is*; yet when there are no longer any creatures, Father, Son, and Holy Spirit go back into the ground of the Godhead, in which they are one. Insofar as God gazes upon himself, he sees in himself the *rationes ideales*, the images of all things. As God sees them, they are uncreatable, that is, existing in themselves in unity, and in view of them creatures are created out of nothing. What creatures have as *creatures*, as separated and existing for themselves, namely, their existence, is thus only nonbeing; they are, in themselves, nothing, and have all their being only insofar as they are in the One and from the ground; their being depends on the presence of God. From here it must therefore be said that *esse* in the authentic sense belongs only to God as ground, and indeed the ground is not only uncreated, but remains entirely for itself and untouched by everything qua created and present-at-hand. That means, however, that at this point Eckehart decisively moves beyond the approach of antiquity and Christianity according to which being = being-present-at-hand = being-created or being-produced, where an *analogia attributionis* can be posited between the being of God and the being of creatures as between the being of the uncreated creator and the being of the created that is derived from it. Inasmuch as the being of the Godhead, as ground-being [*Grundsein*], is disengaged from every connection with being as created-being, the meaning of "being" in both cases is only lexically identical: if God is, then the creature is nothing. The obscure problem of analogy (not only in Thomas!) is thus here radically decided in favor of *aequivocatio*, only shortly after Duns Scotus had aligned himself on the side of *univocatio* owing to the need to secure the knowability and provability of God. Eckehart does not pose the question as to how far the concept of being is to be stretched in order for it to be able to encompass all beings.

Eckehart makes the same radical attempt to move beyond the traditional interpretation of the being of God in a few of the early Parisian Questions, which deal with the question of the *relation between <u>esse</u> and <u>intelligere</u>*. Here he takes as his point of departure the following sentence from the *Liber de causis*: "Prima rerum creatarum est esse."[2] At issue for us is not whether he understands this sentence correctly in the sense of the *Liber de causis*, but rather only what consequences he draws from it for himself. He continues, namely: "Unde statim cum venimus ad eum (sc. Esse),[3] venimus ad creaturam.—Ideo Deus, qui est creator et non creabilis, est intellectus et intelligere et non ens vel esse."[4] Thus, here it is clearly seen that the traditional concept of being = being-created, being-produced—Eckehart says explicitly: "est de ratione entis, quod sit causatum"![5]—is not applicable to God; with *intelligere*, the approach is made to a concept of being that is not oriented to what is present-at-hand, just as is the case, later, with ground-being. It is the same thought when Eckehart says '*Deus est esse*,[6] the creature is nothing,' and when he says '*Deus est eius intelligere et non est ens, esse = esse creatum*';[7] only, the word *esse* designates, in the one case, the way of being of God and, in the other, that of the creature, although he himself says: "Si tu intelligere velis vocare esse, placet mihi. Dico nihilominus, quod si in Deo est aliquid, quod velis vocare esse, sibi competit per intelligere."[8] *Intelligere* thus does not belong to God because he *is*, but rather he *is* because he thinks; the principle in God is not the *ens* but rather the *Verbum*, as per John 1:1.[9] Likewise, the *esse formale* of creatures only is because God thinks it: *Deus per intellectum producit res in esse*.[10]

The problem becomes so complicated in Eckehart because *the soul* is always also connected with the being of God. On a superficial level, his psychology agrees in essence with Scholasticism. He distinguishes three supreme powers of the soul—memory, reason, and will—and he compares these with the Trinity: they are, as powers, united in their essence, but distinct in their activity, even though they remain in one another; memory provides the images that reason thinks, and the will loves what reason knows. The soul, however, in this sense is not only a *likeness* of the Trinity; it is also an *image* of God and created in its essence like God. That is to say, memory not only has in itself the images of things that have entered in through the senses, but has in its ground an image that comprises all images in a unity, and that image is the image of God. Yet as long as this image is covered over with the images of the creature, it is not *actually* in the soul, that is to say, the human being is not like God by nature, but only comes to be like God by grace; he is like God, not *actu*, but only *potentia*.[11] If, however, the human being turns away from external things and directs himself solely to his own essence, the Son comes to be born in the ground of the soul, that is, in memory, in the little spark of the soul, in the conscience; the soul comes to be like God, indeed it goes even further, from likeness with God into the unity of the one ground, where understanding and will are extinguished and even the Persons cannot reach. The soul and the Godhead are thus, in their ground, one and unseparated, and therefore the ground of the soul is uncreatable and untouched by any creature.

That Eckehart speaks of an *uncreated ground of the soul* can be proved beyond doubt from his writings, and when, in other passages, he speaks of the createdness of the ground of the soul and of the spark, it is necessary to see that he makes both statements in entirely different dimensions. It is not a part or a power of the soul that is uncreated, nor, therefore, memory and the spark as a power, but rather the ground, which lies before all active powers and, as the authentic essence of the soul, is free of all individual present-at-hand creatures. Ground-being is thus in Eckehart's anthropology as in his theology the concept with which he attempts to overcome the conception of being = being-caused and being-present-at-hand. He sees clearly that being-caused does not, in the ultimate ground, comprise the being of the human, just as causing cannot be constitutive for the being of God. It is from this point that Eckehart's entire philosophical work is to be understood.

Connections to Schelling's doctrine of freedom emerge readily from Eckehart's doctrine of the ground. In the structure of the system, the ground in Eckehart corresponds to the return to the unground in Schelling, which precedes the severing of existence and the ground of existence, and which is neither the one nor the other nor in both equally. For, what Schelling calls the ground in the human being would in Eckehart correspond roughly to memory, although not completely; for memory as a power belongs again on the side of existence. Memory is ground insofar as there is a peculiar dimensional stretching in it, according to which it offers to the powers, that is, to the existing, something that precedes them, preserving something earlier for the present, just as, for Schelling, in God the ground of his existence precedes him as existing and yet also could not be as such if God did not exist *actu*.[12]

Appendix Three

"Nietzsche's Zarathustra and Meister Eckhart," by Nishitani Keiji

TRANSLATED FROM THE JAPANESE
BY S. P. K. CERDA AND HIROSHI ABÉ

Translated into English here for the first time is Nishitani's 1938 essay on Nietzsche's Zarathustra and Meister Eckhart, which Nishitani first gave as a presentation in one of Heidegger's classes. See §4 of chapter 1, above, for discussion. All of the endnotes come from the translators.

1. Nietzsche and the Elemental Nature of Living

After speaking to the sun on the mountaintop at dawn, Zarathustra went down toward the town of human beings. On the way, he encountered none but an old saint, who lived hidden away in the woods at the base of the mountain where he gave praise to God. After parting with the saint, Zarathustra turned to his heart and spoke. "Could it be possible! This old saint in his woods has not yet heard the news that God is dead!"[1] Saying this, he went down to the town. This opening section intimates the basic disposition[2] from which the entirety of *Zarathustra* is developed. Zarathustra had once passed through these woods before. At that time, he was a person dead to the human world. The saint says, "many years ago he passed by here. . . . Back then, you carried your ashes to the mountain."[3] Yet, during the ten years on the mountain top where "he enjoyed his spirit and his solitude,"[4] Zarathustra was reborn. His ashes transfigured[5] into overflowing life.⁶ This life drove Zarathustra's going under toward the world of human beings. The woods are found at the beginning of the mountain, which towers over the world of human beings. There, the saint lives like "a bear among bears, a bird among birds." "I make songs and sing them, and when I make songs I laugh, weep, and growl: thus I praise God. / With singing, weeping, and growling I praise the god who is my god."⁷ Rising above the human being, the saint finds himself with God. He is carried in the bosom of God, like an innocent little child. Taking one step within the inner recesses of human life, we find an innocence where good and evil have yet to branch off, where malice has yet to sprout. There human life has its origin, but in a blink it becomes caught up in a world brimming with malice, a world of surging pandemonium. Only a young child could remind us of this origin. And not until one makes oneself childlike can one enter heaven. The old saint became childlike once again; that is to say, he became a saint. The state of the saint is where the human being returns home to its innate natural nature. Although the human being is a natural entity, birthed by nature like any stone, grass, or beast, it becomes intoxicated by the ferment brewed by interhuman relations, by "society," and forgets that it was churned up from the earth. By wrapping itself in clothes, it forgets the infinite depths lying at the bottom of its naked self; by surrounding itself with four walls, it forgets that endless heavens envelop it, and envelop even its sheltering roof. They are perhaps a rarity—those who could, from the bit of fish on their plate, envisage its swimming figure in the Kuroshio Current. Indeed, rarer still are those who feel, directly beneath them, that life runs in common through the fish and themselves. Though I make no claims to be the author of *Sartor Resartus*,⁸ I would say that all disaster and evil began by wrapping the body in clothes. Clothing beckons the need for a mirror. Since the time early humans painted their faces in clay and saw themselves mirrored in reflecting waters, the human being lost an immediate feeling of itself, and obtained the now deep-rooted habit of grasping itself within the reflective eyes of others. The mirror is the universal eye of the other. How one is seen or heard has taken the place of natural "being" as the self's *Existenz*. "Being" seen trespasses into the deepest layers of the soul, and the soul's natural "being" has become wrapped up in "being" seen just as the body is wrapped in clothes. The human being grasps within itself a self imagined without the real self. With the countless threads spun out from this specious *Existenz*, human beings tie themselves up with each other and form a society divorced from nature. In this separate-world, they forget themselves within the imagined self and give special treatment to the pretentious ("*eingebildet*") self as a rational entity. Reason is divorced from its natural nature, but in rising above the all-too-human "town," one can return it to its elemental source where it becomes a great manifestation of natural life on par with animal instinct. Here, reason is simultaneously brought down and raised up. This bringing down and raising up negates the *superbia* (arrogant loftiness) of reason and causes it to merge with the depths of life. Lofty reason is not real, but a mere *Bild* (imagined figure) subordinate to the imagination. But here it is liberated from the imagination and brought home to its reality as something originating from the infinite depths of great life, as something that sprouted from the earth. Here rational activity becomes a way of living on par with the singing of birds and the growling of bears, and, at the same time, it goes to the bottom of nature and becomes a gently undulating wave on the surface of the sea of bottomless and divine life. There is an infinite fullness of life to be had even in weeping and laughing. These too are a praising of God. When we die to the human, all-too-human world and return to its inner recesses in nature, we find the saintly state. There, even a crowded line of tall buildings stands equal with a row of trees, and conversing humans are the equals of singing birds. The person whom Zarathustra thus encountered was a saint who had risen out of the town and made his home in these woods.

Nevertheless, the woods are found only on the way. Even here, the form of Hegel's dispassionate logic finds its application. A negation must be further negated. Yet this is a necessity belonging to life before it belongs to logic. It is an urgency that seeps up from the bottom depths of life. The saint was able to unite with the life of God in the great natural world by dying to his life in the human world. Seen from this rebirth, living in the human world probably looks like a dying. Nevertheless, no matter how lofty a life his rebirth may attain, it would still be one that places its wellspring before itself. It is a living that places God before itself, and thereby remains two with God. To rest within God is to be apart from God. This is not to say that the saint has taken that *other* path to God, that of listening for God's graceful word in the midst of a deep self-awareness of one's own sinfulness. Thus, the wicked trail lurking on that path, that *Koketterie* or "humble loftiness" that intentionally rips itself even farther from God for the purpose of trying to pay for divine mercy with its needless sins, is something quite foreign to the saint. Yet, he still remains two with divine life, and to the extent that he sees God as his object, divine life has not yet truly made itself present to him as life. Seeing one's life as one's object is actually the dying of one's life. Therefore, because it is a oneness of two with divine life, even the saint's reclaimed life is still a living of dying. Likewise, because he stands before God, he turns his back on human beings. For him, human living is a dying. Because his life submerges into that of God, he has lost the path to human living. Inasmuch as the state of the saint is one of a higher living, it turns out to be a state belonging to the death of God, the death of the self, and the death of the human being. By draping himself in death toward both God and human, his living itself is a dying. This is what it means to live in the woods lying on the way between the human town and the mountain. The saint hidden away in these woods, then, is unaware that latent within his higher living lies a state of thoroughgoing death. Zarathustra did not lay his ashes to rest in the woods, but instead had to pass by the woods and, on the mountain peak, await a higher transfiguration, the negation of his life's negation. As is well known, Plotinus once saw the intelligible world to be higher than the sensible, and taught that when a soul transcends the sensible world, it unites with God. Furthermore, while it is often believed that the soul finds its peace in this basic disposition, Plotinus explains that it still includes a view of God as one's object, it is still a oneness of two, and so one must ascend beyond it toward a still higher, purer oneness. He expressed such a oneness variously as *ekstasis,* awakening, or that which is good itself, yet cannot be called good; it is the far side of good and evil, the yonder side of thought and existence; he called this will, or life. Does the figure of Zarathustra leaving the woods and seeking the mountain peak not remind us of a soul ascending the stages of Plotinus's *Hypostasen*?

"Zarathustra is transformed [*henshin*], Zarathustra has become a child, an awakened one is Zarathustra," proclaims the saint.[9] What does this transfiguration mean? Zarathustra turns to the sun and speaks. "Bless the cup that wants to flow over, such that water flows golden from it and everywhere carries the reflection of your bliss!"[10] His transfiguration is a transfiguration toward overflowing will. Instead of *the self* being filled by great life, as with the saint, *great life* fills the self. When the self is filled, the shape of the self still remains. The self is still an *eidos*. Here, the water of life merely fills the space of the cup. But when great life fills the self, the water of life breaks through the shape of the cup and overflows. Any *eidos* that remains, even if the self were to become empty, is rejected from within. The self is no longer something "substantial." Neither is it the fixed center of conscious activity. It can take on infinite *eidē* without ever becoming fixed. "Does he not stride like a dancer?"[11] asks the saint. Indeed, within Zarathustra's own teaching, it is often said one must learn to dance. Rather than fixating on some particular *eidos,* he instructs us to transition to the life of a dancing current wherein infinite *eidē* interfuse. In overflowing will—and even here we may find a trace of what Plotinus called the "ecstatic soul" or the "will of the emanating One"—the saint's resignation to God has vanished as well. Instead of a unity of two wills, all that remains is one will, Zarathustra's will, which has rejected the *eidos* of the self. While the lofty life of the saint still contained a deep dying, in this one will, a life becomes a life truly lived; it becomes creative living. Just as the water flows golden down over the cup, this life, then, must go under. Creating must necessarily become a going under (*Untergang*). The water has filled the cup to its breaking point. Zarathustra grew weary of the fullness of his wisdom. A fruit born at the top of a tree is most separated from the earth, but in becoming good and ripe, it must free itself from the encompassing life in the tree, the life that has, until now, nurtured, constrained, and driven it; it must fall and return itself to the earth.[12] By the same necessity of life, Zarathustra descends the mountain toward the town to join human living. Zarathustra himself says, "This cup wants to become empty again, and Zarathustra wants to become human again."[13] It is said that God's Word became flesh through love, but in the same way we could say that it was from love that Zarathustra, transfigured on the lonely peak overlooking the "holy" woods, turned to the human realm and went under. When a life reaches its peak and becomes truly creative, it cultivates a will to *Untergang* (to going under or to falling).[14] To become truly creative is to become truly capable of falling. Bearing fruit is the pinnacle of life in a tree, and yet the tree performs its most creative act at the moment its fruit breaks off and falls to the earth. All true creating is completed in true falling, and true falling can only be attained by a truly creative living. That is the final leap of creating, a progression one step beyond one's peak. This is why a life's absolute negation of itself is at the same time its absolute affirmation. Only here can what we earlier called thoroughgoing death turn into a thoroughgoing living. It remains a question as to whether this point is found in Hegelian philosophy. It seems even his penetrating logic, which reaches into the deep corners of life, retains the limits of logic at that final point where the negation of a negation immediately turns into an affirmation. In a manner and direction quite unlike that intended by historical materialism, can we not find in this point a new possibility of tearing down and rebuilding his logic? Perhaps we can say that the respective standpoints of Fries, Schelling, and Schopenhauer turn out to yield criticisms that grasp this very point. In any case, what is interesting is that Nietzsche's Zarathustra, just like Hegel's religious critics, attempted to express the self's basic disposition using the word *love*. Yet, Zarathustra immediately abandoned this attempt. When the saint tries to persuade him from descending to the town, he replies, "I love human beings." The saint retorts, "Why did I go into the woods and the wilderness in the first place? Was it not because I loved human beings all too much? / Now I love God: human beings I do not love. Human beings are too imperfect a thing for me. Love for human beings would kill me."[15] With these words, Nietzsche draws a contrast between the saint's Achilles heel, which remains by the fact that even love for God, as noted above, has a halfway quality (as coming to rest halfway through the dialectical movement of life), and Zarathustra's basic disposition, which, in the conclusion of this movement, drained the thoroughgoing possibility of destruction off into overflowing will. Upon hearing the words of the saint, Zarathustra at once retracts the word *love*. "Why did I speak of love? I bring human beings a gift."[16] And when the saint tells him to give human beings not even alms, Zarathustra answers: "No, I do not give alms. For that I am not poor enough." We could say that these ironic words show the reverse side of the halfway quality of loving God. They seem to mean that when one's life has not yet become overflowing will, one tries to supplement one's own inner unfulfillment through others, as with so-called neighborly love. Even in neighborly love, one speculates that by warming others, one's own chilly poverty will be warmed. In contrast, Zarathustra tries to "carry [his] fire into the valley."[17] His fire was not one meant to warm the self and other, but was one that set them ablaze; it was the fire of absolute negation. It is the negation of the human being's "human nature," its all-too-human part, and, likewise, a negation of its dependence on God. The human being clings to itself in the *eidos* of the ego. Or rather, such self-attachment is the *eidos* of the ego itself. Yet, when the human being negates itself or is negated by God, even when it clings to God, such attachment still contains traces of self-attachment insofar as it is "for oneself." To make the negation of human nature absolute, even the human nature contained within its dependence on God must be negated. When human nature is negated and yet God is still clung to, we are still on the way to an absolute negation-*sive*-affirmation. (Much theology, even so-called dialectical theology, satisfies itself with such a halfway dialectic.) For this reason, even neighborly love must be transmuted into a new shape. Love of one's neighbor (those who are closest) must be turned into a "love of those farthest." An immediately granted affirmation of human nature must be turned into an absolute, negative affirmation. The fire Zarathustra carries into the valleys was a fire of love for those thus farthest.

Even the words "God is dead" must be understood in the above sense. They can be interpreted as indicating an abyss in one's life, an abyss that has yet to manifest in a life described as facing God or having love for God, that is, a life that dies as a human being to be born toward God. Even a life that is described as a unity with God does not encounter this abyss. Elsewhere, Nietzsche says, "when you stare for a long time into an abyss, the abyss stares back into you" (*Jenseits v. Gut u. Böse*, 146).[18] Although these words appear in a completely different context, I think the gist of what is meant can be found here as well. It is something that only appears in what Bergson calls a moment of *élan vital*, a moment of creating. Such creating appears in the culmination of the dialectical movement of living, and, it goes without saying, does not belong to a so-called immediate, simple life. Zarathustra says, "Creating—that is the great redemption from suffering, and life's becoming light. But in order for the creator to be, suffering is needed and much transformation [*henshin*]. / Indeed, much bitter dying must be in your life, you creators!" (II. Auf d. glückl. Inseln).[19] What he demands, then, as the final transfiguration, is a transfiguration away from the final schism of a life of facing God, resting in God, or unifying with God. He demands the self-presentation of a life's deepest "oneness." "Away from God and gods this [creating] will lured me; what would there be to create, after all, if there were gods?" (ibid.).[20] "Oh that Someone [God] would yet redeem them from their redeemer!" (II. Von d. Priestern).[21] Earlier, in his "On the Use and Abuse of History for Life," Nietzsche contrasts the "eternally masculine" and the "eternally feminine," but the same spirit operates here as well. "Truthful—thus I call the one who goes into godless deserts and has broken down his revering heart" (II. V. d. berühmt. Weisen).[22] A revering heart is a heart of faith. Hence, Zarathustra thoroughly rejects both one who believes in God and the God in whom belief is placed. His attitude toward faith is perhaps best expressed in the following words addressed to his believers: "You are my believers, but what matter all believers! / You had not yet sought yourselves, then you found me. All believers do this; that's why all faith amounts to so little. / Now I bid you lose me and find yourselves; and only when you have all denied me will I return to you" (I. V. d. Schenkenden Tugenden).[23] Those from the standpoint of faith must lose the person they believe, seek themselves, and find themselves; only then will the person they believed return. Does this not clearly indicate what it means for the standpoint of faith to be transcended? This makes up the background for why Zarathustra enthusiastically calls himself "the godless." "I am Zarathustra, the godless who says, 'Who is more godless than I, so that

I can enjoy his instruction?' / I am Zarathustra, the godless: where do I find my equal? And all those are my equal who give themselves their own will and put aside all resignation" (III. V. d. Verkleinernden Tugenden).[24] Based on what has been written, it seems clear that this standpoint is something entirely different from ordinary "atheism" and its temperament.

2. Eckhart and the Elemental Nature of Living

The teaching of the thirteenth-century German mystic Meister Eckhart[25] centered on what he called the birth of God in the soul.[26] This birth of God implied becoming purely one with God. For Eckhart, this further implied that one must not be satisfied with entering into a unity with God. Pure "oneness" must truly present itself. This distinction between unity and oneness was something he repeatedly emphasized. "It is neither a being enveloped nor a unifying, but a oneness."[27] "Not a mere unifying, but a single oneness (*ein einic ein*)."[28] "Giving nothing to God, taking nothing from God, it is a oneness, a pure becoming one (*ein ein und ein lûter einunge*)."[29] Such oft-repeated expressions demonstrate the effort with which Eckhart tried to express a basic disposition beyond that which is called "a unity with God." That being said, why must this distinction between unity and pure oneness be emphasized? The reason derives from the fact that Eckhart took God, the human being, and their relationship to be, in the truest sense, life. He saw them as life even in their ultimate essence, or rather, precisely in their ultimate essence. Therefore, these moments must each be lived as a life rising from their deepest inner grounds. Taking God to be the source of life that must be lived out is the foundation of the mystical tradition. Originating with Augustine, who claimed that God is the "life of lives,"[30] Augustinianism rested on a standpoint that accepts that the light of God flows directly within the human soul and that there is a source of life flowing in common between both. It opposed standpoints that establish definite limits to the expandable sphere of the human soul so as to deny that the soul has immediate contact with God; it opposed the intellectualist tendencies that found their completion in Thomas, and became the riverbed of medieval mysticism. While the stream of Eckhart's thought finds its source in Thomism, eventually it was to flow into that riverbed. For him, too, life is both first and last. Life cannot take root in anything outside itself. If we could place some transcendental roothold outside of life, life would transcend itself and live through that roothold. We cannot establish a limit on life, for life manifests precisely in surmounting its limits. Likewise, there is no reason that could give meaning to life. Life is reason-less. Life will ascend to the highest realms to live out any reason posited therein. Life will then render itself reason-less. Such an elemental nature of life runs throughout Eckhart's thought. He says, for example, that life lives in order to live, that life lives from its ground; it lives without a "why," and it lives itself. In applying Aristotle's realism, Thomas constrained the human intellect's possible sphere of knowledge to the world of sensible things connected to matter. Yet, Aristotle's thought also emphasizes the dynamic and developmental nature of life. Perhaps if this aspect of Aristotle's thought were to be radicalized, it would come to display a necessary tendency to return to its source in Platonism, which teaches of the intuition of ideas as supersensible reality. Eckhart too comes from the thought of Thomas while being influenced by Augustinianism, Platonism's medieval configuration. While Bonaventure and others' influence on him is just as indicated by historians of philosophy, at the same time, we cannot say that his radicalization of the developmental nature of life stops at Platonism. This pattern—where the dynamic moment in Aristotle's thought sublates his thought from within and leads to Platonism, which is passed through and outstripped—we find already in Plotinus. Eckhart's thought flows through the riverbed of Platonism and into the abyss of Neoplatonism. He says, for example, "Justice is living, justly living. Justice is being with this way of being itself,"[31] and, "The being of justice and the being of the just person are the same one being"[32] (Käte Otermanns, Meister Eckhart, S. 28).[33] Clearly, this must be a transcendence of Platonism. In Plato, as is well known, justice itself or the idea of justice is the original image, while the justice appearing in the just person is a copy image. Though Augustine thought that knowledge was established by the human intellect perceiving eternal truth through divine light flowing into the soul, even he could not help but settle with accepting that there was some relation of similarity or reproduction between an original image and its copy. Nevertheless, Eckhart's claim that the being of justice and the being of the just person are one could only ever be said from the standpoint of radicalized living. Only if the relationship between justice and the just person is penetrated by living could it be said that justice is living, justly living, or that justice is being with this way of being itself. Only in living can the original and the copy become one image. Not until we have reached the standpoint of radicalized living, where living is being and being is living, can we say that the being of justice and the being of the just person are the same one being. Here,

Platonism is broken through by the developmental nature of living. It is broken through by the life of the copy that lives the original. Therefore, what Eckhart expresses in the above words is not something to be understood or criticized from the Platonic or, much less, Aristotelian perspective (that is, from the two fundamental ways of thinking ruling philosophical and theological thought). For that, we require a perspective from a horizon completely different. Yet, from the above, it should be clear that what is here called "living" is not a direct, unmediated living, but one that includes within it a deep rift of various negations, a living that incorporates the trembling of a landslide. It is a living of dialectical movement. It should be equally clear that, in the end, every aspect of this movement is living. Even the negation of living is a self-negation of living within a life, and, in the grounds of this negation, there awaits a negating life's self-affirmation. This self-affirmation, then, manifests fundamentally as the force of direct, unmediated living in its primordial mode. In the negation of negation, it is the primordial *dynamis* that grants surging vibrancy to life. In self-negation, this unmediated, primordial mode becomes the supporting basis of negation, and in the negation of negation, it becomes the original driving force of surging progress. In this sense, even mediation in the dialectical movement of living is, in its grounds, unmediated. The dialectical movement of living always mediates the unmediated. Unmediated living serves as the grounds of this movement and is always its beginning and end. Movement always emerges thenceforth and thereto it sinks. By this process, negativity, as a mediation, and unmediation are mediated and become unmediated. The negation of the standpoint of the copy-image mediates perceiving the original-image, and the negation of the standpoint of the original-image mediates the appearance of the life of the copy that lives the original. Here, the original and the copy are mediated and unmediated living appears as a single image of both the life of the original and the life of the copy. The life of the just person only has its being by living out justice, and justice only has its being in the life of the just person. To speak even of a unity is insufficient. They must be a pure oneness. There, the elemental nature of living makes its appearance as having neither roothold nor limit. When it is said that the birth of God in the human soul implies the pure oneness of God and the human being, it must be understood by taking the elemental nature of living as a premise. Only then will what Eckhart calls pure oneness or nothingness appear as the elemental nature of living itself. But in what sense is this so?

Although absolute affirmation, as the elemental and reason-less nature of living, as living just to live, is present as a wellspring wherever living may move, it cannot be said, conversely, that all of life's motion emerges from this wellspring. The elemental nature of living only truly appears in the completion of the dialectical movement of living. "Living just to live" could just as well be the slogan of those who live completely for the moment and give themselves up to reckless self-abandonment. Even there we find something that easily lends itself to the elemental nature of living. In self-abandonment, which arises from despair not unlike the absolute negation of living, there is a distorted trace of life's absolute affirmation. In reckless self-abandonment, to use an expression used earlier, the eidetic ego is broken through. Because the eidetic ego is an ego of self-attachment that seizes upon itself, in reckless self-abandonment there is an *ekstasis,* albeit an inverted one. In fact, many find their way into the world of religion by first passing through reckless self-abandonment. Reckless self-abandonment touches upon the elemental and reason-less nature of life; notwithstanding, it is still a way of life that seeks the most incoherent reasons outside of itself, thereby diverting itself from the elemental nature of living. To that extent, the elemental nature of living is a mere void to this way of life, and its supporting roothold, its reasons for living, are, in their grounds, brought to self-awareness as an emptiness. To keep this emptiness from rising to self-awareness, living seeks its roothold in one thing or another, and so manages to establish a life of incoherence upon the emptiness of such grounds.—And yet, the facts are reversed for a normal life, which is unified by some consistent reason it grasps within itself. (There, the reason for living cannot avoid becoming extremely varied in accordance with what each individual takes to be their occupation, *Beruf.*) In contrast to a life of abandonment, this way of living has its roothold within itself. It roots itself in the "reason for living" it has granted to itself. A reason is, furthermore, an end, something that traverses into the future and defines a way of living. It rests in the grounds of present living, establishing its roothold, while traversing into the future and ever defining that way of life. Present, past, and future are enveloped therein, and a life thus divided and uncoupled from elemental living establishes itself by closing up within itself. The unity that allows this closed-up life to establish itself, then, is none other than the eidetic ego. Living expands limitlessly toward the future without ever separating from itself. Such self-attachment is the fixed, eidetic ego. This *eidos* separates living from its elemental nature. By returning home within itself, by becoming for-itself and self-aware, living becomes separated from its elemental source. There, the standpoint of the "substantial" ego, of the understanding, is established in isolation from all others. By standing before itself, living also stands before everything else and from here the distinction between inner and outer arises. With this we may understand Bergson's well-known claim that the spatial perspective, which in its discernment of the flow of living sees things as resting beside each other in space, has the same elemental source as the so-called reflective consciousness or understanding. Thus the standpoint of "spirit," divorced from living, nevertheless arises within living, as spirit is ultimately a living. Even where spirit is divorced from the elemental source of living, the elemental nature of living appears. Nothing demonstrates this better than subjectivity, or rather intentionality, which first establishes itself in "spirit." Where there is being for-itself-*sive*-for-another in spirit, we have what is called intentionality. Subjectivity and its noetical, absolute uniqueness appear along with the establishment of an "ego" that distinguishes itself from all others while taking the other in view. Amidst countless entities traversing infinite past and infinite future, the absolute uniqueness of the self establishes itself as absolutely noetical through seeing, hearing, and thinking. It establishes itself in the fact that no one can see, hear, or think in place of itself. Being noetical, then, is the self-presenting of the elemental source of living immediately beneath it. Yet, despite the fact that the elemental source of living presents itself in the ego, even here we cannot say that the ego is in the elemental source of living. In other words, the ego is not aware of itself as the self-presentation of the elemental source of living, but instead thinks that being noetical is something that emerges from out of the ego itself. Lacking self-awareness, the ego is not yet in the elemental source of living, and precisely in this condition we find the establishment of the fixed, eidetic ego, the substantial ego, that is, the noematicized ego that is taken to be thingly. If the ego were in the elemental source of living, such an *eidos* would be broken through from within, and it would truly become aware of itself as absolutely noetical. Yet, because the elemental source of living presents itself in the ego without the ego being in the elemental source of living, its absolute noetical nature still appears in seeing, hearing, and knowing, but the ego thinks of this as the activity of a noematicized ego. This "thinking" is the foundation of all "thinking" of this species (what the Greeks called *doxa*). It is fundamental *doxa*. The eidetic ego establishes itself in this fundamental *doxa*, thereby divorcing itself from the roothold of living. If this is so, how is this *eidos* broken through? How does it return to its source in the roothold of living?

On the one hand, the substantial ego is for-itself and knows itself. On the other, it stands before all others, seeing them (as its objects) from without. Or rather, by obtaining the mode of seeing which sees all others as its objects (as things resting beside each other), it comes to know itself. This is the meaning of the discerning understanding. The so-called representation, then, is but an *indicium* of this subject-object opposition, this mode of seeing from without. Representations make up the content of the isolated ego's activity when it sees all others from without (as its objects). When the ego adopts this mode of seeing and sees something as its object, a representation comes to intervene between the two, even when the ego itself thinks that it is immediately seeing the object. Representing is emblematic of the estrangement between the ego and the thing seen as its object. It intervenes between them and holds them apart. Representations arise as scales before the eye, which sees everything as its objects, and seeing through these scales interferes with perceiving others directly from within. It interferes with what Bergson calls "lived sympathy" or "intuition." (For that reason, we should not think that first there is an ego and its objects, and that only then do representations arise from their relationship. The ego, seen as a substance, others, seen as its objects, and representations all arise simultaneously with the mode of seeing from without.) Nevertheless, representations function not only to intervene between and hold apart the ego and its object, but, as what mediates between them, representations at the same time bring them closer together. As an object's representative, representations allow for objects to present themselves to the ego, and, as the content of the ego's activity, they allow the ego to intend its objects. When the ego's activity takes representations as its content, the ego turns to its objects and relates to them. Representations are the tractive power of objects the ego has grasped. For that reason, breaking through the eidetic ego and returning to the elemental source of living first requires that representations be purged from the ego. The eidetic ego establishes itself as being for-itself-*sive*-for-others. For that reason, if being for-others is negated, being for-itself will be negated as well. If the ego's relation with objects is severed, the fixed *eidos* of the ego may also be broken through, and, conversely, a connection may appear between the ego and the elemental source of living. Thus, what is first required is the negation of being for-others, the purging of representations.

Such a purging of representations was, for Eckhart too, undoubtedly a precondition for the birth of the Son in the soul. Following the tradition since Aristotle, Eckhart uses the concept of "image" (*Bild*). The Word of

God cannot be heard past the cacophony in a soul that has yet to shed itself of all images. But once it becomes an emptied *eidos,* the Word of God reverberates throughout it. By becoming an empty locus,[34] the soul becomes a womb that receives a new *eidos.* To become an empty locus is to immediately receive the Word of God. Or rather, the Word of God, which had already originated within the soul from the eternal beginning, then appears to the soul. The soul was created in time. Nevertheless, within it there is something that pre-exists the creation of the world, time, and the soul itself; there is something "uncreated." This uncreated something is the living connection with God, the unity of life. The grounds of one's soul are, so to speak, penetrated by the spearhead of divine life. Or better yet, this spearhead is none other than the inner depths of the soul itself. And when the soul becomes an empty locus, it encounters this spearhead, this connection with divine life. The self-presentation of this uncreated something, which Eckhart variously calls the "ground of the soul," the "spark" of divine life, "spiritual poverty," "stillness," or "silence," is none other than the birth of God in the soul. In this birth, the soul is in a state of unity with God and it knows God. Because this knowing establishes itself where there is neither representation nor "image," it is by no means the ratiocination of a discerning understanding, but rather an intuitive knowing. If knowing by means of representations is to be called knowing, then it is a non-knowing. For this reason, Eckhart called this intuitive knowing a "knowing of non-knowing."—However, Eckhart finds even this point, which has traditionally been taken as the most final of destinations, to be only a final step that must still be transcended. This is due to the fact that even when the soul receives the Word of God by becoming an empty locus, even when the soul encounters the divine life that penetrates it, so long as we are satisfied with this unity, the soul is still a oneness of two with God, and intuitive knowing still includes a distinction between that which intuits and that which is intuited. God still remains as an object against which one stands, as something represented, as something seen from without through an "image." The image of God (*imago Dei*) and the Word of God (the Son) within the soul become things that, just as earlier with thingly knowledge, bring the soul closer to God from without, only to estrange one from God. There, the soul still maintains its being for-itself, its self-attachment; it maintains its eidetic fixedness. To that extent, even the divine life that enters it cannot yet enter as something truly lived. To borrow a metaphor used earlier, it enters as water that fills only the fixed shape of an emptied cup. When God enters as a truly lived God, the *eidos* of the ego is broken through and the cup overflows with the water of life. As long as the ego maintains its eidetic nature and remains a locus, God is still a God which is thought. "In intuition, we are not one with what we intuit. For when there is nothing outside of oneness, one sees nothing. Therefore, one can see God only with blindness, one can know God only with non-knowing, and one can accept God only with reasonlessness"[35] (Büttner II. S. 151). "So long as the soul has God, accepts God, and knows God, it is apart from God"[36] (II. S. 165). "The soul must become too poor to be or contain the place wherein God works. So long as the human being secures a place within himself, he secures discrimination" (I. S. 206).[37] These words indicate that a unity is still a oneness of two. If that is so, what could constitute the leap from unity to pure oneness? What fuses God and the soul, while nevertheless bringing them face-to-face, is their penetrating through one another. In this way, God breaks through the *eidos* of the ego and the ego breaks through the image of God. Eckhart goes so far as to claim, "I must become God, and God must become me" (op. cit. I. S. 178).[38] Without considering the dialectical movement of mutual negation, this kind of talk could only be understood as mere falsehood. Intuition, which includes a distinction between perceiver and perceived, that is, the two eyes that meet, the two glances that are exchanged, must become a single eye and a single glance. "The eye by which I see God is the same eye by which God sees me. My eye and God's eye are one eye, one glance" (Pf. 96).[39] The elemental nature of living presents itself as the absolute, noetical uniqueness in the seeing of my eye, as my uncreated life, as that which I "must have been" since the eternal beginning. Yet, so long as this seeing is thought to be the activity of an eidetic ego divorced from the elemental source of living, my being-for-itself qua being an ego places me as a dam in an undammed stream. Although such being-for-itself is required for the appearance of its absolute, noetical nature and absolute, subjective uniqueness, that is, for the appearance of the elemental nature of living itself, at the same time it causes the ego to be divorced from the elemental source of living. The elemental nature of living appears most clearly in the ego while remaining most deeply hidden. The ego's noetical activity is an immediate appearance of the elemental nature of living, while also being the absolute negation of the elemental source of living and the absolute, negative mediation required for a return to its elemental source. That is to say, as noted previously, here the immediate nature of unmediation itself has become a mediation. In this way, so long as the ego is an absolute negation of the elemental source of living, the elemental source of living stands against the ego on its far side as an absolute other, and the ego with its egoity builds a dam within its life, thereby imposing a limit on itself. For the ego to return home to its elemental source, its limit must be broken through from the far side of that limit. (Here we find what, in Eckhart, could be spoken of as "God's grace" or "God's love.") The *eidos* of the ego's egoity, then, must be broken through by being penetrated from within by a new, higher *eidos*. Or to use Eckhart's expression, we require a *durchformen* by a new, higher *eidos*. Yet, for this *durchformen* to truly be a *durchformen,* that which forms and that which is formed must not stop at being two. The higher *eidos* must be for the ego a higher way of living; it must be a new ego. When the ego's *eidos* is broken through and rebuilt with a new ego, the ego is transfigured. The ego's new life gushes forth from within the ego, transforming it. Or, the ego's new life, which flows over the limit it had erected in itself, and its new birth, which breaks through and flows over it, appear within the ego. This living transcends limits and lives a higher *eidos* situated on the far side. To once again borrow an expression from Eckhart, we may call this *überformen,* to overcome limits and to make the far side the near side. Only in such a *durchformen-sive-überformen* can we say that, "God's eye and my eye are one eye, one glance," and only there does the elemental source of living reveal its absolute, noetical nature in its true figure. "I must become God, and God must become me. This 'He' and this 'I' become one, and must be one, and in this 'being' there must be a single work working (*ein werc wirkent*)" (I. S. 178).[40]

In these words we find the reason for why I said earlier that Eckhart, by seeing being as living, transcended Aristotelianism (Thomism) and even Platonism (Augustinianism). That is, to see being as living is, in one regard, to transcend being. Of course, the usual meaning of being, taken as the being of ideas, or better yet, taken even as the being of God, so long as it stands as one's object, is something that blocks the effluence of pure acting. As Bergson ascertained in his sharp analysis, fixing living as being is living's death. Pure acting must transcend even the being of God, and from there turn back home to ideas, and then back to the being of sensual things. The being of sensual things are the shadows of ideas, and ideas are true reality, a higher dimension of being. Yet, even if ideas are true reality (or rather because they are true reality), from the standpoint of pure activity that transcends being, they are "shapes" formed on emptiness, shadows drawn on emptiness, and yet are nevertheless truly real just as so. Even if sensual things, as the shadows of ideas, are thereby the transient shadows of shadows, they are a concrete reality that transcends mere "shapes" and are, in a different sense, true reality. By transcending Platonism and Aristotelianism, there may here be a path toward vitalizing them. Yet for that, the grounds of living must be the nothingness of all being. When the opposition between God and the person is noetically transcended, the being of God and the being of the person are transcended as well. By transcending the being of God in the deep recesses of God (what Eckhart called the "Godhead"), by transcending the being of the self (the substantial ego) in the deep recesses of the self, God and the person become a pure oneness in nothingness and they enact a single activity. When a person stands in the bottom depths of God beyond even the being of God, that is, when one returns most deeply to God, one truly returns home to oneself and becomes an acting self, a free self. Eckhart says, "God's ground is my ground, and my ground is God's ground"[41] (I. S. 127). Thus, when God's eye and my eye become a single eye, a single glance, the "now-here" in which seeing activity takes place is the uncreated place of God, the yonder side of even God's being. Where the opposition between the far side and the near side is transcended, the far side of the far side becomes the near side of the near side. This is also why Eckhart says that in the "nothingness" of the Godhead, a person becomes free, or that when a person stands in the "groundless ground" that makes up their own ground, they are free. Even Bergson, who began his philosophical career studying the problem of freedom, ultimately arrived at the standpoint of his *Two Sources of Morality and Religion*, the standpoint of creative acting that, by becoming one with the creative activity of God, takes over that activity.

3. Religious Living and the Positivist Spirit

In the above, I have tried to pick out what are thought to be the respective fundamental dispositions of Nietzsche's Zarathustra and Meister Eckhart without traversing the entirety of their individual teachings. In doing this, I am not trying to say that their teachings belong to identical categories in the history of philosophy. Neither have I forgotten that Eckhart, a preaching monk who led a monastic life from the end of the thirteenth century to the beginning of the fourteenth, and Nietzsche, the late-nineteenth-century card-carrying atheist and withdrawn philosopher of the will to power, had backgrounds nearly opposite in demeanor, and that each possessed his own historical atmosphere colored by the characteristics of his time. The shape of the problems brewed in that atmosphere and the shape of the answers provided are in no way the same. In Eckhart we may even find a superbly medieval spirit, while in Nietzsche one superbly modern. Nevertheless, I find I must acknowledge that there is something in the recesses of such historical differences that flows in common at the bottom of their respective ways of thinking. Where one endeavors to lead the soul past the complications of theological knowledge and toward unhindered freedom, the other offers a radical and originary critique of modern mentalities and endeavors to rise out of the various mazes lying therein. Yet, can we not see that both paths unexpectedly meet at the peak (or the elemental source) of great life? The fundamental attitude common to both is the radicalization of the dialectical movement of living. It is the radicalization of human affirmation through human negation. In both, this radicalization of human affirmation appears in seeing a mediating stage that must be transcended even in a state of fusion (or even unity) with God. Fusing or unifying with God is still a oneness of two. So long as there are still two, so long as one stands before God, represents God, and takes God as one's object, there remains an estrangement from the ultimate reality of living, a negation of living, and death. Although the ultimate reality of living is, on the one hand, the "here-now" and, on the other, the bottomless ground of living, the former has been hidden on the hind side of the self standing before God and the latter has been hidden on the hind side of God standing before the self. While even fusing and unifying already establish themselves on a pure oneness of these hind sides, so long as they are separated and hidden from each other, they remain two. When this is transcended, the two hind sides become one fore side. The fore side of God and the fore side of the self are one. Eckhart expresses this absolute noetical nature through such expressions as "God's ground is my ground, and my ground is God's ground," "God's eye and my eye are one," or as freedom standing on nothingness, and Nietzsche expresses it with, "Peak and abyss—they are now merged as one!,"[42] "noon and midnight have become one,"[43] or as an overflowing life that flows over the ego and as the godless one's creative activity. When Eckhart says, "When I will to stand in a state of pure oneness in God's will, and will to stand above from God's will, all of God's work, and God himself, then I have risen beyond all creatures and am neither God nor creature"[44] (I. S. 185), and when Nietzsche says, "Away from God and gods this [creating] will lured me; what would there be to create, after all, if there were gods?" (cited above), they stand together in the blazing present moment of living's bottomless depths; they stand, so to speak, in a life of living. So long as he stands before God as a "creature," for him there is no living qua creating.

"Peak and abyss—they are now merged as one! . . . [I]t must be your best courage that there is no longer a way behind you! . . . Your foot erased the path behind you" (*Zarath*. III. Der Wanderer).

Yet this radicalization of affirmation is the radicalization of negation. A person must at one point thoroughly become a "creature." Nietzsche too states that, "To always say hee-yaw—only the ass learned that, and whoever is of its spirit!" (*Zarath*. III. Vom Geist d. Schwere).[45] By negating itself living enlightens itself. Its self-negation includes the path to knowledge in the true, that is to say, philosophical sense. Nietzsche does not, as is popularly thought, simply assert immediate living or will. What he calls living or will is a living purified by a strict knowledge that negates the all-too-human part within itself. It is knowledge in this sense that Nietzsche spoke fondly of. For example, he says, "To me you are lukewarm, but every deep knowledge flows cold. Ice-cold are the innermost wells of the spirit, invigorating for hot hands and human doers" (II. V. d. berühmt. Weisen).[46] Although Eckhart had come to be quite distant from Thomas, he nevertheless emphasized the intellect and knowledge in contrast to the voluntarists of his time who challenged Thomas's intellectualism. Appearing at the bottom of a thoroughgoing removal of every *Bild* and representative knowing, Eckhart's "knowing of non-knowing," too, expresses living's self deepening through a deepening of the intellect as life's negative side. It expresses that what results from this deepening is that negativity, just as it is, turns into affirmation. (Corresponding with the removal of representations in Eckhart, the weak-stomached Nietzsche offers the symbol of nausea. Zarathustra cries out, "*Ekel, ekel, ekel!*")[47] Just as negation was radical, such a turning into affirmation is radical. The absolute noesis appearing here, the acting of free creating, obtains its highest reality in bodily activity. In that sense, the body is the deepest soul, a soul even deeper than the soul. "Soul" and "spirit" are but one part of the total life focused and consolidated in the body. The body transcends them and finds its support in the bottomless abyss of living. In Eckhart's words, "God positioned the spirit in its own freedom. Thus, God cannot rise above the soul's free will and force it to do anything, and neither does He demand anything that the soul does not will. Therefore, the soul in its body can choose with its free will and with that the soul can securely rest"[48] (I. S. 197). Any further elaboration of Nietzsche's emphasis on the body is probably unnecessary, so let the following words suffice. " 'Body am I and soul'—so speaks a child. And why should one not speak like children? / But the awakened, the knowing one says: body am I through and through, and nothing besides; and soul is just a word for something on the body." "The body is a great reason," " 'I'[49] you say and are proud of this word. But what is greater is that in which you do not want to believe—your body and its great reason. It does not say I, but *does* I" (*Zarath*. I. V. d. Verächtern d. Leibes).[50]

Yet, I do not think that such a fundamental commonality in the basic dispositions of these two thinkers can be conceived as merely coincidental. Perhaps, despite completely different states of affairs, there is already some shared, fundamental characteristic to be found in the historical atmosphere each breathed. Even superficially we see that in the periods following the death of Thomas and that of Hegel, great spasms[51] spread from the bottom depths of history out over the entire surface of culture. The confusion of the intellectual world following Thomas's death was deeper than and quite distant from that which preceded him. Perhaps we can say that it has its foundation in the opposition between faith and knowledge, that is, between supernatural revelation, which had come to expose an increasingly overwhelming question mark in the course of the history of medieval thought, and natural reason. This opposition had been lurking in Christian theology since the Greek Church Fathers and especially since Augustine had taken up Greek philosophy. Or, to put it more boldly, we could even say that this opposition is as old as the awakening of the human intellect and is a problem that began to sprout when this awakening brought about the collapse of early religion and, therefore, early society and the dawn of the historical age of humankind. After Augustine, Scholasticism, which prospered in the wake of the long history of the Christianization of the Germanic peoples, is the rise of Greek thinking within the Christian doctrinal system, and with it this opposition—the opposition of completely different human attitudes—once again began to appear on the surface. Especially as we enter the twelfth and thirteenth centuries, Aristotle's philosophy, which is said to have already given rise to a great changeover in the Islamic world two centuries prior, had infiltrated the Christian cultural sphere through his own works and Averroes's commentary, and Averroism, which eliminated the limits of supernatural revelation and natural reason, was greeted with enthusiasm by thinkers with enlightenment tendencies, and, in Thomas's generation with Paris University at the center, it became greatly energized. In this way, the intellectual world at the time was the scene of an entanglement between, on the one hand, the faith of Christian revelation and, on the other, Averroes's Aristotelianism that stood on the standpoint of the speculation of natural reason, and then Augustinianism and others who tried to mediate this opposition. Augustine's Platonism could not readily reconcile this opposition. For Augustine, eternal ideas (*rationes*) are true reality, and human reason can obtain true knowledge by passing through the world of sensual things and intuiting the ideas as the original image of these things. Furthermore, when this happens, the light of divine reason flows into human reason, illuminating it, and by this light and only in it, can reason intuit ideas. Yet, it goes without saying, this standpoint, where all things are intuited in eternal ideas and through divine light, causes us to feel a deep estrangement from the positivist spirit of objective knowledge of sensual things (what in modern times appeared as scientific knowledge) and its self-awareness of the autonomy of the human intellect. Although we already find something arising from this same feeling in Aristotle's criticism of Plato, the same matter gradually formed in the Middle Ages and came to a head with the infiltration of Averroism. Thomas's great task was to grant order and unity to this intellectual disarray. On the one hand, he drew on Aristotelianism and revised or reinterpreted Augustine's thought, acknowledging the relative autonomy of natural reason by contending that natural reason does not obtain knowledge through the immediate influx of or contact with God's light, but that when human beings were created the highest principles of thought were already implanted in their reason and, by these principles, reason can obtain knowledge of sensual things. On the other hand, in true accordance with this, he contended that natural reason cannot transcend beyond knowledge of sensual things, and so established a limit to natural reason. He then acknowledged the world of revelation on the yonder side of this limit, thereby vanquishing Averroism while keeping Augustine's Platonism alive on the yonder side of natural reason's limit. Nevertheless, not even this grand synthesis and harmonizing of systems, which could be called the culmination of medieval thought, could dam up the various currents of thought that would scatter to the poles of every direction. What demands special attention is the fact that many religious free-thinking groups dispensed with the church's creed and grew together as a counteraction to the terminal symptoms of Scholastic currents that had been competing with exquisite conceptual analysis, and that these free-thinking groups rapidly spread and ultimately collapsed into intellectual self-indulgence and moral depravity, leading to the further darkening of the intellectual disarray. Such conditions were ripe for an effort to be born that keeps one foot deeply planted in the intellectual tradition, while thoroughly maintaining the standpoint of free living. For only living is immediately real, while at the same time being something that could readily take on thoroughgoing negation and infinite self-deepening—this moment, as noted earlier, is found in the Aristotelianism Thomas drew upon. By radicalizing this moment, Eckhart transcended Aristotelianism, thereby breaking through the limits Thomas had erected, and at last transcended even Platonism. In this return home to the plain fact of living, there appears the collapse of the old and a re-departure toward the new.

It is the consensus of many that the middle of the nineteenth century was a turning point where a deep spasm occurred within European spiritual life. We today remain in this spasm and shall probably remain so for the considerable future. By bearing this spasm both vividly and most deeply, Nietzsche casts his shadow over the future. While I think there is a significant similarity between the intellectual worlds following Hegel's death and that of Thomas, I would like to draw particular attention to whether there may not lie between both a relation of, so to speak, world intellectual history. The reconciliation between faith and knowledge once accomplished in Thomas was completely torn asunder in the changeover from the Middle Ages to the modern period. This is indicated by, on the one hand, religious reformation and, on the other, by the sudden rise of humanism, the natural sciences, and Bacon's logic. (These are immediately continuous with the various currents of medieval thought. For example, there is the relation between the Averroists and the humanists, or the effect of Arabic science on that of Europe.) Humanism and the natural sciences induced a decisive revolution in the religious, historical, and natural view that ruled the Middle Ages and created a deepening rift between itself and the religious worldview that extended into modern times. Despite the attempts at reconciliation made by Descartes, Leibniz, and others, this deep rift appeared as a landslide in the enlightenment movements brought on by the eighteenth-century freethinkers. Only then were the Middle Ages decisively bid farewell. It goes without saying that it was Kant who would once again try to bring order and unity to this disarray inherited from the Middle Ages from its deep grounds up. In him the Protestant spirit, Newton's natural-scientific method of thinking, empiricism since Bacon, and rationalism since Descartes all flowed into each other. His fundamental orientation in unifying them was, as with Thomas, to establish a limit on knowledge to make room for faith. Moreover, as Kant himself says in the Dialectic of his first critique, in the world of knowledge he inherits the intention of Aristotle's emphasis on the sensual and his categories, while, in the supersensual world of morality, he draws on Platonic insights. This indicates that the same problem in medieval thought was flowing in the bottom depths of modern thought. Yet, regardless of such cursory concordance, Kant's so-called Copernican

Revolution distinguishes him from Thomas fundamentally and indicates to us the direction in which this same problem developed during the history spanning from the Middle Ages into modern times. The development of modern natural sciences, and the development of the human sciences that followed, were taken as unable to shake the autonomy of the positivist spirit, of the human being's natural reason. The problem here is not one of science's individual achievements. While those are susceptible to change, the mentality of scientific inquiry itself, the self-awareness of natural reason's autonomy, will not. (Many theorists who study the relationship between science and religion or modern culture and religion overlook this point.) *The Critique of Pure Reason* is a philosophical confession of the self-awareness of autonomy that natural reason has secured. This same self-awareness of natural reason's autonomy is linked to the spirit of Protestantism and appears even in its moral view. As explained in *The Critique of Practical Reason*, the will's autonomy as self-legislator takes even acting morally by a commandment from God to be heteronomous. None of this is to be found in Thomas, and it endows Kantian philosophy with the monumental significance of giving deep expression to the modern mentality. Yet, for that very reason, it became even more difficult to secure a place for faith. Kant's theory of the postulates of practical reason, his theory of religion, and other places indicate to us how sparse this place had been left. By reining in English and French Enlightenment, Kant actually deepened, or heightened, it. German Idealism, which was to follow him, would progress in this direction. Natural reason would envelop the sparse world of faith left over by Kant and thereby try to take what were once granted as the contents of faith and reinstate them as the contents of natural reason. We could say that this was the last great attempt to keep the contents of faith alive in an era that had established the autonomy of reason. Meanwhile, the natural and human (historical and social) sciences had been ceaselessly progressing, and when Hegel died, they resisted the natural philosophy or historical-social philosophy of those like Schelling and Hegel, and asserted themselves. At that time, faith became powerless, and a generalized indifference toward religion began. That is to say, the period following the middle of the nineteenth century was the time for the eighteenth-century enlightenment movement, after a brief counteroffensive, to realize its success. For, while the enlightenment movement was a battle against the religious worldview, now that battle was unnecessary. And yet, as various materialisms and various idealisms fell into utter confusion, a deep sense of living rose up within people once again. What became the greatest trigger for this was Darwin's theory of evolution, and this sense of living, unlike that following Thomas's death, was based on something biological and psychological. But at any rate, people obtained a deep sense of a great life penetrating both self and other as something most real and, at the same time, most elemental. One could, broadly speaking, call this era the period of the philosophy of living. Nietzsche and Bergson have become its representatives in Western thought through their deep grasp of this sense of living. While each made their departure from different aspects of living, in the end, they came to approach the same state attained by Eckhart.—What gave life to the harmonic synthesis of systems in those like Thomas and Kant was the disarray brewed by the development of the autonomy of human reason that swiftly penetrates through the bottom of the history of humankind. Furthermore, this development transcends these attempts at harmony and continues to develop. It is coming to expose its own inevitability with increasing strength. Earlier, this autonomy was taken to indicate the human being's deepest sinfulness, its so-called "original sin." Even now, many theologians think this way. Yet, no matter how deep an insight may be contained therein, is not ending the conversation there an inadequate response to this mentality that has risen to self-awareness in scientific knowledge and moral self-legislation, this mentality that has claimed an inseverable foothold in all modern people? What scientist or technologist in their own work, what everyday person in their own actions of turning on a light or taking medicine, therein catches wind of original sin? We can say that both Eckhart and Nietzsche, who appeared in those times of deepest crisis following attempts at reconciliation, touched upon that current coursing through the bottom depths of the history of humankind, and by persisting through and intensifying the dialectics of living in human autonomy, they tried to overcome the opposition of faith and knowledge and the crisis to which this opposition gives rise.

(1938, June)

Notes

Chapter 1. The Thinker and the Master

1. Brightman, ed., *Between Friends: The Correspondence of Hannah Arendt and Mary McCarthy*, 353. For Gadamer, see his reports in §6 of Appendix One, below. Pöggeler, *Neue Wege mit Heidegger*, 389. Derrida, "A Time for Farewells," xlii; see also Derrida's interview with Dominique Janicaud in the latter's *Heidegger in France*, 348. Beierwaltes, "Heideggers Gelassenheit," 32.

2. In Sauer's archives, there is a small bound book with three sets of printed pages, each numbered 1–11. They are clearly different drafts for a bibliography titled "Geschichte der mittelalterlichen Mystik," for each contains different marginalia and emendations. Nearly an entire page of each set (pp. 8–9) is devoted to editions and translations of, as well as texts on, Eckhart. The first set includes, *inter alia*, those of Pfeiffer, Jostes, Büttner, and Denifle. The second and third sets date from a later period, for they add, respectively, the edition of Diederichs (1912) and Evans's translation of Pfeiffer (1924), among other texts. UAF C 67/160.

3. Arnold, *Katholizismus als Kulturmacht*, 18, 283.

4. Ott, "Martin Heidegger's Catholic Origins," 149; Arnold, *Katholizismus als Kulturmacht*, 347–48. See also Sauer's 1928 "Mystik und Kunst unter besonderer Berücksichtigung des Oberrheins," in which he discusses some of Eckhart's followers such as Henry Suso and John Tauler. As for Krebs, whose important work on medieval philosophy and mysticism I cannot analyze here, see above all three texts: (1) Krebs's foundational book on Eckhart's colleague Dietrich of Freiberg, which was published in 1906 under the title *Meister Dietrich* and contains more than a dozen references to Eckhart. Krebs had been advised to write on this topic by his dissertation director Heinrich Finke, who would eventually teach and mentor Heidegger and serve as an examiner for Heidegger's PhD and *Habilitationsschrift*. See GA 1: 62, 191; GA 16: 39/9, 42; HAD, 71–72; MH/EB, 36; MH/KL, 87; MH/HR, 28, 91; and Cercel, "'Sur la valeur du comprendre historique pour le philosophe.'" Incidentally, Krebs had advised Heidegger to write his *Habilitationsschrift* on Dietrich, to which Heidegger replied that "the theme would certainly be

219

of interest," but that he felt more comfortable with his work in mathemathics and logic. Quote in von Wolzogen, " 'Gottes Geheimnisse verkosten, bevor sie geschaut werden,' " 205; cf. Ott, "Der Habilitand Martin Heidegger," 146. (2) Krebs's 1912 book *Theologie und Wissenschaft nach der Lehre der Hochscholastik*, which deals with Eckhart's student and companion Hervaeus Natalis, on whom Martin Grabmann had encouraged Krebs to work (Junghanns, "Der Freiburger Dogmatiker Engelbert Krebs," 30). For Heidegger's relation to Grabmann, see pp. 231–32, n. 49, below. (3) Krebs's 1921 *Grundfragen der kirchlichen Mystik*, a copy of which could be found in Fritz Heidegger's library, which Martin would use while in Meßkirch; the library is now located in the Martin-Heidegger-Archiv der Stadt Meßkirch. Krebs discusses Eckhart on pages 29–30 and 129–30. For Krebs's many other works on mysticism and mystics, including Eckhart, see the bibliography in Junghanns, "Der Freiburger Dogmatiker Engelbert Krebs." For Heidegger's relation to Krebs, especially as regards mysticism, see Ott, "Martin Heidegger's Catholic Origins," 143–53, who nevertheless overstates matters when he writes that "Heidegger owed his early encounter with mysticism, that is, medieval mysticism, to . . . Krebs" (143). Finally, I might note that Heinrich Finke's wide-ranging interests included an edition of medieval Dominican letters (*Ungedruckte Dominikanerbriefe des 13. Jahrhunderts*) as well as writings on the history of the German Dominicans in the thirteenth and fourteenth centuries ("Zur Geschichte der deutschen Dominikaner im XIII. und XIV. Jahrhundert").

5. Bernhard Welte relates that, on September 9, 1957, Heinrich Ochsner told him about a seminar held on Lotze, during which Heidegger had connected truth to self-showing and presencing: "O. hat auf dem Spaziergang erzählt: Heidegger hat schon in den Jahren 1915–1917 vor seiner Einziehung in den Krieg, in dem damals gehaltenen Lotze-Seminar den Gedanken vertreten: Wahrheit ist nicht adaequatio, sie ist ursprünglicher: sich zeigen, anwesend [the final 'd' of 'anwesend' is crossed out in pen]." "On our walk O. related that, already in the years 1915–1917, before being drafted into the war, Heidegger had already espoused, in the Lotze-seminar that was being held at the time, the idea that truth is not *adaequatio,* but something more original: self-showing, presencing" ("Aufzeichnungen aus meinen Gesprächen mit Heinrich Ochsner," 5; UAF E 8/934). Perhaps Ochsner is referring to Heinrich Rickert's Summer Semester 1915 seminar on Lotze's *Logik*, in which Heidegger gave a presentation on "Question and Judgment" (GA 80.1: 1–13/56–62). At any rate, according to a recollection by Reiner Schürmann, it was *Eckhart* who helped Heidegger to begin thinking of *being* as presencing (*Anwesen*). See the reports by Schürmann in §6 of Appendix One, below.

6. To cite just one example: Heinrich Rickert, who *did* take Eckhart seriously, was nevertheless criticized for "sympathizing" with him in his essay "Das Eine, die Einheit und die Eins," by which the critic meant: "having nothing in common with positive science and practical life." See Marbe, "Beiträge zur Logik und ihren Grenzwissenschaften," 186. Rickert dismisses the absurdity of this critique on the

final pages of the book version of his essay: *Das Eine, die Einheit und die Eins: Bemerkungen zur Logik des Zahlbegriffs*, 92–93.

7. Heidegger is perhaps referring to the series *Deutsche Mystiker*, published by Kösel Verlag. Volume 1 (on Suso) appeared in 1910, and Volume 3 (on Eckhart) in 1914. In the latter volume, a fourth volume (on Tauler) is announced for publication in Autumn 1914, although it does not appear to have been published until 1919. Heidegger owned copies of Volume 3 and Volume 4. He also owned a copy of Volume 2 (on Mechthild of Magdeburg), published in 1911.

8. "Aber do si ein sein in dem wesen, da ensein si niht geleich, wann geleichheit stet in unterscheid." "But in that they are one in nature they are not equal, for equality resides in separation." Jostes, 94,32–34/Evans, 1, 276; now available in DW 4: 1127,3–1128,1 Pr. 117 ("Ze dem êrsten suochet daz rîche gotes"). GA 1: 218/33–34. Other references to Eckhart can be found in the book version of Rickert's text (92–93), and there is also an Eckhart reference in Rickert's *Die Philosophie des Lebens*, 55. Interestingly, an article by György Lukàcz immediately following the essay version also begins with an epigraph from Eckhart: "Nature makes a man out of a child, and a hen out of an egg, but God makes the man before the child and the hen before the egg." Lukàcz, "Metaphysik der Tragödie," 79; DW 5: 118,6–8/Walshe 563 (VeM).

9. The primary source for Heidegger's footnote appears to be Hermann Leser's "Das religiöse Wahrheitsproblem im Lichte der deutschen Mystik," which deals with the metaphysics of truth and draws heavily on Eckhart. Heidegger also makes reference to the Eckhartian term *breakthrough,* which he connects with the problem of truth: philosophy must "aim . . . at a *breakthrough* [Durchbruch] to true actuality and actual truth" (GA 1: 406/66). This chiasmic structure, which is quite Eckhartian (see Tobin, *Meister Eckhart: Thought and Language*, 167–71), points to another such structure in the *Habilitationsschrift* that may well stem from Eckhart too. In the midst of a discussion of analogy, Heidegger writes: "In the strictest, absolute sense, *only God* is actual. He is the absolute that is *existence existing in essence and in existence 'essencing'* [Existenz ist, die im Wesen existiert und in der Existenz 'west']" (GA 1: 260/77; trans. mod.). Aside from the fact that Eckhart develops a conception of analogy according to which only God *is*, the idea that God "essences" comes directly from Eckhart (as Heidegger will later acknowledge in GA 73.2: 922). In the sermon from which Rickert takes the abovementioned epigraph, Eckhart writes, in Büttner's translation: "Denn der eigenste Ausdruck für die *Gottheit* und die erste Bestimmung, die sich förmlich setzen läßt, ist: sie *west*." "For the most proper expression for the *Godhead* and the first specification that can be formally posited is: it [the Godhead] *essences*" (Büttner 2nd ed., 2, 155). Middle High German in Jostes, 85,25–26 and DW 4: 1093,28–29 Pr. 117 ("Ze dem êrsten suochet daz rîche gotes"). Cf. DW 5: 205,8 (RdU, §6): "einen gewesenden got," rendered misleadingly as "present" and "living" in ES, 253 and

Davies, 10, respectively. Heidegger will later cite from Jostes's version of this sermon, as well as mark up his copy of Büttner's translation of it in the 1938 one-volume edition. Eckhart also uses the language of breakthrough in Pr. 52 ("Beati pauperes spiritu"), from which Heidegger will later copy out a long passage. For other usages of breakthrough in Eckhart, see McGinn, *The Mystical Thought of Meister Eckhart*, 257, n. 153. For the importance of this term, see the following three texts: (1) McGinn, *The Mystical Thought of Meister Eckhart*, passim; (2) Haas, "Durchbruch zur ewigen Wahrheit," who suggests that Eckhart may have coined the term; and (3) the major book by Nishitani Keiji's student Ueda Shizuteru titled *Die Gottesgeburt in der Seele und der Durchbruch zur Gottheit*. For various ways in which Heidegger deploys the language of *brechen* (and its cognates) throughout his corpus, and an attempt to see Eckhart as Heidegger's source, see Lera, "The Fascination of the Origin." Finally, for Heidegger's later use of the phrases "Der Gott west" and "Seyn west," see, respectively, GA 4: 169/194 and GA 65: passim.

    10. For the title of the course, see Kisiel and Sheehan, eds., *Becoming Heidegger*, xlix. Kisiel was the first to identify that certain back pages in the manuscript of the Winter Semester 1925–26 lecture course (DLA 75.7051) belonged originally to Heidegger's Winter Semester 1915–16 course (*Becoming Heidegger*, xlix–l, n. 9). In Summer 2016 I located many other such pages (which are of the same size and written in the hand of Heidegger's earlier years) in the manuscripts of the SS 1926, WS 1926–27, WS 1928–29, and WS 1929–30 lecture courses, as well as in notes for the WS 1925–26 lecture course and for Division III of *Sein und Zeit*. Although most of the pages are numbered (the lowest is 2, the highest 170), suggesting a unified whole, many of the topics (including Kant and questions of logic and judgment) seem to fall outside the confines of "The Basic Trends of Ancient and Scholastic Philosophy." At any rate, Eckhart is not named in the notes, as a comment by Kisiel would seem to suggest: "The numbered fragments found indicate that the young Heidegger in WS 1915–16 lectured at least from Pythagoras to Aristotle and then on to Eckhart" (*Becoming Heidegger*, xlix–l, n. 9). In an email to me from July 11, 2016, Kisiel clarified that "It was probably the reference to Abgeschiedenheit that brought Eckhart to mind."

    11. See especially *On Learned Ignorance*, in Cusa, *Selected Spiritual Writings*. Heidegger occasionally refers to other important aspects of Cusa's thought, which, as Heidegger knew (GA 42: 54/31), was strongly influenced by Eckhart. See UAS 96 (on the world as an unfolding of God), GA 67: 173 (on the derivation of the name for God, *theos*, from the name for seeing, *theōrein*), and GA 84.1: 524 (on human nature as a microcosm). See also GA 3: 307/215; GA 95: 428/334; and DLA 75.7072/23. For Cusa's debt to Eckhart, see Brient, "Meister Eckhart's Influence on Nicholas of Cusa."

    12. Two passages from Bernhart's translation into modern German relate to this. First, he renders §6 of RdU as "Der Mensch soll Gott erleben in allen Dingen" (Bernhart, 82); "The human should experience God in all things." Cf. DW 5: 205,1/

Davies 9. In his personal copy of Bernhart's translation, Heidegger crossed out the word *erleben* (experience) and wrote the Middle High German *nemen* (take, grasp) in the margin. In the second passage, Heidegger underlined four words in red pencil: "Wer Gott so im Wesen inne hat der erfaßt ihn göttlich, und dem leuchtet er in allen Dingen" (Bernhart, 84). "Whoever possesses God in their being, has him in a divine manner, and he shines out to them in all things" (Davies, 10). Cf. DW 5: 205,10–11. According to personal conversations with Friedrich Wilhelm von Herrmann, red pencil often signifies "very important" for Heidegger.

13. This note is published in German and in an English translation in Kisiel, "Notes for a Work on the 'Phenomenology of Religious Life' (1916–19)," 319, 327, n. 35. This note, along with others first published in Kisiel's text, can be found in the Deutsches Literaturarchiv Marbach among those published in GA 60 under the title *Die philosophischen Grundlagen der mittalterlichen Mystik* [Ausarbeitungen und Entwürfe zu einer nicht gehaltenen Vorlesung 1918/19]. I follow Kisiel's dating of them here and in what follows. Kisiel also argues that "Phenomenology of Religious Life" is a better title for most of both of these sets of notes, since only ten of about forty-five pages containing these notes were written in preparation for Heidegger's cancelled Winter Semester 1919–20 (and not 1918–19) lecture course on *The Philosophical Foundations of Medieval Mysticism*. The rest were for a planned, though never completed, "phenomenology of religious consciousness," as Heidegger put it in a letter to Elisabeth Blochmann from May 1, 1919 (MH/EB, 16), or "Phenomenology of Religious Life," as is found on the manuscript title page of the notebooks. Several of these notes may be seen as an initial (though never completed) attempt to evaluate Eckhartian mysticism in light of the material determination of every form and the problem of truth that Heidegger discusses in the conclusion of his *Habilitationsschrift*. Unlike in the latter, however, the relationship between mysticism and scholasticism in the notes is a relationship less of collaborative compatibility than of fundamental antipathy. See Kisiel, *The Genesis of Heidegger's* Being and Time, 82.

Additional evidence for the 1919–20 dating, not mentioned by Kisiel, can be found in Heidegger's letter to Elfride Heidegger from September 9, 1919: "The fact that Fräulein Walter [*sic*] is going to Munich because I'm not lecturing on mysticism is also typical—people would, after all, have experienced & enjoyed the course as something of a sensation albeit without responding in a manly-strong manner or actively getting to grips with an infinite set of problems" (MH/EH, 100/67). (Gerda Walther would later become a parapsychologist and avid defender of mystical experience. On her work and relation to Heidegger, see Mario Fischer, *Religiöse Erfahrung in der Phänomenologie des frühen Heidegger*, 111–22; MH/KL, passim; and GA 56/57: 225/192. See Walther, *Zum anderen Ufer*, 323–24, for her relation to Eckhart.)

14. Heidegger will later refer to the spark of the soul in GA 8: 153/149, and Z, 250/201.

15. In Kisiel, "Notes for a Work on the 'Phenomenology of Religious Life' (1916–19)," 319, 327, n. 36.

16. Heidegger later mentions Eckhart's eternal now in GA 26: 56/45.

17. As Heidegger puts it in 1920–21: "It is peculiar to phenomenological understanding that it can understand the *incomprehensible*, precisely in that it radically *lets* the latter *be* [*beläßt*] in its incomprehensibility. That is itself comprehensible only if one has understood that philosophy has nothing to do with the scientific study of object and subject." GA 60: 131/92–93.

18. See Camilleri, *Phénoménologie de la religion et herméneutique théologique dans la pensée du jeune Heidegger*, 305–306. I might note that Otto's 1917 *Das Heilige: Über das Irrationale in der Idee des Göttlichen und sein Verhältnis zum Rationalen*, of which Heidegger had planned to write a review, contains several significant references to Eckhart (and to Eckhart's successors Tauler, Suso, and Jakob Böhme). It is interesting that Heidegger's sketches for this review (GA 60: 332–34/251–52) deal with the problem of irrationality (signaled in the subtitle of Otto's book), for this topic is under discussion in "Irrationality in Meister Eckhart." Moreover, a note from 1919, titled simply "Irrationality," brings together themes addressed in the earlier notes on Eckhart and Otto (see Camilleri, *Phénoménologie de la religion*, 233), suggesting that, at least for a time, Heidegger was thinking of, and perhaps intending to treat, these two figures together. Cf. Heidegger's letter to Elfride from September 9, 1919, in which Heidegger speaks of both *Gelassenheit* and Otto: "Times of abandonment [*Ver-lassenheit*] & seeming distance from God are only lived genuinely if they are times of trusting composure [*Gelassenheit*]—that is, of the strong, God-assured mastery of life. Since I read Luther's Commentary on Romans, much that before was troubling & dark to me has become bright & liberating—I have quite a new understanding of the Middle Ages & the development of Christn. religiousness; & wholly new perspectives on the problems of the philos. of religion have opened up to me—Otto, for example, seems to me to be on the wrong track" (MH/EH, 100/66–67). Later references to Otto can be found in GA 60: passim. Given Heidegger's interest in Otto during his early Freiburg period, it is quite possible that he would have read some of Otto's later texts while they were colleagues in Marburg (1923–28). See, for example, the following three, all of which touch on Eckhart: "Meister Eckeharts Mystik im Unterschiede von östlicher Mystik" (1925), "Der östliche Buddhist" (1925), and *West-östliche Mystik* (1926). Heidegger at any rate would have been familiar with the last text on account of his student Käte Oltmanns's detailed discussion of Otto's reading of Eckhart in her dissertation (*Meister Eckhart*, 47–56). These later texts by Otto could well have been the first sources for Heidegger's appreciation of Eckhart as a thinker with Eastern resonances, though in a letter to Jaspers from 1949 he contends that people who see an Eastern influence on his thought fail to see that it is Eckhart's influence that gives this illusion. MH/KJ, 181–82/172. Be that as it may, many of Heidegger's Japanese connections would go on to do great work on Eckhart, such as Tanabe

Hajime, Nishitani Keiji, D. T. Suzuki, Tsujimura Kōichi, and Ueda Shizuteru. For texts that discuss and draw on the some of these figures in relation to Heidegger's thought, see Davis, *Heidegger and the Will*, May, *Heidegger's Hidden Sources*, and Parkes, ed., *Heidegger and Asian Thought*. For one of Nishitani's important texts on Eckhart, see Appendix Three, below, and my discussion of it in §4 of the present chapter. I note as well a letter Heidegger wrote to his brother on December 20, 1956, in which he mentions that there is an outstanding Japanese professor in his seminar on Hegel's *Logic* who is a Zen Buddhist and is working on Eckhart. DLA HS.2014.0069.00021.

19. On the role of freedom in Eckhart, see especially Oltmanns, *Meister Eckhart*.

20. In this passage, Heidegger quotes Leser, "Das religiöse Wahrheitsproblem im Lichte der deutschen Mystik," 23.

21. As Camilleri, *Phénoménologie de la religion*, 319, suggests.

22. And not "va à l'encontre de la religiosité vivante," as Camilleri renders it. *Phénoménologie de la religion*, 319. The German reads: "Der neue Motivationszusammenhang für den mystiktheoretischen Überbau entstammt der lebendigen Religiösität, dem lebendigen Subjekt."

23. Gadamer, "Auf dem Rückgang zum Anfang (1986)," 406. Gadamer seems to be confused about when the *Opus tripartitum* was published. See my description of Gadamer's reports in §6 of Appendix One, below. For other ways in which an Eckhartian influence may be traced during this period, see Lera, "The Fascination of the Origin"; McGrath, "Heidegger and Medieval German Mysticism"; Onishi, "Transcendence as Indistinction in Eckhart and Heidegger"; and Flaumbaum, "Meister Eckhart y Martin Heidegger," who boldly declared in 1944 that "[i]f we follow our analysis of existential philosophy, we will find that every one of Eckhart's concepts has its correspondence in Heidegger's philosophy, although they are of course distorted [*deformado*]" (53). Lastly, it is noteworthy that Spanish translations of Heidegger's 1929 "What Is Metaphysics?" and Eckhart's *On Detachment* were published together as the sole texts of a single volume: *Qué es metafísica? por M. Heidegger / Sermón del Maestro Eckehart* (Santiago de Chile/Madrid: Cruz del Sur, 1963). Both translations date back to 1933, when they appeared in different issues of the journal *Cruz y Raya*.

24. As Reiner Schürmann relates, "Heidegger sometimes quotes from Meister Eckhart, and we learned personally from him that he developed his understanding of being as *An-wesen* (a verb, not a noun) in the years in which he also read Meister Eckhart's sermons." *Wandering Joy*, 254, n. 93; cf. xviii, as well as the other reports by Schürmann provided in §6 of Appendix One, below. In a cryptic passage probably dating from 1956 or later, where Heidegger uses the archaic German spelling *Seyn* (beyng) to distinguish being from the mere being of beings, Heidegger nevertheless appears to contrast his understanding of being with that of Eckhart: " '*Wesen*' (im Sinne von: das Seyn west.) / als Name des Seyns des Seyns . . . nicht wie Eckhart: Gott '*west*'—An-wesen, sondern: *einai* als *estin* des *einai*. / Nur das Seyn als Seyn west:

das Selbe Selber und 'Wesen' als Seyn des Seyns ist das Ereignis *des Unterschieds* / Es west: | das Seyn ist |"; " *'Essence' (in the sense of: beyng essences.)* / as name of the *beyng of beyng* . . . not like Eckhart: God *'essences'*—presenc-ing, but rather: *einai* as the *estin* of *einai*. / Only beyng as beyng essences: *the Same Itself* and 'essence' as the beyng of beyng is the appropriative event *of the distinction*. / It essences: | beyng is |" (GA 73.2: 922).

25. Lasson, *Meister Eckhart, der Mystiker*, 109–11.

26. The distinction between *deitas* and *deus* dates back to Gilbert de la Porrée, whose work on this idea Heidegger mentions in a passage from the manuscript which did not make its way into the published version of the lecture course (DLA 75.7054).

27. Heidegger was a mentor to Stadelmann during the Third Reich. See Heidegger's letters to and fond recollections of Stadelmann in GA 16: 174, 179–80, 370–71, 395–96, 405–408, 419–20, 438–39. In a letter of recommendation from 1935, Heidegger praises Stadelmann, noting that he is the best historian when it comes to the Middle Ages. Quote found in Jatho and Simon, *Gießener Historiker im Dritten Reich*, 78. I might note that Stadelmann's *Vom Geist des ausgehenden Mittelalters* (1929) examines, inter alia, mysticism in the late Middle Ages, including Meister Eckhart (see esp. ch. 3). In a piece from 1930 Stadelmann names among his interests "Meister Eckhart up through Dürer, the archetype of Germanness [*das Urbild des Deutschtums*]." Quote found in Jatho and Simon, *Gießener Historiker im Dritten Reich*, 104.

28. The expression *Lese- und Lebemeister* goes back to a proverb about Eckhart that is preserved in the edition of Eckhart's German works with which Heidegger was most familiar, namely, Pfeiffer's, 599,19–20: "Es sprichet meister Eckehart: wêger wêre ein lebemeister denne tûsent lesemeister." "Meister Eckhart says: a master of life would be better than a thousand masters of letters." Part of this line was also taken as the epigraph to the second volume of Büttner's translation of Eckhart: "Ein Lebemeister frommte mehr denn tausend Lesemeister." Heidegger will later cite from the first volume of the second edition of Büttner. Cf. also Bernhart, 22.

It is possible that Tauler was actually Heidegger's source, though. Heidegger owned a copy of Ferdinand Vetter's 1910 edition of Tauler, where, on p. 196,28–31 Pr. 45 ("Beati oculi qui vident quod vos videtis"), one reads: "Lieben kinder, die grossen pfaffen und die lesmeister die tispitierent weder bekentnisse merre und edeler si oder die minne. Aber wir wellen nu *al* hie sagen von den lebmeistern. Als wir dar komen, denne súllen wir aller dinge worheit wol sehen." "Dear children! The great clerics and masters of letters quarrel about the question of whether knowledge or love is better and nobler. We, however, wish to speak about the masters of life here. When we get there [heaven], then we shall indeed behold the truth of all things." Although the only marginalia from Heidegger are the marks he made in red pencil next to some words in the index (*inblic, inblicken, inliuhten, inliuhtunge, insehen, insprâche*), he no doubt had more than a passing engagement with this text, for he also inserted slips of paper between pages 36–37, 58–59, 68–69, 108–109, 128–29, 366–67, 464–65, and 470–71. (The slip of paper between pages 128 and 129 comes from a typescript of "Hegel and the Greeks" and is thus quite late. According to von Herrmann, these slips indicate that Heidegger had planned to come back to these pages.) Heidegger's mark next to *insehen* (seeing-in, insight) was perhaps made while he was taking notes for *The Principle of Reason*, since one note contains a quote by Tauler (which actually comes from Eckhart) on this theme. Heidegger is citing from the Grimm dictionary entry on "abgründig": "abgründig, *immense profundus* . . . got hat ein vollkommen einsehen in sich selber und abgrundiges durchkennen sich selbs mit im selber. TAULER." "abyssal, *immense profundus*, immeasurably deep: God has a perfect insight into himself and abyssal thorough knowledge of himself by himself"; cf. DW 4: 350,87–351,88 Pr. 101 ("Dum medium silentium tenerent omnia") and Walshe's translation, 32. Heidegger then writes out a phrase in modern German that comes from Tauler's sixty-seventh sermon "Flecto genua mea ad Deum et patrem Domini Jhesu Christi," where, in the edition cited above, one reads: "dem abgrúnde der grundeloskeit Gotz" (368,13), "[from] the abyss of the groundlessness of God." Heidegger may well be drawing from Grimm again, where, under the entry on "Grundlosigkeit" (groundlessness) one finds this quote; incidentally, it immediately follows one by Eckhart: "da enkan si (*die seele*) in (*gott*) niemer begrifen in dem mer sîner gruntlôsekeit. MEISTER ECKHARDT 228 *Pfeiffer.*" "It [the soul, or more properly the intellect: *vernünfticheit*] can never grasp Him in the ocean of his unfathomableness [or groundlessness]" (Walshe, 369). Cf. DW 1: 123,2–3 Pr. 7 ("Populi eius qui in te est, misereberis"). DLA 57.7314,2. For other references to Tauler in Heidegger's corpus, see KT, 22/51; GA 6.2: 267; GA 42: 54/31; GA 58: 62/48; GA 61: 7/7. For a comparison between Tauler on the call of God and Heidegger on the call of conscience, see Sikka, *Forms of Transcendence*, chs. 5–6.

Finally, to return to Heidegger's phrase *Lese- und Lebemeister*, what is interesting about this is that it does not privilege the role of *lebemeister* over that of *lesemeister*, as both the proverb and Tauler do, though it is perhaps worth noting that, in one typescript of "The Pathway" bearing Heidegger's signature at the top of the first page, *Lebemeister* is missing. Available in Max Müller's papers at UAF E 3/174. Heidegger could have taken *lesemeister* alone from Pfeiffer, 77,17–18 or 623,13. According to Georg Steer, Tauler and the members of the *Gottesfreunde* (Friends of God) movement were probably the first to use the term *lebemeister*, which would make the abovementioned proverb apocryphal. See Steer, "Eckhart der *meister*," esp. 720–23.

29. For the possibility that Heidegger may be referring to Pr. 53 ("Misit dominus manum suam"), see Pöggeler, *Neue Wege mit Heidegger*, 433, and DW 3: 531,10–13 and 535,39–42/Davies 128–29.

30. Cf. Eckhart's sermon on poverty (Pr. 52, "Beati pauperes spiritu"), which was read and cited by Heidegger as well: "Until creatures came into existence, God was not 'God,' but was rather what he was. Then, when creatures emerged and

received their created being, God was not 'God' in himself but in creatures." "And if I did not exist, then neither would God have existed as 'God.' I am the cause of God's existence as 'God.'" DW 2: 492,8–493,2 and 504,2-3/Davies 204–205 and 208. Here too, there are no inverted commas to be found in the manuscripts.

31. This is repeated nearly verbatim in Pr. 52 ("Beati pauperes spiritu"): "When I flowed forth from God, all things said: God is [*Dô ich ûz gote vlôz, dô sprâchen alliu dinc: got der ist*]." DW 2: 504,5/Davies 208. Drawing on Pr. 109 (with its language of the river of the Godhead) and the Pseudo-Eckhartian *Liber positionum*, Lera makes a case for how "Eckhart himself may be a source for Heidegger's 'Neoplatonic' interpretation of Hölderlin's rivers" ("The Fascination of the Origin," 227).

32. Cf. GA 86: 804–805; GA 15: 153/93; GA 99: 38, 63; and, for a detailed discussion of Heidegger's understanding of speculative sentences and the transitive "is," Schlüter, *Heideggers Rezeption des antiken und mittelalterlichen Neuplatonismus*, 115–25.

33. In §6 of RdU, Eckhart writes: "Thus we should be permeated with the sense of a divine presence and be in-formed with the form of our beloved God and be so established in him [*in im gewesent sîn*, literally: 'be beened' in him] that we see his presence effortlessly and, more than this, remain unencumbered by anything, free of all things" (DW 5: 208,11–209,2/Davies 7). Heidegger marked up this section extensively in his personal copy of Bernhart's translation into Modern German, though not this particular sentence. Bernhart renders the relevant phrase with an accusative: "in ihn eingewest sein," "to be essenced into him" (86). Oltmanns quotes the Middle High German from Pfeiffer's edition in her book *Meister Eckhart*, 72. Cf. DW 5: 306,3–5/Davies 50 (RdU, §23): "sie werdent alsô mit götlîchem wesene überwesent," "they are transformed [literally, 'beened over'] in their essence by the divine essence." Cf. also *Die Predigten Taulers*, 413,19ff. Pr. 77 ("Qui michi ministrat, me sequitur").

34. For Eckhart's uses of *isticheit*, see Morard, "Ist, istic, istikeit bei Meister Eckhart," esp. 170–71; Beccarisi, "*Isticheit* nach Meister Eckhart"; and Beccarisi, "Philosophische Neologismen zwischen Latein und Volkssprache," esp. 338, nn. 26–27.

35. This was one of the lines Eckhart had to defend during his heresy trial in Cologne. The censors translated it into Latin poorly, obscuring the significance of *isticheit*: "secundum quod deus est in se ipso." See LW 5: 231,21 (Acta #47).

36. After the publication of GA 63, Theodore Kisiel wrote to Oltmanns to congratulate her on her fine work, pointing out to her, however, this divergence from the manuscript. Oltmanns replied that Heidegger was actually the one who made the mistake, and that she was absolutely certain he meant "transitive." She mentions Eckhart and Schelling as examples of philosophers who used being transitively. Kisiel ends up agreeing with her, and cites a couple of instances in which Heidegger employs this usage elsewhere. Kisiel, "Edition und Übersetzung," 93–94. Cf. Ochsner's claim about Heidegger's very early use of the transitive "is" on pp. 260–61, n. 9, below.

37. GA 29/30: 533/367; Müller, "Martin Heidegger—Ein Philosoph und die Politik," 192, 206, 212; MH/MM, 113, 130, 138. See Heidegger's seminar books: DLA 75.7437, 75.7438. Oltmanns also attended Heidegger's 1941 seminar on Schelling, and in the manuscript of his 1941 lecture course and seminar *Die Metaphysik des deutschen Idealismus*, there is a letter from Oltmanns arguing for a different interpretation of a passage in Schelling than the one Heidegger had proposed. At the top of the letter, Heidegger writes that her interpretation is "fully convincing." See DLA 75.7176, and GA 49: 115, n. 3. The oral examination for Oltmanns's dissertation was held on February 28, 1934. (For Heidegger's notes on the examination, see §8 of Appendix One, below.) Oltmanns then published her dissertation as a book in 1935 with two different presses, August Osterrieth and Vittorio Klostermann. A copy of Heidegger's imprimatur for the dissertation is available in his 1930–39 letters to her husband (DLA HS.2003.0056; other letters between Heidegger and the couple can be found in DLA 75.16222, 83.668, and 96.146.77). Heidegger was also involved in helping Oltmanns publish it. See his letter to Erich Rothacker from August 11, 1934, in which he asks whether Rothacker might have a place in the series for Oltmanns's text, which, he relates, Oltmanns had been working on since 1927. He describes it as "excellent [*ausgezeichnet*]" and comments that the Freiburg historian Gerhard Ritter also "esteemed it very highly [*sehr hoch eingeschätzt*]" (MH/ER, 223–24). Heidegger was not successful with Rothacker, but, we may assume, this did not stop Heidegger from following up with Klostermann. For Heidegger had been engaged in an "intense correspondence" with Klostermann since 1929, one that had included "many meetings" and recommendations; additionally, other students of Heidegger had published with Klostermann in the first half of the 1930s (including Herbert Marcuse, Hans-Georg Gadamer, Karl Löwith, Otto Friedrich Bollnow, Wilhelm Weischedel, and, in 1935, Oltmanns's husband Walter Bröcker). Thus, it is likely that Heidegger played an important role in Oltmanns's decision to publish with Klostermann as well. See his letter to Walter Bröcker from July 19, 1935 (DLA HS.2003.0056), as well as Klostermann, ed., *Vittorio Klostermann, Frankfurt am Main, 1930–2000*.

38. As she reveals in a 1992 interview with Cornelius Bickel and Jürgen Zander, available on CD at the Martin-Heidegger-Archiv der Stadt Meßkirch. See also Oltmanns, *Meister Eckhart*, 10.

39. Oltmanns's book, which, especially in its later portions, attempts to assimilate Eckhart's thought to the categories of *Being and Time*, or rather to read *Being and Time* back into Eckhart, has received mixed reviews. See Caputo, *The Mystical Element in Heidegger's Thought*, 196–99; Degenhardt, *Studien zum Wandel des Eckhartbildes*, 319–20; Schürmann, *Wandering Joy*, 263; Tanabe, *Philosophy as Metanoetics*, 178–85; and the various reviews of Oltmanns's work cited in the first two texts. Others who have drawn on Oltmanns's work in relation to Heidegger include Pöggeler, "Jean Wahls Heidegger-Deutung," 451–52; and Schmid, "Praeteritio dei," 347. Heidegger himself later expressed his frustration about the unfair

way in which his students' work, including work on Eckhart, was received (GA 97: 478). We may presume he means the book version of Oltmanns's dissertation here.

40. As related in her 1992 interview with Cornelius Bickel and Jürgen Zander, available on CD at the Martin-Heidegger-Archiv der Stadt Meßkirch.

41. Suzuki, *Essays in Zen Buddhism*. Nishitani relates that Suzuki's book led Heidegger to check out the only book on Zen in the university library: *Zen: Der lebendige Buddhismus in Japan*, ed. August Faust, with a preface by Rudolf Otto. Information found in Parkes, ed., *Heidegger and Asian Thought*, 10. (Faust had, incidentally, attended Heidegger's Winter Semester 1920–21 lecture course, and would later go on to edit Böhme's *Sämtliche Schriften*. See MH/HR, 63, 65–66, 131–32.) Barrett, in "Zen for the West," xii, reports that "A German friend of Heidegger told me that one day when he visited Heidegger he found him reading one of Suzuki's books. 'If I understand this man correctly,' Heidegger remarked, 'this is what I have been trying to say in all my writings.' "

42. I draw the information for this paragraph from Parkes, ed., *Heidegger and Asian Thought*, 9–10; May, *Heidegger's Hidden Sources*, 103–104; and Davis, *Heidegger and the Will*, 308, n. 12.

43. Nishitani, "Mon point de départ philosophique," 302; Heisig, *Philosophers of Nothingness*, 183–84. Plotinus, Augustine, Eckhart, and Böhme are the main figures discussed in Nishitani's book-length article "Shinpishisō-shi" (A History of Mystical Thought), which was first published in 1932. I thank Hiroshi Abé and S. P. K. Cerda for this information.

44. Davis, "Zen after Zarathustra," 105–106; Kawamura, "[Review of] The Selected Works of Nishitani Keiji," 307. Its importance is indicated by the fact that Nishitani put it at the beginning of his first book and at the beginning of his collected works, ahead of texts composed earlier.

45. See the report by Ōhashi Ryōsuke in §6 of Appendix One, below.

46. Later, Nishitani will be more critical of Nietzsche (as will Heidegger): "Nietzsche does not seem to have attained Eckhart's standpoint of an absolute nothingness that takes its stand on the immediacy of everyday life. . . . [I]f the *nihilum* of *creatio ex nihilo* (as a negative referring to the relative existence of created being) may be called relative nothingness, and if the nothingness of godhead in Eckhart (as the point at which all of existence, including subjective existence, stands out in its true-to-life reality) may be called absolute nothingness, then perhaps we might say that the nihility of Nietzsche's nihilism should be called a standpoint of *relative absolute nothingness*" (*Religion and Nothingness*, 66).

47. See also GA 42: 54/31. Beierwaltes, while rightly noting the National Socialist connection in deeming Eckhart the founder of German philosophy, nevertheless conflates Heidegger's understanding of German and modern philosophy, claiming, incorrectly, that Heidegger thus contradicts himself. See Beierwaltes, "Heideggers Gelassenheit," 17. Wolz-Gottwald, in contrast, suggests that Heidegger is *criticizing* National Socialism by locating the origin of *modern* philosophy

in Descartes, rather than in Eckhart. See Wolz-Gottwald, "Martin Heidegger und die philosophische Mystik," 69. At any rate, the Nazis were by no means the first to see in Eckhart the emergence of a uniquely German philosophical spirit. For example, in a 1900 article titled "Der entwicklungsgeschichtliche Pantheismus nach seinem geschichtlichen Zusammenhang mit den älteren pantheistischen Systemen," Wilhelm Dilthey maintained that, in Eckhart, "the life constitution of the German spirit is first manifested philosophically" (315). (Republished in 1914 in *Weltanschauung und Analyse des Menschen seit Renaissance und Reformation* [see p. 321], a text to which Heidegger refers in GA 42: 13/8.) Paul Natorp, another philosopher who greatly influenced Heidegger, espoused a similar view in 1918. For further discussion, see Baier, "Heidegger und das Mittelalter," 36–40; and Pöggeler, *Neue Wege mit Heidegger*, 177–78, 238.

48. In response to a 1967 essay that Bernhard Welte had sent him, Heidegger writes that what Welte wanted to accomplish with regard to Aquinas, that is, to show that there is a certain background in his corpus that is not forgetful of being (in Heidegger's sense), can only be accomplished with regard to Eckhart: "Is the 'background' in Thomas actually a background *thought?* In contrast, there actually 'follows' in Meister Eckhart a new step. A sentence like *Sed etiam Deus* [*sic*, should be *dico*] *quod Deo non convenit esse nec est ens, sed est aliquid altius ente* . . . can, as far as I know, be found nowhere else" (MH/BW, 29–30). (I take it that "Deus" is either a slip of the pen or an editorial transcription error, not that Heidegger is trying to "correct" the text, as Schlüter, *Heideggers Rezeption des antiken und mittelalterlichen Neuplatonismus*, 73, n. 2, claims.) Welte's essay (originally titled "Rückblick auf die Metaphysik") can be found under the later title "Thomas von Aquin und Heideggers Gedanke von der Seinsgeschichte." The Eckhart quote can be found in LW 5: 47, no. 12 (Qu. Par. 1). A few days after his letter to Welte, Heidegger wrote to his brother, praising Welte's article, while at the same time remarking that Welte should have emphasized Eckhart's uniqueness more. DLA HS.2014.0069.00027. In an essay from 1968 entitled "Bemerkungen zum Gottesbegriff des Thomas von Aquin," Welte concludes his reflections on Aquinas with a consideration of Eckhart, as he had done the previous year in the 1967 essay, as well as in the conclusion of his 1946 *Habilitationsschrift: Der philosophische Glaube bei Karl Jaspers und die Möglichkeit seiner Deutung durch die thomistische Philosophie*, 278 and note. Heidegger comments on the last-mentioned text in MH/BW, 12.

49. Sturlese, *Homo divinus*, 28, n. 69, 95–106. Heidegger cites from Grabmann's edition in his letter to Welte discussed in the previous endnote, and Heidegger owned a copy as well. Indeed, Grabmann's long introduction is a likely source for Heidegger's appreciation of Eckhart; see especially his discussion the uniqueness of Eckhart's conception of analogy on pages 59–62. See also Oltmanns's seminar presentation in Appendix Two, below.

Grabmann was a leading scholar of medieval philosophy whom Heidegger knew personally and to whose work Heidegger was avowedly indebted. See GA 1:

193–94, 197, n. 4; GA 23: 41–42; HAD, 73–74; and MH/EB, 36. Grabmann, in turn, had written on Heidegger's *Hablitationsschrift* with admiration (in, for example, *Mittelalterliches Geistesleben*, Vol. 1), although he was the first to show that the author of *De modis significandi sive Grammatica speculativa*, on which Heidegger had written the second part of his *Habilitationsschrift*, was not by Duns Scotus, as Heidegger had thought, but rather by Thomas of Erfurt. Grabmann also published on Eckhart in other respects. See, for example, his "Neue Eckhartforschungen im Lichte neuerer Eckhartfunde," Otto Karrer's reply ("Zu Prälat M. Grabmanns Eckehartkritik"), and Grabmann's response ("Erwiderung"). On Grabmann's publication of the Parisian Questions and his philological background, see Vincent, "*Questions on the Attributes (of God)*."

50. Gadamer, "Die Geschichte der Philosophie (1981)," 299. See §6 of Appendix One, below, for Gadamer's quote.

51. This sermon seems to be a plausible candidate as the source of Heidegger's note, for in it Eckhart explains that, "Whoever understands about the just man and justice understands all that I am saying." (On the theme of justice in Eckhart, see §3 of chapter 2, below, as well as Nishitani's discussion in §2 of Appendix Three, below.) Another candidate is Eckhart's Latin Commentary on John, which Heidegger cites elsewhere, including amid another discussion of Nietzsche in the "Leitgedanken über das Entstehen und Vergehen der Metaphysik" (written sometime between 1940 and 1955) (GA 76: 11). *Gelassenheit* makes an appearance here as an alternative to Nietzsche's will to will and the reign of metaphysics (GA 76: 6). For other citations of Eckhart's commentary, see GA 73.2: 995–96; GA 98: 211; and MH/HA, 112/91.

52. "All the love of this world is based on love of self. If you had released [*gelâzen*] this, you would have released the world." DW 1: 108,12–110,1/Walshe 330; trans. mod. Eckhart draws support from Augustine to claim that "[t]he true lover of justice is so established in what he loves that it is his very being" (DW 1: 104,5–6/Walshe 329). Heidegger will pick up on this latter idea in his 1949 lecture "Das Ding": "Thus Meister Eckhart, following a saying of Dionysius the Areopagite <Ed.: Augustine is probably meant>, says: love is of such a nature that it changes man into the things he loves" (GA 79: 15/14–15). It should be noted that the editor of the GA-volume is mistaken here. Heidegger is citing, not from Pfeiffer's edition, but from the eighty-second text in Jostes's edition, from which the quotation, with its reference to Dionysius, derives. Thus, Heidegger is not himself trying to figure out Eckhart's sources, *pace* Schlüter, *Heideggers Rezeption des antiken und mittelalterlichen Neuplatonismus*, 19, 25.

53. "*Denken //* Denken ist das Nahe-Wohnen / ist der stille Dank. // Denken ist das edle Schonen, / ist der kühne Rank. // Eines Wegs der dunklen Zeichen, / Kehren zwischen Nichts und Sein. // Denken ist das Nie-Entweichen / aus dem Bösen, vor der Pein. // Denken ist ohn' greifend Fassen, / ist ein Fragen frank. // Denken ist Sich-sagen-Lassen, / ist der kühle Trank // Auf dem Gang, da sanft sich

lichten / Lichter ohne Zahl, // Rosen ohn' Warum, die dichten, / grüßend Strom und Tal. // Denken bleibt dies Alles-Freyen, / weiseloser Ruf, // daß, die sterblich, seyend seyen: / Heilem der Behuf" (GA 81: 186–87). Cf. the different versions of this poem, which bear the dates January 23, 1946, and January 21, 1946, respectively, and were intended for his wife Elfride, in GA 81: 22–23.

I should also mention Heidegger's 1916 poem "Abendgang auf der Reichenau" (Eventide on Reichenau), which he composed while vacationing with Elfride on the island of Reichnau. The poem resonates with Eckhartian themes such as the simplicity of eternity and the desert of the Godhead, and we know that Heidegger was reading Eckhart at this time. As he recalls in a letter to Elfride: "all the lovely Reichenau days from 1916 come back to me again—the evenings in the boat—the walks—out in the Cove, where we read Meister Eckhart on Sundays" (MH/EH, 97/64). There is, moreover, a draft of the poem (reproduced in MH/EH, 46/24) that is even more Eckhartian, containing words such as "Gottesnähe" (nearness of God) "gotterfüllt" (God-suffused), and "Seele" (soul). The poem reads, in William Richardson's translation (*Heidegger: Through Phenomenology to Thought*, 1): "Over the waters flows a silvern glimmer / Forth to distant, darkened shores, / And in the summer-weary, dew-damp gardens / Falls, like a lover's word withheld, / The night. / From moon-white gabled prison / Neath the ancient tower's roof / A bird sings one last song. / And the yield to me of shining summer day / Rests like heavy fruit– / From long eternities / A burden beyond sense– / For me in the gray desert / Of a great Simplicity." "Seewärts fließt ein silbern Leuchten / zu fernen dunkeln Ufern fort, / und in den sommermüden, abendfeuchten / Gärten sinkt wie ein verhalten Liebeswort / die Nacht. / Und zwischen mondenweißen Giebeln / verfängt sich noch ein letzter Vogelruf / vom alten Turmdach her– / und was der lichte Sommertag mir schuf / ruht früchteschwer– / aus Ewigkeiten / eine sinnentrückte Fracht– / mir in der grauen Wüste / einer großen Einfalt."

54. On letting-be-said see GA 75: 279–85. Heidegger mentions Eckhart on p. 282.

55. Natorp, *Deutscher Weltberuf*, 2, 74. GA 56/57: 75/64; trans. mod. I owe this reference to van Buren, *Rumor of the Hidden King*, 299. Van Buren (see esp. 307–50) devotes considerable attention to the influence of Natorp's book on Heidegger, which Husserl had strongly recommended to Heidegger in 1918 (Husserl, *Briefwechsel*, 4, 136). As regards Eckhart, two additional moments are especially noteworthy. First, Natorp, like Heidegger, saw something unique about Eckhart's role within the history of ideas. In contrast to other mystics, who remained under the sway of the doctrine of Scholasticism and brought only a "religious fundamental attunement [*Grundstimmung*]" to it, Eckhart was able to achieve something new in terms of the doctrine itself (1, 92–93), thereby transforming "Romance mysticism into German philosophy" (2, 111). This distinctively German philosophy can be identified in Eckhart's focus on returning to the self from the dispersions and distractions resulting not only from an excessive focus on works, but also from an

excessive focus on contemplation and flight from the world. Indeed, Natorp contends that this "*self-discovery of the German soul*" was "more important in its consequences for the fate of *humanity* than the opening-up [*Erschließung*] of the earth . . . and all the laws of external nature" (2, 71). Second, Natorp's book may have been responsible for Heidegger's turn toward Luther, as van Buren considers in *Rumor of the Hidden King*, 149. For, as in Heidegger's own subsequent genealogies (GA 58: 61–62/47–48; GA 42: 45/31), both Eckhart and Luther play pivotal roles in Natorp's. Far from a fundamental shift, however, Natorp contends that "Eckehart had already reached in principle," if not in deed, "the essential, perhaps the most essential," things for which Luther would become famous (2, 83). For Heidegger's personal relation to Natorp, and the latter's relation to Eckhart, see the recollection by Gadamer in *Philosophical Apprenticeships*, 26.

There is, finally, a noteworthy anecdote about Natorp and Husserl that Heidegger's oldest student and lifelong friend Heinrich Ochsner (who was also an Eckhart-enthusiast) related to Bernhard Welte. Ochsner would meet with Husserl occasionally during the period of World War I. One day, Husserl told him that Natorp had recently discovered Eckhart and had drawn Husserl's attention to him. As Bernhard Welte tells it: "Now he, Husserl, has been sitting for two days in his room smoking cigars and reading nothing but Meister Eckhart. During this encounter he said to Heinrich Ochsner: 'I envy your religious-historical knowledge.' For indeed Heinrich Ochsner had known Meister Eckhart for a long time and was therefore able to draw Husserl's attention to many things which were important to be able understand him." In Ochwadt and Tecklenborg, eds., *Das Maß des Verborgenen*, 213. In 1932, Husserl would himself relate to Dorian Cairns that "[w]hole pages of Meister Eckehart . . . could be taken over by him [Husserl] unchanged." Cairns, *Conversations with Husserl and Fink*, 91. For Ochsner's interest in Eckhart see Welte, *Meister Eckhart: Gedanken zu seinen Gedanken*, 21; Ochwadt and Tecklenborg, eds., *Das Maß des Verborgenen*, 40, 93–94, 176, 184, 186, 211, 224, 257, 280; and Ochsner's Eckhartian essay "Zur Kritik der Deutsch-Christlichen Studentenvereinigung" (available in *Das Maß des Verborgenen*, 3–10). This was one of Ochsner's few publications, publications with which, incidentally, Heidegger was wont to provide guidance (*Das Maß des Verborgenen*, 94, 284; MH/EH, 102/68–69). For Ochsner's attendance in Heidegger's first seminar, see *Das Maß des Verborgenen*, 263, n. 1; cf. 176, n. 1. For his relation to Heidegger, see, passim, *Das Maß des Verborgenen*; Müller, *Auseinandersetzung als Versöhnung*; MH/MM; MH/E&S; and MH/BW. In MH/EH, 100/67, Heidegger suggests that, in 1919, Ochsner had access to Heidegger's "mysticism lectures [*Mystikkolleg*]."

56. On Eckhart's text, see below. Regarding Suso, Heidegger's nephew Heinrich Heidegger reports that, in honor of Heinrich's investiture as a pastor in Schwandorf in 1962, Martin gave him the collected German writings of "my namesake Henry Suso [referred to in German as Heinrich Seuse, who was beatified in 1831,] and cited from it an essential saying [*Wort*] from the 'Book of Truth' (Ch. VII, fine)" (quote in

Zimmermann, *Martin und Fritz Heidegger*, 167). The text Martin gave Heinrich was Martin's own copy of Bihlmeyer's 1907 edition. See Heinrich Heidegger and Stagi, *Martin Heidegger: Ein Privatporträt zwischen Politik und Religion*, 129. Suso's book not only was written in the spirit of Eckhart around the time of the latter's death, but attempts to vindicate and develop Eckhart's thought as well, especially as regards releasement and discernment. See Frank Tobin's introduction to this work in Suso, *The Exemplar*, 27–32; as well as Piesch, "Seuses 'Büchlein der Wahrheit' und Meister Eckhart." The end of chapter VII of Suso's book, which is also the end of the entire work, confirms, moreover, Heidegger's appreciation of the role of the practical apriori and *gelâzenheit* in Eckhartian thought. In response to the question—"Does such a person [that is, a released person, *ein gelazener mensche*] come to a full knowledge of the truth, or does he remain in the realm of opinion and imagining?"—personified Eternal Truth replies: "Since such a person remains basically human, he continues to have opinions and imaginings. But because he has withdrawn from himself into that which is, he has a knowledge of all truth; for this is truth itself and the person is unaware of himself. But let this be enough for you. One does not arrive at the goal by asking questions. It is rather through releasement [*gelazenheit*] that one comes to this hidden truth. Amen." Bihlmeyer, ed., *Heinrich Seuse: Deutsche Schriften*, 359,22–30; Suso, *The Exemplar*, 331; trans. mod. Indeed, as Heinrich relates in a different report, Martin inscribed the Middle High German of the first two sentences of Eternal Truth's reply in the edition he gave to his nephew (*Martin Heidegger: Ein Privatporträt zwischen Politik und Religion*, 138). For references to Suso in Heidegger's corpus, see KT, 22/51; GA 6.2: 267; GA 42: 54/31. Heidegger also, incidentally, attended the Heinrich-Suso-Gymnasium in Konstanz from 1903 to 1906.

57. This may seem even more striking when one recalls the many pejorative comments Heidegger makes about mysticism throughout his corpus, for example, GA 6.2: 21/182; GA 27: 178; GA 66: 403–404/356–57. A more ambivalent view can be found in Heidegger's 1936 lecture course on Schelling, where Heidegger links Schelling's understanding of the ground of God back to Eckhart: "The whole boldness of Schelling's thinking comes into play here. But it is not the vacuous play of thoughts of a manic hermit, it is only the continuation of an attitude of thinking which begins with Meister Eckart and attains its unique unfolding in Jakob Böhme." Aware of the popular misconceptions surrounding mysticism and theosophy, Heidegger cautions his audience against lackadaisically pigeonholing these thinkers with such terms. While one can certainly call Eckhart a mystic and Böhme a theosophist, "nothing is said by that with regard to the spiritual occurrence and the true creation of thought." When it comes to such figures as Eckhart, Böhme, and Schelling, being a mystic in no way means being "a muddlehead who likes to reel in the obscure and finds his pleasure in veils." GA 42: 204/117; trans. mod. See also Heidegger's comments on the mystical in his review of Karl Jaspers's *Psychologie der Weltanschauung* (GA 9: 20/17). Jaspers's text contains discussions of Eckhart on pages 51–52 and 74–76.

58. Silesius is even blunter: "Wir bethen es gescheh mein Herr und Gott dein wille: / Und sih / Er hat nicht will': Er ist ein Ewge stille." "We pray, 'O Lord my God, Thy will be done, Thy will!' / And yet no will hath He; For e'er and aye He's still." *Cherubinischer Wandersmann*, I, 294; *A Selection from the Rhymes of a German Mystic*, 4. Note that this couplet occurs in close proximity to the one on the rose without why (I, 289).

59. Tauler: "They let [*lossent*] God prepare their ground and release themselves [*lossent sich*] entirely to God. . . . They accept all things from God in humble awe and refer them back to him in a naked self-poverty [*blossen armüte irs selbes*], in a willing releasement [*williger gelassenheit*], bowing lowly to the divine will [*willen*]." *Die Predigten Taulers*, 23,9–15/*Sermons*, 47 Pr. 5 ("An dem zwölften tage usser Ysaias epistele"); trans. mod.; emphasis added. Heidegger could have found this quote translated into modern German already on p. 3 of his 1919 copy of Tauler (ed. Oehl). See also *Die Predigten Taulers*, 108,12–17; Tauler, *Sermons*, 96 Pr. 26 ("Repleti sunt omnes spiritu sancto et ceperunt loqui"); *Tauler* (ed. Oehl), 53–54.

Luther: "this good will in us must be hindered for its own improvement. God's only purpose in thwarting our good will is to make of it a better will. And this is done when it subordinates itself to and conforms to the divine will (by which it is hindered), until the point is reached when man is entirely released [*gantz gelassen*], free, without will [*willelosz*], and knows nothing except that he waits upon the will of God [*gotis willen*]." "Auslegung deutsch des Vaterunsers für die einfältigen Laien," 103–104; "An Exposition of the Lord's Prayer for Simple Laymen," 47; trans. mod. Reference found in Ritter et al., eds., *Historisches Wörterbuch der Philosophie*, s.v. "Gelassenheit."

Böhme: "When one's own will [*Wille*] dies to the self, it is free from sin. Then it desires . . . only that for which God created it, that which God wishes [*will*] to do through it. And although the will is the doing, and must be so, it is nevertheless only a tool of the doing, with which God does what God will. . . . [W]ho does not work and act in the released will [*gelassenen Willen*], in trust in God, only lays waste and scatters. This is not acceptable to God. Nothing pleases God except what God wills with God's Spirit and does through God's tool." "Von wahrer Gelassenheit," 94–95, nos. 39 and 45; "True Yieldedness," 108–109; trans. mod. In his 1945 lecture "Poverty" (see §7, below), Heidegger praises Böhme, all the while placing his spiritual thought under the banner of the "primal will [*Urwille*]" (AR, 6/4). For Heidegger's debt to Böhme, see Bernasconi, "Being Is Evil." Heidegger also refers to Böhme in GA 5: 128/96; GA 42: 54/31, 204/117; GA 49: 113; GA 68: 77/60; GA 85: 39/31, 51/43; GA 86: 232–33, 268, 270, 397; GA 73.1: 875; GA 95: 59/45; GA 97: 50; GA 98: 238–39; EDP, 40/229; DLA 75.7072/23. (Although the editor of the *Gesamtausgabe* volume does not mention this, Heidegger's quotes of Böhme in GA 86: 232–33 undoubtedly come from Berdjajew, "Jakob Böhmes Lehre von Ungrund und Freiheit.") Imma von Bodmershof and Jean Wahl also mention Böhme in letters to Heidegger in MH/IB, 56–57, and Wahl, *Transcendence and the Concrete*, 214. See, finally, Alexandre Koyré's "Die Gotteslehre Jacob Boehmes," which appeared in the Festschrift Heidegger edited for Husserl.

60. In a letter to his brother from Todtnauberg dated September 13, 1946, Heidegger asks him to bring back from Schloß Hausen (that is, from the ruins near where Heidegger was staying at the end of World War II) Pfeiffer's edition of Eckhart, as well as seventy-eight other texts and editions including Thomas à Kempis and the anonymous *Theologia Deutsch*. Böhme too is on the list, although his name is crossed out. DLA HS.2014.0069.00013. For Elfride's gift of Pfeiffer's edition to Heidegger, see MH/HA, 247/208. Regarding Elfride's interest in Eckhart, see MH/EH, 97/64, where we learn that she and Heidegger would read Eckhart on Sundays while on vacation in 1916; see also MH/EH, 93/61–62. Eflride was enrolled in Heidegger's first lecture course (DLA 75.7439), which, as we saw above, concluded in an especially Eckhartian vein. Finally, a marginal note in Heidegger's copy of Bindschedler's edition of Eckhart is especially telling. On the inside of the back cover, one finds, in Elfride's hand: "Sein des Mittelal[ters] / Funktion der Neuzeit / Anliegen des Mittelal / ters: Würde des / Individuum / Ekkard u. Duns / Scotus / Das Desindividuierende / ganz entfernt v. Pantheismus / Eigenschaft ist das grösste Hinder- / nis zu Gott / homo justus / ist keine moralische / Größe [?] / auch Summa übernommen [?] / vacare deo." "Being of Middle Ages / function of modern age / concerns of Middle Ages: / worth of / the individual / Ekkard and Duns / Scotus / that which disindividuates / entirely remote from pantheism / property is the greatest obstacle / to God / *homo justus* [the just man] / is not a moral / greatness [?] / also, summa overtaken [?] / *vacare deo* [to be empty for God]." On the first blank page of this volume is the name "Heidegger" in dark gray pen in non-Sütterlin cursive. The title page bears the following words of thanks in the hand of Hartmut Buchner: "In Dankbarkeit / H. B." "Gratefully / H. B." I thank Friedrich Wilhelm von Herrmann, Alfred Denker, and Peter Trawny for information regarding this text and for suggestions about how to decipher a few of these words.

61. For the story about the Freiburg philosophy faculty's final semester under the Third Reich in the Upper Danube Valley, and Heidegger's teaching of the first "Country Path Conversation," see the introduction to chapter 7, below. The information about the holdings of the Beuron library may be gleaned from the dates written in the copies telling when the library received them. For the Eckhartian current in Beuron, see Ochwadt and Tecklenborg, eds., *Das Maß des Verborgenen*, 93; Engelmann, "Hundert Jahre Bibliothek Beuron," 438; and Schmidtke, "Eine Beuroner Mystikerhandschrift." For Heidegger's relation to Beuron, see Schaber's articles "Phänomenologie und Mönchtum" and "Te lucis ante terminum." Finally, here is what Heidegger's friend Heinrich Ochsner had to say about the archabbey: "Beuron, that is, for me, identical with the unity, the silencing of every dichotomy. But it is precisely for this reason that words fail, and I must at last admit with Eckhart: 'The One that I mean is wordless.'" In Ochwadt and Tecklenborg, eds., *Das Maß des Verborgenen*, 93. (The Eckhart quote can be found in the Pseudo-Eckhartian

text, "Von dem überschale," in Pfeiffer, 517; Evans, 1, 368. It is the same quote that Martin Buber used for the epigraph of his influential 1909 edition of mystical writings titled *Ekstatische Konfessionen*.)

62. In one (Pr. 2, "Intravit Iesus in quoddam castellum"), Eckhart speaks of the spark of the soul being "empty and free, entirely as God is empty and free in himself" (Bernhart, 56). This means that neither the spark of the soul nor God can be conceived in terms of any power, mode, or faculty, for "so elevated" are they "above all powers [*Kräften*]" (Bernhart, 56–57). The will would be one such power. In the other sermon (Pr. 28, "Ego elegi vos"), Eckhart speaks of something that transcends the created aspect of the soul and "is akin to the divine manner," that "is One and so unnameable that it has no names, and is more unknown than known" (Bernhart, 43). Surely not a mere will giving itself over to a great one. It must be noted, however, that Heidegger's underlining and marginalia in his personal copy of Bernhart's edition are confined or indexed only to *Die rede der underscheidunge* and *Daz buoch der götlichen træstunge*.

63. See, for example, GA 81: 187 (cited above); Natorp's *Deutscher Weltberuf*, 1, 80; 2, 73–75; 2, 79; and Appendix Two, below.

64. Baeza, *Die Topologie des Ursprungs*, 101–102; Baier, "Heidegger und das Mittelalter," 39–40; Beierwaltes, "Heideggers Gelassenheit," 14, 24–26, 31; Capelle, "Heidegger et Maître Eckhart," 120–21; Caputo, *The Mystical Element in Heidegger's Thought*, 142–43, 180–81; Dalle Pezze, *Martin Heidegger and Meister Eckhart*, 186–87; Davis, *Heidegger on the Will*, 126, 195–96; Bret W. Davis, "Translator's Foreword" to GA 77, xi; de Libera 188–89, n. 12; De Vitiis, "Das Gebet des Schweigens," 137; D'Helt, *Heidegger et la pensée médiévale*, 151–52; Dobie, "Overcoming Ontotheology," 365; Filippi, "Martin Heidegger y la mística eckhartiana," 37–38; Greisch, *Le Buisson Ardent et les Lumières de la raison*, 3, 693; Greisch, "La contrée de la sérenité et l'horizon de l'ésperance," 181; Haas, *Kunst rechter Gelassenheit*, 250; Helting, "Heidegger und Meister Eckhart," 83, 98; Helting, *Heidegger und Meister Eckehart: Vorbereitende Überlegungen zu ihrem Gottesdenken*, 66; Lera, "The Fascination of the Origin," 209; McGrath, *The Early Heidegger and Medieval Philosophy*, 136, n. 29; Moran, "Meister Eckhart and Modern Philosophy," 694; Pöggeler, *Neue Wege mit Heidegger*, 389–90, 437–38; Schirmacher, *Technik und Gelassenheit*, 86; Schlüter, *Heideggers Rezeption des antiken und mittelalterlichen Neuplatonismus*, 44, 44, n. 3, 46, 97–102, 109; Ingrid Schüßler, "Editor's Afterword" to GA 77: 248/163; Steiner, *Die Aufgabe des Denkens*, 228; Strummiello, "'Alte Wörter,'" 193; Vitiello, "'Abgeschiedenheit,' 'Gelassenheit,' 'Angst,'" 308; von Herrmann, *Wege ins Ereignis*, 377; Wagner, *Meditationen über Gelassenheit*, 14, 135–37, 174; Welte, *Meister Eckhart: Gedanken zu seinen Gedanken*, 43, 82, n. 16; Wolz-Gottwald, "Martin Heidegger und die philosophische Mystik," 69. Zimmermann, *Martin und Fritz Heidegger*, 148, suggests that this is Heidegger's error, but he at least mentions the possibility (without considering it further) that it may have been intentional. (See also Moran's and Wolz-Gottwald's contributions,

which suggest that Heidegger is criticizing, and not so much interpreting, Eckhart's *Gelassenheit* in order to bring his own conception of this term into greater relief. Cf. also Vitiello, who initially attributes the Scholar's comment to Heidegger's intention to distinguish his position from Eckhart's *abegescheidenheit,* but then considers the Sage's response as a sort of redress for the rashness of the former.) Schürmann, "Heidegger and Meister Eckhart on Releasement," 115, is careful not to conflate the Scholar and Heidegger, but he does not explain why Heidegger would have one of his characters say this.

65. This and the following information is taken from Ott, *Martin Heidegger: A Political Life,* 17; Speck, "Vorlesungen im Phantomsemester"; Zimmermann, *Martin und Fritz Heidegger,* 100–101, 108–10; and my own archival research. For more information, see the introduction to chapter 7, below.

66. While Ott and Zimmermann report thirty students, Speck has proven that the actual number is around twenty, most of whom were quite advanced in their studies ("Vorlesungen im Phantomsemester," 169, 181–82).

67. Quote from an unpublished remark in Heidegger's 1942 lecture course on "The Ister," found in Ott, *Martin Heidegger: A Political Life,* 14. Cf. GA 16: 370.

68. Beierwaltes, "Heideggers Gelassenheit," 32.

69. Anonymous, *Liber viginti quattuor philosophorum,* Definition Two: "Deus est sphaera infinita cuius centrum est ubique, circumferentia nusquam."

70. For a brief outline of this history, see Borges, "The Fearful Sphere of Pascal," as well as its supplementation (and correction) by Harries, "The Infinite Sphere," and Brient, *The Immanence of the Infinite,* Part Three.

71. As Federico Bauchwitz, "Contribuições à história de uma metáfora," and Lacoue-Labarthe, "Présentation," 36, respectively argue.

72. Moreover, Heidegger may have already read Eckhart's *Commentary on John,* where this definition appears (LW 3: 527, no. 604 [In Ioh.]), and he would eventually cite from Pr. 9 ("Quasi stella matutina"), where there is an explanation of and citations from *The Book of Twenty-Four Philosophers.* For other places in which Eckhart cites from this book, see Beccarisi, "'noch sint ez allez heidenischer meister wort.'" Additionally, we know that Heidegger makes elliptical reference to Denifle's edition of Eckhart's Latin writings, which includes the first edition of the *Book of Twenty-Four Philosophers* (see §1 of Appendix One, below) and that he was influenced by Clemens Baeumker's work on medieval philosophy, whom he references several times and who also published two versions of the *Book of Twenty-Four Philosophers.* For the influence of Baeumker on Heidegger and their relationship, see GA 1: 193/3; MH/HR, 20, 36; and Heidegger's letter to Grabmann from January 7, 1917, in HAD. For other references to Baeumker, to his works, and to texts he edited, see GA 1: 193/3; GA 22: 33, n. 5/26, n. 35; GA 23: 42, n. 1, 41–42; GA 62: 291–92; and §§1 and 6 of Appendix One, below. For Baeumker on Eckhart, see his *Der Anteil des Elsass an den geistigen Bewegungen des Mittelalters,* passim; and *Die christliche Philosophie des Mittelalters,* 425–27.

73. Brient, *The Immanence of the Infinite*, 170. Cf. Harries, "The Infinite Sphere," 10: "Thus before Cusanus transferred the metaphor of the infinite sphere from God to the universe Meister Eckhart described the soul in ways which suggest its transference from God to man."

74. See AR, 7/5–6, and GA 73.1: 876, n. 29. The latter contains a passage titled "Hölderlin, Das Göttliche" that Heidegger copied out on a loose page and included in the manuscript of "Armut."

75. This quote comes from a different version of the introduction to "Armut" only available in GA 73.1.

76. I owe this connection to Beierwaltes, "Heideggers Gelassenheit," 18–19.

77. This is not to deny the allusion to Hölderlin's *Sophocles*-distich: "Viele versuchten umsonst, das Freudigste freudig zu sagen / Hier spricht endlich es mir, hier in der Trauer sich aus." "Many have tried, but in vain, with joy to express the most joyful; Here at last, in grave sadness [or mourning], wholly I find it expressed" (Michael Hamburger's translation in Hölderlin, *Hyperion and Selected Poems*, 138–39). It is interesting, though, that Eckhart uses both mourning and joy (albeit in a different sense) on the final page of the section from RdU just cited (which is also the final page of the tractate): "And so there is nothing in him [God] that is to be mourned [*zu trûrenne sî*]. / He who has all his will and his wish has all his joy [*vröude*]" (DW 5: 309,1–3/ES 285).

78. Although it is not clear whether this underlining stems from Heidegger or from Friedrich-Wilhelm von Herrmann, Heidegger did underline in red pencil three words from Bernhart's translation of this sentence in his personal copy of the latter: "Merke wohl, daß noch nie ein Mensch im Leben sich so überwand, daß ihm nicht noch etwas zu überwinden übrig blieb" (Bernhart, 80). "Note well that never yet has anyone overcome himself so much in life that something did not still remain left for him to overcome."

79. The Eckhart quote can be found in DW 5: 198,6–7 (RdU, §4). Davies renders it as "Little comes from the works of those whose being is slight" (7). In his personal copy of Bernhart's edition (80–81), Heidegger drew diagonal lines in red pencil before and after the passage he quotes, and there are multiple vertical lines in lead pencil next to it in his personal copy of Diederichs's edition (8). See also GA 77: 158/103, where Heidegger writes "Being of Great Essence," under which he copies out two Eckhart quotes from RdU.

80. This idea is developed above all in Eckhart's sermon cycle on the eternal birth of the Word in the soul (Prr. 101–104), which Heidegger will later cite.

81. The Eckhart quote comes from LW 3: 440, no. 509 (In Ioh.). Heidegger cites it again on the first page of *Anmerkungen VIII* in GA 98: 211.

82. See Martin Heidegger's letters to his brother from December 21, 1951, and March 3, 1956 (DLA HS.2014.0069.00018 and HS.2014.0069.00021, respectively). See also MH/HA, 247/208. In a letter to me from July 31, 2016, Fritz's son Heinrich Heidegger explained that Martin was also probably responsible for ordering Fritz's copy of another important edition of Eckhart as well, namely, Quint's

translation into modern German, which Fritz marked up extensively, writing on the front cover page "Zweite Lesung, Mai-Juni 1963; unterbrochen Ende Mai 1964. (zu viele Wiederholungen.)." "Second reading, May-June 1963; interrupted at the end of May 1964. (too many repetitions.)." Other texts by mystics that Fritz marked up include Suso, *Des Mystikers Heinrich Seuse* O. Pr. *Deutsche Schriften*, and Saint John of the Cross, *Dunkle Nacht*. He also owned a copy of Nigg, *Das Leben des seligen Heinrich Seuse*, which was a gift from his son Heinrich. These books can be found in the library of the study in Fritz's home where Martin would work, now available in the Martin-Heidegger-Archiv der Stadt Meßkirch. It is also noteworthy how frequently Martin mentions Eckhart in his letters to Fritz (I was able to find six instances), especially in light of how sparse his references to other classical philosophers are in their correspondence. Finally, Fritz's deep interest in Eckhart has been explored by Hans Dieter Zimmermann, *Martin und Fritz Heidegger*, 133–39, 146–52, 156. Especially noteworthy is a quote from one of Fritz's aphorisms that recalls Pr. 52 ("Beati pauperes spiritu"), a sermon to which Fritz refers in the index he made in his personal copy of Quint's translation of Eckhart. The quote speaks, among other things, of "The art of willing nothing in all things" (138). Martin himself seemed to recognize Fritz's interest in these topics when, on Fritz's eightieth birthday, Martin delivered the following tribute to his brother: "In our old age the span of the future narrows ever more quickly. For this reason it is good, if we are in a position to do so, to build in advance a completely different expanse than this narrow span yet remaining, in order to embrace with releasement [*gelassen*] the descent into the poverty of spirit" (GA 16: 737).

83. For an attempt to see the notes as a critique of Eckhart's "Christian philosophy," see Schlüter, *Heideggers Rezeption des antiken und mittelalterlichen Neuplatonismus*, 65–69. While Schlüter's argument is in large part persuasive, it is not clear that Heidegger's own remarks always pertain to Eckhart (let alone to Eckhart's thought as a whole). On the other hand, after pointing to a few passages in which Heidegger's own thought comes to the fore, Schlüter does wonder whether Heidegger saw Eckhart's "metaphysical, Neoplatonically informed doctrine of creation" as a sort of "surface ('mask')," on which "the prevailing of the appropriative event is indicated" (69; cf. 32). At any rate, it is important not to deny Heidegger's occasional ambivalence about Eckhart. For example, despite the many passages I cited above in which Heidegger identifies Eckhart as a thinker who is mindful of being, one reads, in a recently published note from "1949/50 (May)": "The human being, in the essence of the ground of the soul, is not merely the same with the ground of God, as is the case for Meister Eckhart. Here the human being is still thought from God as the *esse entium*, and *esse* itself is left unthought" (GA 98: 240).

84. However, like Eckhart, he will also say that being is nothing, that is, not a being, as we saw above. See, for example, GA 9: 123/97. Moreover, at times, Heidegger's understanding of the nothing also resembles Eckhart's understanding of the nothingness of the Godhead as more than the mere being of beings. See my essay "Science, Thinking, and the Nothing as Such."

85. Cf. DW 4: 601,19–20/Davies 46 Pr. 104 ("In his, quae patris mei sunt, oportet me esse").

86. Based on the range of dates Heidegger provides for the material contained in this section of GA 81: 276–334.

87. While I could not find this term, as Heidegger writes it, in Eckhart's corpus, Eckhart does use the term *gestelnisse* in Pfeiffer's edition: "dem ougen daz eigen ist sehen gesteltnisse unde varwe," "the eye is for seeing form and color" (Pfeiffer, 172,1–2; Walshe, 277). This term appears as "gesteltnisse," which one finds more frequently, in DW 2: 143,2 Pr. 32 ("Consideravit semitas domus suae"). *Gesteltnisse* also appears a few times in Pfeiffer, ed., *Deutsche Mystiker des vierzehnten Jahrhunderts*, Vol. 1, 104,6, 156,25, 423; as well as in Par. an. (see the index on p. 150), which contains sixty-four sermons, half of which are attributed to Eckhart. The closest example I could identify for what Heidegger might have in mind can be found on p. 29,18–20 of Par. an., although the sermon in which it is found is not ascribed to Eckhart, but rather to one Bruder Erbe: "ein figure ist ein gesteltnisse, ein ummecreizin eines wesines. also ist der son ein gesteltnisse, ein ummecreizin eines wesines. also ist der son ein gesteltnisse gotlicher substancien oder wesines." "a figure is a *gesteltnisse*, a circling around of a being. Thus the Son is a *gesteltnisse*, a circling around of a being. Thus the Son is a *gesteltnisse* of divine substance or being." This quote can also be found in Preger, 2, 446,1–4.

88. *Gestellung* seems to mark a sort of middle station on the way to the naming of *Gestell* as the consummate epoch of metaphysics. For other uses of *Gestellung*, see GA 79: passim, and GA 76: 353, 367.

89. GA 81: 286, 290, 301, 312; GA 12: 249; GA 13: 232. For a discussion, see Ma and van Brakel, "Out of the *Ge-stell?*," esp. 530–32.

90. In January, the two men had a conversation about Eckhartian detachment. See the present book's conclusion and §6 of Appendix One, below.

91. In a letter to Arendt from 1974, Heidegger writes: "How nice that you are studying Meister Eckhart. What he set down in his German texts is astonishing in terms of linguistic creativity, but it can hardly be seen anymore in our age, when language is being destroyed by linguistics. It is perhaps in this way that his thinking will most likely be saved [*gerettet*]—but for whom?" MH/HA, 247/208; trans. mod.

92. See Welte, *Meister Eckhart: Gedanken zu seinen Gedanken*, and Welte, "Der mystische Weg des Meisters Eckhart und sein spekulativer Hintergrund"; also Schürmann, *Maître Eckhart ou la joie errante*; revised English edition available under the title *Wandering Joy*. Welte had already taught Eckhart in Summer Semester 1952 ("Übung zu ausgewählten Texten des Meister Eckhart") and Winter Semester 1952–53 ("Übungen zu Meister Eckhart II. Die Problematik der lateinischen Schriften"). The latter, incidentally, was attended by Heidegger's nephew Heinrich Heidegger. UAF E 8/159, E 8/216, and E 8/904. For earlier texts by Welte on Eckhart, see the material compiled in Welte, *Gesammelte Schriften II/1*.

Part Two: Introduction

1. See Nishitani's essay in Appendix Three, below, as well as Bernhart, *Meister Eckhart und Nietzsche*; and Schoeller-Reisch, "Die Demut Zarathustras." Nietzsche, *Kritische Studienausgabe*, 3, 533; for other references see 1, 372; 11, 151.

2. Bullivant, "A Meister among the Moderns," 15–18; Cage, "Meister Duchamp or living on water."

3. Piper, *Alfred Rosenberg: Hitlers Chefideologe*. See above all Rosenberg's *Der Mythus des 20. Jahrhunderts* and the excerpt from it *Die Religion des Meister Eckehart*. Rosenberg was also the editor of the journal *Nazionalsozialistische Monatshefte: Zentrale politische und kulturelle Zeitschrift der NSDAP*, which published at least three articles on Eckhart between the years 1934 and 1937: Raschke, "Meister Eckhart der Deutsche"; Baeumler, "Ignatius und Meister Eckhart"; Seeberg, "Die verlorene Handschrift: Zur Geschichte der Eckhart-Ausgabe." Büttner's translation of Eckhart's "Von der Abgeschiedenheit" also appeared in Vol. 5, no. 47 (February 1934): 148–54. For Rosenberg's Eckhart (and the influence of Büttner's introduction on his reading, an introduction which, incidentally, Heidegger considered "worthless" [MH/EH, 93/61–62; cf. pp. 272–73, n. 4, below]), see Largier, "Mystik und Tat," 30–34. Although there is at present no dust jacket on Heidegger's 1938 copy of Büttner's one volume edition, if there was at one point, Heidegger would have been able to read on the inside flap a blurb from Rosenberg's *Der Mythus*: "In Meister Eckehart tritt zuerst unbewußt der neue, der wiedergeborene germanische Mensch in Erscheinung. Heute scheint es wie ein Dämmern durch das Volk zu gehen, das anzieht, als sei es reif geworden für den Apostel der Deutschen, den 'heiligen und seligen Meister.'—Die beste Arbeit und zugleich eine in die Tiefe gehende Würdigung hat Herman Büttner gegeben; sein Werk gehört als erste Schrift in jedes deutsche Haus." "In Meister Eckehart there first appears, unwittingly, the new, the reborn German human being. Today, like a dawning, it seems to pass through the people, who indicate that they have become ready for the apostle of the Germans, the 'holy and blessed Meister.'—Herman Büttner has given us the best work and at the same time a profound evaluation; his text belongs as the first writing [or perhaps 'scripture'] in every German house." For Heidegger's relation to Rosenberg, see p. 252, n. 8, below. I might note, finally, that Heidegger's old friend Engelbert Krebs boldly criticized the Nazi appropriation of Eckhart, noting that the putatively "German" features of Eckhart's thought (the unification of the soul and God, the focus on God's simplicity) in fact stem from not only Greek and Arabic roots, but Jewish ones as well. See Krebs, "Arteigenes Christentum," 90.

4. See the final three poems of *Lightduress*. The second even contains a quotation from Pr. 71 ("Surrexit autem Saulus de terra"). For an extensive discussion of these and other Eckhartian poems by Celan, see von Perger, "Mystik unter Zwang." When Celan gave a reading of this collection in Freiburg in 1970,

Heidegger was in attendance, and, according to Celan, "really listened." Celan and Wurm, *Briefwechsel*, 238–39. (In another letter, however, Celan suggests that his poems did not have such an effect, which Gerhart Baumann challenges. See Celan and Shmueli, *Briefwechsel*, 135–36, 236, n. 2.)

5. Reference and translation found in O'Meara, *Romantic Idealism and Roman Catholicism*, 89, 214, n. 29. See also Hegel, *Frühe Exzerpte*, 215–16; Rosenkranz, *Georg Wilhelm Friedrich Hegel's Leben*, 102; and Hegel, *Vorlesungen über die Philosophie der Religion*, 1, 257.

6. Quote from Schopenhauer's *Senilia* found in Haas, *Gottleiden—Gottlieben*, 189.

7. Bloch, *Atheism in Christianity*, 63–65; Bloch, *The Principle of Hope*, passim; Ley, *Studie zur Geschichte des Materialismus im Mittelalter*, 378–401.

8. McGinn, *The Mystical Thought of Meister Eckhart*, 172.

9. And not, as is often claimed, just to nuns (and Beguines). Indeed, Sturlese, *Homo divinus*, 31, n. 85, holds that only three sermons can be said to have been delivered before women. Cf. *Homo divinus*, 15, n. 1, as well as Ruh, "Meister Eckharts Pariser Quaestionen 1–3," 308.

10. Certain topics, because there are passages in which Eckhart tells his readers not to worry about understanding everything; he does not, however, say that all understanding must come about through equaling *in esse* the truth of that which one understands.

11. For Schürmann's exchange with Heidegger, see §6 of Appendix One, below. Schürmann's interpretation also received support from Bernhard Welte, who served as a mentor to him and, as we saw in chapter 1, whose own reading of Eckhart was influenced and encouraged by Heidegger. For Schürmann's exchange with Welte, see "Reiner Schürmann's Report of His Visit to Martin Heidegger"; Schürmann, *Wandering Joy*, xxi; and the letters from Welte to Schürmann that can be found in Box 1, Folder 4 of the unprocessed Reiner Schürmann Archives.

12. Schürmann, *Wandering Joy*, xx–xxi. For commentaries on Schürmann's reading of Eckhart, see Bernasconi, "Eckhart's Anachorism"; Casteigt, "La métaphysique eckhartienne"; Gonzalez Nuñez, "Infrapolitical Reflection"; Kurak, "The Epistemology of Illumination in Meister Eckhart"; Martinengo, *Introduzione a Reiner Schürmann*, chapter 3; and Schmidt, "*Solve et coagula*."

13. Schürmann, *Wandering Joy*, 183.

Chapter 2. Thinking, Being, and the Problem of Ontotheology in Eckhart's Latin Writings

1. See Heidegger's references to Parmenides in his 1964 essay "The End of Philosophy and the Task of Thinking" (GA 14: 67–90/55–73), as well as in GA 7, GA 8, and GA 54. See also chapter 6, below.

2. Ruedi Imbach, *Deus est Intelligere*, 1–4, 148–50, 183; Flasch, *Das philosophische Denken im Mittelalter*, 466, 470; Grabmann, 58; E. Hirsch, "[Review of] *Grabmann, Martin: Neuaufgefundene Pariser Quaestionen Meister Eckharts*," 43. Heidegger recognized this as well: see MH/BW, 29.

3. Flasch, *Das philosophische Denken im Mittelalter*, 466, speaks of the texts in which this move occurs as "documents of the prehistory of modern subjectivity." Regarding Eckhart's First Parisian Question, E. Hirsch writes, "In Eckhart's Question about *intelligere* and *esse* in God, there in fact stirs nothing less than a bit of German idealism." "[Review of] *Grabmann, Martin: Neuaufgefundene Pariser Quaestionen Meister Eckharts*," 43; cf. 44. Winkler, "Zwischen strukturalistischer und intentionalistischer Interpretation," makes a strong case for the idealist strand in Eckhart's First Parisian Question, a question which I discuss in great detail, below. Caputo, "The Nothingness of the Intellect in Meister Eckhart's 'Parisian Questions,'" points out parallels with Fichte, Hegel, Husserl, and Sartre. For further references, see Schüßler, "Gott—Sein oder Denken?," 164, nn. 8–9. For a similar claim by one of Heidegger's students, see Weischedel, *Der Gott der Philosophen*, 1, 156. Finally, regarding Weischedel's book, it is perhaps worth noting that, on January 11, 1972, Heidegger wrote to his brother about a series of theological texts, including Weischedel's. He says that such literature is ephemeral, whereas a mere few pages of Meister Eckhart are more enduring and fruitful. HS.2014.0069.00028.

4. Ley, *Studie zur Geschichte des Materialismus im Mittelalter*, 378–401. For a critique of Ley's thesis, see Albert, *Meister Eckharts Thesen vom Sein*, 75–96.

5. Drawing on recent archival discoveries, Loris Sturlese has challenged this traditional chronology, suggesting that the Prologues of the *Opus tripartitum* were actually composed *before* the early Parisian Questions. See his *Homo divinus*, 28, n. 69, and 95–106. I discuss the significance of Sturlese's paleographic findings, below.

6. Cf. Flasch, *Das philosophische Denken im Mittelalter*, 470.

7. Zum Brunn, "Dieu n'est pas être," 85.

8. Joseph Koch maintains that Eckhart was actually a student at Paris in 1277, though this has been contested. See the discussion in LW 5: 156, n. 4 (Acta #2).

9. As Bernard McGinn notes, "Theologians had often been investigated for censure of erroneous views in the Middle Ages, but Eckhart's trial *for heresy* before the inquisition was unprecedented." McGinn, *The Mystical Thought of Meister Eckhart*, 15; cf. 1, 14. Senner, however, disputes that the trial was for heresy. "Meister Eckhart's Life, Training, Career, and Trial," 61–62.

10. Unless otherwise indicated, all translations of Eckhart's Parisian Questions are my own.

11. This discovery, made by Walter Senner, was first published in 2012 in Vinzent, "*Questions on the Attributes (of God),*" 182–84, and then in LW 1,2: 488 (Frag. Par. #4). Senner, "Meister Eckhart's Life, Training, Career, and Trial," 16, maintains that this fragment is "most likely" from 1302–03. Vincent, however, says "there are arguments that make me consider the later date, too" (186, n. 89; cf. 184–85).

12. See von Perger, "*Disputatio*," 117, n. 5, 131–32; MAP, 8, 157–66.
13. Flasch, *Meister Eckhart: Philosopher of Christianity*, 88.
14. Schüßler, "Gott—Sein oder Denken?," 165.
15. *Meister Eckhart*, 14. See also Heribert Fischer, "Thomas von Aquin und Meister Eckhart," 229.
16. Unlike most commentators, in the few pages of "*Disputatio* in Eckharts frühen Pariser Quästionen und als Predigtmotiv" (131–36) devoted to the First Parisian Question, Mischa von Perger discusses Eckhart's initial response and also speaks of that which follows his final argument as "a sort of excursus," without, however, unpacking the full significance of what von Perger appropriately calls the Question's "rhetorically and carefully calculated layout" (131). While most have taken Eckhart's turn toward the understanding at face value, there have been some who have stepped back and surveyed the operation of the Question as a whole, thereby seeing less a change of doctrine than a shift in perspective that would not amount to a complete break with or contradiction of Aquinas. See Beierwaltes, *Platonismus und Idealismus*, 50–54; Grotz, "Meister Eckharts Pariser Quaestio I"; Krieger, "Mystik und Scholastik"; Lossky, *Théologie négative et connaissance de Dieu chez Maître Eckhart*, 207–20; Schüßler, "Gott—Sein oder Denken?"; and Zum Brunn, "Dieu n'est pas être." In contrast, those who argue for the preeminence of the understanding in Eckhart's question (and thus a consequent distancing from Aquinas) include Albert, *Meister Eckharts These vom Sein*, 76; Caputo, "The Nothingness of the Intellect"; Flasch, *Das philosophische Denken im Mittelalter*, 466–71, 476; Flasch, *Meister Eckhart: Philosopher of Christianity*, 88–94 (though Flasch's interpretation here is more subtle with regard to the status of being than in the previous text); Gilson, *History of Christian Philosophy in the Middle Ages*, 438–39; Grabmann, 48, 55; Halfwassen, "Gibt es eine Philosophie der Subjektivität im Mittelalter?"; Imbach, *Deus est Intelligere*, 147, 160, et passim; Koch, "Neue Forschungen über Meister Eckhart," 414–16; LaZella, "As Light belongs to Air"; Ruh, "Meister Eckharts Pariser Quaestionen 1–3"; and Winkler, "Zwischen strukturalistischer und intentionalistischer Interpretation." As will become clear in what follows, I side ultimately with the former position. While I do agree with the latter position that Eckhart distances himself from Aquinas, I hold that such distancing is not due to the intellectualist strand of the Question per se, but rather to the overall methodological strategy of the Question in general.
17. Angled brackets signify Geyer's editorial interpolations.
18. According to Zum Brunn, "Dieu n'est pas être," 85–86, Eckhart may be referring to his no longer extant *Commentary on the Sentences*, as there are indications of this position in the inaugural lecture of Eckhart's commentary, which does survive. See Collatio 1 and Collatio 2. Albert, *Meister Eckharts These vom Sein*, 76, agrees. For the possibility that it was Eckhart's first *Commentary on Genesis* (In Gen. I), see Flasch, *Meister Eckhart: Philosopher of Christianity*, 88–89.
19. As Grotz, "Meister Eckharts Pariser Quaestio I," 373, 375, points out.

20. Though cf. von Perger's attempt to see an implicit rational identity in Eckhart's proof. "*Disputatio*," 132.

21. Lossky, *Théologie négative et connaissance de Dieu*, 214. Cf. Beierwaltes, *Platonismus und Idealismus*, 50–54; and Krieger, "Mystik und Scholastik," 136–37.

22. Maurer, 45 (emphasis added; trans. mod.). Cf. Bernhard Geyer's German rendering in LW 5: 40: "Drittens zeige ich, daß ich nicht mehr der Meinung bin, daß Gott erkennt, weil er ist; sondern, weil er erkennt, deshalb ist er"; as well as Zum Brunn's French version, MAP, 179: "En troisième lieu, je montre ceci: il ne me semble plus maintenant que c'est parce que Dieu est qu'il connaît, mais que c'est parce qu'il connaît qu'il est." Winkler, "Zwischen strukturalistischer und intentionalistischer Interpretation," 200, opts for: "daß es mir jüngst nicht so scheint, daß . . . sondern . . ." ("that recently it does not appear to me that . . . but rather . . .").

23. "Drittens zeige ich, daß ich *nicht nur* der Meinung bin, daß Gott denkt, weil er ist, *sondern vielmehr*, daß er ist, weil er denkt." Sturlese, *Homo divinus*, 22–23, n. 36; emphasis added. Von Perger, "*Disputatio*," 133, n. 31, concurs. Although he does not consider an alternate translation, Lossky wrote in his 1960 *Théologie négative et connaissance de Dieu chez Maître Eckhart*: "certain rapprochements between the 'Parisian Questions' and other texts of Meister Eckhart allow us, it seems, to interpret the declaration *non ita videtur mihi modo* in a sense that does not imply the hypothesis of a radical change of doctrine" (211).

24. Zum Brunn, "Dieu n'est pas être," 88–89 and note 17, contends that Eckhart is not so much opposed to Aquinas here as he is to those who would interpret Exodus 3:14 in an "anti-intellectualist" fashion. She adduces a passage from Pr. 9 ("Quasi stella matutina"), where, in the critical edition, Eckhart writes: "Grobe *meister* sprechent, got sî ein lûter wesen" (DW 1: 145,7–8). "Unsophisticated teachers [Zum Brunn has "maîtres frustes"] say that God is pure being" (TP, 256). While Zum Brunn's argument seems plausible—if, that is, we opt to render *non ita modo . . . sed* as "no longer now . . . but rather"—there is yet another difficulty that would need to be accounted for, namely, that one of the Middle High German manuscripts has "Grôze" instead of "Grobe": "*Great* teachers say that God is pure being." While most commentators follow the critical edition (see also the editor's explanation and the texts he cites in DW 1: 146, n. 1), Schüßler, "Gott—Sein oder Denken?," 177 and 177, n. 103, favors "Grôze," citing Pr. 53 ("Misit dominus manum suam") for support. There, Eckhart explains that, "When I preach, I am accustomed to speak about . . . the purity of the divine nature [*von götlîcher natûre lûterkeit*]" (DW 2: 528,5–529,1/ES 203). Steer, "Eckhart der meister," 734 and note 72, also prefers "Grôze." I will return to the question of purity (*puritas, lûterkeit*), below.

25. Grabmann, 53: "This interpretation was completely foreign to the medieval exegetes of the Gospel of John."

26. See Flasch, *Dietrich von Freiberg*, 56–59; and Flasch, *Meister Eckhart: Philosopher of Christianity*, 89–90. On Heidegger's relation to Dietrich, especially as regards the question of time, see Roesner, "Continu, individu, esprit."

27. Gonsalvus's citations can be found in Qu. Par. 3 (LW 5: 65–66, no. 24). Eckhart's own citations of the verse from John can be found in LW 3: 326, no. 383; 422–23, no. 490 (In Ioh.); and of the verse from Job in LW 2: 29, no. 22 (In Exod.). I have rendered the relevant portion of the latter verse (*ipse . . . solus est*) as "he alone is" rather than following Douay-Rheims's "he is alone." See also Eckhart's citation of Job 14:4 ("thou who only art"), in support of the idea that only God is being, in the Prologue to the Book of Propositions (LW 1: 168, no. 5 = LW 1,2: 42–43/Maurer 94).

28. Cf. LW 1,2: 53, no. 21 (Prol. op. prop. (rec. L)): "Et hoc est quod Ioh. 1 dicitur: 'omnia per ipsum facta sunt, et sine ipso factum est nihil.' Li sunt enim et li est esse significant." "Thus, according to John 1, 'All things made by him are, and without him nothing is made'; for 'are' and 'is' signify being" (Maurer, 101–102; trans. mod.).

29. Anonymous, *The Book of Causes*, 22.

30. I take this division into three assumptions and four arguments from von Perger, "*Disputatio*," 133.

31. Zum Brunn speculates that Eckhart's forceful assertion was directed at someone who maintained not only a conceptual priority of being over understanding, but also a real priority. Zum Brunn, "Dieu n'est pas être," 91. Regarding Eckhart's vacillation between "brutal negations" and concessions to ontotheology, see "Dieu n'est pas être," 89.

32. Grabmann (52) said of this last passage that its "sense is somewhat enigmatic on account of the poor text of the manuscript."

33. Cf. Grotz, "Meister Eckharts Pariser Quaestio I," 387–91, who nicely distinguishes the human intellect's relation to beings as one of *Nachdenken* (a thinking after or in response to beings), from the divine intellect's relation to beings as one of *Er-Denken* (a thinking that produces beings). Cf. also Krieger, "Mystik und Scholastik," 140.

34. This reading has precedence in Boethius and Aquinas. See MAP, 183, n. 21.

35. Von Perger, "*Disputatio*," 132–33.

36. Take, for example, Euclid's *Elements*, where a straight line is defined in such a way as to presuppose the existence of points: "A *straight line* is a line which lies evenly with the points on itself" (I.Def.4). This would suggest that a line in general (defined as "breadthless length" [1.Def.2]) would be dependent on the point, for a non-straight line would simply be a breadthless length that does *not* lie evenly with the points on itself.

37. "This expression [*puritas essendi*] . . . does not signify an additional way of designating being, but rather, as Gilson claimed, a purity from being." Beccarisi, "Eckhart's Latin Works," 92. Cf. LaZella, "As Light Belongs to Air," 582, who

also follows Gilson, *History of Christian Philosophy in the Middle Ages*, 438–39. As Gilson writes, "In these Questions, then, Eckhart considers God as One who has the privilege of being pure of all being (*puritas essendi*), and One who, by reason of that very purity with regard to being, can be its cause." Sturlese, *Homo divinus*, 23, n. 37, points out both possibilities, but says that he is inclined to follow Gilson. Ley, *Studie zur Geschichte des Materialismus im Mittelalter*, 395, reads *puritas essendi* as "emptiness of being [*Leerheit vom Sein*]," yet curiously interprets this as a "deficiency [*Mangel*]." See Albert's discussion in *Meister Eckharts These vom Sein*, 85.

38. I follow Schüßler and Grotz in their wariness of Mojsisch's distinction between God as intellect, on the one hand, and being in God as founded by his intellect, on the other. Mojsisch understands *puritas essendi* in this latter sense, which means that, when we call God being, we are speaking of the being that his intellect founds and that is nonetheless distinct from creatures. As Mojsisch writes, "Eckhart distinguishes between this something in God which is being or purity of being and the cognition (or essence) of God which in every respect is without being and yet the ground of this something in God, of being" (*Meister Eckhart: Analogy, Univocity, and Unity*, 45). As Schüßler "Gott—Sein oder Denken?," 172–73, shows, the passages on which Mojsisch's approach relies need not be read as establishing a foundational relation between God's intellect and being in God. See also Grotz, "Meister Eckharts Pariser Quaestio I," 376–77, who emphasizes the incompatibility between Mojsisch's approach and Eckhart's exegeses of Exodus 3:14 (which I discuss in some detail, below). While Mojsisch's distinction is ingenious, there are numerous moments in the First Parisian Question that suggest Eckhart is after something less clear-cut.

39. Grotz, "Meister Eckharts Pariser Quaestio I," 380, 383. For Eckhart's reading of 3:14, especially in his *Commentary on Exodus*, see de Libera, "L'être et le bien: Exode 3,14 dans la théologie rhénane"; as well as Beierwaltes, *Platonismus und Idealismus*, 38–67. Cf. also Eckhart's ontological reading of 3:14 in Prol. gen. and Prol. op. prop. On Eckhart's frequent disregard of plot, even for a medieval exegete, see McGinn, *The Mystical Thought of Meister Eckhart*, 27.

40. Grotz, "Meister Eckharts Pariser Quaestio I," 377–78.

41. In his 1927 edition, Grabmann has *nego*, explaining in a footnote that "Longpré inserts here *non nego*, though the context requires *nego*" (Grabmann, 104, note c). In their editions, Geyer (LW 5: 48, no. 12), Mojsisch (196), and Zum Brunn (MAP, 187) all follow suit with *nego*. Koch, in his 1928 review of Longpré's edition, is in agreement with Grabmann on this point (though not, significantly, as Grotz points out, with the interpolation of "quod suum non est" discussed above). Koch, "Neue Forschungen über Meister Eckhart," 415; Grotz, "Meister Eckharts Pariser Quaestio I," 384–85, n. 48. Dondaine's edition (9) has *sic etiam ego ab ipso Deo <tollo> ipsum esse et talia*, "So also I <remove> from God himself being itself and such things." Even if *ab ipso* is the correct reading (which would suggest a verb

such as *tollo*), interpolating a negation (*non tollo*) would be equally viable: "So also I <do not remove> from God himself being itself and such things."

42. On the authenticity of this text and the legitimacy of its usage, as well as its import for the question of analogy vis-à-vis univocity in Eckhart's corpus, see Schiffhauer, "'*nos filii dei sumus analogice*': Die Analogielehre Meister Eckharts in der Verteidigungsschrift," as well as Sturlese's introduction in LW 5: 249–73. Beccarisi, "Eckhart's Latin Works," 121, refers to portions of this text from which I quote below as "a sort of *summa* of Eckhartian thought." While I agree with Schiffhauer's description of analogy as "a real unity between God and creature . . . which nevertheless does not transform into univocity through the moment of difference and nothingness belonging to the secondary analogate" (373), I still think there are moments in Eckhart's corpus in which he does intend an identity between God and the human being, or rather not so much between God and the human being—and perhaps here is the crucial difference—as between the Godhead and the spark of the soul (cf. 382, 389). See chapter 3, below.

43. Sturlese, "Eckhart as Preacher, Administrator, and Master of the Sentences," 134.

44. Sturlese, *Homo divinus*, 25, 28, 28, n. 69, 75–96.

45. Mojsisch, *Analogy, Univocity and Unity*, 60. See also Schiffhauer, "'*nos filii dei sumus analogice*,'" 370. As for the role of analogy in general in Eckhart's thought, Josef Koch writes that "this doctrine forms the linchpin of Eckhartian thought" ("Zur Analogielehre des Meister Eckharts," 369). Regarding the status of the *Sermons and Lectures on Ecclesiasticus* as such, see Sturlese, *Homo divinus*, 28.

46. The intellectualist stance they did condemn concerned the uncreated spark of the soul qua intellect, a stance that Eckhart curiously denied holding, though it can be found in DW 1: 220,4–9/Walshe 161 Pr. 13 ("Vidi supra montem Syon") and is evoked elsewhere throughout his writings. As the papal bull has it: "There is something in the soul that is uncreated and not capable of creation; if the whole soul were such, it would be uncreated and not capable of creation, and this is the intellect." LW 5: 599/ES 80 (Acta #65). For a discussion, see ES, 42. For a commentary on and selection of texts in which Eckhart speaks of the spark of the soul and related terms, which he sometimes associates with the intellect, sometimes with being, and sometimes with that which is beyond being, see Wéber, "Petite étincelle et fond de l'âme." We will return to this issue in chapters 3 and 4, below.

47. "[T]he just man is equal to justice, not less than it. . . . Half of justice is no justice" (LW 3: 15, 18/ES 127, 129, nos. 17, 22 [In Ioh.]).

48. With respect to justice, we read, on the one hand: "The just man proceeds from and is begotten by justice and by that very fact is distinguished from it. . . . Nonetheless, the just man is not different in nature from justice, both because 'just' signifies only justice, just as 'white' signifies only the quality of whiteness, and because justice would make no one just if its nature changed from one place to another, just as whiteness does not make a man black or grammar make him

musical" (LW 3: 14/ES 127, no. 16 [In Ioh.]). On the other hand: "The just man in justice itself is not yet begotten nor Begotten Justice, but is Unbegotten Justice itself" (LW 3: 16/ES 128, no. 19 [In Ioh.]).

49. Cf. LW 1,2: 45/Maurer 97, no. 11 (Prol. op. prop. [rec. L]).

Chapter 3. Become Who You Are

1. Heidegger may have taken this idea from Pr. 52 ("Beati pauperes spiritu"). The lexical parallels are at any rate striking. Of the grace conferred upon Paul the Apostle, Eckhart writes: "[I]t was God's grace working in him that brought [*volbrâchte*] what was accidental to the perfection of the essential [*daz wesen*]. When grace had finished and accomplished [*volbrâchte*] its work, then Paul remained what he was" (DW 2: 502,1–3/ES 202; trans. mod.).

2. Schürmann, "Neoplatonic Henology as an Overcoming of Metaphysics," 31.

3. While this may seem like an old Neoplatonic or Dionysian schema of emanation, what Eckhart is ultimately after is a leveling of grades of being. God gives himself fully to creatures. If, *gelâzen,* I see this, they can become God to me. If not, they are nothing. Walter Haug examines groups of Eckhart's German sermons to show how Eckhart's thought develops from an early Dionysianism to this more mature, radical position—a position that, Haug contends, is really what got him into trouble with his inquisitors. I would be more inclined to speak of a radicalization or thematization of aspects of Eckhart's thought which are already operative even in some of the Latin works examined in chapter 2, above. See Haug, *Die Wahrheit der Fiktion,* 521–37.

4. Cf. DW 1: 170,1–2/TP 264 Pr. 10 ("In diebus suis"), and DW 2: 487,6–7/ES 199 Pr. 52 ("Beati pauperes spiritu"). In the latter, Eckhart says that "if you are unlike this truth of which we want to speak, you cannot understand me." This motif appears to be a product of Eckhart's late thought. Prr. 10, 12, and 52 all likely date to Eckhart's final years in Cologne. Largier, 1, 739–40; Colledge and Marler, "'Poverty of the Will,'" 46–47; Ruh, *Meister Eckhart: Theologe, Prediger, Mystiker,* 157–59. Cf. also DW 4: 1131,384–86, 1138,470–71/Davies 248, 251 Pr. 117 ("Ze dem êrsten suochet daz rîche gotes"). On the idea of *being* released, see DW 5: 283,7–9/Davies 42 (RdU, §21), and DW 1: 203,2–5/Davies 179–80 Pr. 12 ("Qui audit me").

5. That is, I will not draw on the Pseudo-Eckhartian material Heidegger cites in 1916, in 1927, and in or after 1956, nor primarily on other sermons of Eckhart (except to supplement the authentic texts Heidegger cites). See §§3–5 of Appendix One, below.

6. The sermon was well known initially: in 1934, Schulze-Maizier could speak of this "clearly much-loved . . . sermon" (SM, 435). Due to questions concerning its

authenticity, however, and to its longstanding absence in the critical edition, it would later fall into oblivion. In 1981, Haas could claim that it was "barely acknowledged in Eckhart scholarship" ("Christliche Aspekte des 'Gnothi seauton,'" 88; cf. Haas's similar statements in his 1989 book *Gottleiden—Gottlieben*, 192, 216). Although Jostes argued against its authenticity back in 1895 (conceding nevertheless that "much points to Eckhart," xi), the following individuals included it (or portions of it) in their editions: Büttner (1909), Evans (1924), Schulze-Maizier (1934), Davies (1994), de Libera (1995), and Döll (2014). Georg Steer included it in the critical edition, not because he deemed it fully authentic, but rather because he could not rule out the possibility that it derives from portions of an earlier, though no longer extant, sermon composed by Eckhart himself (DW 4: 1083). For arguments in favor of its authenticity, see Büttner 2nd ed., 2, 185; SM, 435; McGinn, *The Mystical Thought of Meister Eckhart*, 145–47; Haas, "Christliche Aspekte des 'Gnothi seauton,'" 88, 88, n. 97; Haas, *Gottleiden—Gottlieben*, 426, n. 21; and de Libera, 509–12. Earlier, in his 1984 *Introduction à la mystique rhénane*, de Libera refrained from weighing in on its authenticity, preferring "by simple prudence" to call it "apocryphal" (298, n. 38).

7. "one of the most powerful uses of breakthrough language" (McGinn, *The Mystical Thought of Meister Eckhart*, 144); "eine summa mytica," "umfasst die Hauptgedanken der Mystik" (Jostes, xi); "un véritable *compendium* de la théologie eckhartienne" (de Libera, 509, n. 763).

8. Heidegger would have been familiar with this sermon earlier thanks to his mentor Heinrich Rickert, who culled an epigraph from it for his 1911–12 "Das Eine, die Einheit und die Eins." As mentioned in chapter 1, Heidegger refers to Rickert's epigraph in his *Habilitationsschrift*. The sermon was also the source for the epigraph to Alfred Rosenberg's *Der Mythus des 20. Jahrhunderts* (1930), which, along with *Mein Kampf*, was among the best-selling and "probably most influential" books during the Third Reich (Piper, *Alfred Rosenberg*, 200). Although there is no strong evidence to suggest that Heidegger read Rosenberg's book closely, he does critique it by name in 1938–39, suggesting at least some engagement with it (GA 95: 412–13/321–22). For further references to Rosenberg, see GA 16: 398–99, 402–403, 410–13; GA 39: 26/27; GA 86: 892; and GA 97: 462. See also p. 243, n. 3, above.

9. Regarding its authenticity, see Schaefer, 97–147; Quint, "Das Echtheitsproblem des Traktats 'Von abegescheidenheit' "; and DW 5: 392–99. Kurt Ruh has argued against it. See his *Geschichte der abendländischen Mystik*, 3, 349–58. For a critique of some of Ruh's arguments and a summary of his debate with Quint, see Enders, "Abgeschiedenheit des Geistes," 63–65; and Gottschall, "Eckhart's German Works," 179–80.

10. See the rectos of Part Two of Löser, 325–497. The material included in Pfeiffer's third tractate from Vab can be found in DW 5: 410,7–411,10; 419,8–421,1; 426,6–428,11; 431,4–432,13 (see Löser, 371–81, 397; cf. DW 5: 382). These passages correspond roughly to passages in Pfeiffer, 398–39, 402 (Evans, 1, 292–93, 295).

11. He might well have read this tractate in his personal copy of the one volume edition of Büttner's translation, which appears as the second text in his collection. Büttner 1 vol., 48–57. Heidegger would have also been able to consult the first edition (published in two volumes in 1903 and 1909) in the library of the Benedictine Archabbey of Beuron. He at any rate consulted a reprint of the first edition at the home of his friend Theophil Rees in 1919. Regarding the latter consultation, see pp. 272–73, n. 4, below.

12. One manuscript of "On Detachment," N4, nonetheless has other instances. See DW 5: 380, and the variations for lines containing *abegescheidenheit* in the critical edition of the tractate. I discuss this further in §3 of this chapter, below.

13. Regarding *gelâzenheit*, no earlier instances have been documented at any rate. See the references to various lexica in Panzig, "*gelâzenheit* und *abegescheidenheit*," 338, n. 11. Regarding *abegescheidenheit*, see DW 5: 438, n. 1 and the various lexica to which the editor refers.

14. Nevertheless, there are, in accordance with Eckhart's dialectical thought, moments throughout his German writings when even sheer being is inadequate to describe the divine ground of God and the soul. See DW 1: 144,4–46,6/TP 256 Pr. 9 ("Quasi stella matutina"); also DW 3: 231,1–2/TP 324–25 Pr. 71 ("Surrexit autem Saulus de terra"). For the different ways in which Eckhart refers to that divine aspect of the soul, see his own list in DW 1: 39,1–45,3/ES 180–81 Pr. 2 ("Intravit Iesus in quoddam castellum").

15. As we will see in chapter 4, below, there is a way in which to speak positively of God as nothingness.

16. See DW 4: 578,149–581,177/Walshe 48 Pr. 104 ("In his, quae patris mei sunt, oportet me esse"), and especially Pr. 86 ("Intravit Iesus in quoddam castellum, etc."). For an outstanding monograph on Pr. 86, see Mieth, *Die Einheit von Vita activa und Vita contemplativa in den deutschen Predigten und Traktaten Meister Eckharts und bei Johannes Tauler*, esp. 182–233; see also Mieth's commentary on the sermon in LE, 2, 156–75.

17. See DW 4: 1133,403–1135,414/Davies 249 Pr. 117 ("Ze dem êrsten suochet daz rîche gotes"), and Schürmann, *Wandering Joy*, xix.

18. Ueda, *Die Gottesgeburt in der Seele und der Durchbruch zur Gottheit*, 23.

19. The description of creaturely corporeality, temporality, and multiplicity is a red thread running throughout Eckhart's corpus, including texts Heidegger had read, such as DW 4: 1133,407–408/Davies 249 Pr. 117 ("Ze dem êrsten suochet daz rîche gotes"); and DW 4: 488,2–3/Davies 227 Pr. 103 ("Cum factus esset Iesus annorum duodecim"). See also Pr. 12 ("Qui audit me").

20. DW 4: 1113,224–28/Davies 242 Pr. 117 ("Ze dem êrsten suochet daz rîche gotes"): "I have sometimes said, and this is what I still affirm, that no external devotional practice leads to very much, for they serve only to tame nature. You should understand that all the external works which we may practise serve only to constrain nature and not to eradicate [*ertætent*] it. In order to eradicate nature

[*Sterben der natûre*] it is spiritual works that we must perform. . . . God is no more likely to be found in external observances than he is in sin."

21. See Eckhart's sermon "The Nobleman" (VeM); also DW 4: 1111,214–1114,242/Davies 242–43 Pr. 117 ("Zu dem êrsten suochet daz rîche gotes"), and DW 4: 767–68/Walshe 293 Pr. 109 ("Nolite timere eos, qui occidunt corpus"). Heidegger may have had the latter sermon in mind when he refered to Eckhart in "The Pathway"; see §2 of chapter 1, above.

22. Ueda has also written on the trope "God must" in Eckhart's corpus. See his "Über den Sprachgebrauch Meister Eckharts: 'Gott muß. . . .' "

23. See Sturlese, *Homo divinus*, 20.

24. See his commentary on Pr. 52 ("Beati pauperes spiritu") in LE, 1.

25. See Largier, 1, 767 and 848–50.

26. Latin versions of some of these phrases can be found in LW 3: 265,12–266,1 (In Ioh.). See Panzig, "*gelâzenheit* und *abegescheidenheit*," 346–47 for discussion and further parallels.

27. In notes on Eckhart from 1956 or later, Heidegger copies out a portion of the just-cited passage from Pr. 69 about reason breaking into the ground, but then expresses reservations about calling the agent of this activity reason. DLA 75.7305,9. For passages in which reason is problematized, see p. 256, n. 1, below. For knowledge, see Pr. 52 ("Beati pauperes spiritu"). As for the intellect, Pr. 2 ("Intravit Iesus in quoddam castellum") is a good example. Although Eckhart does not name the intellect and will as such in the sermon, his description of the former correlates with what he says elsewhere about the intellect in contrast to discursive reason as a power or faculty of the soul, despite his use of the word *kraft* in the sermon. Eckhart then goes on to say, however, that neither of the "powers" of which he just spoke suffices to capture the ground of the soul (also called the spark or, in this sermon, the little town) that is absolutely identical with God beyond the Trinity (or the Godhead), so much so that God (as Person of the Trinity) would have to give himself up were he to gaze upon it (DW 1: 42,1–43,5/ES 181). This finds support in Eckhart's Cologne defense, where he says of the doctrine of the little town that "it has no proper name and is higher than *intellectus*" (LW 5: 347, no. 122 [Acta #48]).

28. On this tradition in medieval German mysticism, including Eckhart (449–58), see Haas, "Mors mystica—Ein mystologisches Motiv." On the theme of death in Eckhart in particular, see the article by Heidegger's student Ernesto Grassi, "Tod und Schmerz."

29. This and other points in this paragraph are echoed in other sermons cited or paraphrased by Heidegger, such as Pr. 52 ("Beati pauperes spiritu") and Pr. 109 ("Nolite timere eos, qui occidunt corpus"), respectively.

30. Although Eckhart does employ the latter doctrine too. For an example in the Middle High German work, its mistranslation into Latin by Eckhart's inquisitors, and the subsequent charge of pantheism, see Schürmann, *Wandering Joy*, 241, n. 96.

31. This is also how McGinn, *The Mystical Thought of Meister Eckhart*, 146, reads the soul's third death.

32. On transcending receptivity, see DW 4: 1133,402–1135,414/Davies 249 Pr. 117 ("Ze dem êrsten suochet daz rîche gotes"), where Eckhart begins by speaking of the need for grace, only to say that such grace is innate and that on the most fundamental level the soul is God: "This [the uncovering of the kingdom of God in the soul] can only happen through grace and not by the soul's own powers. The soul can discover the kingdom only with the help of the grace which inheres naturally within the highest image. Here the soul is God, savoring and delighting in all things as God. And here the soul receives nothing from God nor from creatures, since she it is who contains herself and receives all things from herself. Here the soul and the Godhead are one, and here the soul has discovered that she herself is the kingdom of God." See also Pr. 52 ("Beati pauperes spiritu"), and §3 of this chapter, below.

33. I leave aside the role of nothingness in Eckhart's thought, although I do not think it is altogether incompatible with the verbal understanding of *wesen*. I would argue that, just as, in the First Parisian Question, Eckhart negates God's being in order to elevate it (*puritas essendi*), so too in the German work does he negate to elevate: "But when I have said God is not a being [*wesen*] and is above being, I have not thereby denied Him being: rather I have exalted it in Him." DW 1: 146,4–6/Walshe 342 Pr. 9 ("Quasi stella matutina"). The theme of the nothing in Eckhart has been analyzed by Haas, "The Nothing of God and its Explosive Metaphors" and Ueda, "'Nothingness' in Meister Eckhart and Zen Buddhism," among others. On the role of the nothing in Heidegger, see my essay "Science, Thinking, and the Nothing as Such."

34. There is also the description of God as detached (*abegescheiden*) in DW 4: 1108 187–88/Evans 1, 272 Pr. 117 ("Ze dem êrsten suochet daz rîche gotes"), although here it is a matter of creatures' inability to understand God.

35. I borrow this phrase from Haas, "The Nothing of God and its Explosive Metaphors," who himself takes it from Hans Blumenberg (15).

36. Grace is nevertheless problematized in the tractate by Eckhart's rather scant explanation for why unity must occur through grace, as well as in his subsequent ontological, and not charismatic, description of human/divine reciprocity vis-à-vis creatures: "[E]quality must come about in grace, for it is grace that draws a man away from all temporal things, and makes him pure of transient things. And you must know that to be empty of all created things is to be full of God, and to be full of created things is to be empty of God." DW 5: 413,1–4/ES 288 (Vab).

37. For a brief account of the reception and development of *gelâzenheit* up through Böhme, see Völker, "'Gelassenheit.'"

38. This similarity might be explained, in part, by the fact that N4 contains portions of RdU, immediately followed by *Von abegescheidenheit*. For details on this manuscript, see Schaefer, 51–52; and Untersuchungen 1, 147–54.

39. Although it does not do so as frequently as *abegescheidenheit*, perhaps out of a desire to resist a more positive attribution when it comes to God. It is therefore misleading to say, as Schaefer does and Bundschuh and Enders repeat, that in this manuscript "*abegescheidenheit/abegescheiden* is almost never used alone, but rather always in the combination *abegescheidenheit vnd gelassenheit/abegescheiden vnd gelassen*." Schaefer, 52; Bundschuh, *Die Bedeutung von gelassen und die Bedeutung der Gelassenheit in den deutschen Werken Meister Eckharts unter Berücksichtigung seiner lateinischen Schriften*, 108; Enders, "Abgeschiedenheit—der Weg ins dunkle Licht der Gottheit," 19. For, as much as one might wish otherwise, there are many crucial passages in which this does not happen, especially when it comes to God's *abegescheidenheit*. The closest the redactor comes to doing so is the passage I cite in Table 3.2, on p. 78.

40. Schürmann, "Neoplatonic Henology as an Overcoming of Metaphysics," 33.

Chapter 4. Eckhart's Strategies for Cultivating Releasement

1. DW 1: 42,1–43,3/ES 181 Pr. 2 ("Intravit Iesus in quoddam castellum"); DW 1: 123,1–3/Walshe 368–69 Pr. 7 ("Populi eius"); DW 2: 66,1–11/Walshe 131 Pr. 28 ("Ego elegi vos"). For becoming the Son of God, see in general Pr. 2. This experience is taken even farther when Eckhart speaks of transcending the Trinity to reach "the silent desert" of the Godhead. DW 2: 420,9/Walshe 311 Pr. 48 ("Ein meister sprichet: alliu glîchiu dinc minnent sich under einander"). The Godhead is "above grace and being [*wesene*] and understanding and will and longing . . . and distinction [*underscheide*]." DW 2: 501,7–8 and 502,7/ES 202 Pr. 52 ("Beati pauperes spiritu"); trans. mod. It is "more unknown than it is known [*mê unbekant, dan ez bekant sî*]." DW 2: 66,7/Walshe 131 Pr. 28 ("Ego elegi vos"). On the relationship between the birth of the Son in the soul and the breakthrough to the Godhead in Eckhart's thought, see Ueda, *Die Gottesgeburt in der Seele und der Durchbruch zur Gottheit*, and Caputo, *The Mystical Element in Heidegger's Thought*, 127–34.

2. A few examples among many: Haas, "The Nothing of God and its Explosive Metaphors"; Hasebrink, *Formen inzitativer Rede bei Meister Eckhart*; Grassi, *La preminenza della parola metaforica*; Milem, *The Unspoken Word*; Tobin, *Meister Eckhart: Thought and Language*.

3. McGinn, *The Mystical Thought of Meister Eckhart*, 90–100, quote on 92–93. What follows in this section takes its inspiration from McGinn's analysis. For more on dialectic in Eckhart, see de Gandillac, "La 'dialectique' du Maître Eckhart"; Sikka, *Forms of Transcendence*, ch. 3; Oltmanns, *Meister Eckhart*; and Schürmann, *Wandering Joy*. See also Heidegger's evaluation of Oltmanns's dissertation and oral examination in §§7–8 of Appendix One, below.

4. See Eckhart's commentary on Ws. 7:27a in LW 2: 481–94/TP 166–71, nos. 144–57 (In Sap.). On p. 490/TP 169, no. 154, one finds: "Everything which is distinguished by indistinction is the more distinct the more indistinct it is, because it is distinguished by its own indistinction. Conversely, it is the more indistinct the more distinct it is, because it is distinguished by its own distinction from what is indistinct. Therefore, it will be the more indistinct insofar as it is distinct and vice versa. . . . But God is something indistinct which is distinguished by his indistinction. . . . For God is a sea of infinite substance, and consequently indistinct."

5. This ground is also that of God taken as distinct. As Eckhart's other ways of describing it indicate, including abyss (*abgrunt*), wasteland (*einœde*), and desert (*wüeste*), it should not be thought in terms of efficient causality, though. (See Largier, 1, 803 for a catalogue of such terms.) Even though, as Eckhart suggests in his Commentary on the Book of Genesis (LW 1: 186/ES 83, no. 3 [In Gen. I]), it can be understood as *causa essentialis* ("you must recognize that the 'principle' in which 'God created the heaven and earth' is the ideal reason [*ratio idealis*]"), we have seen in chapter 3 that this, too, does not go far enough; for we must transcend the Word as the exemplar of creation and even God as a potential creator.

6. I do not follow the editor (or the translator) here in placing quotations marks around the second instance of the word God. There are no such marks in the manuscripts, and interpolating them mitigates the shock value of Eckhart's paradoxical prayer. Georg Steer, in his new version of Pr. 52, in LE, 1, 163–99, omits them as well. Cf. Michael A. Sells's different reason for omitting them in his *Mystical Languages of Unsaying*, 188–89, as well as Thomas Merton's reservations, in *Zen and the Birds of Appetite*, 9–10.

7. For the desert motif, see, for example, DW 1: 193,4/Walshe 295 Pr. 12 ("Qui audit me"), DW 2: 77,1–2/Walshe 125 Pr. 29 ("Convescens praecepit eis"), and DW 2: 420,8–10/Walshe 311 Pr. 48 ("Ein meister sprichet: alliu glîchiu dinc minnent sich under einander").

8. Other passages have been mentioned in chapters 2 and 3. For more, see Schürmann, *Wandering Joy*, 9–10; McGinn, *The Mystical Thought of Meister Eckhart*, 55, 211, n. 8; and Bray, "Deutsche Bibelzitate in den Predigten Meister Eckharts."

9. While it may be too quick to place quotations marks around Eckhart's sentence, as Josef Quint does in the critical edition of Eckhart's works, one finds a similar "translation" of the Bible verse in Pr. 10 ("In diebus suis"), this time in conjunction with an apparent rendering of Luke 9:23: "Dar umbe sprichet unser herre: wer mîn jünger wil werden, der muoz sich selben lâzen; nieman enmac mîn wort hœren noch mîne lêre, er enhabe denne sich selben gelâzen." DW 1: 169,11–170,2. Cf. TP, 264. Panzig, "*gelâzenheit* und *abegescheidenheit*, 342–44, is nevertheless skeptical, and points instead to Eccli. 24:30–31: "He that hearkeneth to me, shall not be confounded: and they that work by me, shall not sin. They that explain me shall have life everlasting." Given Eckhart's other interpretive translations

of the Vulgate, though, the phrase "no one hears my word nor my teaching" seems a plausible gloss on not being able to be Jesus's disciple.

Part Three: Introduction

1. Schürmann, *Heidegger on Being and Acting*, 235.
2. As with my discussion of Eckhart, I will not treat Heidegger's modus operandi in great detail, as this would undoubtedly call for a separate study. Were I to do so, I would begin by taking up the work of Schöfer, *Die Sprache Heideggers*, and Botet, *Langue, langage et stratégies linguistiques chez Heidegger*.
3. For instance, GA 15: 399/80; GA 73.1: 507, 526; EGI, 12. For a contrast between ontology and the method of twentieth-century physics, which Heidegger ties back to Galileo and to Descartes's *Discourse on the Method*, see GA 15: 355/53–54.
4. If this occurs only for a few, it is not because only a few are capable of it. "In truth," as Heidegger says a few lines later in his conversation with the Buddhist monk, "every human, insofar as he is a thinking being, can carry out this thinking" (GA 16: 589). In 1928–29, Heidegger even says that Dasein as such philosophizes, albeit implicitly (MH/EB, 25; GA 27, §1). I discuss this latter point more in chapter 5.
5. Take, for example, the following quote from a transcript of the final, extemporized session (April 8, 1919) of Heidegger's lecture course *The Idea of Philosophy and the Problem of Worldview*: "Aim of phenomenology: the investigation of life itself. . . . [P]hilosophy can progress only through an absolute sinking into life as such, for *phenomenology* is never concluded, only *preliminary*, it always sinks itself into the preliminary. . . . [T]heories do not struggle with one another here, but only genuine with ungenuine insights. The genuine insights, however, can only be arrived at through honest and uncompromising sinking into the genuineness of life as such, in the final event only through the genuineness of *personal life* as such" (GA 56/57: 220/187–88). Here, Heidegger lays out a phenomenology *of* life, wherein phenomenology both investigates life (*genetivus objectivus*) and demands a self-investigation of life itself (*genetivus subjectivus*). For Heidegger at this period, phenomenology is not theoretical or scientific, but happens in accord with what he in calls the "pre-theoretical something" (which is another name for being) (GA 56/57: 219/186). The task is to let this happen and to describe it without objectifying it. To do so, a practical apriori is necessary (here a preparatory "immersion in life"), and Heidegger deploys new strategies and terms to convey and cultivate this (for example, the neologism *es weltet*, "it is worlding," which, though grammatically impersonal, still involves us, and which conveys a verbal, pre-subjective/objective dynamism at the heart of things; GA 56/57: 73/61). Such personal immersion also requires a kind of Eckhartian detachment. Just over two weeks later (April 24, 1919), Heidegger wrote to Husserl's daughter Elisabeth: "From an expansiveness

in a plurality of objects, our life must return to the original swelling [*ursprünglichen Quellung*] of a growing formation. No shattering of life into programs, no aestheticizing cosmetics, no ingenious gestures, but the strong trust in the bond to God and the originary force of the deed, with its pure consequences. Only life overcomes life—not objects or things—not even logical 'values' and 'norms' " (MH/EHuss, 8/126–27). As Eckhart's conception of detachment seeks to return to the origins, to the original energetic identity between the Godhead and the spark of the soul, so does Heidegger's conception of phenomenology seek to return to the original movedness of life, to the "living spirit" mentioned in the conclusion of his *Habilitationsschrift*. For spiritual detachment, as for detachment in phenomenology, existentiell engagement is crucial. See Kisiel, *The Genesis of Heidegger's* Being and Time, 81–83, 112.

6. Reiner Schürmann argues for the connection between being and method as a practical apriori with regard to authentic temporality in *Being and Time* in his lecture course on the latter. See Critchley and Schürmann, *On Heidegger's* Being and Time; see also Schürmann, *Heidegger on Being and Acting*, 235, 377, n. 28. Such a reading might find support in Heidegger's move in GA 27 to ground Dasein's transcendence, which is a form of letting-be that can only be understood on the basis of letting-be, in temporality (p. 218). There are, moreover, a number of Eckhartian strategies in play in *Being and Time* that challenge its putatively scientific-theoretical orientation. These include the recurring need for ontic-existentiell testimony and involvement; the need for an increasingly more profound deconstruction of Western philosophy (which can be traced back philosophically to Eckhart via Luther and Tauler); and the need for a comportment of letting and openness that is in tension with, though not necessarily opposed to, the language of *Entschlossenheit,* which must be understood not just as resoluteness, but literally, as un-closedness. For more on the supposedly scientific stance of *Being and Time* (and the Summer Semester 1927 lecture course *The Basic Problems of Phenomenology*) as itself a deconstructive strategy, see §3 of my "Homesickness, Interdisciplinarity, and the Absolute." At any rate, by 1928–29, Heidegger comes to view scientific philosophy as a "non-concept" and a "misunderstanding" (GA 27: 219; cf. p. 224).

Chapter 5. The Middle Voice of Releasement in Heidegger's Lecture Courses, 1928–30

1. See the references to works by Karl Löwith, Jürgen Habermas, and Richard Wolin in Davis, *Heidegger and the Will*, 322–23, n. 6.

2. For the date, see Kisiel, "Notes for a Work," 312.

3. Heidegger was also discussing the role of *Abgeschiedenheit* (detachment, departedness) in Eckhart with Bernhard Welte less than two months prior to his (Heidegger's) death. See the book's conclusion and §6 of Appendix One, below.

Heidegger himself brings *Gelassenheit* and *Abgeschiedenheit* together in a marginal note in "Time and Being" (GA 14: 20, n. 6). For a much earlier parallel, see GA 60: 308–309/234–35. For the role of *Abgeschiedenheit* in Heidegger's corpus, especially as it pertains to his reading of the poet Georg Trakl, see my essay "For the Love of Detachment." For the role of a different poet in Heidegger's corpus, one whom Julia Ireland has called "the poet of *Gelassenheit*," namely, Johann Peter Hebel, see Ireland's "Heidegger's *Hausfreund* and the Re-enchantment of the Familiar."

4. Two senses of *Gelassenheit* I do not discuss are the early theological sense and Heidegger's use of *Gelassenheit* in relation to the divine in Hölderlin. I discuss *Gelassenheit* as a comportment vis-à-vis technology in chapter 7. For a specifically Christian reading of *Gelassenheit*, see the sixteen-page book by Viktor Emil von Gebsattel, the physician who treated Heidegger during his mental breakdown in 1946: *Von der christlichen Gelassenheit*. (On p. 11, Gebsattel discusses Eckhart's disciple Suso.) For Heidegger's relation to Gebsattel, see Mitchell, "Heidegger's Breakdown."

5. One of the few extensive commentaries on this course of which I am aware is an important lecture course given by Jean Wahl at the Sorbonne in 1946 and published under Wahl, *Introduction à la pensée de Heidegger*. For more details on the French reception of Heidegger's *Einleitung in die Philosophie* long before its publication in German, see Moore and Schrift, "Existence, Experience, and Transcendence," 11, n. 30.

6. Though see, for example, Benveniste, "Active and Middle Voice in the Verb," and Rutger, *The Middle Voice in Ancient Greek*.

7. See the texts listed in note 10 (p. 261), below, as well as, for example, Gadamer, *Wahrheit und Methode*, 109–15 (on the middle voice of play); Derrida, "Différance," 9 (on the middle voice of *différance*); Schürmann, *Broken Hegemonies*, passim (on middle-voiced language and phenomena as they appear throughout the history of philosophy and on the middle voice as a way in which to think an-archically); and Lewin, "The Middle Voice in Eckhart and Modern Continental Philosophy." It is no accident that these authors find inspiration in Heidegger.

8. See also GA 7: 214/60, 272/108; GA 8: 160/156; GA 9: 430/325; GA 17: 28/21; GA 20: 111/81; GA 22: 129/107; GA 29/30: 449/310; GA 34: 137/98–99, 142/102, 203/146–47, 222–23/159; GA 40: 71/74; GA 46: 37; GA 54: 152, 159; GA 55: 338; GA 60: 207, n. 11/153, n. 127, 271/203–204; GA 62: 357, n. 39/157, n. 18; GA 97: 262.

9. Gadamer relates that in 1920–21 Heinrich Ochsner informed him that Heidegger had used the phrase *es weltet* in a 1915 lecture course. This led Gadamer to believe that Ochsner may have been the first to know that "the young Heidegger already at that time in no way whatsoever thought in a transcendental-philosophical fashion." In Ochwadt and Tecklenborg, eds., *Das Maß des Verborgenen*, 230. Bernhard Welte, however, in an unpublished record of a conversation he had with Ochsner on September 21, 1957, writes that Ochsner told him Heidegger had used the phrase *die Welt weltet* in a transitive sense in 1915. The entire passage is worth citing in

full: "Auf einem Spaziergang erzählte ich O., Gustav Siewerth habe mir gesagt, er glaube einen Anstoß zu Heideggers Interesse an der Sprache gegeben zu haben. / O. meinte dazu, dies sei wohl bis zu einem gewissen Grade möglich, indessen stehe es fest, daß Heidegger selbst schon sehr früh auf diese Spur gekommen sei. Er, O., habe etwa im Jahre 1915 mit Heidegger zusammen das Buch von Lask über das Urteil gelesen. Damals schon habe Heidegger alētheia als a-letheia verstanden. Damals schon habe er die Formel gehabt, 'die Welt weltet' und hinzugefügt: in transitivem Sinn, damals schon habe er die Bedeutungstheorie der Sprache verworfen und damit den Gedanken (dies vor allem gegen Rickert), daß allein das Urteil die entscheidende signifikative Form der Sprache sei. Damals schon habe der Sinn des 'ist' ihn am meisten beschäftigt. / Dies sind lauter Dinge, so bemerkten wir zusammen, die im veröffentlichten Werk Heideggers zum Teil erst sehr viel später ausgesprochen wurden. Er blieb in seinen Anfängen und kehrte später nur tiefer in diese ein." "On a walk I related to O. that Gustav Siewerth had told me he believed that it was he [Siewerth] who had prompted Heidegger's interest in language. / O. reckoned that this may well have been possible to a certain degree, but said it's certain that Heidegger had already got on this track very early on. For instance, in 1915, he, O., had read with Heidegger [Emil] Lask's book on judgment. Already at that time, Heidegger had understood *alētheia* as *a-lētheia*. Already at that time, he had had the formulation, 'the world worlds,' and added: in a transitive sense; already at that time, he had rejected the semantic theory of language and thus also the thought (this above all against Rickert) that judgment alone is the decisive significative form of language. Already at the time had the sense of the 'is' occupied him most of all. / Then we remarked together that these are so many things that would in part be vocalized in Heidegger's published work only much later. He remained in his beginnings and later turned back to them only more deeply." Welte, "Aufzeichnungen aus meinen Gesprächen mit Heinrich Ochsner," 3, UAF E 8/934. Compare the rather different published version in Ochwadt and Tecklenborg, eds., *Das Maß des Verborgenen*, 215. For a comment about the inadequacy of propositional logic when it comes to impersonal expressions, see GA 27: 54.

10. Crowe, "Resoluteness in the Middle Voice"; Llewelyn, "Heidegger's Kant and the Middle Voice"; Llewelyn, *The Middle Voice of Ecological Conscience*; Scott, "The Middle Voice of *Being and Time*." There is, however, one reference to *Gelassenheit* in a later comment made in the margins of the Kant book. Here, Heidegger indicates his reservations about the language by which the "happening" wherein "Dasein holds itself out into the nothing" is expressed, writing in the margins after the word *Geschehen*: "the nihilating comportment; but this is grounded in *Gelassenheit*" (GA 3: 238/166–67 and note a). Friedrich Wilhelm von Herrmann, the editor of *Gesamtausgabe* edition of the Kant book, explains that Heidegger only made comments in the margins of his copy of the first edition of the Kant book, and that many of these comments stem from the period in which Ernst Cassierer's and Rudolf Odebrecht's reviews of the Kant book appeared, in 1931 and 1931/32,

respectively (GA 3: 314/220). Although it may seem that this note should be counted among those few that "make note of the later level of consideration pertaining to the history of Being," in light of the other references to *Gelassenheit* as well as the tension between action and letting during the late 1920s and early 1930s, it seems quite plausible that the note belongs to the earlier period. At any rate, cf. GA 29/30: 433/299: "The task is to understand the innermost power of the nothing, precisely in order to let beings be [*sein zu lassen*] as beings, in order to have and to be beings in all their powerfulness as beings."

11. Though see, for example, Biraut, *Heidegger et l'expérience de la pensée*, 519–20, and Crowe, "Resoluteness in the Middle Voice." Davis, *Heidegger and the Will*, 24–59, argues for the fundamentally ambiguous status of the will in *Being and Time*.

12. As Theodore Kisiel and John van Buren, the translator of GA 63, have pointed out, the middle-voiced character of *begegnen* is present also in GA 63: 85/65, where Heidegger writes: "*Welt ist, was begegnet*" ("World is what encounters/what is encountered") (rendered by van Buren as "World is something being encountered"; see his note 53 on pages 118–19 of the translation). Kisiel, *The Genesis of Heidegger's* Being and Time, 329–30.

13. This course, more than any other writing of Heidegger's, develops the idea of *Mitsein* (being-with) in astounding detail. Interestingly, according to Preger, 1, 344 and 344, n. 1, it was Eckhart who coined the term *Mitsein*. While I could not find the word in this form, Eckhart does use *mitewesen* in the sense of accidents such as goodness and truth, which do not properly belong to God's pure being (*wesen*). DW 3: 341,3–6/Walshe 264 Pr. 77 ("Ecce mitto angelum meum").

14. Pages 101–103 contain a plethora of words built on the root *Lassen*: not only *Liegen-lassen* and *Seinlassen*, but also *Überlassen, Unterlassen, Lässigkeit*, and *Lassen* itself: "Dieses unser Seinlassen, unser Überlassen der Dinge an sie selbst und ihr Sein ist eine eigene Gleichgültigkeit unsererseits. . . . Die Lässigkeit in diesem Überlassen ist kein Unterlassen schlechthin. Das Seiende sein lassen ist nicht etwa nichts. . . . [D]ieses Seinlassen [ist] ein 'Tun' der höchsten und ursprünglichsten Art." "Our letting-be, our leaving things to themselves and their being, is a unique indifference on our part. . . . The laxity in this leaving is not pure abstention. . . . To let beings be is not nothing. . . . [T]his letting-be [is] a 'doing' of the highest and most originary sort." Later in the course, this "indifference" is tied to *Gelassenheit* itself (214). We will see a similar deployment of words stemming from *Lassen* in chapters 6 and 7, below. Like Eckhart, Heidegger is able to deploy the inner connections among words to philosophical ends, with the result that language appears to be less an arbitrary way to express things than an essential part of the matter itself. To the extent that such language resists discursive formalization, it too may be considered an extradiscursive strategy.

15. Cf. GA 27: 3, 218–20, 223, 226; as well as Heidegger's letter to Elisabeth Blochmann from August 8, 1928 (MH/EB, 25). Later in the lecture course, Heidegger retracts the statement about implicit philosophizing, explaining that it

was initially said in order that it could now, at the end of the lecture course, be taken back. The reason: "Because in this explicit retraction we see something essential: that the one philosophizing must explicitly transpose himself into the mode of existence determined by taking a stance" (GA 27: 398–99; quote on 399). That is to say, the retraction makes more explicit the need for each of us to undertake to philosophize for ourselves, which Heidegger also highlighted at the beginning of the course. The retraction is thus part of the strategic pedagogy of the course, whose task is to "let philosophy become free [*frei werden lassen*] here and now in our Dasein" (GA 27: 8; cf. 4–6). Regardless of whether we should retain an essential implicit valence of philosophizing, this retraction does not change the need explicitly to let our implicit happening of transcendence be, which is of primary concern to me here. One argument, *en passant*, for retaining it would be that, in the second version of his lecture "On the Essence of Truth," held in Bremen on October 8, 1930, more than a year after *Einleitung in die Philosophie*, Heidegger connects philosophizing with the letting-be of beings *prior to* all explicit philosophy: "Dasein is the essence of the human, to whose own essence he liberates himself in the freedom of the letting-be [*Seinlassens*] of beings. Philosophizing begins with this liberation . . . even before all explicit philosophy (GA 80.1: 365 and 365, n. 40). Cf. the end of the lecture "What Is Metaphysics?" from July 24, 1929, where Heidegger quotes a line in Greek from Plato's *Phaedrus* (*phusei gar, ō phile, enesti tis philosophia tēi tou andros dianoiai*) (279a–b), and then provides the following, misleading gloss/translation: "As long as human beings exist, philosophizing of some sort occurs" (GA 9: 122/96). (In the original version of the lecture, there are even quotes around Heidegger's rendering: " 'By nature, philosophy is in the essence of every human being, in a certain way,' as Plato says at the end of the *Phaedrus*" [WMU, 743].) This is misleading, because the context indicates that Socrates is talking about a specific person (namely, Isocrates), not about the human being as such: "By nature . . . some philosophy is in *the* man's thought." We might consider this an instance of creative translation à la Eckhart, or perhaps Heidegger is simply taking things out of context to suit the needs of the moment.

16. This turnabout is intriguingly intimated with regard to truth in GA 27: 109 and 109, n. 1. Heidegger writes that "its [truth's] place is not the sentence, but Dasein (or even vice versa)." The footnote reproduces a supplementary sentence from Hildegard Feick's copy of the lecture course, a sentence which the editor surmises was written not at the time of the lecture course itself, but later, at the time the copy was made: "(or even vice versa: that the essential place of Dasein is truth as unconcealment)." By October 1930, Heidegger will at any rate have affirmed Dasein's belonging to truth rather than the other way around. See GA 80.1: 365.

17. Such terms and inconsistencies include affection, the drive to return home, being held captive, leeway, and play, among many others.

18. For example, Heidegger at one point says that the three primary metaphysical questions of the lecture course—world, finitude, and solitude or

individuation—must themselves arise out of a fundamental attunement (GA 29/30: 87/57). Cf. GA 29/30: 434/300: "we must aim . . . to let *the intrinsic relationships between world, individuation, and finitude* emerge together [*heraustreten zu lassen*]."

19. My concern in what follows will be to expose the various aspects of letting-be that must precede and support the moment of vision. While it would be fruitful to investigate the extent to which such letting-be is still operative within the activity of the moment of vision itself, I will not take this up here. I should note, however, that *Entschlossenheit*, with which the moment of vision is essentially connected in *Being and Time* (SZ, 338/323), has been interpreted in terms of letting-be, including by Heidegger himself, as we will see in the next two chapters.

20. It is no accident that Heidegger will bring philosophy up in this context, for it too "*must first form its own interrogative space*" in the act of questioning, and only in the act of questioning is it capable of *keeping* this interrogative space *open*"; only in this way will it be able "*to evoke the Dasein in man*" (GA 29/30: 258/174). Indeed, "acting" within metaphysics means "nothing other than the fact that we must now really and properly question" (GA 29/30: 86/56–57).

21. Cf. GA 27: 214–15 and 410, where freedom is associated with the middle-voiced letting-be of primal action (which is ultimately neither passive nor active), and where freedom is said to be found only in liberation as a letting-happen of transcendence.

Chapter 6. Violent Thinking and Being in Heidegger's *Introduction to Metaphysics*, 1935

1. See the early drafts of, and notes for, "On the Essence of Truth" from 1930 (GA 80.1: 342, 401), the 1930–31 seminar on Augustine (GA 83: 81), and the lecture "Die gegenwärtige Lage und die künftige Aufgabe der deutschen Philosophie" from November 1934 (GA 16: 330).

2. Capobianco, *Engaging Heidegger*, 55. For Heidegger's own reflections on its importance, see GA 40: 232/249–50.

3. Kisiel, "Heidegger's Philosophical Geopolitics in the Third Reich," 226.

4. There is also the issue concerning the date and status of Heidegger's appeal to National Socialism (GA 40: 208/222), which sparked a fervent controversy already at the time of the lecture course's publication in 1953. For details, see Kisiel, "Heidegger's Philosophical Geopolitics." I will not address such issues in what follows, although I might note in passing that Heidegger's own justification in 1968 for this appeal—that he was throwing the National Socialists in the audience a crumb, but that those with ears to hear could perceive his critique of the reigning regime—points to a possible exoteric/esoteric methodological dimension in the lecture course that would deserve further treatment. See GA 40: 233/251 and 232/249.

5. The most conspicuous instance of this is when Heidegger derives willing, resoluteness, unconcealment, and the human's relation to being from letting. He points

to "On the Essence of Truth" to support this position, although it is by no means obvious that Heidegger intended for this earlier work to subtend his entire analysis while he was writing and lecturing on the *Introduction to Metaphysics*. His bracketed interpolation reads: "The essence of willing is traced back here to open resoluteness [*Ent-schlossenheit*]. But the essence of open resoluteness lies in the un-concealment of human Dasein *for* the clearing of being and by no means in an accumulation of energy for 'activity.' Cf. *Being and Time*, §44 and §60. But the relation to being is letting. That all willing should be grounded in letting strikes the understanding as strange. See the lecture 'On the Essence of Truth,' 1930" (GA 40: 23/23–24; trans. mod.; see also 159/167). A similar attempt is made in the first "Country Path Conversation" (to be discussed in chapter 7, below). The Researcher in the dialogue notes that words such as resoluteness "misinterpret releasement [*Gelassenheit*] as pertaining to the will," to which the Scholar replies, "One would then have to think the word 'resoluteness,' for example, as it is thought in the book mentioned earlier [*Being and Time*]: as the self-opening for the open." The Researcher concludes that "the essence of thinking, namely releasement to the open-region, would then be a resolute openness [*Entschlossenheit*] to the essential occurring of truth" (GA 77: 143–44/93).

6. *Walten* does not, in and of itself, necessarily bear a violent valence. It is not obvious that Heidegger intends it this way when he begins to use it as a term for the "being of nature in the happening of history" in 1928–29 (GA 27: 393–94), or when he starts to use it as a translation for originary *physis* in 1929–30 (GA 29/30). Given Heidegger's frequent deployment of more violent terms deriving from the same root in the 1935 lecture course, however, he seems to want us to think it does have this valence at this time. On the significance and polysemy of *Walten*, see Derrida's final seminar, *The Beast and the Sovereign: Volume II*.

7. Cf. GA 40: 122–23/126–27 for the language of *Kampf* with respect to the distinctions between being and becoming and between being and semblance. On *polemos* in Heidegger in general, see Fried, *Heidegger's* Polemos.

8. Heidegger even quotes from the Rectoral Address in GA 40: 53/54.

9. In an unpublished typescript titled "Tracing the Rift," William McNeill discusses the significance of a nonviolent deployment of *Riß* in Heidegger's contemporaneous "Origin of the Work of Art," which is to be thought of as an inscription of ecstatic temporality and in connection with letting-be.

10. Heidegger's language of letting in the original version of the lecture course, which includes *sich einlassen auf, sein lassen, erscheinen lassen, aufgehen lassen, zukommen lassen, ankommen lassen, beiseitelassen*, and *überlassen*, can be found in GA 40: 10, 14, 66, 82, 109, 146, 170, 172, and 175.

11. On Heidegger's self-interpretations, including those with respect to *Entschlossenheit*, see von Herrmann, *Die Selbstinterpretation Martin Heideggers*, esp. 141–47.

12. Davis, *Heidegger and the Will*, 92–99.

13. See Heidegger's 1939 essay on Hölderlin's "Wie wenn am Feiertage . . . ," where Heidegger explains that the inceptive character of *physis* prevailed as "releasement [*Gelassenheit*]." GA 4: 65/87; trans. mod.

14. The word *Gelassenheit*, to say nothing of its cognates, appears in GA 71: 87/73, 311/270; GA 53: 68/55; and GA 97: 52, 67, 71, 73–74, 78, 89. For other usages of *Gelassenheit* around this time, see, for example, GA 9: 305/232; GA 82: 365, 369 (1943); and GA 75: 307–308 (1944).

Chapter 7. Releasement as the Essence of Thinking and Being in Heidegger's First "Country Path Conversation," 1945

1. Heidegger also points to the gathering in *Gelassenheit* by hyphenating the term. See especially GA 97: 296, and one of his notes for *Der Satz vom Grund* (DLA B 74); also GA 73.1: 23; GA 73.2: 1199–1200; GA 90: 296; GA 99: 41; and UDS 50.

2. Neither term suffices as a translation, since neither captures the sense of a gathering (*Ge-*) of language (*Sprache*) that the German *Gespräch* indicates. The formal Latinate term *colloquy*, meaning "to talk" (*loqui*) "together" (*com-*), works best etmologically, but reminds one less of Platonic philosophy than Erasmian humanism (cf. the *Colloquia familiaria*).

3. The conversation should therefore perhaps be dated 1945, and not 1944–45, as one finds in G1, 72/58, note, and in the title (*Feldweg-Gespräche (1944/45)*) and editorial note (246/161) of GA 77. The date of 1945 is also supported by an unpublished typescript of the dialogue bearing the title "ΑΓΧΙΒΑΣΙΗ / das erste Feldweggespräch 1945" (DLA D 86.298), although a different typescript that I discuss below has Winter 1944–45.

4. Another source for Heidegger's inspiration to write dialogues might have come from the ancient Chinese text *Zhuangzi*, which contains a conversation about the necessity of the unnecessary that Heidegger has one of the interlocutors cite at the end of the third "Country Path Conversation" (GA 77: 239/156). It is presumably the dialogue from the *Zhuangzi* that Heidegger sent to his wife on March 2, 1945 (see MH/EH, 234/187). Three days later, he sent it to his brother (DLA HS.2014.0069.00012).

5. See also Heidegger's letter to his wife from March 23, 1945: "Even though my condition is still physically delicate, in the last few days I've gained such remarkable momentum that I'm almost completely oblivious to food & sleep. I suddenly found a form of saying I would never have dared use, if only because of the danger of outwardly imitating the Platonic dialogues. I'm working on a '*Gespräch*'; in fact I have the 'inspiration'—I really have to call it this—for several at once. In this way, poetic & thoughtful saying have attained a primordial unity, & everything flows along easily & freely. Only from my own experience have I now understood Plato's mode of presentation" (MH/EH, 234–35/187; trans. mod.; cf. 235/188).

6. As Heidegger writes to his wife from Meßkirch on April 15, 1945, "On Monday I'll be cycling to [Castle] Wildenstein & Beuron" (MH/EH, 236/188). See also MH/KB, 101.

7. The typescript is titled "Über das Wesen des Denkens (Ein Gespräch zwischen einem Forscher, einem Gelehrten und einem Weisen)." DLA 84.2110.

8. In a letter to his brother from June 28, 1945, Heidegger thanks him for sending a transcript of the dialogue. He also mentions that he is ruminating on ten (!) interrelated evening dialogues, and that the first serves as a sort of introduction to the others and contains all of the themes that will be developed in them (DLA HS.2014.0069.00012).

9. Lossmann, "Die Verlagerung der Philosophischen Fakultät der Universität Freiburg auf die Burg Wildenstein (14.April 1945 bis 8.August 1945)" (UAF D 14/21): "Gelegentlich kam Heidegger, der bei der Fürstin Leiningen [sic] auf der Burg Werenwag (gegenüberliegende Talseite) ein Refugium gefunden hatte, zu einem Seminar im großen Saal der Burg herüber. Einmal . . . kamen die anderen nach der Sitzung lachend zurück. 'Heute hast Du was verpaßt, er hat geredet über die Nacht als Näherin der Sterne ohne Naht und Saum!' Wir hatten am Abend vorher im Halbdunkeln, wie so oft, Morgenstern-Gedichte auswendig rezitiert, darunter auch 'Die Nähe' " (p. 4). Morgenstern's humerous, hardly translatable poem indeed bears striking resemblance to Heidegger's wordplay. See in particular the second and third stanzas (which I will render literally, providing explanations in brackets): "Doch eines Nachts, derweil sie [die Nähe] schlief / da trat wer an ihr Bette hin / und sprach: 'Steh auf, mein Kind, ich bin / der kategorische Komparativ! // Ich werde dich zum Näher steigern, / ja, wenn du willst, zur Näherin!' / Die Nähe, ohne sich zu weigern, / sie nahm auch dies als Schicksal hin." "Yet one night, while she [nearness, *die Nähe*] was asleep / someone came to her bed / and said: 'Get up, my child, I am / the categorical comparative! // I will elevate you to a seamster [*Näher*, literally a man who is nearer], / indeed to a seamstress [*Näherin*, literally a woman who is nearer] if you wish!' / Nearness, without hesitating / accepted this as fate." For the German and a looser translation, see Morgenstern, *The Gallows Songs*, 11, n. 25.

The Freiburg faculty decided on the location of Wildenstein in February 1945, although the university had already been discussing possible places of refuge in January 1940. See Speck, "Vorlesungen im Phantomsemester," as well as MH/KB, 99–102 and Heidegger's letters to his brother from January 13, 15, and 29, 1945 (DLA HS.2014.0069.00012). According to Heidegger's nephew Heinrich Heidegger, it may well have been Elfride Heidegger who had made the recommendation to the Freiburg philosophy faculty; for, in the 1910s, she had tried, together with Ernst Laslowski and Heinrich Ochsner, to arrange to have Wildenstein serve as a meeting place for the circle of students and friends gathered around Heidegger at the time. See Heinrich Heidegger and Stagi, *Martin Heidegger: Ein Privatporträt zwischen Politik und Religion*, 80–81.

10. Denker and Büchin, eds., *Martin Heidegger und seine Heimat*, 145. See Heidegger's letter to Mayor Siegfried Schühle from August 17, 1955, available in the Martin-Heidegger-Archiv der Stadt Meßkirch.

11. A report of the whole event was first published in the newspaper "Südkurier" and can be found in Denker and Büchin, eds., *Martin Heidegger und seine Heimat*, 148–49; cf. 253, n. 63.

12. He renamed the dialogue: "Zur Erörterung der Gelassenheit: Aus einem Feldweggespräch über das Denken" ("Toward an Emplacing Discussion of *Gelassenheit*: From a Country Path Conversation on Thinking"). Like the book title, Heidegger's speech appeared under the title "Gelassenheit," although the manuscript has "Über die Bodenständigkeit" ("On Autochthony"); see the facsimile in G2, 35; also available under DLA B 54. It can also be found in GA 16: 517–29, and in G2, 9–26. The truncated dialogue appears also in GA 13: 37–74.

13. Although rendered as "the Scientist" in the published translation of the conversation, *der Forscher*, as Keiling ("Letting Things Be for Themselves," §2) points out, is more general and would be better rendered as "the Researcher." *Der Weise* would typically be rendered as "the Sage" or "the Wise One," as it is related to the adjective *weise* (wise) and the noun *Weisheit* (wisdom). However, during the course of the conversation, *der Weise* says that "there are presumably no wise ones, no sages [*Weisen*]. However, this does not preclude that one may be a *Weiser* in the sense of a guide, where by this word I do not mean one who knows [*Wissenden*], but rather one who is capable of pointing [*weisen*] into that wherefrom hints come to humans. Such a guide [*Weiser*] is also able to show [*weisen*] the manner [*Weise*], the way, in which these hints are to be followed" (GA 77: 84–85/54). Nonetheless, it still seems to me to be more appropriate to translate *der Weise* as "the Sage" than to translate it as Bret Davis does in his translation, namely as "the Guide," since "the Sage" is how the German reader would first hear it. Moreover, as Keiling argues, we may think of the wisdom of *der Weise* as an alternative to two other Aristotelian intellectual virtues represented, respectively, by the Researcher and the Scholar, namely, *technē* and *epistēmē*. At any rate, perhaps it was the ambiguity surrounding the Sage's name that led Heidegger to rename him "the Teacher" (*der Lehrer*) in the later version of the dialogue. This seems puzzling, though, for two reasons: (1) ambiguity is important for the movement and reflection of the dialogue (see GA 77: 79–80/50); and (2) the word *teacher* may contain connotations of *imparting* knowledge, rather than participating in an exchange in which insight *happens* (although it should be noted that Heidegger himself does not always understand teaching in this fashion, but rather as a "letting-be-learned").

14. Heidegger has the Scholar introduce it in a lowercased form (*gegnet*), implying that it is Old or Middle High German. The translator of GA 77 explains in a footnote that it is in fact a Middle High German contraction of *gegenōte* (73–74, n. 44), although Beierwaltes, "Heideggers Gelassenheit," 11, n. 33, doubts whether

gegnet is actually Middle High German. At any rate, I find it best to think of this word as an example of Heidegger's attempts to deploy old or uncommon words (as well as neologisms) to creative ends.

15. Capobianco, *Engaging Heidegger*, 8, 142; Davis, *Heidegger and the Will*, 198. In his translation of a passage from the 1959 version of the first "Country Path Conversation," William Richardson even interpolates the word *Being* in place of a translation of *Gegnet* to indicate more clearly what the releasement of our essence toward the open-region amounts to: " 'Thus, the essence of thought, i.e., release unto [Being], would be resoluteness unto truth in its presencing' (*Dann wäre das Wesen des Denkens, nämlich die Gelassenheit zur Gegnet, die Entschlossenheit zur wesenden Wahrheit*)." Richardson, *Heidegger: Through Phenomenology to Thought*, XXXI; cf. 502, 509.

16. The editor notes that the material in which this passage is included probably dates from the first half of the 1930s (GA 73.2: 1493). Incidentally, the very next note (GA 73.1: 23) speaks of letting-be:

Sein-lassen
↓
die *Ge-lassenheit*—in die Wahr-heit—*nicht bloß 'moralisch'*; verhaltungsmäßig
↓
der Dank.

Letting-be
↓
gathered releasement—into sheltering trueness—*not merely "moral"*; pertaining to comportment
↓
thanks.

A later note from this volume even asks whether "Gegnet" in the first "Country Path Conversation" serves "als Vornahme für Ereignis" (GA 73.2: 1258). For other usages of "Gegnet" in proximity with "Sein," see GA 13: 206–207/6, 210/8; GA 81: 297; GA 82: 362–64.

17. Though Heidegger uses the word *Geschehnis* in the block quote above, the language of *Ereignis* and its cognates does appear throughout the dialogue. See GA 77: 57/36, 114/74, 119/77, 121/79, 142/92, 146–47/95–96, 157/103.

18. Note that, in the 1959 version of the conversation, the Sage, now called the Teacher, goes farther, saying, "authentic releasement [*eigentliche Gelassenheit*] can come to pass without it necessarily being preceded by that being-let-loose [*Losgelassensein*] from horizontal transcendence" (G1, 49/73; trans. mod.).

19. See Davis, *Heidegger and the Will*, 18–22, for an explanation of this phrase.

20. Note that this word can also mean "conception" in the sense of conceiving a child, as in the German phrase for the Immaculate Conception: *Mariä Empfängnis*. Eckhart plays on this ambiguity in Pr. 2, where he translates, in characteristically peculiar fashion, Luke 10:38 (*Intravit Jesus in quoddam castellum et mulier quaedam, Martha nomine, excepit illum in domum suam*) as "unser herre Jêsus Kristus der gienc ûf in ein bürgelîn und wart enpfangen von einer juncvrouwen, diu ein wîp was." *Gelassenheit* would then not only receive, but also be involved in genesis.

21. The word for letting in German is *Lassen*, which, in its verbal form, means "to let" or "to have something done," as in, "I'm having my car fixed" (*ich lasse mein Auto reparieren*). From this root a number of important terms and phrases employed throughout the conversation are derived. In addition to the ones I mention below, one finds: *fallen lassen* (to let fall by the wayside, to abandon); *sein lassen* (to let be); *walten lassen* (to let prevail); and, of course, *Gelassenheit*. *Schmuck, kosten, wollen, stellen, fallen,* and *Mut* all serve as roots for further word clusters and wordplays throughout the dialogue.

22. Von Herrmann, *Wege ins Ereignis*, 371–86. I have added #4 to von Herrmann's list.

23. For the fourth, see GA 77: 120/78. For the last, see GA 77: 117/76 and 122/79. The others appear on and off throughout the conversation.

24. For the locution *Gelassenheit zu*, see G1, 23–26/54–57, where Heidegger speaks of "releasement toward things [*Gelassenheit zu den Dingen*]."

25. Although Heidegger in "The Essence of Language" says that it is an attunement (GA 12: 159/66; see also GA 83: 81), it is certainly no ordinary attunement. For it seems to be a condition for, yet at the same time to belong essentially to, thinking as such (rather than just enabling thinking in a particular way, such as attunements). It would thus be an attument more fundamental than all fundamental attunements, a *fundamental* fundamental attunement, an *Urgrundstimmung*.

26. This was changed in the 1959 version to "the open-region, regioning everything [*die Gegnet, alles gegnend*]" (G1, 66/86; trans. mod).

27. Another example is when Heidegger writes: "The essence of thinking which, as an indwelling releasement to the worlding of the world [*Gelassenheit zum Welten der Welt*], bears that relationship by means of which the human dwells in nearness to farness" (GA 77: 151/99).

28. This passage comes from a bundle of notes written between 1943 and 1945. Heidegger also connects *Gelassenheit* to originary freedom in these notes: "Das Lassen—als Gelassenheit in die äußerste Weite der Weile der Freyheit." "Letting—as releasement into the utmost expanse of the whiling of freedom" (GA 73.1: 666; cf. 705, and GA 82: 369). See chapter 5, above, for the role of freedom in Heidegger's earlier thought.

29. For the origins of this procedure in Aristotle, see Aubenque, "The Relationship between Hermeneutics and Ontology in the Case of Aristotle's *PERI HERMENEIAS*."

Conclusion

1. On being's independence from Dasein, see, above all, Capobianco's books, *Engaging Heidegger* and *Heidegger's Way of Being*.
2. In the *Beiträge*, for example, beyng is frequently described as "riven" or "fissured" (*zerklüftet*) (GA 65: passim).
3. As Walter Biemel reports Husserl having once said to Heidegger. "The Transformation in Husserl's Later Philosophy," 115.
4. For different approaches to this question that have appeared just in English over the past few years, see, for example, the contributions in Björk and Svenungsson, eds., *Heidegger's Black Notebooks and the Future of Theology*; Farin and Malpas, eds., *Reading Heidegger's* Black Notebooks 1931–1941; and Mitchell and Trawny, eds., *Heidegger's* Black Notebooks. Each of these volumes, incidentally, contains no more than a couple passing references to Eckhart.
5. On Heidegger's "metaphysical anti-Semitism," see Di Cesare, *Heidegger, die Juden, die Shoah*. For a contrasting view, see von Herrmann and Alfieri, *Martin Heidegger: Die Wahrheit über die* Schwarzen Hefte.
6. The eulogy is titled "Suchen und Finden." In it, Welte refers to their conversation, as well as to the themes of death, the nothing, the fourfold, and the Godhead, though not explicitly to Eckhart.
7. Welte, *Meister Eckhart*, 21.
8. Welte, "Erinnerung an ein spätes Gespräch," 149–50. Max Müller interprets this Eckhartian conversation as transpiring beyond the contentious contrast Heidegger draws between thinking and faith. See *Auseinandersetzung als Versöhnung*, 109–11.

Appendix One. Materials on Heidegger's Relation to Eckhart

1. Von Herrmann, *Wege ins Ereignis*, 376–77, n. 4. Other editions of medieval mystics owned by Heidegger that von Herrmann specifies, but that are not provided below, include Mechthild of Magdeburg, *Das fließende Licht der Gottheit*, ed. Oehl; Mechthild of Magdeburg, *Das fließende Licht der Gottheit*, ed. Schleussner; *Tauler*, ed. Oehl; *Die Predigten Taulers*, ed. Vetter; Suso, *Horologium Sapientiae*; and H. A. Grimm, trans., *Von Gottes- und Liebfrauenminne*. Three additional texts of Heidegger's that von Herrmann does not mention, but that he made available to me, are Bernard of Clairvaux, *Ausgewählte Sermone des Heiligen Bernhard über das Hohelied*; Abraham a Sancta Clara, *Auswahl*; and a secondary source on "the Meister Eckhart of the sixteenth century," Sebastian Franck: Hegler, *Geist und Schrift bei Sebastian Franck*. (Quote in Borngräber, *Das Erwachen der philosophischen Spekulation der Reformationszeit*, 57.) Von Herrmann also owns Heidegger's copy of an old edition of Francis of Assisi, as well as the 1928 edition of the patristic and scholastic volume of Ueberweg's history of philosophy. Additionally, we know that

Heidegger owned Bihlmeyer's edition of Suso, a book by Thomas à Kempis, the anonymous *Theologia Deutsch*, and a volume of Böhme's writings. Heinrich Heidegger and Stagi, *Martin Heidegger: Ein Privatporträt zwischen Politik und Religion*, 129; DLA HS.2014.0069.00013. We may assume that Heidegger's edition of the *Theologia Deutsch* was Bernhart's, since, on May 10, 1930, Heidegger recommended this edition to Blochmann, mentioning the "vast [*Große*] introduction" (MH/EB, 36), which, incidentally, contains many references to Eckhart. See Anonymous, *Der Frankfurter: Eine deutsche Theologie*, 1–90, esp. 70–71, 78–79. (For parallels between Bernhart's introduction and Heidegger's notes on mysticism, see Baier, "Heidegger und das Mittelalter," 36, 36, n. 68, 38, n. 72. However, we need not follow Baier when one very close parallel misleads him to suggest that one of Heidegger's notes must have been composed after 1920, when Bernhart's translation appeared with Insel Press; for Heidegger may well have consulted the first edition for his notes, which appeared in 1910 with Hermann Rinn.) I might note here as well that, in addition to his edition of the *Theologia Deutsch*, Bernhart published his dissertation on Bernard of Clairvaux and Eckhart in 1912 (*Bernhardische und Eckhartische Mystik in ihren Beziehungen und Gegensätzen*); a translation of Eckhart in 1914, on which see more below; a history of medieval mysticism in 1922 (*Die philosophische Mystik des Mittelalters von ihren antiken Ursprüngen bis zur Renaissance*; see 175–99 and passim for Eckhart); and a comparative study of Eckhart and Nietzsche in 1934.

 2. I thank Ulrich von Bülow and Arnulf Heidegger for this information. Email correspondence: July 11, 2016 and July 12, 2016.

 3. Daniels's edition can be found in the fifth number of the twenty-third volume of the series to which Heidegger refers when recommending material on the Middle Ages to his students in Winter Semester 1926–27: "Beiträge zur Geschichte der Philosophie des Mittelalters. Texte und Untersuchungen. Earlier edited by Bäumker, now by Grabmann 1891 ff. Only the text-editions are worthwhile" (GA 23: 42). Heidegger refers to texts in this series elsewhere, for example, GA 1: 205, n. 9/258–59, n. 9, and GA 22: 33, n. 6, and many figures he was associated with published in it, including Clemens Baeumker, Martin Grabmann, Engelbert Krebs, and Arthur Schneider. Denifle's edition can be found in the second of seven volumes of the *Archiv für Literatur und Kirchengeschichte des Mittelalters* to which Heidegger also refers his students in Winter Semester 1926–27: "H. Denifle u. Fr. Ehrle, Archiv für Literatur und Kirchengeschichte des Mittelalters. Bd. I–VII, 1885–1900" (GA 23: 42). Denifle's "Meister Eckharts lateinische Schriften und die Grundanschauung seiner Lehre" contains, in addition to a long introduction and the first modern edition of the *The Book of Twenty-Four Philosophers*, many texts or portions of texts from Eckhart's Latin writings, as well as a note on Nicholas of Cusa's copy of them. For further evidence that Heidegger may have been familiar with Daniels's and Denifle's editions, see my discussion of Gadamer's reports in §6, below.

 4. The second edition first appeared in 1912. It is not clear which printing Heidegger used for his citations; however, Heidegger does appear to have exam-

ined this edition in 1919. In a letter to his wife Elfride (née Petri) from April 17, 1919, Heidegger writes: "At Theophil's I had a look at the new edition of Eckhart's writings (Diederichs), which is much more thoroughly edited—apart from the worthless introduction—Did you know by the way that Adam Petri first printed Tauler's sermons in Basel in 1521 & along with them some of Eckhart's?" (MH/EH, 93/61–62). Here he is referring to Büttner's edition (published by Eugen Diederichs Verlag), and *not* to Ernst Diederichs's 1913 edition *Meister Eckharts Reden der Unterscheidung*. For, in the second edition of the first volume of Büttner's 1903 edition, which, as mentioned, first appeared in 1912, but was reprinted in 1917 and 1919, one finds a note by Büttner on Adam Petri's 1521 edition: "Der erste Herausgeber Eckeharts, *Adam Petri* (in: Johannes Tauleri des heiligen Lehrers Predigten, Basel 1521)" (Büttner 2nd ed., 1, 208). It is possible that Heidegger could mean the first edition (1, 206), which also contains this note, although it is not clear why he would call it new. Perhaps he was unaware of the first edition and intends a comparison with a different edition, such as Pfeiffer's? At any rate, it would not make sense to speak of Ernst Diederichs's edition, which contains only the Middle High German of RdU and a short, two-page editorial note at the beginning.

5. It is possible, though not certain, that Heidegger's Eckhart epigraph was a part of the version he presented on July 27, 1915. The published version dates from 1916.

6. For this and the following two references, the dates are based on Kisiel, "Notes for a Work," 312–13.

7. More exactly, Heidegger is here referring to Käte Oltmanns's dissertation on Eckhart. For more details, see §§6–8, below.

8. Based on the date of the lecture "Europa und die deutsche Philosophie."

9. Because Heidegger refers to his manuscript on "Nietzsche's Metaphysics" in this collection of notes, we may assume that it was written sometime during or, more likely, after 1940. Heidegger's editor misses this in his dating of this text to as early as 1936 (GA 76: 395–96). The editor gives the terminus ante quem of 1955 (GA 76: 395).

10. See my discussion in the introduction to chapter 7 for the possibility that these references date from 1945.

11. In light of other texts Heidegger cites in proximity to this Eckhart reference, as well as of his reference in GA 73.2: 995–96 to LW 4 (published in 1956).

12. See Büttner 2nd ed., 1, 229–30; also Gottschall, "Eckhart and the Vernacular Tradition," 526–27.

13. In this and the following entries for 1916, I first quote the note as Kisiel has reproduced it in translation on page 319. Then I quote the German as found on page 327. I have not corrected slight typographical discrepancies between Heidegger's citations here and Pfeiffer's edition.

14. Heidegger takes this material from Lasson, *Meister Eckhart, der Mystiker*, 109–11, although he must have looked up the material for the second and third

quotes in his edition of Pfeiffer, since they are not identical with Lasson's renderings. Cf. Lasson's text on Eckhart in the tenth edition of the second volume of Ueberweg's history, *Die patristische und scholastische Philosophie*, 646. Heidegger refers to this edition in GA 23: 42, and in MH/KL, letter of March 19, 1924.

15. Translation of Eckhart mine. The published English translation of Heidegger's course, p. 4, leaves the quote in the original.

16. The editor of GA 76 interpolates the ellipsis, explaining that it indicates an illegible word. Yet this sentence is simply a quote from Meister Eckhart: "Et *Augustinus* l. VII Confessionum dicit se in libris Platonis legisse *in principio erat verbum* et magnam partem huius primi capituli Iohannis." I have accordingly filled in the ellipsis in my translation, below.

17. See my discussion in chapter 7 of the possibility that these references date from 1945.

18. In his unpublished preparatory notes for "Das Ding" (DLA 75.7305,3), Heidegger cites more of Eckhart's sentence: "got ist etwaz hœhste und oberste dinc, daz gemeine ist aller gebrûchunge."

19. Heidegger does not mean Augustine here, as the editor supposes. Heidegger is not citing from Pfeiffer's edition, but from the eighty-second text of Jostes's edition (= Pr. 117 in the critical edition), where Eckhart himself cites Dionysius. This is proven by Heidegger's own specification of the quote's source in his unpublished preparatory notes for "Das Ding" (DLA 75.7305,3). The correct citation is provided below, and I have accordingly deleted the editor's interpolation in the English translation. For the source in Dionysius and other references to it in Eckhart's corpus, see DW 4: 1116, n. 12.

20. Heidegger's references here derive from the editorial note in LW 4: 51, n. 4. On this basis alone, one would not be able to deduce that he had read Pr. LXXXVII in Pfeiffer (Pr. 52 in the enumeration of the critical edition, "Beati pauperes spiritu"); however, he does cite Büttner's translation of this sermon in 1956 or later, and he did consult Pfeiffer while taking these notes in GA 73.2. Although Heidegger may not have followed up on his reference to no. 103 of In Ioh., his citation of this text on June 27, 1950, proves that he was acquainted with it.

21. Heidegger's citation here probably derives from the editorial note in LW 4:52, n. 3, although Heidegger does cite from this same passage in 1949.

22. Here Heidegger's citation seems to derive in part from the editorial note in LW 4: 52, n. 3 (which cites Pr. 9 in the critical edition) and in part from Pfeiffer's edition. Perhaps Heidegger had both texts in front of him when taking these notes.

23. Heidegger's citation here derives from the editorial note in LW 4:57, n. 5, although he does cite from In Ioh. elsewhere. See above.

24. On account of his citations from S. VI,2 in LW 4 on the same sheet as his quotation of Pfeiffer Pr. L, we may assume that the latter comes from an editorial foonote on LW 4: 56–57, n. 5. On account of his mention of Boethius on the sheet as well, Heidegger certainly read more of the footnote than the single sentence he

quotes, and perhaps all of it. I accordingly cite the whole footnote here: "*Cf. Pr. L 166,11–18:* Werlt sprichet als vil als reine; er meinet die sêle. Boetius sprichet: dar umbe heizet diu werlt der sêle reine, want si gebildet ist nâch der reiner schoener werlt, diu in gote ist, in der alliu reinikeit unde schoenheit ist. Diu sêle, diu dâ în getreten ist in daz lûter bilde, daz dâ gebildet ist nach der reinen unde schoenen werlte, diu in gote ist unde gote ist, und allez in ime belîbende ist, in dem bilde, unde niht ûzluogende ist und ze mâle gescheiden ist unde gesundert von der ûzern werlte, in die liehte werlt, in die sêle kumet der sun unde gebirt sich dar in. *166,36–38:* 'in die werlt,' daz ist; in die liehten werlt, in die sêle, diu zemâle gescheiden ist von der ûzern werlt und ist in alle wîs gebildet nâch der götlîchen werlt. In die werlt kumet der sun, reht als er ûzer dem vater vellet, unde wirt geborn in der sêle. *Pr. 5a* (QUINT) *I 80,7–11:* 'Er sant inn in die wellt.' 'Mundum' betútet in ein wys 'rein.' Merckend! Got enhat kein eygner statt dann ein rein hertz und ein reine sel; do gebirt der vatter sinen sun, . . . was ist ein rein hercz? daz ist rein, daz von allen creaturen ist gesúndert und gescheiden." "*World* meaning pure or virgin. He is referring to the soul. Boëthius says the world of the soul is called pure because she is fashioned like the fair and virgin world in God. And God is that soul which has gotten her into the perfect image of the divine world and wholly there abides, not peering forth but, all aloof from the outside world, standing still in the light-world in God. Into this soul comes the Son, begotten there in all the panoply of God . . . 'into this world,' into the light-world, that is. The soul, [which is completely detached from the outer world and is a] true reflection of the divine world, into her enters the Son; just as he falls from the Father he is born in the soul" (Evans, 1, 131; Pfeiffer, Pr. L, "Exivi a patre et veni in mundum"). "'He sent him into the world.' One meaning of the Latin word *mundum* is 'pure.' Now take note! There is no place more suited to God than a pure heart and a pure soul: there the father gives birth to his Son. . . . What is a pure heart? That heart is pure which is [separated and] detached from all creatures" (Davies, 189; Pr. 5a in the critical edition, "In hoc apparuit").

25. This should be "Abhandlung," as is found in Grabmann's text. Accordingly rendered as "treatise," rather than "series," in the translation, below.

26. Kisiel, "Notes for a Work," 309.

27. Bernhart adds the following footnote here: "Pahncke, Kleine Beiträge, S. 18, verweist auf die Stelle Pfeiffer II, 612, 12 f.: Das Herz wird nicht rein vom äußeren Gebet, vielmehr wird das Gebet rein vom reinen Herzen."

28. The Middle High German has *sachet* rather than the modern German *verursachet*. Both mean "to cause," but Heidegger appears here to be wondering about the prefix "verur-." At any rate he writes: "to cause and to hold within the essence."

29. *Vollbringen*: to bring about, to accomplish. *Wirken*: to cause, to effect.

30. *i. S. v. gegenständlich Vorstellen*: in the sense of objectively representing. The next line is the Middle High German of "dieses wahre Gotthaben—daß man ihn wirklich habe": "this true possession of God, whereby we really possess him" (Davies, 10).

31. Bernhart adds the following footnote here: "Nach Büttner II, 216, zu S. 9."
32. Bernhart adds the following footnote here: "Vgl. hiezu Pfeiffer 179, 4–6 den Vergleich mit dem Maler."
33. Bernhart adds the following footnote here: "Gott muß Prinzip unseres Handelns werden."
34. This sermon, along with Prr. 102, 103, and 104 were grouped together in Büttner's edition under the title "Von der ewigen Geburt: Vier Predigten" (pp. 63–92 of the second edition). Since Heidegger makes two excerpts from the third and fourth sermons (Prr. 103 and 104 in the critical edition), it is reasonable to assume he read the first two as well.
35. There are nevertheless portions of some of these tractates that are in the critical edition, such as the material from *Von abegescheidenheit* that can also be found in "Von der sêle werdikeit und eigenschaft."
36. Gadamer, "Auf dem Rückgang zum Anfang (1986)," 406, n. 6: "Vgl. dazu die Edition von Cl. Baeumker (1924)." This footnote is absent in the original publication of Gadamer's text under the title "Heideggers Rückgang auf die Griechen."
37. Koch, "Neue Forschungen über Meister Eckhart," 414.
38. Hans-Georg Gadamer, "Der eine Weg Martin Heideggers (1986)," 425; "Martin Heidegger's One Path," 28.
39. Gadamer, "Auf dem Rückgang zum Anfang (1986)," 406. In the original publication of this text, Gadamer writes "deus est suum esse" instead of "Esse est Deus." See "Heideggers Rückgang auf die Griechen," 414.
40. Gadamer, "Geschichtlichkeit und Wahrheit (1991)," 255.
41. Gadamer, "Die Geschichte der Philosophie (1981)," 299; *Heidegger's Ways*, 156; trans. mod.; my interpolation. Referring to Gadamer in a footnote, Otto Pöggeler writes: "Als er [Heidegger] in den zwanziger Jahren mit dem *Opus tripartitum* des Meisters Eckhart bekannt wurde, war er so begeistert, daß seine Schüler erneut eine Arbeit über Eckhart von ihm erwarteten." "When, in the '20s, he [Heidegger] became acquainted with Meister Eckhart's *Opus tripartitum*, he was so exited that his students once again expected a work from him on Eckhart." *Neue Wege mit Heidegger*, 387. It is not clear whether Pöggeler is overinterpreting Gadamer's report or whether he has a different source for the expectation of Heidegger's students. At any rate, their earlier expectation would have at least come from the conclusion of Heidegger's *Habilitationsschrift*, where he had projected future work on Eckhart.
42. Guitton, "Visite à Heidegger," 155. Cf. Guitton's later republication of the article, in which one finds the date "October 1956." *Profils parallèls*, 470–86.
43. Heinrich Heidegger and Stagi, *Martin Heidegger: Ein Privatporträt zwischen Politik und Religion*, 138.
44. Elisabeth F. Hirsch, "Reminiscences of Heidegger in Marburg," unpublished typescript, 4–5, 7. This typescript seems to have been the source for Hirsch's 1977 presentation at the Heidegger Circle, titled "In Memory of Martin Heidegger: Observations on Heidegger as Teacher and Scholar." See Saas, *Martin Heidegger: Bibliography and Glossary*, 412. Although the typescript may provide further evidence

for Heidegger's engagement with Eckhart in his Marburg period, it is necessary to mention two emendations in pen that make this less certain. In the first sentence, "on" is crossed out and "besides" is written above it, and "on" is inserted before "Luther." Thus, the line would read: "Despite his Catholic upbringing, Heidegger's religious interests soon focused besides Augustine, Eckhart, on Luther and Kierkegaard." In a shortened, published version of her recollections, which does not contain the discussion of Eckhart and Otto, Hirsch writes, "Despite his Catholic upbringing, Heidegger's religious interests soon focused beyond Augustine and Eckhart on Luther and Kierkegaard. The latter two theologians attracted Heidegger because they started their reflection with a religious experience: faith." See Elisabeth F. Hirsch, "Remembrances of Martin Heidegger in Marburg," 343.

45. Ôhashi, "Die frühe Heidegger-Rezeption in Japan," 34; my interpolations.

46. Davis, in "Zen after Zarathustra," 134, n. 47, and *Heidegger and the Will*, xiv, 308, n. 12, has the years 1937–39, which are corroborated by Heisig, *Philosophers of Nothingness*, 184.

47. Nishitani's text was actually published while he was abroad in Germany. *Nishitani Keiji Chosakushū Daiikkan*, 302. I am grateful to S. P. K. Cerda for this information.

48. Oltmanns, *Meister Eckhart*, 10. Oltmanns's comment is confirmed in an interview she gave with Cornelius Bickel and Jürgen Zander, available on CD at the Martin-Heidegger-Archiv der Stadt Meßkirch. See §3 of chapter 1, above, for more information.

49. This letter, originally written in German, is, to my knowledge, only available in the English translation by Pierre Adler cited here. See Schürmann, "Reiner Schürmann's Report of His Visit to Martin Heidegger," 67–68.

50. Schürmann, "Recit de l'entretien avec Heidegger," 157; "Reiner Schürmann's Report of His Visit to Martin Heidegger," 71.

51. Unlike in the reports that follow, Schürmann speaks in the plural in "Heidegger and Meister Eckhart on Releasement," 95: "Heidegger in private conversations emphasizes the authenticity of Meister Eckhart's experience of Being." See also Schürmann's unpublished text, "Heidegger and the Mystical Tradition," 7.

52. Schürmann, *Maître Eckhart ou la joie errante*, 295, n. 1; cf. 11.

53. Schürmann, *Wandering Joy*, 254, n. 93; cf. xviii, as well as Schürmann, "Heidegger and the Mystical Tradition," 12; "Neoplatonic Henology as an Overcoming of Metaphysics," 31; and "Meister Eckhart's 'Verbal' Understanding of Being as a Ground for Destruction of Practical Teleology," 808.

54. Welte, "Erinnerung an ein spätes Gespräch," 149–50.

55. There is an additional "l" that is partially crossed out, and the "a" is blurry (probably from a letter being placed on top of another), which suggest that Heidegger (or his typist) had initially had *existentiellen*.

56. Protocols of Heidegger's tutorials have been published in HSS. Oltmanns's presentation, given on January 28, 1928, can be found therein under the title "Wesenheit, Dasein und Grund bei Meister Eckehart," 356–62. See §3 of chapter

1, above, for a discussion of her presentation, and Appendix Two, below, for my translation of it.

57. See note 55 (p. 277), above.

Appendix Two. "Essentiality, Existence, and Ground in Meister Eckehart," by Käte Oltmanns

1. The original German is available in HSS, 356–62. Oltmanns uses the word *Dasein* in the title, but never in the body of the text, where the word *Existenz* (which I have also rendered as "existence") appears instead.

2. Anonymous, *Von Bagdad nach Toledo: Das "Buch der Ursachen" und seine Rezeption im Mittelalter*, prop. 4, 46; *The Book of Causes*, 22: "The first of things created is being." Quoted by Eckhart in Grabmann, 102 and LW 5: 41/Maurer 45, no. 4 (Qu. Par. 1).

3. Oltmanns's parenthetical interpolation.

4. Oltmanns refers to Grabmann, 102ff.; the quote can be found on p. 102. Cf. LW 5: 41, no. 4 (Qu. Par. 1), and Maurer, 45–46: "Hence as soon as we come to it [sc. being] we come to a creature. . . . So God, who is the creator and is not creatable, is intellect and understanding; he is not being or a being" (trans. mod.).

5. Oltmanns refers to Grabmann, 104. Cf. LW 5: 46, no. 10 (Qu. Par. 1), and Maurer, 49: "it belongs to the essential account of a being that it is caused" (trans. mod.).

6. "God is being."

7. "God is his understanding and is not a being, to be = to be created."

8. Oltmanns refers to Grabmann, 103. Cf. LW 5: 45, no. 8 (Qu. Par. 1), and Maurer, 48: "[I]f you wish to call understanding being I do not mind. Nevertheless I say that if there is anything in God that you want to call being, it belongs to him through his understanding" (trans. mod.).

9. Oltmanns refers to Grabmann, 102. Cf. LW 5: 40, no. 4: "Quia dicitur Ioh. 1: 'in principio erat verbum, et verbum erat apud deum, et deus erat verbum.' Non autem dixit evangelista: 'in principio erat ens et deus erat ens.' Verbum autem se toto est ad intellectum et est ibi dicens vel dictum et non esse vel ens commixtum"; Maurer, 45: "It is said in John 1: 'In the beginning was the Word, and the Word was with God, and the Word was God.' The Evangelist did not say: 'In the beginning was a being, and God was a being.' A word is completely related to an intellect, where it is either the speaker or what is spoken, and not being or a composite being" (trans. mod.).

10. Oltmanns refers to Grabmann, 81, and notes that this quote is "according to a manuscript from [Nicholas of] Cusa." Cf. LW 4: 268, no. 301, S. XXIX ("Deus unus est"), and Davies, 261: "God calls things into being through the intellect."

11. "Actually," "potentially."

12. Here Oltmanns refers simply to page 30, which the editors of HSS link to Schelling, *Philosophische Untersuchungen über das Wesen der menschlichen Freiheit*, 358. In English as *Philosophical Investigations into the Essence of Human Freedom*, 27–28.

Appendix Three. "Nietzsche's Zarathustra and Meister Eckhart," by Nishitani Keiji

1. Nietzsche, *Thus Spoke Zarathustra*, 5; henceforth TSZ.

2. Nishitani makes use of three related terms throughout the text. *Chi* 地, rendered as "earth," *sakai* 境, rendered as "state," and the combination of these two Chinese characters in *kyōchi* 境地. By translating this last word as "basic disposition," we aim to emphasize the spatial motif. While *kyōchi* too can mean something like "mental state," it is also used in the sense of "attaining the (state of) enlightenment" or "being caught up in a (state of) ecstasy." One must keep in mind that Nishitani would certainly warn against psychologizing such "dispositions." Also, we do not mean for this word to imply something like an "elemental disposition." For Nishitani, there are various "basic dispositions," some, as it were, more "basic" than others.

3. TSZ, 4.

4. Ibid., 3.

5. Nishitani uses several words beginning the with the character 変, meaning "change." We have tried to distinguish these while maintaining the connection with the prefix "trans-". Thus, "*henshin* 変身" (lit. "change in body") we render as "transfigure" and "*henkei* 変形" (lit. "change in form or shape") as "transform." Note that Nietzsche's three "metamorphoses" (*Verwandlungen*) can be translated in Japanese as "*henkei*" or "*henten* 変転" ("change-around"). In fact, Nishitani translates Nietzsche's *verwandeln* below as *henshin suru*.

6. We have tried to maintain a clear distinction between "*seimei* 生命" and "*sei* 生." Where the former normally implies "life" or "life force," and its antonym is "death," the latter means "human life" or "living." We generally achieve this by translating "*sei*" alternatively as "a life," "one's life," "living," or "way of life," depending on the context. For clarity, we sometimes translate "*seimei*" as "source of life."

7. TSZ, 5.

8. A reference to Thomas Carlyle's 1836 novel. Nishitani's translation of the title is *ishou no tetsugaku* 衣裳の哲学, *A Philosophy of Clothes*.

9. TSZ, 4.

10. Ibid., 3. Note the German: "welcher überfliessen will."

11. Ibid., 4.

12. Nishitani is certainly alluding to the opening lines of "On the Blessed Isles" (TSZ, 65), which he cites below.

13. TSZ, 3.

14. The word *botsuraku* 没落 carries the same negative connotation as the English "fall" and German "*Untergang*," as in "the fall of the Roman Empire." When something reaches its prime, it has nowhere to go but down. Nishitani will emphasize this negative moment below. This, of course, is not to be confused with Heidegger's *Verfallen*, which, in any case, is translated in Japanese as "*tairaku* 頽落."

15. TSZ, 4. For consistency, we have modified the translation of "*Menschen*" to "human beings."

16. Ibid.; trans. mod. See the previous note.

17. Ibid.

18. Nietzsche, *Beyond Good and Evil*, 69.

19. TSZ, 66.

20. Ibid., 67. Nishitani replaces Nietzsche's "*dieser Wille*" with "*kono seisan no ishi* この生産の意志," which we mark with the addition in brackets.

21. Ibid., 70. Nishitani picks up on Nietzsche's capitalization of "*Einer*," which gets glossed over in Del Caro's translation, and translates it as "*yuiitsu-naru mono* 唯一なる者." We have added the capitalization, but the brackets in the quote are Nishitani's own.

22. Ibid., 80.

23. Ibid., 59. There is a small error in Nishitani's citation. "Schenkenden Tugenden" should read "schenkenden Tugend."

24. Ibid., 136. "Verkleinernden Tugenden" should read "verkleinernden Tugend."

25. Unless otherwise noted, Nishitani's quotations of Meister Eckhart are direct translations from his Japanese. Where an English translation of Eckhart was available, we have supplied it in the notes. The references to Meister Eckhart's work, the source language, and the available English translations have all been procured by Ian Alexander Moore, to whom the translators extend our deepest gratitude. Moore has also indicated where Nishitani's citations are mistaken and indicated where material is lacking from the critical edition of Meister Eckhart's works.

26. Nishitani maintains a distinction between Plotinus's "*psyche*" and Eckhart's "*Seele*," translating the former as "*tamashī* 魂" and the latter as "*rei* 霊." Keeping with the English literature, we render both as "soul."

27. "niht în geslozzen, niht vereiniget, mêr: ez ist ein" (Pfeiffer, 86,4; cf. DW 2: 341,9 Pr. 44 ["Postquam completi erant dies"]). "not included, not united, but *one*" (Walshe, 144).

28. "niht alleine vereinet, mêr: ein einic ein" (Pfeiffer, 431,17; cf. DW 5: 33,8–9 [BgT]). In ES we find the following rendering of this section: "And our Lord prayed his Father that we might become one with him and in him, not merely that we should be joined together" (222).

29. "Er gap gote nie niht noch er enpfiene nie niht von gote: ez ist ein ein und ein lûter einunge" (Pfeiffer, 310,40–311,2; cf. DW 1: 197,5–6 Pr. 12 ["Qui

audit me"]). "He never gave God anything, nor did he receive anything from God: it is a single oneness and a pure union" (Walshe, 296). In Japanese, the subject of a sentence can be dropped, which Nishitani has done in his translation. We have tried to maintain this sense in our translation of Nishitani's rendering.

30. Augustine, *The Confessions*, Book III, vi (10), 42. Nishitani's translation is "*moromoro no seimei no seimei* 諸々の生命の生命." Cf. note 6 (p. 279), above, on the implications of the term "*seimei*."

31. "Justitia vita est et vivere justo, et est justitia ipsi esse inquantum huiusmodi." (Cf. LW 2: 596, no. 265 [In Sap.]).

32. "Unicum est et idem est esse justitiae et justi." (Cf. LW 2: 391, no. 63 [In Sap.]).

33. There is a mistake in Nishitani's citation, which should read Käte Oltmanns, *Meister Eckhart*, 82.

34. The word is *basho* 場所, a term which had a central place in the thinking of the founder of the Kyoto School, Nishida Kitarō (1870–1945).

35. "Solange wir beim Schauen stehn, sind wir noch nicht in dem, den wir schauen, solange ein Etwas Gegenstand unseres Bemerkens ist, sind wir nicht Eines in dem Einen. Denn wo nichts als eines ist, da sieht man nichts! Woher man denn Gott nicht sehen kann, als mit Blindheit, nicht erkennen, als mit Unerkenntnis, und nicht vernehmen, als mit Unvernunft" (Büttner 2nd ed., 2, 151 ["Von den Hindernissen an wahrer Geistlichkeit"]). This sermon is not included in the critical edition of Eckhart's works; however, the material before and after this quote in Büttner's edition may be found in Pfeiffer, 248–49.

36. "Denn solange sie [die Seele] einen Gott hat, Gott erkennt, von Gott weiß, so lange ist sie getrennt von Gott" (Büttner 2nd ed., 2, 165; cf. DW 4: 1121,295 Pr. 117 ["Ze dem êrsten suochet daz rîche gotes"]). "for as long as the soul has God, knows God and is aware of God, she is far from God" (Davies, 244).

37. "der Mensch solle so arm stehn, daß er 'eine Stätte, darin Gott wirken möge' weder selber sei noch gar in sich habe! Solange der Mensch in sich Raum behält, solange behält er *Unterschiedenheit*" (Bütter 2nd ed., 1, 185; cf. DW 2: 502,4–6 Pr. 52 ["Beati pauperes spiritu"]). Note that the citation should read p. 185 and not p. 206. "man should be so poor that he should not be or have any place in which God could work. When man clings to place, he clings to distinction" (ES, 202).

38. "Gott muß geradezu ich werden, und ich geradezu Gott" (Bütter 2nd ed., 1, 179; cf. DW 3: 447,5 Pr. 83 ["Renouamini spiritu"]). Note that the quote is on p. 179, not 178. "God must become me and I must become God" (Davies, 238). In the Japanese, Nishitani does in fact switch the order of "*Gott*" and "*ich*."

39. Nishitani's citation refers to German Sermon 96 in Pfeiffer's edition. "mit dem ougen, dâ inne ich got sihe, daz ist daz selbe ouge, dâ inne mich got siht: mîn ouge unde gotes ouge daz ist ein ouge und ein gesiht" (Pfeiffer, 312,8–10; cf. DW 1: 201,5–7 Pr. 12 ["Qui audit me"]). "The eye with which I see God is exactly the same eye with which God sees me. My eye and God's eye are one eye,

one seeing" (Davies, 179). We translate "*shi* 視" in Nishitani's quote as "*glance*" in order to maintain the connection Nishitani makes with the previous line, where he uses the word "*shisen* 視線."

40. "Gott muß geradezu ich werden, und ich geradezu Gott: so ganz eins, daß dieses Er und dieses Ich Eines werden und es bleiben und—als das reine Sein selber—in Ewigkeit desselben Werkes walten!" (Bütter 2nd ed., 1, 179; cf. DW 3: 447,5–6 Pr. 83 ["Renouamini spiritu"]). The quote is on page p. 179, not p. 178. Nishitani takes the Middle High German ("ein werc wirkent") from Pfeiffer, 320,11. "God must become me and I must become God, so entirely one that this 'he' and this 'I' become one 'is' and act in this 'isness' as one" (Davies, 238).

41. The English translation is from ES, 183. "Hier ist Gottes Grund mein Grund und mein Grund Gottes Grund" (Bütter 2nd ed., 1, 127; cf. DW 1: 90,8 Pr. 5b ["In hoc apparuit"]).

42. TSZ, 121.

43. The reference is likely to "The Sleepwalker Song," where Nietzsche writes, "*Mitternacht ist auch Mittag*" ("midnight is also noon," TSZ, 262).

44. "da ich ledig stehn will im Willen Gottes, und ledig auch von diesem Gotteswillen, und aller seiner Werke, und Gottes selber—da bin ich mehr als alle Kreaturen, da bin ich weder Gott noch Kreatur" (Büttner 2nd ed., 1, 185; cf. DW 2: 504,7–8 Pr. 52 ["Beati pauperes spiritu"]). "when I come to be free of will of myself and of God's will and of all his works and of God himself, then I am above all created things, and I am neither God nor creature" (ES, 203).

45. TSZ, 155.

46. Ibid., 81.

47. In "The Convalescent." See ibid., 174.

48. "Gott hat die Seele in freie Selbstbestimmung eingesetzt, so daß er über ihren freien Willen hinweg ihr nichts antun, noch ihr etwas zumuten will, was sie nicht will. Was sie also in diesem Leibe mit freiem Willen erwählt, darauf vermag sie wohl zu bestehen" (Büttner 2nd ed., 1, 196, "Von dem Zorne der Seele und von ihrer rechten Stätte"). Nishitani's citation should refer to p. 196, not p. 197. This passage is not to be found in the critical edition of Eckhart's works.

49. Nishitani translates "*Ich*" here as "*jiga* 自我," which we have rendered throughout as "ego."

50. TSZ, 22–23.

51. The word is *hendō* 変動. Note the connection to *henkei* and *henshin*. Cf. note 5 (p. 279), above.]

Bibliography

Published Primary Sources

Eckhart

Throughout the book, I refer mostly to the critical edition of Eckhart's writings: Meister Eckhart, *Die deutschen und lateinischen Werke,* herausgegeben im Auftrag der deutschen Forschungsgemeinschaft (Stuttgart/Berlin: Kohlhammer, 1936–). I refer to Eckhart's Latin works with the cipher "LW" and to his German works with the cipher "DW," followed by volume, page, and, for the German works, line numbers. For the Latin works, rather than line numbers, I provide subsection numbers, referring to them with the ciphers "no." or "nos." I employ the following abbreviations of Eckhart's works:

Eckhart's Latin Works in the Critical Edition

Acta	Acta Echardiana (LW 5: 149–655)
Collatio 1	Collatio in Libros Sententiarum (LW 5: 3–26)
Collatio 2	Collatio in Libros Sententiarum (denuo recognita) (LW 1,2: 475–79)
Frag. Par.	Fragmenta Parisiensia (LW 1,2: 481–88)
In Eccli.	Sermones et Lectiones super Ecclesiastici c. 24,23–31 (LW 2: 229–300)
In Exod.	Expositio Libri Exodi (LW 2: 1–227)
In Gen. I	Expositio Libri Genesis (LW 1: 185–444)
In Gen. II	Liber Parabolorum Genesis (LW 1: 447–702)

In Ioh.	Expositio sancti Evangelii secundum Iohannem (LW 3)
In Sap.	Expositio Libri Sapientiae (LW 2: 301–643)
Prol. gen.	Prologus generalis in opus tripartitum (LW 1: 148–65)
Prol. gen. (rec. L)	Prologus generalis in opus tripartitum (Recensio L) (LW 1,2: 20–39)
Prol. op. prop.	Prologus in opus propositionum (LW 1: 166–82)
Prol. op. prop. (rec. L)	Prologus in opus propositionum (Recensio L) (LW 1,2: 41–57)
Qu. Par.	Quaestiones Parisienses (##1–5 in LW 5: 27–83, ##6–9 in LW 1,2: 453–69)
S. and SS.	*Sermo* and *Sermones* (LW 4)

Eckhart's Middle High German Works in the Critical Edition

BgT	*Daz buoch der götlichen træstunge* (DW 5: 1–105)
Pr. and Prr.	*Predigt* and *Predigten* (DW 1–4)
RdU	*Die rede der underscheidunge* (DW 5: 137–376)
Vab	*Von abegescheidenheit* (DW 5: 400–61)
VeM	*Von dem edeln menschen* (DW 5: 106–36)

Manuscript Analyses in the Critical Edition

Untersuchungen 1   *Untersuchungen*, Vol. 1: *Neue Handschriftenfunde zur Überlieferung Meister Eckharts und seiner Schule: Eine Reisebericht von Josef Quint*. Stuttgart: W. Kohlhammer, 1940.

Translations of Eckhart and Other Editions

Bernhart   Bernhart, Joseph, ed. and trans. *Meister Eckhart* (*Deutsche Mystiker*, Vol. 3). Kempten: Jös. Kösel'sche, 1914.

Bindschedler   Bindschedler, Maria, ed. and trans. Meister Eckhart, *Vom mystischen Leben: Eine Auswahl aus seinen deutschen Predigten*. Klosterberg/Basel: Schwabe, 1951.

Büttner 2nd ed.   Büttner, Herman, ed. and trans. *Meister Eckehart Schriften*. 2nd ed. 2 vols. Leipzig: Eugen Diederichs, 1921. The two volumes were originally published in 1903 and 1909, respectively.

BIBLIOGRAPHY 285

Büttner 1-vol.	Büttner, Herman, ed. and trans. One-volume edition. *Meister Eckehart Schriften*. Leipzig: Eugen Diederichs, 1934.
Davies	Davies, Oliver, ed. and trans. *Meister Eckhart: Selected Writings*. London: Penguin, 1994.
Daniels	Daniels, Augustinus, ed. *Eine lateinische Rechtfertigungsschrift des Meister Eckhart*. With a foreword by Clemens Baeumker. Münster i. W.: Aschendorff, 1923.
De Libera	De Libera, Alain, trans. Maître Eckhart, *Traités et sermons*. 3rd ed. Paris: Flammarion, 1995.
Denifle	Denifle, Heinrich, ed. "Meister Eckharts lateinische Schriften und die Grundanschauung seiner Lehre." *Archiv für Literatur und Kirchengeschichte des Mittelalters* 2 (1886): 417–652, 673–87.
Diederichs	Diederichs, Ernst, ed. *Meister Eckharts Reden der Unterscheidung*. Bonn: A. Marcus and E. Weber, 1925. Anastatic reprint of the 1913 edition.
Dondaine	Dondaine, Antonius, ed. *Magistri Eckardi Opera Latina XIII: Quaestiones Parisienses*. Commentariolum de Eckardi Magisterio adiunxit Raymundus Klibansky. Lipsiae in aedibus Felicis Meiner, 1936.
Döll	Döll, Ermin, ed. and trans. *Das Buch der ewigen Weisheit: Die Originaltexte der bedeutendsten Mystiker in der Sprache unserer Zeit*. Petersberg: Via Nova, 2014.
Jostes	Jostes, Franz, ed. *Meister Eckhart und seine Jünger: Ungedruckte Texte zur deutschen Mystik*. Freiburg, Switzerland: Universitätsbuchhandlung, 1895.
Evans	Evans, C. de B., trans. *Meister Eckhart*. 2 vols. London: John M. Watkins, 1924, 1931.
ES	*Meister Eckhart: The Essential Sermons, Commentaries, Treatises, and Defense*. Translated and edited by Edmund Colledge, O.S.A. and Bernard McGinn. New York: Paulist Press, 1981.
Grabmann	Grabmann, Martin, ed. *Neuaufgefundene Pariser Quaestionen Meister Eckharts und ihre Stellung in seinem geistigen Entwicklungsgange: Untersuchungen und Texte*. Munich: Verlag der Bayerischen Akademie der Wissenschaften in Kommission des Verlags R. Oldenbourg, 1927.
Largier	Largier, Niklaus, ed. *Meister Eckhart Werke*. 2 vols. Frankfurt: Deutsche Klassiker Verlag, 1993.

LE	*LECTURA ECKHARDI: Predigten Meister Eckharts von Fachgelehrten gelesen und gedeutet.* 3 vols. Edited by Georg Steer and Loris Sturlese. Stuttgart: Kohlhammer, 1998–2008.
Löser	Löser, Freimut. *Meister Eckhart in Melk: Studien zum Redaktor Lienhart Peuger; Mit einer Edition des Traktats 'Von der sel wirdichait vnd aigenschafft.'* Tübingen: Max Niemeyer, 1999.
Longpré	Longpré, E., ed. "Questions inedites de Maître Eckhart, O. P. et de Gonzalve de Balboa, O. F. M." *Revue néoscholastique de philosophie* 26 (1927): 69–85.
MAP	*Maître Eckhart à Paris: Une critique médiévale de l'ontothéologie; Les Questions parisiennes no. 1 et no. 2.* Edited by Émilie Zum Brunn, Zénon Kaluza, Alain de Libera, Paul Vignaux, and Edouard Wéber. Paris: Presses Universitaires de France, 1984.
Maurer	Meister Eckhart. *Parisian Questions and Prologues.* Translated by Armand A. Maurer, C.S.B. Toronto: Pontifical Institute of Mediaeval Studies, 1974.
Mojsisch	Von Hochheim, Eckhart. "Utrum in deo sit idem esse et intelligere? / Sind in Gott Sein und Erkennen identisch?" Edited, translated, and introduced by Burkhard Mojsisch. *Bochumer Philosophisches Jahrbuch für Antike und Mittelalter* 4 (1999): 179–97.
Par. an.	*Paradisus anime intelligentis (Paradis der fornunftigen sele).* Edited by Philipp Strauch. Second edition edited and with an afterword by Niklaus Largier and Gilbert Fournier. Hildesheim: Weidmann, 1998.
Pfeiffer	Pfeiffer, Franz, ed. *Meister Eckhart (Deutsche Mystiker des vierzehnten Jahrhunderts,* Vol. 2). Leipzig: Göschen, 1857.
Preger	Preger, Wilhelm. *Geschichte der deutschen Mystik im Mittelalter nach den Quellen untersucht und dargestellt.* 3 vols. Leipzig: Dörffling und Franke, 1874–1893.
Quint	Quint, Josef, ed. and trans. *Meister Eckhart: Deutsche Predigten und Traktate.* Munich: Carl Hanser, 1965.
Schaefer	Schaefer, Eduard, ed. *Meister Eckeharts Traktat "Von Abegescheidenheit."* Bonn: Ludwig Röhrscheid, 1956.
SM	Schulze-Maizier, Friedrich, ed. and trans. *Meister Eckharts deutsche Predigten und Traktate.* 2nd ed. Leipzig: Insel, 1934.

TP	*Meister Eckhart: Teacher and Preacher.* Edited by Bernard McGinn with the collaboration of Frank Tobin and Elvira Borgstadt. New York: Paulist, 1986.
Walshe	Walshe, Maurice O'C., ed. and trans. *The Complete Mystical Works of Meister Eckhart.* Revised with a foreword by Bernard McGinn. New York: Crossroad, 2009.

Heidegger

Heidegger's Gesamtausgabe

Throughout this book, when texts from Heidegger's *Gesamtausgabe* are cited, page numbers to the German are given first, then, followed by a slash, page numbers to the published English translation, if one exists. To make cross-referencing easier, in the volumes listed below, page numbers to Heidegger's German texts are provided when the English translation only covers a small portion of the German volume. "GA" stands for Heidegger's *Gesamtausgabe* (Frankfurt am Main: Vittorio Klostermann, 1975–).

GA 1 Frühe Schriften.
    Pp. 189–398: *Duns Scotus' Theory of the Categories and of Meaning.* Translated by Harold Robbins. Ann Arbor: University Microfilms International. Dissertation reprint (DePaul University, 1978).
    Pp. 399–411: "Conclusion: The Problem of Categories (1916)." Translated by Roderick M. Stewart and John van Buren. In Heidegger, *Supplements: From the Earliest Essays to* Being and Time *and Beyond*, edited by John van Buren, 62–68. Albany: State University of New York Press, 2002.
    Pp. 413–33: "The Concept of Time in the Science of History (1915)." Translated by Harry S. Taylor, Hans W. Uffelmann, and John van Buren. In Heidegger, *Supplements*, 49–60.

GA 3 Kant und das Problem der Metaphysik.
    Kant and the Problem of Metaphysics. Translated by Richard Taft. 5th ed. Bloomington: Indiana University Press, 1997.

GA 4 Erläuterungen zu Hölderlins Dichtung.
    Elucidations of Hölderlin's Poetry. Translated by Keith Hoeller. Amherst, NY: Humanity, 2000.

GA 5 Holzwege.
    Off the Beaten Track. Edited and translated by Julian Young and Kenneth Haynes. Cambridge: Cambridge University Press, 2002.

GA 6.2 Nietzsche II.
   Pp. 7–29: "The Eternal Recurrence of the Same as Will to Power." Translated by Frank A. Capuzzi and David Farrell Krell, in Heidegger, *Nietzsche. Volume Three: The Will to Power as Knowledge and as Metaphysics*; *Volume IV: Nihilism*, 159–83. New York: HarperCollins, 1991.

GA 7 Vorträge und Aufsätze.
   Pp. 212–34: "Logos (Heraclitus, Fragment B 50)." In Martin Heidegger, *Early Greek Thinking*, translated by David Farrell Krell and Frank A. Capuzzi, 59–78. New York: Harper and Row, 1984.
   263–88: "Aletheia (Heraclitus, Fragment B 16)." In Heidegger, *Early Greek Thinking*, 102–23.

GA 8 Was heißt Denken?
   What Is Called Thinking? Rev. ed. Translated by J. Glenn Gray. New York: Perennial Library, 1976.

GA 9 Wegmarken.
   Pathmarks. Edited by William McNeill. Cambridge: Cambridge University Press, 1998.

GA 10 Der Satz vom Grund.
   The Principle of Reason. Translated by Reginald Lilly. Bloomington: Indiana University Press, 1991.

GA 11 Identität und Differenz.
   Pp. 27–81: *Identity and Difference*. Translated by John Stambaugh. Chicago: University of Chicago Press, 1969.

GA 12 Unterwegs zur Sprache.
   On the Way to Language. Translated by Peter D. Hertz. New York: Harper and Row, 1971.

GA 13 Aus der Erfahrung des Denkens: 1910–1976.
   Pp. 87–90: "The Pathway." Translated by Thomas F. O'Meara, O.P., with revisions by Thomas J. Sheehan. *Listening* 8 (1973): 32–39.
   Pp. 203–10: "Art and Space." Translated by Charles H. Seibert. *Man and World* 6, no. 1 (1973): 3–8.

GA 14 Zur Sache des Denkens.
   Pp. 3–104: *On Time and Being*. Translated by John Stambaugh. New York: Harper and Row, 1972.

GA 15 Seminare.
 Pp. 11–263: *Martin Heidegger and Eugen Fink. Heraclitus Seminar 1966/67.* Translated by Charles H. Seibert. University, AL: University of Alabama Press, 1979.
 Pp. 271–407: *Four Seminars.* Translated by Andrew Mitchell and François Raffoul. Bloomington: Indiana University Press, 2003.

GA 16 Reden und andere Zeugnisse eines Lebensweges.
 Pp. 37–39: "Curriculum Vitae 1915." In Kisiel and Sheehan, eds., *Becoming Heidegger,* 7–9.
 Pp. 107–17: "Rectorship Address: The Self-Assertion of the German University." In *The Heidegger Reader,* edited by Günter Figal, translated by Jerome Veith, 108–16. Bloomington: Indiana University Press, 2009.
 Pp. 652–83: "Der Spiegel Interview with Martin Heidegger." In Figal, ed., *The Heidegger Reader,* 313–33.

GA 17 Einführung in die phänomenologische Forschung.
 Introduction to Phenomenological Research. Translated by Daniel O. Dahlstrom. Bloomington: Indiana University Press, 2005.

GA 20 Prolegomena zur Geschichte des Zeitbegriffs.
 History of the Concept of Time: Prolegomena. Translated by Theodore Kisiel. Bloomington: Indiana University Press, 1985.

GA 22 Die Grundbegriffe der antiken Philosophie.
 Basic Concepts of Ancient Philosophy. Translated by Richard Rojcewicz. Bloomington: Indiana University Press, 2008.

GA 23 Geschichte der Philosophie von Thomas von Aquin bis Kant.

GA 24 Die Grundprobleme der Phänomenologie.
 The Basic Problems of Phenomenology. Translated by Albert Hofstadter. Rev. ed. Bloomington: Indiana University Press, 1988.

GA 26 Metaphysische Anfangsgründe der Logik im Ausgang von Leibniz.
 The Metaphysical Foundations of Logic. Translated by Michael Heim. Bloomington: Indiana University Press, 1992.

GA 27 Einleitung in die Philosophie.

GA 29/30 Die Grundbegriffe der Philosophie: Welt, Endlichkeit, Einsamkeit.
 The Fundamental Concepts of Metaphysics: World, Finitude, Solitude. Translated by

William McNeill and Nicholas Walker. Bloomington: Indiana University Press, 1995.

GA 31 Vom Wesen der menschlichen Freiheit.
The Essence of Human Freedom: An Introduction. Translated by Ted Sadler. London: Continuum, 2002.

GA 33 Aristoteles, Metaphysik Θ, 1–3: Von Wesen und Wirklichkeit der Kraft.
Aristotle's Metaphysics Θ: On the Essence and Actuality of Force. Translated by Walter Brogan and Peter Warnek. Bloomington: Indiana University Press, 1995.

GA 39 Hölderlins Hymnen "Germanien" und "Der Rhein."
Hölderlin's Hymns "Germania" and "The Rhein." Translated by William McNeill and Julia Ireland. Bloomington: Indiana University Press, 2014.

GA 40 Einführung in die Metaphysik.
Introduction to Metaphysics. Translated by Gregory Fried and Richard Polt. 2nd ed. New Haven: Yale University Press, 2014.

GA 41 Die Frage nach dem Ding: Zu Kants Lehre von den transzendentalen Grundsätzen.
What Is a Thing? Translated by W. B. Barton, Jr. and Vera Deutsch. Chicago: H. Regnery, 1967.

GA 42 Schelling: Vom Wesen der menschlichen Freiheit.
Schelling's Treatise on the Essence of Human Freedom. Translated by Joan Stambaugh. Athens: Ohio University Press, 1985.

GA 46 Zur Auslegung von Nietzsches II. Unzeitgemässer Betrachtung "Vom Nutzen und Nachteil der Historie für das Leben."
Interpretation of Nietzsche's Second Untimely Meditation. Translated by Ullrich Haase and Mark Sinclair. Bloomington: Indiana University Press, 2016.

GA 49 Die Metaphysik des deutschen Idealismus: Zur erneuten Auslegung von Schelling: Philosophische Untersuchungen über das Wesen der menschlichen Freiheit und die damit zusammenhängenden Gegenstände (1809).

GA 50 1. Nietzsches Metaphysik. 2. Einleitung in die Philosophie: Denken und Dichten.
Pp. 83–87: "Appendix to Nietzsche's Metaphysics." In Martin Heidegger, *Introduction to Philosophy—Thinking and Poetizing*, translated by Phillip Jacques Braunstein, 63–67. Bloomington: Indiana University Press, 2011.

GA 53 Hölderlins Hymne "Der Ister."
Hölderlin's Hymn "The Ister." Translated by William McNeill and Julia Davis. Bloomington: Indiana University Press, 1996.

GA 54 Parmenides.
Parmenides. Translated by André Schuwer and Richard Rojcewicz. Bloomington: Indiana University Press, 1998.

GA 56/57 Zur Bestimmung der Philosophie.
Towards the Definition of Philosophy. Translated by Ted Sadler. London: Continuum, 2000.

GA 58 Grundprobleme der Phänomenologie (1919/20).
Basic Problems of Phenomenology: Winter Semester 1919/1920. Translated by Scott Campbell. New York: Bloomsbury Academic, 2013.

GA 60 Phänomenologie des religiösen Lebens.
The Phenomenology of Religious Life. Translated by Matthias Fritsch and Jeniffer Anna Gosetti-Ferencei. Bloomington: Indiana University Press, 2004.

GA 61 Phänomenologische Interpretationen zu Aristoteles: Einführung in die phänomenologische Forschung.
Phenomenological Interpretations of Aristotle: Initiation into Phenomenological Research. Translated by Richard Rojcewicz. Bloomington: Indiana University Press, 2001.

GA 62 Phänomenologische Interpretationen ausgewählter Abhandlungen des Aristoteles.
Pp. 345–75: "Phenomenological Investigations with Respect to Aristotle: Indication of the Hermeneutical Situation." In Kisiel and Sheehan, eds., *Becoming Heidegger*, 144–79.

GA 63 Ontologie: Hermeneutik der Faktizität.
Ontology—The Hermeneutics of Facticity. Translated by John van Buren. Bloomington: Indiana University Press, 1999.

GA 64 Der Begriff der Zeit.
Pp. 3–103: *The Concept of Time: The First Draft of* Being and Time. Translated by Ingo Farin with Alex Skinner. London: Continuum, 2011.

GA 65 Beiträge zur Philosophie (Vom Ereignis).
Contributions to Philosophy (Of the Event). Translated by Richard Rojcewicz and Daniela Vallega-Neu. Bloomington: Indiana University Press, 2012.

GA 66 Besinnung.
Mindfulness. Translated by Parvis Emad and Thomas Kalary. New York: Continuum, 2006.

GA 70 Über den Anfang.

GA 71 Das Ereignis.
The Event. Translated by Richard Rojcewicz. Bloomington: Indiana University Press, 2013.

GA 73.1 Zum Ereignis-Denken.

GA 73.2 Zum Ereignis-Denken.

GA 75 Zu Hölderlin—Griechenlandreisen.

GA 76 Leitgedanken zur Entstehung der Metaphysik, der neuzeitlichen Wissenschaft und der modernen Technik.

GA 77 Feldweg-Gespräche (1944/45).
Country Path Conversations. Translated by Bret W. Davis. Bloomington: Indiana University Press, 2010.

GA 79 Bremer und Freiburger Vorträge.
Bremen and Freiburg Lectures. Translated by Andrew Mitchell. Bloomington: Indiana University Press, 2013.

GA 80.1 Vorträge. Teil I: 1915 bis 1932.
Pp. 1–13: "Question and Judgment." In Kisiel and Sheehan, eds., *Becoming Heidegger*, 56–62.

GA 81 Gedachtes.

GA 82 Zu eigenen Veröffentlichungen.

GA 83 Seminare: Platon—Aristoteles—Augustinus.

GA 84.1 Seminare: Kant—Leibniz—Schiller.

GA 86 Seminare: Hegel—Schelling.

GA 90 Zu Ernst Jünger.

GA 95 Überlegungen VII–XI (Schwarze Hefte 1938/39).
Ponderings VII–XI: Black Notebooks 1938–1939. Translated by Richard Rojcewicz. Bloomington: Indiana University Press, 2017.

GA 96 Überlegungen XII–XV (Schwarze Hefte 1939–1941).
Ponderings XII–XV: Black Notebooks 1939–1941. Translated by Richard Rojcewicz. Bloomington: Indiana University Press, 2017.

GA 97 Anmerkungen I–V (Schwarze Hefte 1942–1948).

GA 98 Anmerkungen VI–IX (Schwarze Hefte 1948/49–1951).

GA 99 Vier Hefte I und II (Schwarze Hefte 1947–1950)

Other Editions of Heidegger

AR	"Die Armut." *Heidegger Studies* 10 (1994): 5–11. Republished in GA 73.1, 873–81. "Poverty." Translated by Thomas Kalary and Frank Schalow. In *Heidegger, Translation, and the Task of Thinking: Essays in Honor of Parvis Emad*, edited by Frank Schalow, 3–10. Dordrecht: Springer, 2011.
EDP	"Europa und die deutsche Philosophie." In *Europa und die Philosophie*, edited by Hans-Helmuth Gander, 31–41. Frankfurt am Main: Klostermann, 1993. "Europe and German Philosophy." Translated by Andrew Haas. *New Yearbook for Phenomenology and Phenomenological Philosophy* 6, no. 1 (2006): 331–40.
EGI	Ein gefährliches Irrnis. Meßkirch: Martin-Heidegger-Gesellschaft, 2008.
G1	Gelassenheit. 14th ed. Pfullingen: Neske, 1992. *Discourse on Thinking*. Translated by John M. Anderson and E. Hans Freund. New York: Harper and Row, 1966.
G2	*Gelassenheit: Zum 125. Geburtstag von Martin Heidegger; Heideggers Meßkircher Rede von 1955*. 2nd ed. Freiburg: Karl Alber, 2015.
HAD	*Heidegger Jahrbuch 1: Heidegger und die Anfänge seines Denkens*. Edited by Alfred Denker, Hans-Helmuth Gander, and Holger Zaborowski. Freiburg: Karl Alber, 2004.

HNS	*Heidegger Jahrbuch 4: Heidegger und der Nationalsozialismus I: Dokumente*. Edited by Alfred Denker and Holger Zaborowski. Freiburg: Karl Alber, 2009.
HSS	*Heideggers Schelling-Seminar (1927/28)*. Edited by Lore Hühn and Jörg Jantzen in cooperation with Philipp Schwab and Sebastian Schwenzfeuer. Schellingiana 22. Stuttgart-Bad Cannstatt: frommann-holzboog, 2010.
KT	"Das Kriegs-Triduum in Meßkirch." In HAD 22–25. Freiburg: Karl Alber, 2004. "The War Triduum in Messkirch." In Kisiel and Sheehan, eds., *Becoming Heidegger*, 51–54.
SZ	*Sein und Zeit*. 19th ed. Tübingen: Max Niemeyer, 1993. *Being and Time*. Translated by John Stambaugh. Revised and with a forward by Dennis J. Schmidt. Albany: State University of New York Press, 2010.
UAS	*Übungen für Anfänger: Schillers Briefe über die ästhetische Erziehung des Menschen. Wintersemester 1936/37. Seminar-Mitschrift von Wilhelm Hallwachs*. Edited by Ulrich von Bülow. Marbach am Neckar: Deutsche Schillergesellschaft, 2005.
UDS	*Über den Schmerz*. Meßkirch: Martin-Heidegger-Gesellschaft, 2017/2018.
WMU	"Was ist Metaphysik? Urfassung / What is Metaphysics? Original Version." Dual-language edition. Edited by Dieter Thomä. Translated by Ian Alexander Moore and Gregory Fried. *Philosophy Today* 62, no. 3 (Summer 2018): 733–51.
Z	*Zollikoner Seminare: Protokolle—Zwiegespräche—Briefe*. Edited by Medard Boss. 2nd ed. Frankfurt am Main: V. Klostermann, 1994. *Zollikon Seminars: Protocols—Conversations—Letters*. Edited by Medard Boss. Translated by Franz Mayr and Richard Askay. Evanston, IL: Northwestern University Press, 2001.

Heidegger's Published Correspondence

MH/BW	*Martin Heidegger/Bernhard Welte: Briefe und Begegnungen*. Edited by Alfred Denker and Holger Zaborowski. Stuttgart: Klett-Cotta, 2003.
MH/E&S	Heidegger, Martin. *Briefwechsel mit seinen Eltern (1907–1927) und Briefe an seine Schwester (1921–1967)*. Edited by Jörg Heidegger und Alfred Denker. Freiburg: Karl Alber, 2013.

MH/EB	*Martin Heidegger/Elisabeth Blochmann: Briefwechsel 1918–1969.* 2nd ed. Edited by Joachim W. Storck. Marbach am Neckar: Deutsche Schillergesellschaft, 1990.
MH/EH	*"Mein liebes Seelchen!": Briefe Martin Heideggers an seine Frau.* Edited by Gertrud Heidegger. Munich: Deutsche Verlags-Anstalt, 2005. Heidegger, Martin. *Letters to His Wife 1915–1970.* Translated by R. D. V. Glasgow. Cambridge: Polity, 2008.
MH/EHuss	"Brief Martin Heideggers an Elisabeth Husserl." *Aut Aut* 223–24 (January–April 1988): 6–14. "Heidegger's Letter to the Boss's Daughter." Translated by Russell A. Berman and Paul Piccone. *Telos* 77 (Fall 1988): 125–27.
MH/ER	Heidegger's letters to Erich Rothacker. In Joachim W. Storck and Theodore Kisiel, eds., "Martin Heidegger und die Anfänge der 'Deutschen Vierteljahrsschrift für Literaturwissenschaft und Geistesgeschichte': Eine Dokumentation." *Dilthey-Jahrbuch für Philosophie und Geschichte der Geisteswissenschaften* 8 (1992/1993): 181–226.
MH/HA	*Hannah Arendt/Martin Heidegger: Briefe 1925 bis 1975; Und andere Zeugnisse.* Edited by Ursula Ludz. 2nd ed. Frankfurt am Main: Klostermann, 1999. *Hannah Arendt/Martin Heidegger: Letters 1925–1975.* Translated by Andrew Shields. Orlando: Harcourt, 2004.
MH/HF	"Der Briefwechsel zwischen Martin Heidegger und dem Freiburger Romanisten Hugo Friedrich." In HNS 89–139.
MH/HR	*Martin Heidegger/Heinrich Rickert: Briefe 1912 bis 1935 und andere Dokumente aus den Nachlässen.* Edited by Alfred Denker. Frankfurt am Main: Vittorio Klostermann, 2002. Pp. 95–97: "Evaluation of Heidegger's Habilitation Work (July 1915): The Doctrine of Categories and Meaning in Duns Scotus; by Heinrich Rickert." In Kisiel and Sheehan, eds., *Becoming Heidegger,* 341–43.
MH/IB	*Martin Heidegger/Imma von Bodmershof: Briefwechsel 1959–1976.* Edited by Bruno Pieger. Stuttgart: Klett-Cotta, 2000.
MH/KB	*Martin Heidegger/Kurt Bauch: Briefwechsel 1932–1975.* Edited by Almuth Heidegger. Freiburg: Karl Alber, 2010.
MH/KJ	*Martin Heidegger/Karl Jaspers: Briefwechsel 1920–1963.* Edited by Walter Biemel and Hans Saner. Frankfurt am Main: Vittorio Klostermann, 1990. *The Heidegger-Jaspers Correspondence (1920–1963).* Translated by Gary E. Aylesworth. Amherst, NY: Humanity Books, 2003.

MH/KL   *Martin Heidegger/Karl Löwith: Briefwechsel 1919–1973.* Edited by Alfred Denker. Freiburg: K. Alber, 2017.

MH/MM   Heidegger, Martin. *Briefe an Max Müller und andere Dokumente.* Edited by Holger Zaborowski and Anton Bösel. Freiburg: Karl Alber, 2003.

Unpublished Sources

Here and in the body of the text I refer to material housed at the Deutsches Literaturarchiv Marbach and the Universitätsarchiv in Freiburg with the ciphers "DLA" and "UAF," respectively, followed by call number.

Bröcker-Oltmanns, Käte. 1992 interview with Cornelius Bickel and Jürgen Zander. Available on CD at the Martin-Heidegger-Archiv der Stadt Meßkirch.

———. Letter to Heidegger dated July 4, 1941. Available in the manuscript of Heidegger's *Die Metaphysik des deutschen Idealismus*. DLA 75.7176.

Heidegger, Martin. "ΑΓΧΙΒΑΣΙΗ / das erste Feldweggespräch 1945." DLA D 86.298.

———. An undated note, presumably for "Das Ding," contained as the first page of several bundles of notes for the third division of *Sein und Zeit*, which are catalogued under the misleading title "'Logik. Die Frage nach der Wahrheit.' Dr. T." DLA 75.7051. (Note that the call number and the title are identical to the folder containing the actual manuscript of Heidegger's 1925–26 lecture course *Logik. Die Frage nach der Wahrheit*.)

———. An undated note, presumably from the conclusion of Heidegger's Winter Semester 1915–16 lecture course, available on the back page of one of the sheets of the manuscript of the Winter Semester 1925–26 lecture course *Logik. Die Frage nach der Wahrheit*. DLA 75.7051.

———. Notes for "Das Ding." DLA 75.7305,3.

———. Notes for "Europa und die deutsche Philosophie." DLA 75.7072/23.

———. Notes for *Der Satz vom Grund*. DLA B 74.

———. "Der Feldweg." Typescript available in Max Müller's papers at UAF E 3/174.

———. Evaluation, dated January 29, 1934, of Käte Oltmanns's dissertation on Eckhart, as well as notes on her oral examination from February 28, 1934. UAF B 42/2457. (See §§7–8 of Appendix One, above.)

———. "Gelassenheitsrede." Manuscript for the 1955 lecture "Gelassenheit." DLA B 54.

———. Note in Heidegger's manuscript for the Summer Semester 1927 lecture course *Die Grundprobleme der Phänomenologie*. DLA 75.7054.

———. "Inskriptions-, Subskriptions-, und Einzeichnungslisten." Lists of Heidegger courses and the attendees in the second half of the 1910s. DLA 75.7439.

———. "Seminarbuch SS 1919–SS 1926." Lists of Heidegger's seminars and the attendees. DLA 75.7437.

———. "Seminarbuch WS 1928/29–WS 1956/57." Lists of Heidegger's seminars and the attendees. DLA 75.7438.

———. "Über das Wesen des Denkens (Ein Gespräch zwischen einem Forscher, einem Gelehrten und einem Weisen)." DLA 84.2110.

———. "Zum Weltbegriff" and "Der Meister Eckehart." Two fascicles in a collection of notes. DLA 75.7305,9.

Heidegger, Martin, Walter Bröcker, and Käte Oltmanns/Bröcker-Oltmanns. Copies of correspondence. DLA 75.16222, 83.668, 96.146.77, and HS.2003.0056. Originals located at the Schleswig-Holsteinische Landesbibliothek in Kiel.

Heidegger, Martin, and Fritz Heidegger. Correspondence. DLA HS.2014.0069.00001– HS.2014.0069.00030.

Heidegger, Martin, and Siegfried Schühle. Transcribed correspondence available at the Martin-Heidegger-Archiv der Stadt Meßkirch.

Hirsch, Elisabeth F. "Reminiscences of Heidegger in Marburg."

Lossmann, Hermine (née Frentzen). "Die Verlagerung der Philosophischen Fakultät der Universität Freiburg auf die Burg Wildenstein (14.April 1945 bis 8.August 1945)" UAF D 14/21.

McNeill, William. "Tracing the Rift: Heidegger, Hölderlin, and 'The Origin of the Work of Art.'"

Sauer, Joseph. "Geschichte der mittelalterlichen Mystik." Three versions of a bibliography. UAF C 67/160.

Schürmann, Reiner. "Heidegger and the Mystical Tradition." Available in Box 3, Folder 43 of the unprocessed Reiner Schürmann Archives, housed in the Kellen Design Archives, The New School for Social Research.

Von Wulffen, Barbara. Interview from September 14, 2006, available on DVD in the Martin-Heidegger-Archiv der Stadt Meßkirch.

Welte, Bernhard. "Aufzeichnungen aus meinen Gesprächen mit Heinrich Ochsner." UAF E 8/934.

———. Materials for "Übung zu ausgewählten Texten des Meister Eckhart." Summer Semester 1952. UAF E 8/216, E 8/159, and E 8/904.

———. Materials for "Übungen zu Meister Eckhart II. Die Problematik der lateinischen Schriften." Winter Semester 1952–53. UAF E 8/159 and E 8/904. (The last call number also contains material on Eckhart from 1955.)

———. "Seminarübung zum Liber de Causis des Thomas v. A." UAF E 8/189.

———. Letters to Reiner Schürmann. Available in Box 1, Folder 4 of the unprocessed Reiner Schürmann Archives, housed in the Kellen Design Archives, The New School for Social Research.

Secondary Sources

Abraham a Sancta Clara. *Auswahl aus Abraham a S. Clara.* Edited by Karl Bertsche. Bonn: A. Marcus und E. Weber, 1911.

Albert, Karl. *Meister Eckharts These vom Sein: Untersuchungen zur Metaphysik des Opus tripartitum*. Saarbrücken: Universitäts- und Schulbuchverlag/Kastellaun: Aloys Henn, 1976.

Anonymous. *Der Frankfurter: Eine deutsche Theologie*. Translated by Joseph Bernhart. Leipzig: Insel, 1920. First published in Munich: Hermann Rinn, 1910.

Anonymous. *Von Bagdad nach Toledo: Das "Buch der Ursachen" und seine Rezeption im Mittelalter*. Edited by Alexander Fidora and Andreas Niederberger. Mainz: Dieterich, 2001. Treatise translated by Dennis J. Brand as *The Book of Causes*. Milwaukee: Marquette University Press, 2012.

Anonymous. *Liber viginti quattuor philosophorum*. Edited by Françoise Hundry. Turnholt: Brepols, 1997.

———. "Das pseudo-hermetische 'Buch der vierundzwanzig Meister' (Liber XXIV philosophorum)," edited by Clemens Baeumker. In *Abhandlungen aus dem Gebiete der Philosophie und ihrer Geschichte: Eine Festgabe zum 70. Geburtstag des Freiherrn Georg von Hertling*, edited by Clemens Baeumker, 17–40. Freiburg im Breisgau: Herder, 1913. Revised and corrected edition under the same title in Clemens Baeumker, *Studien und Charakteristiken zur Geschichte der Philosophie, insbesondere des Mittelalters: Gesammelte Vorträge und Aufsätze von C. Baeumker*, edited by Martin Grabmann, 194–214. Münster i. W.: Aschendorff, 1927.

Arnold, Claus. *Katholizismus als Kulturmacht: Der Freiburger Theologe Joseph Sauer (1872–1949) und das Erbe des Franz Xaver Kraus*. Paderborn: Ferdinand Schöningh, 1999.

Aubenque, Pierre. "The Relationship between Hermeneutics and Ontology in the Case of Aristotle's *PERI HERMENEIAS*." Translated by Tom Krell and Ian Alexander Moore. *Graduate Faculty Philosophy Journal* 34, no. 1 (2013): 3–20.

Augustine. *The Confessions*. Translated by Henry Chadwick. Oxford: Oxford University Press, 2008.

Baeumker, Clemens. *Der Anteil des Elsass an den geistigen Bewegungen des Mittelalters*. Strasbourg: Heitz, 1912.

———. *Die christliche Philosophie des Mittelalters*. Leipzig: Teubner, 1913.

Baeumler, Alfred. "Ignatius und Meister Eckhart, oder Schmidt contra Ungenannt." *Nationalsozialistische Monatshefte* 7, no. 71 (February 1936): 166–68.

Baeza, Ricardo. *Die Topologie des Ursprungs: Der Begriff der Gelassenheit bei Eckhart und Heidegger und seine Entfaltung in der abendländischen Mystik und im zeitgenössischen Denken*. Berlin: Lit, 2009.

Baier, Karl. "Heidegger und das Mittelalter." In *Heidegger und das Mittelalter*, edited by Helmut Vetter, 13–40. Frankfurt: P. Lang, 1999.

Barrett, William. "Zen for the West." Introduction to *Zen Buddhism: Selected Writings of D. T. Suzuki*, vii–xxiii. New York: Three Leaves, 2004.

Beccarisi, Alessandra. "Eckhart's Latin Works." In *A Companion to Meister Eckhart*, edited by Hackett, 85–124.

———. "*Isticheit* nach Meister Eckhart: Wege und Irrwege eines philosophischen Terminus." In *Meister Eckhart in Erfurt*, edited by Speer and Wegener, 314–34.

———. "'noch sint ez allez heidenischer meister wort, die niht enbekanten dan in einem natiurlîchen liehte': Eckhart e il *Liber vigintiquattuor philosophorum*." In *Studi sulle fonti di Meister Eckhart*, Vol. 2, edited by Loris Sturlese, 73–101. Freiburg, Switzerland: Academic Press Fribourg, 2012.

———. "Philosophische Neologismen zwischen Latein und Volkssprache: istic und isticheit bei Meister Eckhart." *Recherches de Théologie et Philosophie médiévales* 70, no. 2 (2003): 329–58.

Beierwaltes, Werner. "Heideggers Gelassenheit." In *Amicus Plato magis amica veritas: Festschrift für Wolfgang Wieland zum 65. Geburtstag*, 1–35. Berlin: Walter de Gruyter, 1998.

———. *Platonismus und Idealismus*. Frankfurt am Main: V. Klostermann, 1972.

Benveniste, Émile. "Active and Middle Voice in the Verb." In *Problems in General Linguistics*, translated by Mary Elizabeth Meek, 145–52. Miami: University of Miami Press, 1971.

Berdjajew, Nikolai. "Jakob Böhmes Lehre von Ungrund und Freiheit." Translated by Hans Ruoff. *Blätter für deutsche Philosophie* 6 (1932–33): 315–36.

Bernasconi, Robert. "Being Is Evil: Boehme's Strife and Schelling's Rage in Heidegger's 'Letter on 'Humanism.'" *Gatherings: The Heidegger Circle Annual* 7 (2017): 164–81.

———. "Eckhart's Anachorism." *Graduate Faculty Philosophy Journal* 19, no. 2 (1997): 81–90.

Bernard of Clairvaux. *Ausgewählte Sermone des Heiligen Bernhard über das Hohelied*. Edited by Otto Baltzer. Freiburg i. B.: Mohr, 1893.

Bernhart, Joseph. *Bernhardische und Eckhartische Mystik in ihren Beziehungen und Gegensätzen: Eine dogmengeschichtliche Untersuchung*. Kempten: Kösel, 1912.

———. *Die philosophische Mystik des Mittelalters von ihren antiken Ursprüngen bis zur Renaissance*. Munich: Reinhardt, 1922.

———. *Meister Eckhart und Nietzsche: Ein Vergleich für die Gegenwart*. Berlin: Greif, 1934.

Biemel, Walter. "The Transformation in Husserl's Later Philosophy." Translated by Michael Heim. In *The Question of Hermeneutics: Essays in Honor of Joseph J. Kockelmans*, edited by Timothy J. Stapelton, 113–25. Dordrecht: Springer, 1994.

Biraut, Henri. *Heidegger et l'expérience de la pensée*. Paris: Gallimard, 1978.

Björk, Mårten, and Jayne Svenungsson, eds. *Heidegger's Black Notebooks and the Future of Theology*. Cham: Palgrave Macmillan, 2017.

Bloch, Ernst. *Atheism in Christianity: The Religion of the Exodus and the Kingdom*. Translated by J. T. Swann. New York: Herder and Herder, 1972.

———. *Principle of Hope*. 3 vols. Translated by Neville Plaice, Stephen Plaice, and Paul Knight. Cambridge: MIT Press, 1995.
Böhme, Jakob. *Sämtliche Schriften*. Edited by August Faust and Will-Erich Peuckert. 11 vols. Stuttgart: Frommann, 1955–61.
———. "Von wahrer Gelassenheit." In *Christosophia oder Der Weg zu Christo*, 86–108. Amsterdam, 1730. Translated by Michael L. Birkel and Jeff Bach as "True Yieldedness" in *Genius of the Transcendent: Mystical Writings of Jakob Boehme*, 99–123. Boston: Shambhala, 2010.
Borges, Jorge Luis. "The Fearful Sphere of Pascal." Translated by Anthony Kerrigan. In *Labyrinths: Selected Stories and Other Writings*, edited by Donald A. Yates and James E. Irby. New York: New Directions, 1964.
Borngräber, Otto. *Das Erwachen der philosophischen Spekulation der Reformationszeit, in ihrem stufenweisen Fortschreiten beleuchtet an Schwenkfeld, Thamer, Sebastian Franck von Wörd*. Schwarzenberg i. Sa.: C. M. Gärtner, 1908.
Botet, Serge. *Langue, langage et stratégies linguistiques chez Heidegger*. Bern: Peter Lang, 1997.
Bray, Nadia. "Deutsche Bibelzitate in den Predigten Meister Eckharts." In *Meister Eckhart in Erfurt*, edited by Speer and Wegener, 409–26.
Brient, Elizabeth. *The Immanence of the Infinite: Hans Blumenberg and the Threshold to Modernity*. Washington, DC: Catholic University of American Press, 2002.
———. "Meister Eckhart's Influence on Nicholas of Cusa." In *A Companion to Meister Eckhart*, edited by Hackett, 553–85.
Brightman, Carol, ed. *Between Friends: The Correspondence of Hannah Arendt and Mary McCarthy 1949–1975*. New York: Harcourt Brace, 1995.
Buber, Martin, ed. *Ekstatische Konfessionen*. Jena: Eugen Diederichs, 1909.
Bullivant, Stephen. "A Meister among the Moderns: Hegel, Rosenberg, Bloch and Cage." *Eckhart Review* 18, no. 1 (2009): 4–21.
Bundschuh, Adeltrud. *Die Bedeutung von gelassen und die Bedeutung der Gelassenheit in den deutschen Werken Meister Eckharts unter Berücksichtigung seiner lateinischen Schriften*. Frankfurt am Main: P. Lang, 1990.
Cage, John. "Meister Duchamp or living on water / Maître Duchamp ou vivre sur l'eau." In *Voici Maître Eckhart*, edited by Zum Brunn, 429–31.
Cairns, Dorian. *Conversations with Husserl and Fink*. The Hague: M. Nijhoff, 1976.
Camilleri, Sylvain. *Phénoménologie de la religion et herméneutique théologique dans la pensée du jeune Heidegger: Commentaire analytique des* Fondements philosophiques de la mystique médiévale (1916–1919). Dordrecht: Springer, 2008.
Capelle, P. "Heidegger et Maître Eckhart." *Revue des Sciences Religieuses* 70, no. 1 (1996): 113–24.
Capobianco, Richard. *Engaging Heidegger*. Toronto: University of Toronto Press, 2010.
———. *Heidegger's Way of Being*. Toronto: University of Toronto Press, 2014.
Caputo, John D. *The Mystical Element in Heidegger's Thought*. Revised reprint. New York: Fordham University Press, 1986.

———. "The Nothingness of the Intellect in Meister Eckhart's 'Parisian Questions.'" *The Thomist* 39 (1975): 85–115.
Casteigt, Julie. "Le métaphysique eckhartienne: 'Explication à mort' ou anarchie? Une lecture du commentaire eckhartien de Jn 1, 3–4 à partir des *Hégémonies brisées de R. Schürmann*." In *Autour de Reiner Schürmann*, edited by Vaysse, 23–46.
Celan, Paul. *Lightduress*. Translated by Pierre Joris. Copenhagen: Green Integer, 2005.
Celan, Paul, and Ilana Shmueli. *Briefwechsel*. Edited by Ilana Smueli and Thomas Sparr. Frankfurt am Main: Suhrkamp, 2004.
Celan, Paul, and Franz Wurm. *Briefwechsel*. Edited by Barbara Wiedemann in connection with Franz Wurm. Frankfurt am Main: Suhrkamp, 1995.
Cercel, Gabriel. "'Sur la valeur du comprendre historique pour le philosophe': Heidegger et Heinrich Finke." Translated by Sylvain Camilleri. *Bulletin Heideggérien* 1 (2011): 4–13.
Colledge, Edmund, and J. C. Marler. "'Poverty of the Will': Ruusbroec, Eckhart, and The Mirror of Simple Souls." In *Jan van Ruusbroec: The Sources, Content, and Sequels of his Mysticism*, edited by Paul Mommaers and N. De Paepe, 14–47. Leuven: Leuven University Press, 1984.
Critchley, Simon, and Reiner Schürmann. *On Heidegger's Being and Time*. Edited by Steven Levine. London: Routledge, 2008.
Crowe, Benjamin. "Resoluteness in the Middle Voice: On the Ethical Dimensions of Heidegger's *Being and Time*." *Philosophy Today* 45, no. 3 (2001): 225–41.
Cusa, Nicholas of. *Selected Spiritual Writings*. Translated by H. Lawrence Bond. New York: Paulist, 1997.
Dalle Pezze, Barbara. *Martin Heidegger and Meister Eckhart: A Path Towards Gelassenheit*. Lewiston, NY: Edwin Mellen, 2008.
Davis, Bret W. *Heidegger on the Will: On the Way to Gelassenheit*. Evanston, IL: Northwestern University Press.
———. "Zen after Zarathustra: The Problem of the Will in the Confrontation between Nietzsche and Buddhism." *Journal of Nietzsche Studies* 28 (2004): 89–138.
Degenhardt, Ingeborg. *Studien zum Wandel des Eckhartbildes*. Leiden: E. J. Brill, 1967.
De Gandillac, Maurice. "La 'dialectique' du Maître Eckhart." In *La mystique rhénane*, 59–94. Paris: Presses Universitaires de France, 1963.
De Libera, Alain. "L'être et le bien: Exode 3,14 dans la théologie rhénane." In *Celui qui est: interprétations juives et chrétiennes d'Exode 3–14*, edited by Alain de Libera and Émilie Zum Brunn, 127–62. Paris: Les Éditions du Cerf, 1986.
———. *Introduction à la mystique rhénane: D'Albert le Grand à Maître Eckhart*. Paris: O.E.I.L., 1984.
Denker, Alfred, and Elsbeth Büchin, eds. *Martin Heidegger und seine Heimat*. Stuttgart: Klett-Cotta, 2005.
Derrida, Jacques. *The Beast and the Sovereign: Volume II*. Translated by Geoffrey Bennington. Chicago: University of Chicago Press, 2011.
———. "Différance." In *Margins of Philosophy*, translated by Alan Bass, 1–27. Chicago: University of Chicago Press, 1982.

———. "A Time for Farewells: Heidegger (Read by) Hegel (Read by) Malabou." Preface to Catherine Malabou, *The Future of Hegel: Plasticity, Temporality and Dialectic*, translated by Lisabeth During, vii–xlvii. London: Routledge, 2005.

De Vitiis, Pietro. "Das Gebet des Schweigens: Überlegungen zu Martin Heidegger und Bernhard Welte." In *Mut zum Denken, Mut zum Glauben: Bernhard Welte und seine Bedeutung für eine künftige Theologie*, edited by Ludwig Wenzler, 120–47. Freiburg: Verlag der Katholischen Akademie der Erzdiözese Freiburg, 1994.

D'Helt, Alexandre. *Heidegger et la pensée médiévale*. Bruxelles: Ousia, 2010.

Di Cesare, Donatella. *Heidegger, die Juden, die Shoah*. Frankfurt am Main: Vittorio Klostermann, 2016.

Dilthey, Wilhelm. "Der entwicklungsgeschichtliche Pantheismus nach seinem geschichtlichen Zusammenhang mit den älteren pantheistischen Systemen." *Archiv für Geschichte der Philosophie* 13, no. 3 (1900): 307–60.

———. *Weltanschauung und Analyse des Menschen seit Renaissance und Reformation*. Vol. 2 of *Gesammelte Schriften*. Leipzig: Teubner, 1914.

Dobie, Robert. "Overcoming Ontotheology: Heidegger and Meister Eckhart on *Gelassenheit*." In *Martin Heidegger's Interpretations of Saint Augustine: Sein und Zeit und Ewigkeit*, edited by Frederick Van Fleteren, 351–82. Lewiston: Edwin Mellen, 2005.

Enders, Markus. "Abgeschiedenheit des Geistes—höchste 'Tugend' des Menschen und fundamentale Seinsweise Gottes: Eine Interpretation von Meister Eckharts Traktat: *Von abegescheidenheit*." *Theologie und Philosophie* 71 (1996): 63–87.

———. "Abgeschiedenheit—der Weg ins dunkle Licht der Gottheit. Zu Bernhard Weltes Deutung der Metaphysik und Mystik Meister Eckharts." In *Heinrich-Seuse Forum* Vol. 4, 5–29. Berlin: LIT, 2015.

Engelmann, P. Usmar. "Hundert Jahre Bibliothek Beuron." In *Beuron 1863–1963*, 395–440. Beuron: Beuroner Kunstverlag, 1963.

Euclid. *Elements*. Translated by Thomas L. Heath. Edited by Dana Densmore. Santa Fe, NM: Green Lion, 2013.

Farin, Ingo, and Jeff Malpas, eds. *Reading Heidegger's* Black Notebooks *1931–1941*. Cambridge: MIT Press, 2016.

Faust, August, ed. *Zen: Der lebendige Buddhismus in Japan. Ausgewählte Stücke des Zen-Textes*. Translated into German by Schûej Ôhasama. With a preface by Rudolf Otto. Gotha: Perthes, 1925.

Federico Bauchwitz, Oscar. "Contribuições à história de uma metáfora: Heidegger e Nicolau de Cusa." In *O que é metafísica? Atas do III Colóquio Internacional de Metafísica*, edited by Jaimir Conte and Oscar Federico Bauchwitz, 267–78. Lagoa Nova: Natal, 2011.

Filippi, Silvana. "Martin Heidegger y la mística eckhartiana." *Invenio* 6, no. 11 (November 2003): 33–39.

Finke, Heinrich. "Zur Geschichte der deutschen Dominikaner im XIII. und XIV. Jahrhundert." *Römische Quartalschrift* 8 (1894): 367–92.

———. *Ungedruckte Dominikanerbriefe des 13. Jahrhunderts*. Paderborn: Ferdinand Schöningh, 1891.

Fischer, Heribert. *Meister Eckhart: Einführung in sein philosophisches Denken*. Munich: Alber, 1974.

———. "Thomas von Aquin und Meister Eckhart." *Theologie und Philosophie* 49 (1974): 213–35.

Fischer, Mario. *Religiöse Erfahrung in der Phänomenologie des frühen Heidegger*. Göttingen: Vandenhoeck und Ruprecht, 2013.

Flasch, Kurt. *Dietrich von Freiberg: Philosophie, Theologie, Naturforschung um 1300*. Frankfurt am Main: Vittorio Klostermann, 2007.

———. *Meister Eckhart: Philosopher of Christianity*. Translated by Anne Schindel and Aaron Vanides. New Haven: Yale University Press, 2015.

———. *Das philosophische Denken im Mittelalter: Von Augustin zu Machiavelli*. 3rd ed. Stuttgart: Reclam, 2013.

Flaumbaum, Isidoro. "Meister Eckhart y Martin Heidegger." *Minerva: Revista continental de filosofía* 1 (1944): 50–54.

Fried, Gregory. *Heidegger's Polemos: From Being to Politics*. New Haven: Yale University Press, 2000.

Gadamer, Hans-Georg. "Auf dem Rückgang zum Anfang (1986)." In *Neuere Philosophie I*, 394–416.

———. "Der eine Weg Martin Heideggers (1986)." In *Neuere Philosophie* I, 417–30.

———. "Die Geschichte der Philosophie (1981)." In *Neuere Philosophie* I, 297–307.

———. "Geschichtlichkeit und Wahrheit (1991)." In *Gesammelte Werke*, Vol. 10, *Hermeneutik im Rückblick*, 247–58. Tübingen, J. C. B. Mohr (Paul Siebeck), 1995.

———. "Heideggers Rückgang auf die Griechen." In *Theorie der Subjektivität: Festschrift für D. Henrich*, edited by Konrad Cramer et al., 397–424. Frankfurt am Main: Suhrkamp, 1987.

———. *Heidegger's Ways*. Translated by John W. Stanley. Albany: State University of New York Press, 1994.

———. "Martin Heidegger's One Path." In *Reading Heidegger from the Start: Essays in His Earliest Thought*, edited by Theodore Kisiel and John van Buren, 19–34. Albany: State University of New York Press, 1994.

———. *Neuere Philosophie I: Hegel-Husserl-Heidegger*. Vol. 3 of *Gesammelte Werke*. Tübingen, J. C. B. Mohr (Paul Siebeck), 1987.

———. *Philosophical Apprenticeships*. Translated by Robert R. Sullivan. Cambridge: MIT Press, 1985.

———. *Wahrheit und Methode: Grundzüge einer philosophischen Hermeneutik*. Vol. 1 of *Gesammelte Werke*. Tübingen, Mohr Siebeck, 1990.

Gebsattel, Viktor Emil von. *Von der christlichen Gelassenheit*. Würzburg: Werkbund-Verl., Abt. Die Burg, 1940.

Gilson, Étienne. *History of Christian Philosophy in the Middle Ages*. New York: Random House, 1955.

Gonzalez Nuñez, Huberto. "Infrapolitical Reflection: Schürmann and the Existential *Durchbruch*." *Política Común* 11 (2017). http://dx.doi.org/10.3998/pc.12322227.0011.001.

Gottschall, Dagmar. "Eckhart and the Vernacular Tradition: Pseudo-Eckhart and Eckhart Legends." In *A Companion to Meister Eckhart*, edited by Hackett, 509–51.

———. "Eckhart's German Works." In *A Companion to Meister Eckhart*, edited by Hackett, 137–83.

Grabmann, Martin. *Mittelalterliches Geistesleben*. Vol. 1. Munich: Hueber, 1926.

———. "Neue Eckhartforschungen im Lichte neuerer Eckhartfunde: Bemerkungen zu O. Karrers und G. Thérys Eckhartarbeiten." *Divus Thomas* 5 (1927): 74–96.

———. "Erwiderung." *Divus Thomas* 5 (1927): 218–22.

Grassi, Ernesto. *La preminenza della parola metaforica: Heidegger, Meister Eckhart, Novalis*. Modena: Mucchi, 1986.

———. "Tod und Schmerz: Zu einer Interpretation von Meister Eckhart." In *Im Angesicht des Todes: Ein interdisziplinäres Kompendium II*, edited by Hansjakob Becker, Bernhard Einig, and Peter-Otto Ullrich, 1391–1420. St. Ottilien: EOS, 1987.

Greisch, Jean. *Le Buisson Ardent et les Lumières de la raison*. 3 vols. Paris: Les Éditions du Cerf, 2002–04.

———. "La contrée de la serenité et l'horizon de l'ésperance," in *Heidegger et la question de Dieu*, edited by Richard Kearney and Joseph Stephen O'Leary, 168–93. Paris: Grasset, 1980.

Grimm, H. A., trans. *Von Gottes- und Liebfrauenminne: Lieder aus der deutschen Mystik*. Leipzig: Insel, n.d.

Grimm, Jacob and Wilhelm. *Deutsches Wörterbuch von Jacob und Wilhelm Grimm*. Leipzig: 1854–1961.

Grotz, Stephan. "Meister Eckharts Pariser Quaestio I: Sein oder Nichtsein—ist das hier die Frage?" *Freiburger Zeitschrift für Philosophie und Theologie* 49, no. 3 (2002): 370–98.

Guitton, Jean. *Profils parallèles: Pascal—Leibniz, Renan—Newman, Teilhard—Bergson, Claudel—Heidegger*. Paris: Fayard, 1970.

———. "Visite à Heidegger." *La Table ronde* 123 (1958): 143–55.

Haas, Alois Maria. "Christliche Aspekte des 'Gnothi seauton': Selbsterkenntnis und Mystik." *Zeitschrift für deutsches Altertum und deutsche Literatur* 110, no. 2 (1981): 71–96.

———. "Durchbruch zur ewigen Wahrheit." *Meister-Eckhart-Jahrbuch* 2 (2008): 171–87.

———. *Gottleiden—Gottlieben: Zur volkssprachlichen Mystik im Mittelalter*. Frankfurt am Main: Insel, 1989.

———. *Kunst rechter Gelassenheit: Themen und Schwerpunkte von Heinrich Seuses Mystik.* 2nd ed. Bern: Peter Lang, 1996.

———. "The Nothing of God and its Explosive Metaphors." *The Eckhart Review* no. 8 (1999): 6–17.

———. "Mors mystica—Ein mystologisches Motiv." In *Sermo mysticus: Studien zu Theologie und Sprache der deutschen Mystik*, 392–480. Freiburg, Switzerland: Universitätsverlag, 1979.

Hackett, Jeremiah M., ed. *A Companion to Meister Eckhart*. Leiden: Brill, 2012.

Halfwassen, Jens. "Gibt es eine Philosophie der Subjektivität im Mittelalter? Zur Theorie des Intellekts bei Meister Eckhart und Dietrich von Freiberg." *Theologie und Philosophie* 72 (1997): 337–59.

Harries, Karsten. "The Infinite Sphere: Comments on the History of a Metaphor." *Journal of the History of Philosophy* 13, no. 1 (January 1975): 5–15.

Hasebrink, Burkhard. *Formen inzitativer Rede bei Meister Eckhart: Untersuchungen zur literarischen Konzeption der deutschen Predigt*. Tübingen: M. Niemeyer, 1992.

Haug, Walter. *Die Wahrheit der Fiktion: Studien zur weltlichen und geistlichen Literatur des Mittelalters und der frühen Neuzeit*. Tübingen: Max Niemeyer, 2003.

Hegel, G. W. F. *Frühe Exzerpte*. Edited by Friedhelm Nicolin with the collaboration of Gisela Schüler. Vol. 3 of Hegel's *Gesammelte Werke*, edited by the Rheinisch-Westfälische Akademie der Wissenschaften. Hamburg: Felix Meiner, 1991.

———. *Vorlesungen über die Philosophie der Religion*. 2 vols. Edited by Georg Lasson. Hamburg: Felix Meiner, 1966.

Hegler, Alfred. *Geist und Schrift bei Sebastian Franck: Eine Studie zur Geschichte des Spiritualismus in der Reformationszeit*. Freiburg i.B.: Mohr, 1892.

Heidegger, Heinrich, and Pierfrancesco Stagi. *Martin Heidegger: Ein Privatporträt zwischen Politik und Religion*. Meßkirch: Gmeiner, 2012.

Heidegger, Martin, and Meister Eckhart. *Qué es metafísica? por M. Heidegger / Sermón del Maestro Eckehart*. Santiago de Chile/Madrid: Cruz del Sur, 1963.

Heisig, James W. *Philosophers of Nothingness: An Essay on the Kyoto School*. Honolulu: University of Hawai'i Press, 2001.

Helting, Holger. "Heidegger und Meister Eckhart." In *'Herkunft aber bleibt stets Zukunft': Martin Heidegger und die Gottesfrage*, edited by P. L. Coriando, 83–100. Frankfurt am Main: Klostermann, 1988.

———. *Heidegger und Meister Eckehart: Vorbereitende Überlegungen zu ihrem Gottesdenken*. Berlin: Duncker u. Humblot, 1997.

Hirsch, Elisabeth F. "Remembrances of Martin Heidegger in Marburg." *Philosophy Today* 23, no. 2 (Summer 1979): 336–45.

Hirsch, E. "[Review of] Grabmann, Martin, *Neuaufgefundene Pariser Quaestionen Meister Eckharts und ihre Stellung in seinem geistigen Entwicklungsgange*." *Theologische Literaturzeitung* 53, no. 2 (1928): 41–44.

Hölderlin, Friedrich. *Hyperion and Selected Poems*. Edited by Eric L. Santner. New York: Continuum, 1990.

Husserl, Edmund. *Briefwechsel*. 10 vols. Edited by Karl Schuhmann in association with Elisabeth Schuhmann. Dordrecht: Kluwer, 1994.

Imbach, Ruedi. *Deus est Intelligere: Das Verhältnis von Sein und Denken in seiner Bedeutung für das Gottesverständnis bei Thomas von Aquin und in den Pariser Quaestionen Meister Eckharts*. Freiburg, Switzerland: Universitätsverlag, 1976.

Ireland, Julia A. "Heidegger's *Hausfreund* and the Re-enchantment of the Familiar." *Gatherings: The Heidegger Circle Annual* 7 (2017): 142–63.

Janicaud, Dominique. *Heidegger in France*. Translated by François Raffoul and David Pettigrew. Bloomington: Indiana University Press, 2015.

Jaran, François, and Christophe Perrin. *The Heidegger Concordance*. 3 vols. London: Bloomsbury, 2013.

Jaspers, Karl. *Psychologie der Weltanschauungen*. Berlin: Julius Springer, 1919.

Jatho, Jörg-Peter, and Gerd Simon, *Gießener Historiker im Dritten Reich*. Gießen: Focus, 2008.

John of the Cross. *Des Heiligen Johannes vom Kreuz Dunkle Nacht*. Translated by P. Aloysius. 3rd ed. Munich: Kösel-Pustet, 1956.

Junghanns, Albert. "Der Freiburger Dogmatiker Engelbert Krebs (1881–1950): Ein Beitrag zur Theologiegeschichte." Diss.-Theol., Albert-Ludwigs-Universität Freiburg, 1979.

Karrer, Otto. "Zu Prälat M. Grabmanns Eckehartkritik." *Divus Thomas* 5 (1927): 201–18.

Keiling, Tobias. "Letting Things Be for Themselves: *Gelassenheit* as Enabling Thinking." In *Heidegger on Technology*, edited by Aaron James Wendland, Christopher Merwin, and Christos Hadjioannou, 96–114. London: Routledge, 2018.

Kisiel, Theodore. "Edition und Übersetzung: Unterwegs von Tatsachen zu Gedanken, von Werken zu Wegen." In *Zur philosophischen Aktualität Heideggers*, Vol. 3, *Im Spiegel der Welt: Sprache, Übersetzung, Auseinandersetzung*, edited by Dietrich Papenfuss and Otto Pöggeler, 89–107. Frankfurt am Main: Klostermann, 1992.

———. *The Genesis of Heidegger's* Being and Time. Berkeley: University of California Press, 1993.

———. "Heidegger's Philosophical Geopolitics in the Third Reich." In *A Companion to Heidegger's* Introduction to Metaphysics, edited by Gregory Fried and Richard Polt, 226–49. New Haven: Yale University Press, 2001.

———. "Notes for a Work on the 'Phenomenology of Religious Life' (1916–19)." In *A Companion to Heidegger's* Phenomenology of Religious Life, edited by S. J. McGrath and Andrzej Wierciński, 309–28. Amsterdam: Rodolpi, 2010.

———, and Thomas Sheehan, eds. *Becoming Heidegger: On the Trail of His Early Occasional Writings, 1910–1927*. 2nd ed. *The New Yearbook for Phenomenology and Phenomenological Philosophy* IX. Seattle: Noesis, 2009.

Klostermann, Vittorio, ed., with the assistance of Siegfried Blasche et al. *Vittorio Klostermann, Frankfurt am Main, 1930–2000: Verlagsgeschichte und Bibliographie*. Frankfurt: Klostermann, 2000.

Koch, Josef. "Neue Forschungen über Meister Eckhart." *Theologische Revue* 26, no. 11 (1928): 414–22.

———. "Zur Analogielehre Meister Eckharts." In *Kleine Schriften*, Vol. 1, 367–97. Rome: Edizioni di storia e letteratura, 1973.

Koyré, Alexandre. "Die Gotteslehre Jacob Boehmes." Translated by Hedwig Conrad-Martius. In *Jahrbuch für Philosophie und phänomenologische Forschung, Ergänzungsband. Festschrift, Edmund Husserl zum 70. Geburtstag gewidmet*, edited by Martin Heidegger, 225–81. Halle: Niemeyer, 1929.

Krebs, Engelbert. "Arteigenes Christentum." *Stimmen der Zeit* 129 (1935): 81–94.

———. *Grundfragen der kirchlichen Mystik: Dogmatisch erörtert und für das Leben gewertet*. Freiburg im Breisgau: Herder: 1921.

———. *Meister Dietrich (Theodoricus Teutonicus de Vriberg): Sein Leben, seine Werke, seine Wissenschaft*. Münster: Aschendorfische Buchhandlung, 1906.

———. *Theologie und Wissenschaft nach der Lehre der Hochscholastik: An der Hand der bisher ungedruckten Defensa doctrinae D. Thomae des Hervaeus Natalis mit Beifügung gedruckter und ungedruckter Paralleltexte*. Münster i. W.: Aschendorff, 1912.

Krieger, Gerhard. "Mystik und Scholastik: Zur Diskussion um Meister Eckhart im Blick auf seine 'Quaestiones parisienses.'" *Trierer theologische Zeitschrift* 107 (1998): 123–47.

Kurak, Michael. "The Epistemology of Illumination in Meister Eckhart." *Philosophy and Theology* 13, no. 2 (2001): 275–86.

Kawamura, Eiko. "[Review of] The Selected Works of Nishitani Keiji." *Buddhist-Christian Studies* 11 (1991): 307–10.

Lacoue-Labarthe, Philippe. "Présentation." In Martin Heidegger, *La pauvreté (die Armut)*, translated by Philippe Lacoue-Labarthe and Ana Samardzija, 5–65. Strasbourg: Presses Universitaires de Strasbourg, 2004.

Largier, Niklaus. "Mystik und Tat: Zur popular-publizistischen Eckhart-Rezeption zwischen 1900 und 1940." In *Mittelalter-Rezeption IV: Medien, Politik, Ideologie, Ökonomie*, 27–49. Göppingen: Kümmerle, 1991.

Lasson, Adolf. *Meister Eckhart, der Mystiker: Zur Geschichte der religiösen Speculation in Deutschland*. Berlin: Wilhelm Hertz, 1868.

LaZella, Andrew T. "As Light Belongs to Air: Thomas Aquinas and Meister Eckhart on the Existential Rootlessness of Creatures." *American Catholic Philosophical Quarterly* 87, no. 4 (2013): 567–91.

Lera, Luca. "The Fascination of the Origin: Meister Eckhart as the Neoplatonic 'Hidden Source' of Heidegger's Thought." *Dionysius* XXVI (December 2008): 201–36.

Leser, Hermann. "Das religiöse Wahrheitsproblem im Lichte der deutschen Mystik." *Zeitschrift für Philosophie und philosophische Kritik* 160 (1916): 15–71.

Lewin, David. "The Middle Voice in Eckhart and Modern Continental Philosophy." *Medieval Mystical Theology* 20 (2011): 28–46.

Ley, Hermann. *Studie zur Geschichte des Materialismus im Mittelalter*. Berlin: Deutscher Verlag der Wissenschaften, 1957.

Llewelyn, John. "Heidegger's Kant and the Middle Voice." In: *Time and Metaphysics: A Collection of Original Papers*, edited by David Wood and Robert Bernasconi, 87–120. Coventry: Parousia Press, 1982.

———. *The Middle Voice of Ecological Conscience: A Chiasmic Reading of Responsibility in the Neighbourhood of Levinas, Heidegger, and Others*. London: Macmillan, 1991.

Lossky, Vladimir. *Théologie négative et connaissance de Dieu chez Maître Eckhart*. Paris: Vrin, 1960.

Lukàcz, Georg von. "Metaphysik der Tragödie." *Logos* 2 (1911–12): 79–91.

Luther, Martin. "Auslegung deutsch des Vaterunsers für die einfältigen Laien, 1519." In *Werke. Kritische Gesamtausgabe*, Vol. 2, 80–130. Weimar: Hermann Böhlau, 1884. Translated as "An Exposition of the Lord's Prayer for Simple Laymen, 1519." In *Luther's Works*, Vol. 42, 19–81. Philadelphia: Fortress, 1969.

Marbe, Karl. "Beiträge zur Logik und ihren Grenzwissenschaften." *Vierteljahrsschrift für wissenschaftliche Philosophie und Soziologie* XXXVI (Neue Folge XI), no. 2 (1912): 139–94.

Ma, Lin, and Jaap van Brakel. "Out of the *Ge-stell?* The Role of the East in Heidegger's *Das Andere Denken*." *Philosophy East and West* 63, no. 3 (July 2014): 527–62.

May, Reinhard. *Heidegger's Hidden Sources: East Asian Influences on His Work*. Translated by Graham Parkes. London: Routledge, 1996.

McGinn, Bernard. *The Mystical Thought of Meister Eckhart: The Man from Whom God Hid Nothing*. New York: Crossroad, 2001.

McGrath, S. J. *The Early Heidegger and Medieval Philosophy: Phenomenology for the Godforsaken*. Washington, DC: Catholic University of America Press, 2006.

———. "Heidegger and Medieval German Mysticism." *Heinrich-Seuse-Jahrbuch* 1 (2008): 71–100.

Mechthild of Magdeburg. *Das fließende Licht der Gottheit* (*Deutsche Mystiker*, Vol. 2). Edited and translated by Wilhelm Oehl. Kempten: Kösel, 1911.

———. *Das fließende Licht der Gottheit*. Edited and translated by Wilhelm Schleussner. Mainz: Grünewald, 1929.

Merton, Thomas. *Zen and the Birds of Appetite*. New York: New Directions, 1968.

Mieth, Dietmar. *Die Einheit von Vita activa und Vita contemplativa in den deutschen Predigten und Traktaten Meister Eckharts und bei Johannes Tauler: Untersuchungen zur Struktur des christlichen Lebens*. Regensburg: Pustet, 1969.

Milem, Bruce. "Meister Eckhart's Vernacular Preaching." In *A Companion to Meister Eckhart*, edited by Hackett, 337–57.

———. *The Unspoken Word: Negative Theology in Meister Eckhart's German Sermons*. Washington, DC: Catholic University of America Press, 2002.

Mitchell, Andrew J. "Heidegger's Breakdown: Health and Healing Under the Care of Dr. V.E. von Gebsattel." *Research in Phenomenology* 46 (2016): 70–97.

Mitchell, Andrew J., and Peter Trawny, eds. *Heidegger's* Black Notebooks: *Responses to Anti-Semitism*. New York: Columbia University Press, 2017.

Mojsisch, Burkhard. *Analogy, Univocity, and Unity*. Translated by Orrin F. Summerell. Amsterdam: B. R. Grüner, 2001.
Moore, Ian Alexander. "For the Love of Detachment: Trakl, Heidegger, and Derrida's *Geschlecht III*." *International Yearbook for Hermeneutics* 18 (2019): 232–55.
———. "Homesickness, Interdisciplinarity, and the Absolute: Heidegger's Relation to Schlegel and Novalis." In *A Companion to Early German Romantic Philosophy*, edited by Elizabeth Millán and Judith Norman, 280–310. Leiden: Brill, 2018.
———. "Science, Thinking, and the Nothing as Such: On the Newly Discovered Original Version of Heidegger's 'What Is Metaphysics?' " *The Review of Metaphysics* 72, no. 3 (March 2019): 529–62.
Moore, Ian Alexander, and Alan D. Schrift, "Existence, Experience, and Transcendence: An Introduction to Jean Wahl." In Wahl, *Transcendence and the Concrete*, 1–31.
Moran, Dermot. "Meister Eckhart and Modern Philosophy." In *A Companion to Meister Eckhart*, edited by Hackett, 669–97.
Morard, Meinrad Stéphane. "Ist, istic, istikeit bei Meister Eckhart." *Freiburger Zeitschrift für Philosophie und Theologie* 3, no. 2 (1956): 169–86.
Morgenstern, Christian. *The Gallows Songs: Christian Morgenstern's* Galgenlieder; *A Selection*. Translated by Max Knight. Berkeley: University of California Press, 1963.
Müller, Max. *Auseinandersetzung als Versöhnung:* polemos kai eirēnē; *Ein Gespräch über ein Leben mit der Philosophie*. Edited by Wilhelm Vossenkuhl. Berlin: Akademie-Verlag, 1994.
———. "Martin Heidegger—Ein Philosoph und die Politik." In *Antwort: Martin Heidegger im Gespräch*, edited by Günther Neske and Emil Kettering, 190–220. Pfullingen: Neske, 1998.
Natorp, Paul. *Deutscher Weltberuf: Geschichtsphilosophische Richtlinien*. 2 vols. Jena: E. Diederichs, 1918.
Nietzsche, Friedrich. *Kritische Studienausgabe*. Edited by Giorgio Colli and Mazzino Montinari. 15 vols. Munich: Deutscher Taschenbuch, 1999.
———. *Beyond Good and Evil: Prelude to a Philosophy of the Future*. Translated by Judith Norman. Cambridge: Cambridge University Press, 2002.
———. *Thus Spoke Zarathustra*. Translated by Adrian Del Caro. Cambridge: Cambridge University Press, 2006.
Nigg, Walter. *Das Leben des heiligen Heinrich Seuse*. Düsseldorf: Patmos, 1966.
Nishitani, Keiji. "Mon point de départ philosophique." Translated by Sylvain Isaac. *Laval théologique et philosophique* 64, no. 2 (June 2008): 295–303.
———. "Niiche no Tsaratsusutora to Maisutā Ekkuharuto," Kongenteki Shutaisei no Tetsugaku. *Nishitani Keiji Chosakushū Daiikkan* ["Nietzsche's Zarathustra and Meister Eckhart," in *A Philosophy of Elemental Subjectivity. Collected Writings of Nishitani Keiji Vol. 1*], 5–32. Tokyo: Sōbunsha, 1986. First published in 1938.
———. *Religion and Nothingness*. Translated by Jan Van Bragt. Berkeley: University of California Press, 1982.

———. "Shinpishisō-shi," Seiyō Shinpishisō no Kenkyū. *Nishitani Keiji Chosakushū Daisankan* ["A History of Mystical Thought," in *A Study of Western Mystical Thought. Collected Writings of Nishitani Keiji Vol. 3*], 3–154. Tokyo: Sōbunsha, 1986. First published in 1932.

Ochwadt, Curd, and Erwin Tecklenborg, eds. *Das Maß des Verborgenen: Heinrich Ochsner 1891–1970 zum Gedächtnis.* Hannover: Charis, 1981.

Ôhashi, Ryôsuke. "Die frühe Heidegger-Rezeption in Japan." In *Japan und Heidegger*, edited by Hartmut Buchner, 23–37. Sigmaringen: Jan Thorbecke, 1989.

Oltmanns, Käte. *Meister Eckhart.* Vol. 2 of the series *Philosophische Abhandlungen.* 2nd ed. Frankfurt am Main: Vittorio Klostermann, 1957. First edition published by Klostermann in 1935.

———. *Die Philosophie des Meister Eckhart.* Frankfurt am Main: August Osterrieth, 1935.

———. "Wesenheit, Dasein und Grund bei Meister Eckhart." In HSS 356–62, 437–38.

O'Meara, Thomas F. *Romantic Idealism and Roman Catholicism: Schelling and the Theologians.* Notre Dame: University of Notre Dame Press, 1982.

Onishi, Bradley B. "Transcendence as Indistinction in Eckhart and Heidegger." *Religions* 8, no. 4 (2017).

Ott, Hugo. "Der Habilitand Martin Heidegger und das von Schaezler'sche Stipendium: Ein Beitrag zur Wissenschaftsförderung der katholischen Kirche." *Freiburger Diözesan-Archiv* 106 (1986): 141–60.

———. *Martin Heidegger: A Political Life.* Translated by Allan Blunden. London: BasicBooks, 1993.

———. "Martin Heidegger's Catholic Origins." *American Catholic Philosophical Quarterly* 69, no. 2 (1995): 137–56.

Otto, Rudolf. *Das Heilige: Über das Irrationale in der Idee des Göttlichen und sein Verhältnis zum Rationalen.* Breslau: Trewendt und Granier, 1917.

———. "Meister Eckeharts Mystik im Unterschiede von östlicher Mystik." *Zeitschrift für Theologie und Kirche* 6 (1925): 325–50 and 418–36.

———. "Der östliche Buddhist." *Die Christliche Welt* (1925): 978–82.

———. *West-östliche Mystik: Vergleich und Unterscheidung zur Wesensdeutung.* Gotha: Leopold Klotz, 1926.

Panzig, Erik A. "*gelâzenheit* und *abegescheidenheit*—zur Verwurzelung beider Theoreme im theologischen Denken Meister Eckharts." In *Meister Eckhart in Erfurt*, edited by Speer and Wegener, 334–56.

Parkes, Graham, ed. *Heidegger and Asian Thought.* Honolulu: University of Hawaii Press, 1987.

Pfeiffer, Franz, ed. *Deutsche Mystiker des vierzehnten Jahrhunderts.* Vol. 1. Leipzig: Göschen, 1845.

Piesch, Herma. "Seuses 'Büchlein der Wahrheit' und Meister Eckhart." In *Heinrich Seuse: Studien zum 600. Todestag, 1366–1966*, edited by Ephrem M. Filthaut, 91–134. Cologne: Albertus Magnus, 1966.

Piper, Ernst. *Alfred Rosenberg: Hitlers Chefideologe*. Munich: Karl Blessing, 2005.
Plato. *Phaidros*. In *Platonis opera*, Vol. II. Oxford: Clarendon, 1901.
Pöggeler, Otto. "Jean Wahls Heidegger-Deutung." *Zeitschrift für philosophische Forschung* 12, no. 3 (July-September, 1958): 437–58.
———. *Neue Wege mit Heidegger*. Freiburg: Alber, 1992.
Quint, Josef. "Das Echtheitsproblem des Traktats 'Von abegescheidenheit.'" In *La mystique rhénane*, 39–58. Paris: Presses Universitaires de France, 1963.
Raschke, Hermann. "Meister Eckhart der Deutsche." *Nazionalsozialistische Monatshefte* 5, no. 47 (February 1934): 129–47.
Richardson, William J. *Heidegger: Through Phenomenology to Thought*. 4th ed. New York: Fordham University Press, 2003.
Rickert, Heinrich. *Das Eine, die Einheit und die Eins: Bemerkungen zur Logik des Zahlbegriffs*. 2nd ed. Tübingen: Mohr, 1924. First published in *Logos* 2 (1911–12): 26–78.
———. *Die Philosophie des Lebens: Darstellung und Kritik der philosophischen Modeströmungen unserer Zeit*. Tübingen: Mohr, 1920.
Ritter, Joachim, Karlfried Gründer, and Gottfried Gabriel, eds. *Historisches Wörterbuch der Philosophie*. 13 vols. Basel: Schwabe, 1971–2007.
Roesner, Martina. "Continu, individu, esprit: La conception du temps chez le jeune Heidegger face à la théorie du temps de Dietrich de Freiberg." *Archives de Philosophie* 67, no. 3 (2004): 465–91.
Rosenberg, Alfred. *Der Mythus des 20. Jahrhunderts: Eine Wertung der seelischgeistigen Gestaltenkämpfe unserer Zeit*. Munich: Hoheneichen, 1930.
———. *Die Religion des Meister Eckehart (Sonderdruck aus dem "Mythus des 20. Jahrhunderts")*. Munich: Hoheneichen, 1934.
Rosenkranz, Karl. *Georg Wilhelm Friedrich Hegel's Leben*. Berlin: Duncker und Humblot, 1844.
Ruh, Kurt. *Geschichte der abendländischen Mystik*. Vol. 3, *Die Mystik des deutschen Predigerordens und ihre Grundlegung durch die Hochscholastik*. Munich: Beck, 1996.
———. *Meister Eckhart: Theologe, Prediger, Mystiker*. 2nd ed. Munich: Beck, 1989.
———. "Meister Eckharts Pariser Quaestionen 1–3 und eine deutsche Predigtsammlung." *Perspektiven der Philosophie* 10 (1984): 307–24.
Rutger, Allan J. *The Middle Voice in Ancient Greek: A Study in Polysemy*. Amsterdam: J. C. Gieben, 2003.
Saas, Hans-Martin. *Martin Heidegger: Bibliography and Glossary*. Bowling Green: Philosophy Documentation Center, 1982.
Sauer, Joseph. "Mystik und Kunst unter besonderer Berücksichtigung des Oberrheins." *Kunstwissenschaftliches Jahrbuch der Görres-Gesellschaft* 1 (1928): 3–28.
Schaber, Johannes, OSB. "Phänomenologie und Mönchtum: Max Scheler, Martin Heidegger, Edith Stein und die Erzabtei Beuron." In *Leben, Tod, und Entscheidung: Studien zur Geistesgeschichte der Weimarer Republik*, edited by Holger Zaborowski and Stephan Loos, 71–100. Berlin: Duncker und Humblot, 2003.

———. "Te lucis ante terminum: Martin Heidegger und das benediktinische Mönchtum." In *Edith Stein Jahrbuch 8: Das Mönchtum*, edited by Sánchez de Murillo, 281–94. Würzburg: Echter Verlag, 2002.

Schelling, Friedrich Wilhelm Joseph. *Philosophische Untersuchungen über das Wesen der menschlichen Freiheit und die damit zusammenhängenden Gegenstände*. In *Sämmtliche Werke*, Abteilung I, Band 7. Stuttgart: J. G. Cotta, 1860. Translated by Jeff Love and Johannes Schmidt as *Philosophical Investigations into the Essence of Human Freedom*. Albany: State University of New York Press, 2006.

Schiffhauer, Angela. "'*nos filii dei sumus analogice*': Die Analogielehre Meister Eckharts in der Verteidigungsschrift." In *Meister Eckhart in Erfurt*, edited by Speer and Wegener, 356–89.

Schirmacher, Wolfgang. *Technik und Gelassenheit: Zeitkritik nach Heidegger*. Freiburg: Karl Alber, 1983.

Schlüter, Jochen. *Heideggers Rezeption des antiken und mittelalterlichen Neuplatonismus: Anmerkungen zur Heidegger-Forschung*. Berlin: LIT, 2016.

Schmid, Holger. "Praeteritio Dei." *Continental Philosophy Review* 47, nos. 3–4 (2014): 335–51.

Schmidt, Dennis. "*Solve et coagula*: Something other than an Exercise in Dialectic." *Research in Phenomenology* 28, no. 1 (1998): 259–71.

Schmidtke, Dietrich. "Eine Beuroner Mystikerhandschrift." *Scriptorium* 34, no. 2 (1980): 278–87.

Schoeller Reisch, Donata. "Die Demut Zarathustras: Ein Versuch zu Nietzsche und Meister Eckhart." *Nietzsche-Studien* 27, no. 1 (1998): 420–39.

Schöfer, Erasmus. *Die Sprache Heideggers*. Pfullingen: Neske, 1962.

Schüßler, Werner. "Gott—Sein oder Denken? Zur Problematik der Bestimmung göttlicher Wirklichkeit in den *Quaestiones parisienses* Meister Eckharts von 1302/03." In *Transzendenz: Zu einem Grundwort der klassischen Metaphysik*, edited by Ludger Honnefelder and Werner Schüßler. Paderborn: Ferdinand Schöningh, 1992.

Schürmann, Reiner. *Broken Hegemonies*. Translated by Reginald Lilly. Bloomington: Indiana University Press, 2003.

———. *Heidegger on Being and Acting: From Principles to Anarchy*. Translated by Christine-Marie Gros in collaboration with the author. Bloomington: Indiana University Press, 1987.

———. "Heidegger and Meister Eckhart on Releasement." *Research in Phenomenology* 3 (1973): 95–119.

———. *Maître Eckhart ou la joie errante: Sermons allemands traduits et commentés*. Paris: Éditions Payot et Rivages, 2005. Originally published in 1972.

———. "Meister Eckhart's 'Verbal' Understanding of Being as a Ground for Destruction of Practical Teleology." In *Sprache und Erkenntnis im Mittelalter*, Vol. 2, edited by Jan P. Backmann, 803–809. Berlin: Walter de Gruyter, 1981.

———. "Neoplatonic Henology as an Overcoming of Metaphysics." *Research in Phenomenology* 13 (1983): 25–41.

———. "Reiner Schürmann's Report of His Visit to Martin Heidegger." Translated by Pierre Adler. *Graduate Faculty Philosophy Journal* 19, no. 2 (1997): 67–71. The original French material (though not the German material) was published later under the title "Recit de l'entretien avec Heidegger," in *Autour de Reiner Schürmann*, edited by Vaysse, 155–57.

———. *Wandering Joy: Meister Eckhart's Mystical Philosophy*. Great Barrington, MA: Lindisfarne Books, 2001.

Scott, Charles E. "The Middle Voice of *Being and Time*." In *The Collegium Phaenomenologicum: The First Ten Years*, edited by John Sallis, Giuseppina Chiara Moneta, and Jacques Taminiaux, 159–73. Dordrecht: Kluwer, 1988.

Seeberg, Erich. "Die verlorene Handschrift: Zur Geschichte der Eckhart-Ausgabe." *Nationalsozialistische Monatshefte* 8, no. 86 (May 1937): 368–97.

Sells, Michael A. *Mystical Languages of Unsaying*. Chicago: University of Chicago Press, 1994.

Senner, Walter, OP. "Meister Eckhart's Life, Training, Career, and Trial." In *A Companion to Meister Eckhart*, edited by Hackett, 7–84.

Silesius, Angelus. *Cherubinischer Wandersmann: Kritische Ausgabe*. Edited by Louise Gnädinger. Stuttgart: Reclam, 1984.

———. *A Selection from the Rhymes of a German Mystic*. Translated by Paul Carus. Chicago: Open Court, 1909.

Sikka, Sonya. *Forms of Transcendence: Heidegger and Medieval Mystical Theology*. Albany: State University of New York Press, 1997.

Speck, Dieter. "Vorlesungen im Phantomsemester: Die Freiburger Philosophische Fakultät in Beuron zwischen Flucht und Fiktion." In *Mittelalterliches Mönchtum in der Moderne? Die Neugründung der Benediktinerabtei Beuron 1863 und deren kulturelle Ausstrahlung im 19. und 20. Jahrhundert*, edited by Karl-Heinz Braun, Hugo Ott, and Wilfried Schöntag, 169–89. Stuttgart: Kohlhammer, 2015.

Speer, Andreas, and Lydia Wegener, eds. *Meister Eckhart in Erfurt*. Berlin: W. de Gruyter, 2005.

Stadelmann, Rudolf. *Vom Geist des ausgehenden Mittelalters: Studien zur Geschichte der Weltanschauung von Nicolaus Cusanus bis Sebastian Franck*. Halle/Salle: Max Niemeyer, 1929.

Steer, Georg. "Eckhart der *meister*." In *Literarische Leben: Rollenentwürfe in der Literatur des Hoch- und Spätmittelalters*, edited by Matthias Meyer and Hans-Jochen Schiewer, 713–53. Tübingen: Niemeyer, 2002.

Steiner, Wolfgang. *Die Aufgabe des Denkens: Martin Heidegger und die philosophische Mystik*. Marburg: Tectum, 2010.

Strummiello, Giusi. "'Alte Wörter': Gelassenheit und Gottheit bei Heidegger und Eckhart." *Heidegger Studies* 28 (2012): 191–211.

Sturlese, Loris. "Eckhart as Preacher, Administrator, and Master of the Sentences: From Erfurt to Paris and Back: 1294–1313; The Origins of the *Opus tripartitum.*" In *A Companion to Meister Eckhart*, edited by Hackett, 125–35.

———. *Homo divinus: Philosophische Projekte in Deutschland zwischen Meister Eckhart und Heinrich Seuse.* Stuttgart: W. Kohlhammer, 2007.

Suso, Henry. *The Exemplar, with Two German Sermons.* Translated, edited, and introduced by Frank Tobin. New York: Paulist, 1989.

———. *Heinrich Seuse: Deutsche Schriften.* Edited by Karl Bihlmeyer. Stuttgart: W. Kohlhammer, 1907.

———. Henrici Susonis seu Fratris Amandi. *Horologium Sapientiae.* Edited by Josephus Strange. Cologne: Heberle, 1861.

———. *Des Mystikers Heinrich Seuse O. Pr. Deutsche Schriften: Vollständige Ausgabe auf Grund der Handschriften.* Translated by Nikolaus Heller. Heidelberg: Kerle, 1926.

———. *Seuse* (*Deutsche Mystiker*, Vol. 1). Edited and translated by Wilhelm Oehl. Kempten: Kösel, 1910.

Suzuki, D. T. *Essays in Zen Buddhism.* New York: Grove, 1949. First published in 1927.

Tanabe, Hajime. *Philosophy as Metanoetics.* Translated by Yoshinori Takeuchi with Valdo Viglielmo and James W. Heisig. Berkeley: University of California Press, 1986.

Tauler, John. *Tauler* (*Deutsche Mystiker*, Vol. 4). Translated by Wilhelm Oehl. Kempten: Kösel u. Pustet, 1919.

———. *Die Predigten Taulers.* Edited by Ferdinand Vetter. Berlin: Weidmann, 1910.

———. *Sermons.* Translated by Maria Shrady. New York: Paulist, 1985.

Thomas Aquinas. *Opera omnia S. Thomae.* http://www.corpusthomisticum.org/.

Tobin, Frank. *Meister Eckhart: Thought and Language.* Philadelphia: University of Pennsylvania Press, 1986.

Ueberweg, Friedrich. *Die patristische und scholastische Philosophie.* 10th ed. Edited by Matthias Baumgartner. Berlin: Ernst Siegfried Mittler und Sohn, 1915. 11th ed. Edited by Bernhard Geyer. Berlin: E. S. Mittler u. Sohn, 1928.

Ueda, Shizuteru. *Die Gottesgeburt in der Seele und der Durchbruch zur Gottheit: Die mystische Anthropologie Meister Eckharts und ihre Konfrontation mit der Mystik des Zen-Buddhismus.* Gütersloh: Mohn, 1965.

———. "'Nothingness' in Meister Eckhart and Zen Buddhism." Translated by James W. Heisig. In *The Buddha Eye: An Anthology of the Kyoto School and Its Contemporaries,* edited by Frederick Frank, 157–69. Bloomington, IN: World Wisdom, 2004.

———. "Über den Sprachgebrauch Meister Eckharts: 'Gott muß . . .': Ein Beispiel für die Gedankengänge der spekulativen Mystik." In *Glaube, Geist, Geschichte. Festschrift für Ernst Benz zum 60. Geburtstag am 17. November 1967,* edited by Gerhard Müller and Winfried Zeller, 266–77. Leiden: E. J. Brill, 1967.

Van Buren, John. *The Young Heidegger: Rumor of the Hidden King.* Bloomington: Indiana University Press, 1994.

Vaysse, Jean-Marie, ed. *Autour de Reiner Schürmann.* Hildesheim: Georg Olms, 2009.

Vinzent, Markus. "*Questions on the Attributes (of God)*: Four Rediscovered *Parisian Questions* of Meister Eckhart." *The Journal of Theological Studies* 63, no. 1 (April 2002): 156–86.

Vitiello, Vincenzo. "'Abgeschiedenheit,' 'Gelassenheit,' 'Angst': Tra Eckhart e Heidegger." *Quaestio* 1 (2001): 305–16.

Völker, Ludwig. "'Gelassenheit': Zur Entstehung des Wortes in der Sprache Meister Eckharts und seiner Überlieferung in der nacheckhartschen Mystik bis J. Böhme." In *Getempert und gemischet: Für Wolfgang Mohr zum 65. Geburtstag von seinen Tübinger Schülern*, edited by Franz Hundsnurscher and Ulrich Müller, 281–312. Göppingen: A. Kümmerle, 1972.

Von Herrmann, Friedrich-Wilhelm. *Die Selbstinterpretation Martin Heideggers.* Meisenheim am Glan: Anton Hain, 1964.

———. *Wege ins Ereignis: Zu Heideggers "Beiträgen zur Philosophie."* Frankfurt am Main: Vittorio Klostermann, 1994.

Von Herrmann, Friedrich-Wilhelm, and Francesco Alfieri. *Martin Heidegger: Die Wahrheit über die Schwarzen Hefte.* Berlin: Duncker & Humblot, 2017.

Von Perger, Mischa. "*Disputatio* in Eckharts frühen Pariser Quästionen und als Predigtmotiv." In *Meister Eckhart: Lebensstationen—Redesituationen*, edited by Klaus Jacobi, 115–48. Berlin: Walter de Gruyter, 1997.

———. "Mystik unter Zwang: Erlösungsworte Meister Eckharts bei Paul Celan." *Zeitschrift für deutsches Altertum und deutsche Literatur* 133, no. 4 (2004): 433–71.

Von Wolzogen, Christoph. "'Gottes Geheimnisse verkosten, bevor sie geschaut werden': Martin Heidegger und der Theologe Engelbert Krebs." In *Heidegger und die Anfänge seines Denkens*, edited by Denker, Gander, and Zaborowski, 201–13.

Wahl, Jean. *Introduction à la pensée de Heidegger: Cours donnés en Sorbonne de janvier à juin 1946.* Paris: Librairie Générale Française, 1998.

———. *Transcendence and the Concrete: Selected Writings.* Edited by Alan D. Schrift and Ian Alexander Moore. New York: Fordham University Press, 2017.

Walther, Gerda. *Zum anderen Ufer: Vom Marxismus und Atheismus zum Christentum.* Remagen: Otto Reichl, 1960.

Wagner Jürgen. *Meditationen über Gelassenheit: Der Zugang des Menschen zu seinem Wesen im Anschluß an Martin Heidegger und Meister Eckhart.* Hamburg: Kovač, 1995.

Wéber, Édouard Henri. "Petite étincelle et fond de l'âme." In *Voici Maître Eckhart*, edited by Zum Brunn, 105–18.

Weischedel, Wilhelm. *Der Gott der Philosophen: Grundlegung einer philosophischen Theologie im Zeitalter des Nihilismus.* 2 vols. Darmstadt: Wissenschaftliche Buchgesellschaft, 1971–72.

Welte, Bernhard. "Bemerkungen zum Gottesbegriff des Thomas von Aquin." In *Gesammelte Schriften II/1*, 307–15.
———. "Der mystische Weg des Meisters Eckhart und sein spekulativer Hintergrund." In *Gesammelte Schriften II/1*, 234–39.
———. "Erinnerung an ein spätes Gespräch." In MH/BW, 147–50.
———. *Gesammelte Schriften II/1. Denken in Begegnung mit den Denkern I: Meister Eckhart—Thomas von Aquin—Bonaventura.* Freiburg: Herder, 2007.
———. *Meister Eckhart: Gedanken zu seinen Gedanken.* In *Gesammelte Schriften II/1*, 21–215.
———. *Der philosophische Glaube bei Karl Jaspers und die Möglichkeit seiner Deutung durch die thomistische Philosophie.* In *Denken in Begegnung mit den Denkern III: Jaspers*, edited by Klaus Kienzler, 15–291. Freiburg: Herder, 2008.
———. "Suchen und Finden: Ansprache zur Beisetzung am 28. Mai 1976." In MH/BW, 124–27.
———. "Thomas von Aquin und Heideggers Gedanke von der Seinsgeschichte." In MH/BW, 74–90. Originally published under the title "Rückblick auf die Metaphysik." *Wort und Wahrheit* 12 (1967): 747–57.
Winkler, Norbert. "Zwischen strukturalistischer und intentionalistischer Interpretation—Fallbeispiel: Meister Eckharts *Quaestio Parisiensis I*." In *Philosophiegeschichte und Hermeneutik*, edited by Volker Caysa and Klaus-Dieter Eichler, 218–37. Leipzig: Leipziger Universitätsverlag, 1996.
Wolz-Gottwald, Eckard. "Martin Heidegger und die philosophische Mystik." *Philosophisches Jahrbuch* 104, no. 1 (1997): 64–79.
Zimmermann, Hans Dieter. *Martin und Fritz Heidegger: Philosophie und Fastnacht.* Munich: C. H. Beck, 2005.
Zum Brunn, Émilie, ed. *Voici Maître Eckhart.* Grenoble: Jérôme Millon, 1998.

Index

abyss (*abgrunt, Abgrund*), 3, 11, 59, 62–63, 74–75, 80, 87, 138, 140, 159, 191, 201, 213, 227n28, 257n5; of Neoplatonism, 203; and peak, 16, 212–213; without why (*abgrunt sunder warumbe*), 59

activity, xiv, 37, 63–64, 72–74, 92, 95, 97, 99–102, 106–107, 112, 134, 137, 139–140, 193, 197–198, 206–207, 209–213, 265n5; of being, 62, 80; of the human being, 61–62, 76–77, 80, 115, 117, 130; and letting-be, 98, 103–105, 108–109

actuality (*actus*), 11, 47, 106, 152; and potentiality (*potentia*), 10, 14, 73, 139, 191

affirmation, 51, 205; of life, 16, 191, 205; and negation, 17, 52, 191, 200, 212–213; radicalization of, 212–213; self-, 204

Albert the Great, 41, 69

Albertinism, 36

alētheia / a-lētheia (Greek noun). *See* truth: as unconcealing

ambiguity: between letting-be and activity, xvi, 102, 108

analogy, doctrine of: Eckhart's, 14, 17–18, 39–40, 49, 54–55, 57, 59, 181, 192, 221n9, 231n49, 250n42

Anaxagoras, 53

animality, 103

anthropology, 130; Eckhart's, 194

anti-Semitism: in Heidegger's *Black Notebooks*, 140–142, 271n5

anxiety, 116

apatheia, Stoic (Greek noun): as distinct from releasement (*gelâzenheit*), 66

apophainesthai (Greek verb): in *Being and Time*, 98, 101

appropriative event (*Ereignis*), 15, 62, 95, 123, 132, 226n24, 269n17; as en-"owning" (*Er-"eignen"*), 30

Aquinas. *See* Thomas Aquinas, Saint

Arendt, Hannah, 3, 28, 145, 242n91

Aristotle, 5, 17, 26, 36, 51, 57, 64, 103, 138, 190, 203, 207, 214, 216, 222n10, 270n29; and *The Bible*, xviii; Plato and, 59, 215; Pseudo-, 46; Thomas Aquinas and, 39

—works: *De Anima*, 50; *Metaphysics*, 74

Aristotelianism, 36, 69, 183, 204, 214–216, 268n13; and Platonism, 211; as Thomism, 210

artifice: "nature" or spirit and, 113

317

318 INDEX

asceticism, 63, 67, 70, 129
attunement, fundamental, 103, 105–109, 120, 136, 233n55, 264n18; *fundamental* (*Urgrundstimmung*), 270n25; oppressiveness of, 108; philosophy's rootedness in, 105
Aufhebung (sublation): in Eckhart's thought, 84
Augustine, Saint, 155–156, 166, 169, 176, 181, 184, 202, 214–215, 232n52, 274n19; Platonism of, 210, 214–215
—works: *Confessions*, 154, 274n16, 281n30
Augustinianism, 202–203, 210, 214
authenticity (*Eigentlichkeit*): of Eckhart's understanding of being, 35, 277n51
autochthony (*Bodenständigkeit*), 127, 268n12
Averroes (Ibn Rushd), 36; Aristotelianism of, 214
Averroism, 214–215
Avicenna (Ibn Sina), 36

Baader, Franz von, 35
Bacon, Francis: logic and empiricism of, 216
Baeumker, Clemens, 181, 239n72, 272n3, 276n36
Beierwaltes, Werner, 25, 230n47; Derrida and, 3
—works: "Heideggers Gelassenheit," 240n76, 268n14
being (*Sein, einai, esse*): analogy of (*analogia entis*), 17; and appearance, 113–114, 265n7; and becoming, 59, 113, 265n7; as emergence (*physis*), 12, 113, 132, 265n6; etymology of, 113; as event (*Ereignis*), 15, 132; as God (*esse est deus*), xv, 10, 12, 18, 39, 53–60, 181–182, 276n39; grammar of, 113; independence of from Dasein, 140, 271n1; as letting-be, xiii–xiv, 95, 139; as living, 203, 210; and method, 16, 38, 82, 91, 93–95, 112, 121, 259n6; nothingness of, 75, 211, 241n84; and obligation, 113; as the open-region (*die Gegnet*), 126, 132, 137, 269n15; as presencing (*Anwesen*), 15, 30, 186, 220n5; as the prevailing (*Walten*), xiv, 15–16, 112–114, 118, 120, 124, 127, 135, 265n6; purity of (*puritas essendi*), 49–50, 55, 248–249nn37–38, 255n33; question of (*Seinsfrage*), 14–15, 17; reciprocity of with the human being, 96, 113–114; as releasement (*Gelassenheit*), xiii, xvi, 37, 61, 80, 82; and thinking, xiii–xv, 4, 13, 15, 39, 61, 65, 92, 111, 114, 123, 126, 137–139; transitive, 12–13, 25, 79, 228n32; as *wesen* (Middle High German), 13, 42, 61–62, 79, 84
being-let: and letting-be, 86, 134
beings (*das Seiende*): as created (*creata*), 29, 46, 50, 54, 56, 65–67, 73, 75, 83–84, 160–161, 165–166, 185, 192, 228n30, 255n36, 278n2–7, 282n44; as divine, 56; as present-at-hand, 194, 100; as ready-to-hand, 100; refusal of, 108; as a whole, 106–108, 112, 114, 116
being-with (*mitewesen, Mitsein*), 262n13
Bergson, Henri, 201, 206–207, 210–211; Nietzsche and, 218
—works: *Two Sources of Morality and Religion*, 211

Beuron (Benedictine archabbey), 23–24, 124, 237n61, 253n11, 267n6
beyng (*Seyn*), 17, 25, 27, 29, 61, 132, 157–158, 222n9, 225n24, 271n2; as that which underlies changes in the meaning of the beingness of beings, 141
Bible, The, 257n9; and philosophy, xvii
biology, racial, 142
Bloch, Ernst: Ley and, 35
Blochmann, Elisabeth, 223n13, 262n15, 272n1
Bodmershof, Imma von, 236n59
Boethius, 274n24; Aquinas and, 248n34
Böhme, Jakob, 16, 22, 224n18, 230n41, 230n43, 235n57, 236–237nn59–60, 255n37, 272n1
Bollnow, Otto Friedrich, 229n37
Book of Twenty-Four Philosophers, The (anonymous), 25, 239n72, 272n3
Bonaventure, Saint, 203
boredom: as a fundamental attunement, 103, 106–107
breakthrough (*durchbruch, Durchbruch*), 12, 16, 30, 69, 72, 123, 161, 175, 185, 188–189, 198, 209–210, 221n9, 252n7, 256n1
Brentano, Franz
—works: *On the Several Senses of Being in Aristotle*, 5
Brient, Elizabeth, 26, 222n11, 239n70
Bröcker, Walter, 13, 229n37
Bruno, Giordano, 26
Buddha: Eckhart, Schopenhauer, and, 35
Buddhism, 16, 225n18, 230n41

Cage, John
—works: *4'33"* and "Meister Duchamp or living on water," 35

causality: and perfection, 54; as a metaphysical category, 140, 257n5
Celan, Paul, 35
—works: *Lightduress*, 243n4
certainty (*certitudo*): and justice (*iustitia*), 19; and uncertainty, 104
Church Fathers, Greek, 214
circularity: of reasoning, xvii; philosophical, 104, 132
clarity: and distinctness (Descartes), 92
comportment, 68, 107, 114, 123, 127, 134, 137, 259n6, 260n4, 261n10, 269n16; toward ourselves, 63; toward things, 63, 99, 128
concealment: of being, 114, 132, 138; of the heart (*verborgenheit des gemüetes*), 7, 151; and unconcealment, 141
conversation / dialogue (*Gespräch*), 77, 124, 266n5
copula, 12–13, 46, 53, 57
corporeality, 26, 67, 140, 253n19; releasement from, 63
creation, 11–12, 18, 46–47, 62–64, 72–73, 75, 208, 235n57, 241n83, 250n46, 257n5; *ex nihilo*, 192, 230n46
cultivation: for realeasement, 15, 36–38, 64, 67, 81–82, 87, 139
Cusa, Nicholas of, 6, 26, 222n11, 240n73, 272n3, 278n10

Darwin, Charles: theory of evolution of, 217
Dasein, xiv, 97, 103–108, 114, 116–117, 140, 258n4, 261n10, 263nn15–16, 264n20, 265n5, 271n1, 278n1; primordial happening of, 99; and the spark of the soul, 3; transcendence of, xvi, 16, 101, 123, 259n6

Davis, Bret, 120, 225n18, 230n42, 262n11, 268n13, 269n19, 277n46
deconstruction: and cultivation, 36; of metaphysics or Western philosophy, 31, 259n6
deinos, deinon (Greek adjective): as basic feature of the human being, 118; as uncanny (*unheimlich*), 116; as the violent (*das Gewaltige*), 117
Denker, Alfred, 237n60
Derrida, Jacques, 219n1; Beierwaltes and, 3; on the middle voice of *différance*, 260n7
—works: *The Beast and the Sovereign: Volume II*, 265n6
Descartes, René, 231n47; Leibniz and, 216
—works; *Discourse on the Method*, 92, 258n3
desert: of the Godhead, 11, 42, 63, 85–86, 138, 233n53, 256n1, 257n5
detachment (*abegescheidenheit, Abgeschiedenheit*), 3, 6–8, 15, 57, 62–67, 74–79, 81, 84, 91, 121, 143, 187, 222n10, 239n64, 242n90, 253nn12–13, 256n39, 258n5, 259n3; from possessiveness, 63; from self, 6, 70; from world, 6. *See also* releasement
Dietrich of Freiberg, 45, 219n4, 248n26
Dilthey, Wilhelm, 231n47
dialectic, 15–16, 38, 40, 50, 53, 82–84, 86, 189–190, 200–201, 204–205, 209, 212, 216, 218, 256n3
Dionysius the Areopagite, 156, 232n52, 274n19

Dionysianism, 36, 251n3
disclosure, 107. *See also* unconcealment
discursivity, 8, 38, 63, 81, 103, 254n27, 262n14
Dominicans, 8–9, 31, 41, 81 140; German, 220n4
Duchamp, Marcel, 35
Duns Scotus, John, 192, 232n49; Eckhart and, 145, 237n60

Eckhart, Meister: death of, 35, 41; Duns Scotus and, 145, 237n60; German writings of, xv, 14, 38, 40, 59–61, 64–65, 82, 139, 146, 191, 242n91, 253n14; heresy trial of, 41, 56, 228n35, 245n9; iconoclasm of, 23, 40; Latin writings of, xv, 14–15, 18, 29, 37–39, 41, 191, 239n72, 251n3, 272n3; Nazi appropriation of, 35, 231n47, 243n3; Pseudo-, 6, 30, 146–148, 179, 228n31, 237n61, 251n5
—works: Pr. 2 ("Intravit Iesus in quoddam castellum"), 238n62, 253n14, 254n27, 256n1, 270n20; Pr. 4 ("Omne datum optimum"), 56; Pr. 5b ("In hoc apparuit"), 20, 22, 166; Pr. 6 ("Iusti vivent in aeternum"), 19; Pr. 9 ("Quasi stella matutina"), 239n72, 247n24, 274n22; Pr. 10 ("In diebus suis"), 257n9; Pr. 12 ("Qui audit me"), 13, 86; Pr. 13 ("Vidi supra montem Syon"), 250n46; Pr. 28 ("Ego elegi vos"), 238n62; Pr. 52 ("Beati pauperes spiritu"), xiii, 22, 25, 85, 104, 162–163, 222n9, 227–228nn30–31, 241n82, 251nn1–4, 254n24, 254n27, 254n29, 255n32, 257n6, 274n20; Pr. 53 ("Misit dominus

manum suam"), 227n29, 247n24; Pr. 69 ("Modicum et iam non videbitis me"), 69, 254n27; Pr. 71 ("Surrexit autem Saulus de terra"), 83, 243n4; Pr. 86 ("Intravit Iesus in quoddam castellum, etc."), 253n16; Pr. 103 ("Cum factus esset Iesus annorum duodecim"), 6, 253n19; Pr. 109 ("Nolite timere eos, qui occidunt corpus"), 12, 228n31, 254n29; Pr. 117 ("Ze dem êrsten suochet daz rîche gotes"), 64–65, 70, 149, 253n19, 255n32, 274n19; *Commentary on the Book of Genesis,* 257n5; *Commentary on the Book of Wisdom,* 83; *Commentary on John,* 28–29, 54, 59, 158, 232n51, 239n72; *Counsels on Discernment* (*Die rede der underscheidunge*), 21–22, 27–28, 68, 77, 238n62; *On Detachment* (*Von abegescheidenheit*), 65, 75–77, 225n23, 253n12, 255n38, 276n35; *Opus tripartitum,* 9–10, 12, 14, 18, 40–41, 53–54, 56–59, 180–183, 225n23, 245n5, 276n41; *Parisian Questions,* 8, 14, 18, 40–42, 46–47, 50, 52–57, 192, 232n49, 245n3, 245n5, 245n10, 246n16, 247n23, 249n38, 255n33; *Sermons and Lectures on Ecclesiasticus,* 54–56, 58–59, 250n45

—works by Pseudo-Eckhart: *Liber positionum,* 148, 228n31; "Vom Schauen Gottes und von Seligkeit," 149, 165; "Von dem Zorne der Seele und von ihrer rechten Stätte," 30, 164–165; "Von der sêle werdikeit und eigenschaft," 276n35

ekstasis (Greek noun), 198, 205
ego, 183, 200, 205–212, 282n49
eidos (Greek noun), 183, 198–200, 205–210
ein einic ein (German phrase). See oneness: single
emergence: of being, 113; of God from the Godhead, 12; of will in the Godhead, 22; of God into the Trinity, 64
enframing (*Gestell, Gestellnis, Gestellung*), 30–21, 242n88
enlightenment (movement), 214, 216–217
epistemology: impossibility of, 189
epochē (Greek noun), 76
Erasmus. See humanism: Erasmian
essence (*Wesen, essentia*): of being, xiv, 28, 38, 64–65, 112–113, 116, 157, 172, 190; and existence, 10, 14, 191–192; of the human being, xiv, 16, 61, 96, 113, 117, 128, 137; as presencing (*Anwesen*), 181–182
essencing (*wesüng, Wesung*), 3, 121, 132, 178, 221n9
ethics: as way of life, 141; an-archic, 142
event of appropriation (*Ereignis*). See appropriative event (*Ereignis*)
evolution, theory of, 217
Exodus: 3:14, 46, 49–50, 247n24, 249n38

faith, 201, 217, 271n8; and knowledge, xvii, 214, 216, 218
Faust, August, 230n41
Fichte, Johann Gottlieb, 245n3
Finke, Heinrich, 219n4
First World War (World War I), 234n55
Fischer, Heribert, 42

Flasch, Kurt, 69, 245n3, 246n16
formal indication, 92
fourfold, the, 29, 91, 143, 187, 271n6
Franciscans, 8, 41, 81
freedom, 8, 137, 153, 189, 211–213, 225n19; and letting-be, 108, 263n15, 264n21, 270n28; role of in Schelling, 16, 191, 194
Freiburg, xvi, 11, 15–16, 24, 99, 142, 145, 184, 189, 224n18, 229n37, 243n4
Fries, Jakob Friedrich: Schelling, Schopenhauer, and, 199
Führer, 102, 111

Gadamer, Hans-Georg, 3, 9–10, 181, 219n1, 225n23, 229n37, 232n50, 234n55, 260n9, 272n3, 276n36, 276n39, 276n41; Oltmanns and, 18; on the middle voice of play, 260n7
Galileo, 258n3
Genesis: 1:2, 6; as *gignesthai* (Greek verb), 79
German idealism, 39, 115, 217, 245n3
German Romantics, 39
German people (*Volk*), 142
Gilbert de la Porrée, 226n26
God (*got, theos, deus*): as being (*deus est esse*), xv, 53–54, 56–58, 193; death of ("God is dead"), 16, 195, 198, 201; and seeing (*theōrein*), 222n11; as Trinity, 64, 192–193; as understanding (*deus est intelligere*), xv, 18, 47, 54
Godhead (*gotheit, deitas*), xiii, xv, 3, 9–15, 19, 21–22, 30, 40, 42, 61–64, 69, 71–77, 79, 85–86, 92, 126, 138–142, 152, 177–178, 185, 191–192, 194, 211, 221, 226n26, 228n31, 230n46, 233n53, 241n84, 250n42, 254n27, 255n32, 256n1, 259n5, 271n6; as abyssal, 59, 63, 87, 138
Gonsalvus Hispanus, 41, 46, 248n27
Grabmann, Martin, 18, 52, 55, 145, 220n4, 231n49, 239n72, 248n32, 249n41, 272n3, 275n25
grace, 75–76, 166, 193, 210, 251n1, 255n32, 255n36, 256n1
Greek language, xvii, 17, 30–31, 93, 98, 113, 114, 116, 118, 263n15
Grimm dictionary (*Deutsches Wörterbuch*), 145, 158, 227n28
Grotz, Stephan, 48, 51–52, 246n19, 248n33, 249n38, 249n41
Guitton, Jean, 183, 276n42

Habermas, Jürgen, 259n1
habitus (Latin noun), 66
Hausen im Tal (Schloß Hausen), 124, 237
Hebel, Johann Peter, 260n3
Hegel, Georg Wilhelm Friedrich, 39, 197, 199, 245n3; death of, 214, 216; Eckhart and, 11–12, 17, 35; Schelling and, 217; Schopenhauer and, 35
—works: *Science of Logic*, 13, 225n18
Heidegger, Elfride, 22, 145, 223n13, 224n18, 233n53, 237n60, 267n9, 273n4
Heidegger, Fritz, 19, 29, 124, 148, 220n4, 240n82
Heidegger, Heinrich, 183–184, 234n56, 240n82, 242n92, 267n9, 272n1
Heidegger, Martin: and National Socialism, 27, 230n47, 264n4; marginalia of, xv, 27, 167–168, 175–177, 179, 223n12, 226n28, 238n62, 240n78; Rosenberg and, 243n3, 252n8; Sauer and, 4–5;

Welte and, 18, 31, 142, 186, 220n5, 231nn48–49, 244n11, 259n3, 260n9
—works: "*Agchibasië*: A Triadic Conversation on a Country Path between a Scientist, a Scholar, and a Guide" (first "Country Path Conversation"), xvi, 8, 21–24, 68, 96, 107, 120–121, 124, 126–128, 138, 237n61, 265n5, 269n15; "Anmerkungen I," 121; *Basic Problems of Phenomenology*, 9–10, 12, 14, 152, 259n6; *Being and Time* (*Sein und Zeit*), xiv, 92, 94, 96–99, 101, 222n10, 229n39, 259n6, 262n11, 264n19, 265n5; *Black Notebooks*, 140–141; "Concept of Time in the Science of History," 5, 149; *Contributions to Philosophy: Of the Event*, 120, 271n2; "Das Ding," 65, 157, 232n52, 274nn18–19; "Der Meister Eckehart," 29; *Der Spiegel* interview, 92; *Einleitung in die Philosophie*, xvi, 95, 97–99, 102–103, 105, 111, 114, 123, 134, 260n5, 263n15; "On the Essence and Concept of *Physis*," 31; "Evening Conversation: In a Prisoner of War Camp in Russia, between a Younger and an Older Man" (third "Country Path Conversation"), 266n4; *The Event*, 121; *The Fundamental Concepts of Metaphysics: World, Finitude, Solitude*, xvi, 95, 98–99, 102–103, 111; *Gelassenheit*, 126; "Grundlinien der antiken und scholastischen Philosophie," 6; *Habilitationsschrift*, 5, 219n4, 221n9, 223n13, 232n49, 252n8, 259n5, 276n41; "Hegel's Concept of Experience," 57; *Hölderlin's Hymn "The Ister,"* 121; *Introduction to Metaphysics*, xvi, 96, 111–112, 265n5; *Kant and the Problem of Metaphysics*, 99, 261n10; "Kant's Thesis about Being," 58; "Letter on 'Humanism,'" 61–62; "Memorial Address," 126–127, 136; "On the Origin of the Work of Art," 31; *Parmenides*, 93; *The Principle of Reason*, 21, 158, 227n28, 266n1; "Rectorship Address: The Self-Assertion of the German University," 102, 114, 118, 265n8; "Time and Being," 94, 260n3; "The Turning," 28; "What is Metaphysics?," 99, 225n23, 263n15; "Zum Weltbegriff," 29

Heidegger, Martin (Heidegger's paternal grandfather), 24
Heimpel, Hermann, 190
henology; Neoplatonic, 79
Heraclitus: Parmenides and, 17
hermeneutics: of facticity or phenomenological, xiv
Hirsch, Elisabeth Feist, 184, 245n3, 276n44
history, 140–141, 214, 218; of being, xiv, 140, 262n10; of metaphysics as history of oblivion of being, 18
Hitler, Adolf, 35
—works: *Mein Kampf*, 252n8
Hölderlin, Friedrich, 25–26, 64, 228n31, 240n77, 260n4, 265n13
—works: "Der Ister," 24, 239n67; "Patmos," 24; "Remembrance," 25
human being: *dei-formatio* of, 75; essence of, xiv, xvi, 16, 61, 96, 113, 117, 128; finitude of, 17, 140; as image of God (*imago Dei*), 63, 69, 73, 139, 193, 208–

human being *(continued)*
209; as rational animal *(animal rationale)*, 131, 133; reciprocity of with being, 96, 113–114; as releasement *(Gelassenheit)*, xvi, 64, 80; as violence-doing *(gewalttätig)*, xvi, 112–113, 117–119
human sciences, 217
humanism, 216; Erasmian, 266n2
Husserl, Edmund, 21, 141, 183, 233n55, 237n59, 245n3, 258n5, 271n3; chair of, xvi, 95; Natorp and, 234n55
Husserl, Elisabeth, 258n5
hypostases *(Hypostasen)*, Plotinus's, 193

iconoclasm: Eckhart's, 23, 40
illuminationism, 36
In agro dominico (papal bull), 56, 250n46
indwelling *(Inständigkeit)*, 121, 270n27
inner man: and outer man, 67–68
intellect *(vernünfticheit, intellectus)*, 8, 14, 26, 39, 41, 44–48, 56, 59, 62, 69–70, 81–82, 150–151, 161, 193, 203, 213–215, 227n28, 248n33, 249n38, 250n46, 254n27, 278n4
intelligibility, 131
intentionality, 100, 206
Ireland, Julia, 260n3
Isocrates, 263n15
isticheit (Middle High German noun), 13, 228nn34–35

Jaran, François: Perrin and, 147
Jaspers, Karl, 4, 224n18
—works: *Psychologie der Weltanschauung*, 235n57
Jesus Christ, 45, 70, 72, 85–86, 258n9

Job: 14:4, 248n27; 23:13, 46
John: 1:1, 45–47, 154, 193; 1:3, 46–47; 8:58, 46; 14:6, 72; 16:28, 160
John (the Evangelist), 24, 278n9
John XXII (pope), 41
Jungian psychoanalysts, 35
justice *(iustitia)*, 55–56, 59, 203–204, 232nn51–52, 250nn47–48; and certainty *(certitudo)*, 19

Kabbalah, 35
Kant, Immanuel, 58, 64, 99, 111, 222, 261n10; Copernican Revolution of, 216–217; and German idealism, 115; Thomas Aquinas and, 217–218
—works: *Critique of Practical Reason*, 217; *Critique of Pure Reason*, 190, 217
Kierkegaard, Søren, 184, 277n44
Kisiel, Theodore, 147, 222n10, 223n13, 228n36, 262n12, 273n13
knowing *(Wissen)* / knowledge, 6, 8, 59, 70, 73–74, 92, 97, 104, 117–118, 130, 165, 183, 206, 208, 213–215, 226n28, 235n56, 254n27, 268n13; as dependent on sensation, 39, 48, 203; and faith, xvii, 214, 216, 218; traditional sense of, 28; unknown- *(unbekante bekantnisse)*, 28, 74, 104
Kolbe, Walther, 190
Krebs, Engelbert, 5, 243n3, 272n3
—works: *Grundfragen der kirchlichen Mystik*, 220n4; *Meister Dietrich*, 219n4; *Theologie und Wissenschaft nach der Lehre der Hochscholastik*, 220n4
Kreutzer, Conradin, 126
Kyoto School, 281n34

INDEX

language: as inadequate, 83–84, 138; as opposed to linguistics, 242n91; semantic theory of, 261n9
Lask, Emil, 261n9
Lasson, Adolf:
—works: *Meister Eckhart, der Mystiker: Zur Geschichte der religiösen Speculation in Deutschland*, 10, 273n14
Leibniz, Gottfried Wilhelm: Descartes and, 216
Leser, Hermann:
—works: "Das religiöse Wahrheitsproblem im Lichte der deutschen Mystik," 221n9, 225n20
letting-be, xiii–xiv, 13, 16, 38, 63–64, 67, 86, 100, 103–105, 107–109, 111–114, 123, 134, 138–139, 259n6, 262–263n14, 264n19, 269n16; as the essence of being, xvii, 25, 64–65, 95–96, 127–128, 139; as the essence of the human being, 64, 97–99, 101–102, 128, 136; as middle-voiced, xvi, 97, 100, 102, 108, 264n21; as prior to philosophy, 263n15; as transcendence of Dasein, xvi, 101, 259n6
Ley, Hermann, 39, 245n4; Bloch and, 35
Liber de Causis (anonymous, Pseudo-Aristotle), 46, 193
Liber viginti quattuor philosophorum. See *Book of Twenty-Four Philosophers*
life (living): elemental source of, 206–207, 209–210, 212; without why (*sine principio*), 3, 19–20, 91, 142
logic: dialectical, xv, 15, 82, 84, 86; dispassionate, 197; scholastic, 190; traditional, 84; Western, 190

logos (Greek noun), 57; as gathering, 132
Lombard, Peter:
—works: *Sentences*, 41
Longpré, Ephrem, 52, 249n41
Lotze, Rudolf Hermann:
—works: *Logik*, 220n5; *Metaphysik*, 5
Löwith, Karl, 229n37, 259n1
Lukàcz, György, 221n8
Luke: 9:23, 15, 257n9; 10:38, 270n20; 12:31, 70; 14:26, 86–87
Luther, Martin, 22, 184, 234n55, 236n59, 259n6, 277n44
—works: *Commentary on Romans*, 224n18

Maimonides, Moses, 36, 141
Marcuse, Herbert, 229n37
Martin of Tours, Saint, 24
Marxism, 35
Matthew: 6:33, 70; 18:3, 6
Meßkirch, 11, 24, 124, 126, 142, 220n4, 241n82, 267n6
McGinn, Bernard, 55, 83, 245n9, 255n31, 256n3
Mechthild of Magdeburg, 221n7, 271n1
meontology, 40
metaphysics: Western, 3, 21; substance, 79
Method: being and, 38, 82, 91, 94–95, 121, 259n6
Middle Ages, 4, 10, 17, 189, 215–217, 224n18, 226n27, 237n60, 245n9, 272n3
Middle High German language, xiii, 13, 36, 42, 61–62, 64, 82, 94, 131, 139, 148–149, 168, 173, 221n9, 223n12, 228n33, 235n56, 247n24, 254n30, 268n14, 273n4, 275n28, 275n30, 282n40

middle voice, xvi, 95, 97–102, 126, 134–135, 137–138, 260n7
mistranslation, xvii, 15, 38, 70, 82, 125, 254n30, 263n15
modernity, 138
moment of vision (*Augenblick*), 106–108, 264n19
Morgenstern, Christian, 125, 267n9
multiplicity, 7, 26, 61, 67, 71–74, 138, 140, 165, 253n19
mysticism, xvii, 5, 16, 37, 91, 183, 233n55, 235n57; Eckhartian, 5, 7, 9, 21, 31, 42, 223n13; female (*Frauenmystik*), 36; German, 4, 185, 254n28; medieval, 4, 10, 11, 202, 219n4, 226n27, 254n28, 272n1

Natalis, Hervaeus, 220n4
National Socialism (Nazism), xvi, 27, 142, 230n47, 264n4
Natorp, Paul, 231n47, 233n55; Husserl and, 234n55
—works: *Deutscher Weltberuf*, 20–21
natural sciences, 216–217
nature, 10, 47, 113, 127, 140, 152, 157, 196–197, 221n8, 253n20, 263n15, 265n6
negation, 16, 50–51, 59, 207, 212, 215, 250n41; absolute, 199–200, 205, 209; and affirmation, 17, 51–52, 200; of negation, 197–199, 204; radicalization of, 213
neokantianism, 35
neologism, 125, 258n5, 269n14
neoplatonism, 36, 39, 79, 181, 228n31, 241n83, 251n3; abyss of, 203
Newton, Isaac, 216
Nicholas of Cusa, 6, 26, 222n11, 240n73, 272n3, 278n10

Nietzsche, Friedrich, 31, 213, 216, 230n46, 232n51, 279n5, 280nn20–21, 282n43; atheism of, 16, 211; Bergson and, 218; Eckhart and, 16, 19, 35, 59, 184, 195, 200–201, 212, 218, 272n1; Schelling and, 120
—works: "On the Use and Abuse of History for Life," 201
nihilism: European, 185; Nietzsche's, 230n46
Nishida Kitarō, 281n34
Nishitani Keiji, 15–17, 19, 35, 184–185, 195, 222n9, 230n41, 230n44, 230n46, 277n47, 279n2, 279n5, 279n8, 279n12, 280n14, 280nn20–21, 280n23, 280nn25–26, 281nn29–30, 281n33, 281nn38–39, 282n40, 282nn48–49
—works: "Nietzsche's Zarathustra and Meister Eckhart," xv, 185, 225n18, 232n51, 243n1; "Shinpishisō-shi," 230n43
nominative, cognate, 99, 113, 137
nonbeing, 48, 52, 114, 192. *See also* nothingness
nothing, the, (*das Nichts*), 67, 241n84, 261n10, 271n6; as God, 11, 143, 152, 187, 255n33, 255n35
nothingness, 11, 19, 66–67, 75, 204, 212, 230n46, 241n81, 250n42, 253n15, 255n33; of being, 211; of creatures, 29, 54, 56, 65, 83–84, 161, 166

objectification, 100, 123
objectivity: and subjectivity, 7, 95, 98
Ochsner, Heinrich, 220n5, 228n36, 237n61, 260n9, 267n9

—works: "Zur Kritik der Deutsch-Christlichen Studentenvereinigung," 234n55
Ode to Man (Sophocles), 113–114, 116
Oedipus, 114, 117
Ōhashi Ryōsuke, 184, 230n45
Oltmanns, Käte (Käte Bröcker-Oltmanns), 11, 13–15, 17, 147, 185, 187–191, 203, 256n3, 273n7, 277n48, 278n1, 278nn3–5, 278nn8–10, 279n12; Gadamer and, 18; Kisiel and, 228n36
—works: *Meister Eckhart*, 145, 161, 224–225nn18–19, 228n33, 229nn37–39, 281n33; "Wesenheit, Dasein und Grund bei Meister Eckehart," xv, 14–15, 189, 191–194, 231n49, 277n56
oneness, 5, 55, 84, 86, 123, 165, 197–198, 201, 204, 208, 212, 281n29; as opposed to unity, 17, 202, 209; single (*ein einic ein*), 11, 16, 30, 139, 202; of thinking and being, xiii–xv, 61, 72–73, 75, 80; of us with God or the Godhead, xv, 15, 19, 62, 70, 76, 87, 92, 138, 140, 211
ontological difference, 61, 95
ontotheology, xv, 10, 29, 39–40, 53–54, 57–60, 248n31
open-region, the (*die Gegnet*), 95, 126, 130–132, 134–138, 265n5, 269n15, 270n26; as appropriative event (*Ereignis*), being (*Sein*), or beyng (*Seyn*), 132
Otto, Rudolf, 7, 184, 230n41, 277n44
—works: *Das Heilige: Über das Irrationale in der Idee des Göttlichen und sein Verhältnis zum Rationalen*, 224n18

pantheism, 237n60, 254n30
Parmenides, 39, 93, 137, 190, 244n1; Eckhart and, xiii–xiv; Heraclitus and, 17; fragment of: *to gar auto noein estin te kai einai*, 115–116
Pascal, Blaise, 26
path of thought (*Denkweg*), xiv, 25, 28, 64, 125
Paul, Saint, 13, 251n1
pedagogy, 93–94, 96, 263n15
phantasms: intellect's dependency on, 8, 48
Perrin, Christophe: Jaran and, 147
phenomenology, 92, 258n5; of religious life, 4, 6–7, 9, 223n13
philosophy: Eastern, 224n18; first, 57–58; fundamental question of, 113; German, 17, 230n47, 233n55; modern, 230n47; as preparatory, 104–106, 108; and theology, xvii
physics, twentieth-century, 258n3
physis (Greek noun), 265n6; as being, 113; as letting arise, 132
Plato, 31, 190, 203; Aristotle and, 59, 215; dialogues of, 24, 96, 266n5; his idea of the Good, 39, 183
—works: *Phaedo*, 124; *Phaedrus*, 263n15
Platonism, 203–204, 211, 214–216; as Augustinianism, 210
play: eternal, 6–7, 150; middle voice of, 137, 260n7; without why, 91
Plotinus, 181, 198–199, 203, 280n26
Podewils, Sophie Dorothee von: and Heidegger, 186
poiēsis (Greek noun), 118; and *thesis* and *morphē*, 31
Pöggeler, Otto, 3, 227n29, 229n39, 276n41

potentiality (*potentia*), 63, 69, 74, 140; and actuality (*actus*), 73, 139
positivism: spirit of, 211, 215, 217
possessiveness, 66, 86; detachment from, 63
possibility: as higher than actuality, 10. *See also* potentiality
poverty (*Armut*), 12, 24–27, 30, 91, 104, 121, 200, 208, 227, 236n59, 241n82
practical apriori, xiv, xvii, 28, 37, 42, 59, 64, 74, 92–94, 112–113, 117–119, 137–139, 235n56, 258–259nn5–6
presencing (*Anwesen*), 30, 80, 91, 181–182, 269n15; as being, 15, 186, 220n5
principle of noncontradiction, xvi, 83, 103
principle of sufficient reason, 91
progress: philosophical, 103, 258n5
projection, 99–101, 118, 120, 131, 133
Protestantism, 35, 216–217
Pythagoras, 222n10

questioning, 20, 101, 114, 118, 191, 264n20; comportment of, 107

receptivity, 100, 106, 255n32
releasement (*gelâzenheit, Gelassenheit, délaissement*), xiii–xvi, 3, 21–25, 27, 30, 37–38, 40, 42, 57, 59, 62–67, 70, 72, 75–83, 85–87, 91–92, 95–103, 105, 109, 111–112, 114, 116, 120–121, 123–124, 127–130, 132–139, 224n18, 232n51, 235n56, 236n59, 239n64, 241n82, 253n13, 255n37, 260nn3–4, 261n10, 262n14, 265n5, 265–266nn13–14, 269nn15–16, 269n18, 270n21, 270n24, 270nn27–28; and the atomic age, 126. *See also* detachment
religion, 15, 205, 214, 224n18; indifference toward, 217
representation, 12, 48, 123, 126, 130, 132, 207–208, 213
resoluteness (*Entschlossenheit*), 97, 99, 114, 265n5, 269n15; and letting-be, 259n6, 264n5
rest (*Ruhe*), 121
Richardson, William, 269n15
—works: *Heidegger: Through Phenomenology to Thought*, 233n53
Rickert, Heinrich, 220n5, 221n9, 261n9
—works: "Das Eine, die Einheit und die Eins," 5, 220n6, 252n8; *Die Philosophie des Lebens*, 221n8
Rosenberg, Alfred, 35
—works: *Der Mythus des 20. Jahrhunderts: Eine Wertung der seelischgeistigen Gestaltenkämpfe unserer Zeit*, 243n3, 252n8

Sachsen-Meiningen, Princess Margot von, 25, 125
Sartor Resartus (Carlyle), 196
Sartre, Jean-Paul, 245n3
Sauer, Joseph, 4–5, 219n2, 219n4
Schelling, Friedrich Wilhelm Joseph, xv, 14, 16, 194, 199, 229n37, 235n57; Eckhart and, 15, 228n36; Hegel and, 217; Nietzsche and, 120
—works: *Philosophical Investigations into the Essence of Human Freedom*, 191, 279n12
Schneider, Arthur, 272n3
Scholasticism (the Schools), 4, 7, 15, 36, 39–41, 91, 186, 191, 193, 214, 223n13

Schopenhauer, Arthur, 35, 199, 244n6
Schürmann, Reiner, xiv, 36–37, 61, 64, 79, 185–186, 220n5, 225n24, 239n64, 244n11
—works: *Broken Hegemonies*, 260n7; "Heidegger and Meister Eckhart on Releasement," 277n51; *Heidegger on Being and Acting*, 91–92, 259n6
Second World War (World War II), 123, 237n60
seeing (*theōrein*): and God (*theos*), 222n11
self-assertion, 111, 114
semiotics, medieval, 55
Seuse, Heinrich. *See* Suso, Henry
Silesius, Angelus, 20–21, 61, 153, 236n58
Sirach: 24:14, 46
Socrates (Plato's), 263n15
Song of Solomon: 1:8, 70
Sophocles, 119
—works: *Antigone*, 113–114, 116
Soul (*Seele*): as empty, 178, 208; essence of, 7, 13, 151–152, 155–156, 194; threefoldness of, 70
Stadelmann, Rudolf, 11
—works: *Vom Geist des ausgehenden Mittelalters*, 226n27
statesmen: and poets and thinkers, 114, 117–118
struggle (*Kampf, polemos*), 112, 114, 118, 265n7
Sturlese, Loris, 45, 54, 244n9, 245n5, 249n37, 250n42
Suárez, Francisco, 14
subjectivity, 19, 140, 206; modern, 39, 98, 245n3; and objectivity, 7, 95
Suso, Henry (Heinrich Seuse), 5, 219n4, 221n7, 224n18, 260n4, 272n1
—works: *Little Book of Truth*, 21, 234n56
Suzuki, D. T., 225n18
—works: *Essays in Zen Buddhism*, 15–16, 230n41

Tanabe Hajime, 224n18
Tauler, John, 5, 9, 22, 159, 219n4, 221n7, 224n18, 226n28, 236n59, 259n6, 273n4
technē (Greek noun), 126, 131, 268n13; as basic feature of *deinon*, 118; as knowing (*Wissen*), 117
teaching, 93, 124, 268n13
technology, 31, 126–127, 157, 260n4
teleology, 6
temporality, 26, 67, 91, 99, 177, 253n19, 259n6, 265n9; of being and the human being, 141
Theologia Deutsch (anonymous), 237n60, 272n1
theology, xvii, 23, 42, 56, 58, 184, 194; Christian, 214; dialectical, 200; intellectualist, xv, 202; mystical, 10; negative, 84; postmodern, 35
theory: and praxis, 64
theosophy, 35, 235n57
thing (*Ding*): as nothing in itself, 29, 56; and world, 29
thinking: as activity, 29, 37; and being, xiii, 15, 38–39, 61, 65, 114, 123, 126, 137–139; calculative, 126–127; horizontal-transcendental, 130–131, 134, 136; meditative, 126–129, 130, 136; as spark of the soul, 15, 250n42, 250nn45–46
Third Reich, 125, 128, 142, 226n27, 237n61; influential books during, 252n8

Thomas Aquinas, Saint, 10, 12, 41, 59, 152, 192, 202–203, 213, 215, 217, 231n48; Aristotle and, 39; Boethius and, 248n34; Eckhart and, 31, 42–45, 167, 246n16, 247n24; death of, 214, 216, 218
—works: *Summa contra gentiles*, 43; *Summa theologiae*, 41, 43
Thomas of Erfurt, 232n49
Thomas à Kempis, 237n60, 272n1
Trakl, Georg, 260n3
transcendental idealism, 131
transcendentals, 55, 83
Trawny, Peter, 237n60
truth (*Wahrheit, alētheia / a-lētheia*): of being, 62, 123, 139; being the, xiii, 36, 64, 76, 92, 117, 119, 139, 244n10, 251n4; of beings, 19, 226n28; as correspondence, 3; of God, 22, 68, 81; and the intellect, 45, 69, 203; metaphysics of, 5, 221n9; as presencing (*Anwesen*), 220n5, 269n15; as unconcealing, 132, 261n9, 263n16
Tsujimura Kōichi, 225n18

Ueda Shizuteru, 67, 222n9, 225n18, 254n22
unconcealment, 132, 141, 263n16, 264n5
unity, 8, 15, 26, 40, 59, 61–63, 67, 76, 114, 116, 150, 153, 165, 185, 189, 191–194, 199, 201, 205, 208, 212, 215–216, 237n61, 250n42, 255n36, 266n5; as opposed to oneness, 17, 202, 204, 209
University of Freiburg: rectorship of, xvi, 96–97, 111
univocity: and analogy, 57, 250n42

Van Buren, John, 233n55, 262n12
—works: *Rumor of the Hidden King*, 234n55
via negativa, 54
violence (*Gewalt*), 95, 111, 121, 123, 126; of being and of the human being, 96, 112–113, 116–120, 140; and voluntarism, xvi
voluntarism, xvi, 19, 68, 134; Heidegger's, xvi, 112, 120, 128
Von Herrmann, Friedrich-Wilhelm, 135, 167, 237n60, 240n78, 270n22, 271n1; on Heidegger's marginalia, 168, 223n12, 227n28, 261n10
Vulgate, 46, 49, 82, 86, 258n9

Wahl, Jean, 236n59, 260n5
waiting (*Warten*), 107, 136; intransitive, 132
Walther, Gerda, 223n13
Weischedel, Wilhelm, 229n37
—works: *Der Gott der Philosophen*, 245n3
Welte, Bernhard, 18, 31, 142–143, 186, 220n5, 231nn48–49, 234n55, 242n92, 244n11, 259n3, 260n9, 271n6
Wildenstein (castle), 24–25, 124–125, 267n9
will (noun), xvi, 6, 8, 19, 21–23, 41, 68–69, 81, 95, 111, 114, 119–121, 123, 126, 128–130, 134–135, 137–138, 151, 193, 199, 217, 236n59, 238n62, 265n5; in *Being and Time*, 262n11; free, 8, 151, 213; and memory and reason, 15, 193; to power, 19, 211; and self-assertion, 114

will / willing (verb), 102, 113,
  119–120, 128–130, 134, 232n51,
  241n82, 264n5; non- (*Nicht-
  Wollen*), 128–129; to-know,
  114
without why (*ohn' Warum, sine
  principio*), 3, 19–21, 59, 91, 142,
  153, 233n53, 236n58
Wolin, Richard, 259n1

world (*Welt*), 6, 11, 29, 91, 99–100,
  103, 114, 137–138, 261n9,
  262n12, 263n18, 270n27
worldview (*Weltanschauung*): technological,
  128, 136; religious, 216–217
Wulffen, Barbara von, 186

Zarathustra (Nietzsche's), xv, 16, 184,
  195–202, 211, 213

Made in United States
Orlando, FL
10 May 2023